The Short Oxf...

Roman Europe

The Short Oxford History of Europe

General Editor: T. C. W. Blanning

NOW AVAILABLE

Classical Greece
edited by Robin Osborne

Roman Europe
edited by Edward Bispham

The Early Middle Ages
edited by Rosamond McKitterick

The Central Middle Ages
edited by Daniel Power

The Seventeenth Century
edited by Joseph Bergin

The Eighteenth Century
edited by T. C. W. Blanning

The Nineteenth Century
edited by T. C. W. Blanning

Europe 1900–1945
edited by Julian Jackson

Europe since 1945
edited by Mary Fulbrook

IN PREPARATION, VOLUMES COVERING

The Late Middle Ages

The Short Oxford History of Europe

General Editor: T. C. W. Blanning

Roman Europe

Edited by Edward Bispham

CONTRIBUTORS

William Bowden, *Nottingham University*

Guy Bradley, *Cardiff University*

Mary Harlow, *University of Birmingham*

R. W. Benet Salway, *University of College London*

Nicola Terrenato, *University of Michigan*

Peter S. Wells, *University of Minnesota*

Andrew Wilson, *Institute of Archaeology, University of Oxford*

OXFORD

UNIVERSITY PRESS

OXFORD

UNIVERSITY PRESS

Great Clarendon Street, Oxford OX2 6DP

Oxford University Press is a department of the University of Oxford.
It furthers the University's objective of excellence in research, scholarship,
and education by publishing worldwide in

Oxford New York

Auckland Cape Town Dar es Salaam Hong Kong Karachi
Kuala Lumpur Madrid Melbourne Mexico City Nairobi
New Delhi Shanghai Taipei Toronto

With offices in

Argentina Austria Brazil Chile Czech Republic France Greece
Guatemala Hungary Italy Japan Poland Portugal Singapore
South Korea Switzerland Thailand Turkey Ukraine Vietnam

Oxford is a registered trade mark of Oxford University Press
in the UK and in certain other countries

Published in the United States
by Oxford University Press Inc., New York

British Library Cataloguing in Publication Data

Data available

Library of Congress Cataloging in Publication Data

Roman Europe, 1000 BC-AD 400 / edited by Edward Bispham.
p. cm.– (The short Oxford history of Europe)
Includes index.
ISBN 978–0–19–926601–2 (pbk.: acid-free paper) – ISBN 978–0–19–926600–5
(hbk.: acid-free paper) 1. Rome–History. I. Bispham, Edward.
DG209.R594 2008
936'.02–dc22
2008031892

Typeset by Laserwords Private Limited, Chennai, India
Printed in Great Britain
on acid-free paper by
CPI Antony Rowe, Chippenham, Wiltshire

ISBN 978–0–19–926601–2 (Pbk)
ISBN 978–0–19–926600–5 (Hbk)

10 9 8 7 6 5 4 3 2 1

General Editor's Preface

The problems of writing a satisfactory general history of Europe are many, but the most intractable is clearly the reconciliation of depth with breadth. The historian who can write with equal authority about every part of the continent in all its various aspects has not yet been born. Two main solutions have been tried in the past: either a single scholar has attempted to go it alone, presenting an unashamedly personal view of a period, or teams of specialists have been enlisted to write what are in effect anthologies. The first offers a coherent perspective but unequal coverage, the second sacrifices unity for the sake of expertise. This new series is underpinned by the belief that it is this second way that has the fewest disadvantages and that even those can be diminished if not neutralized by close cooperation between the individual contributors under the directing supervision of the volume editor. All the contributors to every volume in this series have read each other's chapters, have met to discuss problems of overlap and omission, and have then redrafted as part of a truly collective exercise. To strengthen coherence further, the editor has written an introduction and conclusion, weaving the separate strands together to form a single cord. In this exercise, the brevity promised by the adjective 'short' in the series' title has been an asset. The need to be concise has concentrated everyone's minds on what really mattered in the period. No attempt has been made to cover every angle of every topic in every country. What this volume does provide is a short but sharp and deep entry into the history of Europe in the period in all its most important aspects.

T. C. W. Blanning

Sidney Sussex College
Cambridge

Editor's Preface

The Roman volume in this series was taken on, and abandoned, by more than one editor. The current editor has lived with this project for some time, and witnessed as many setbacks as steps forward; in that time I have incurred many debts. I would never have had the wonderful but frightening opportunity offered by the volume without Robin Osborne, who initially approached me about it in the last millennium, and once I had naively agreed to take it on, suggested my name to Tim Blanning, whose vision and encouragement have made this series happen. Both he, and Matthew Cotton at OUP, have shown astonishing patience; Matthew has been a source of steady support and sound advice throughout (the volume has outlived more than one commissioning editor, and I must thank Fiona Kinnear for her early encouragement). Kate Hind and Carolyn McAndrew oversaw the transition from typescript to finished product. Chris Noon compiled the index with professionalism and acuity. The illustrations for Chapters 5 and 7 were prepared by Ian Cartwright at the Institute of Archaeology in Oxford.

Much of what little I know about the Roman Empire I know from Fergus Millar, through his writings, and through the regular opportunities I have been lucky enough to have had in the last decade of talking to him. He has played no direct part in the production of this volume, but I conceive of it as, in a very modest way, reopening some of the debates, and more importantly re-adopting the directions of research, presented in Millar's *The Roman Empire and its Neighbours*[2] (London, 1981), at least for the European part of the empire. In addition I must thank Alan Bowman for the invitation to deliver a very early version of Chapter 5 as a lecture to the Roman Society in 2004; and Lawrence Keppie, Adrian Goldsworthy, and Jonathan Pearce for allowing me to pick their brains, and offering useful comments on that occasion; Alan Bowman, Llewelyn Morgan, Andrew Wilson, and Matthew Leigh have also kindly made other suggestions. I also benefited in the early stages of planning from conversations with Guy Bradley, who recommended Peter Wells to me. To all the contributors go my deep thanks for their indefatigability and understanding. The volume is presented more or less as commissioned. Readers who know his impressive scholarship, challenging argumentation, and clarity of exposition will regret that Andreas Bendlin was in the end unable to contribute a chapter on Religions.

The contributors constitute a mix of archaeologists and historians—it seemed inappropriate to let one group rather than another tell the story of the Roman era in Europe, and productive to set their different perspectives side by side, and see what sort of stories each group had to tell; at the same time, the nature of the evidence makes some topics particularly suitable for archaeological approaches. Of course there is no right balance, and not all readers will find the balance adopted in each case between archaeological and textual approaches to their taste.

All the historical contributors have at some time or other been involved in archaeological fieldwork, and are sensitive to the implications of archaeological evidence; and the archaeologists likewise have shown themselves in their published work sensitive to current preoccupations in historical thinking. In fact, some of us find the labels 'historian' or 'archaeologist' unduly restrictive; perhaps we may hope for the day when some scholars can really have a dual intellectual nationality, or, better, when the past, like modern Europe, is without borders and frontiers, and even without disciplinary 'nationalities'.

A guide to the ancient literary sources cited in this volume, with suggestions for further reading, can be accessed at: http://weblearn.ox.ac.uk/site/human/classics/tutorsroom/bispham/

Edward Bispham

Brasenose and St Anne's Colleges

Acknowledgements

ANDREW WILSON would like to thank the Leverhulme Foundation for their award of a Philip Leverhulme Prize, which enabled Chapter 8 to be produced during a period of research leave.

MARY HARLOW: From 1995 I was a tutor on the Open University course, *The Roman Family* (J. Huskinson and P. James); this chapter reflects and acknowledges the work of the course team, discussions with other OU lecturers and students. It also reflects the research undertaken for Harlow & Laurence 2002). I would like to thank Niall McKeown, Leslie Brubaker, Chris Wickham, Ray Laurence and Tim Parkin for reading and commenting on early versions of this chapter.

WILLIAM BOWDEN: I am very grateful to Richard Reece and Ed Bispham for their comments on earlier versions of this text. Any remaining errors are entirely the responsibility of the author.

Contents

List of Illustrations

List of Maps

List of Contributors

EDWARD BISPHAM is Tutorial Fellow in Ancient History at Brasenose College, Oxford, and Lecturer in Ancient History at St Anne's College, Oxford. His research interests lie in the history, epigraphy and archaeology of Italy; he co-directs an excavation project in the Sangro Valley, in Abruzzo, with S.E. Kane. Recent publications include *From Asculum to Actium. The Municipalization of Italy between the Social War and Augustus* (Oxford, Oxford University Press, 2007), *Vita Vigilia Est. Essays in Honour of Barbara Levick* (ed. with G. Rowe and E. Matthews), *BICS* Supplement 100 (London, Institute of Classical Studies, 2007) and *The Edinburgh Companion to Ancient Greece and Rome* (ed. with B.A. Sparkes and T.E. Harrison, Edinbugh, Edinburgh University Press, 2006).

WILLIAM BOWDEN is lecturer in Roman archaeology at the University of Nottingham. His research interests include Roman and late antique urbanism and the use of the past in the creation of modern identities. He has carried out fieldwork in the UK, Italy, Albania and Jordan. He is currently engaged in major field projects at Butrint (Albania) and at Caistor St Edmund (UK). His publications include *Epirus Vetus: the Archaeology of a Late Antique Province* (London, Duckworth, 2003) and *Byzantine Butrint: Excavations and Surveys 1994–1999* (Oxford, Oxbow 2004) (with R. Hodges and K. Lako). He was also co-editor of the first three volumes of the series *Late Antique Archaeology*.

GUY BRADLEY is a Lecturer in Ancient History at Cardiff University. He is co-director of the Iuvanum Survey Project. He is the author of *Ancient Umbria* (Oxford, Oxford University Press, 2000), and a co-editor of *Greek and Roman Colonisation: Origins, Ideologies and Interactions* (Swansea, Classical Press of Wales, 2006) and *Ancient Italy: Regions without Boundaries* (Exeter, Exeter University Press, 2007). He is currently working on a book on early Rome.

MARY HARLOW is Senior Lecturer in Roman History at the University of Birmingham. Her research interests are the Roman life course and the Roman family; Late Antiquity and Roman dress. Recent publications and edited volumes: *The Clothed Body in the Ancient World* (with L. Cleland and L. Llewellyn-Jones, Oxford, Oxbow, 2005);

Age and Ageing in the Roman Empire (with Ray Laurence, *Journal of Roman Studies* Supplementary Series 65, 2007); *Berg Cultural History of Childhood and the Family* vol 1: *Antiquity* (ed. with Ray Laurence, forthcoming) and *Dress and Identity* (ed.) Archeopress, forthcoming.

R. W. BENET SALWAY is Lecturer in Ancient History in the Department of History, University College London, where he is also director of the Projet Volterra on Roman Law. His research interests lie in the later Roman period, principally social aspects of government and administration (on which a monograph is forthcoming) and the surviving evidence for geographical knowledge and understanding, including the Peutinger map (of which he is producing an edition and translation in collaboration with Richard Talbert and Emily Albu).

NICOLA TERRENATO is an Associate Professor of Classical Archaeology at the University of Michigan. He specializes in first millennium BC Italy, with particular reference to northern Etruria, early Rome and the period of the Roman conquest. He has been involved in fieldwork in and around Rome, Volterra, and Potenza. His current projects include excavation of the major Latin city at Gabii, as well as the investigation of long-term social processes at the tower of Donoratico, in coastal Tuscany. Other interests include field survey methods, history of archaeology and especially the role of elite loyalties in the formation of cities and empires in the Mediterranean. His publications include S. Keay & N. Terrenato, eds., *Italy and the West. Comparative Issues in Romanization* (Oxford, Oxbow 2001); P. Van Dommelen & N. Terrenato, eds., *Articulating Local Cultures: Power and Identity under the Expanding Roman Republic. Journal of Roman Archaeology* Supplement 63 (Portsmouth, RI, Journal of Roman Archaeology, 2007) and J.A. Becker & N. Terrenato, eds., *Roman Republican Villas: Architecture, Context, and Ideology* (forthcoming).

PETER S. WELLS is Professor of Anthropology at the University of Minnesota. Among his publications are *The Barbarians Speak: How the Conquered Peoples Shaped Roman Europe* (Princeton, Princeton University Press, 1999), *Beyond Celts, Germans and Scythians: Archaeology and Identity in Iron Age Europe* (London, Duckworth 2001), *The Battle that Stopped Rome: Emperor Augustus, Arminius, and the Slaughter of the Legions in the Teutoburg Forest* (New York, W.W. Norton 2003), and, most recently, *Image and Response in Early Europe*

(London, Duckworth 2008) and *Barbarians to Angels: The Dark Ages Reconsidered* (New York, W.W. Norton 2008).

ANDREW WILSON is Professor of the Archaeology of the Roman Empire at the University of Oxford, and has published extensively on Roman aqueducts, technology, and the ancient economy. His publications include chapters on 'Hydraulic Engineering', 'Machines', and 'Large-scale manufacturing, standardization, and trade' in J. P. Oleson (ed.), *Handbook of Engineering and Technology in the Classical World* (Oxford, Oxford University Press 2008), and on "The Metal Supply of the Roman Empire", in E. Papi (ed.), *Supplying Rome and the Roman Empire* (Portsmouth, Rhode Island, Journal of Roman Archaeology 2007): 109–25.

Introduction

Edward Bispham

In about AD 298 the orator Eumenes delivered a formal speech of thanks to the Tetrarchs (see Chapter 9), possibly in the forum of the Gallic town of Autun. At the end of the speech he praises the restoration of the city's schools, and imagines schoolboys gazing at a map of the empire in the portico (probably of the forum): every day, he says, they may see all the lands and seas of the empire, all the cities restored by the tetrarchs, all the peoples subjected or cowed by their might; and learn all the names and extent of the lands of the empire, how far apart they are, as well as the natural features of the world ... : 'Now at last it is a pleasure to look at the world depicted, since we see nothing in it which belongs to anyone other than the Romans' (*Latin Panegyrics* 9. 21. 3). The learned culture of imperial Gaul was particularly impressive (that of Roman Germany is suggestively hinted at by the image on the cover of this book, part of a relief from a high-status classicizing funerary monument from Neumagen on the Moselle in Germany, showing a school lesson in progress): one of the clearest formulations of the Roman achievement comes from the Romano-Gallic writer Rutilius Namatianus (*On His Return* 1. 66), written shortly after Alaric's sack of Rome in AD 410. Addressing the Romans, he says: 'you have made one city what was before the whole world.' This 'globalization', one of the most important of Rome's achievements, makes it illegitimate to consign the appreciation of any part of the empire to the ghetto of 'specialist studies'.

Yet despite flourishing scholarship on the north-western provinces, especially their archaeology, northern and Mediterranean Europe remain conceptually divided. To be sure, some scholars operate with the breadth of vision to integrate the northern European data into a wider imperial picture, to combine the local and the global: the work of David Mattingly and Greg Woolf, to name but two, is fundamental here. Yet the tendency is for the 'Mediterranean' and 'northern' parts of the empire to be studied as two separate spheres. Some of the reasons for this are scholarly: 'core-periphery' theory, so influential at the end of the twentieth century, inadvertently gives respectability to age-old prejudices (see Arafat and Morgan 1994 for the weaknesses of the 'supply and demand' model which underlies this approach), and underplays variation in terms of the reception of material objects and modes of their exchange in different areas. More recently, cogent arguments have been put forward for the ecological distinctiveness of the Mediterranean as a unity (Horden and Purcell 2000), perhaps unintentionally further encouraging this kind of cleavage.

Other reasons are ideological. Reactions against 'colonial' inter-pretations of Romanization prevalent for much of the last century have led to a welcome shift in perspective. The active input of indi-genous societies into creating Romano-provincial hybrids, and the extent to which Rome adapted rather than extirpated existing sys-tems, have been given more weight in scholarly discussions. Another reaction, this time against classical archaeology, part of archaeology's wider search for identity as an autonomous discipline, has led to a change of emphasis in archaeology departments and curricula. This emancipation from the 'antiquated master' represented by classics in part reflects a legitimate unwillingness on the part of archaeology to be treated as ancient history's handmaid (but this horse long ago bolted from the stable). One consequence is the effective killing-off of old-style classical archaeology, understood as effectively a distinct-ive, Wincklemannesque art history. Less happily, it has led to an ideological positioning which openly parades its dislike of the Greeks and Romans, and defines the objects of its study as the 'northern European Iron Age', the 'Balkan Iron Age', the 'Cycladic Bronze Age', and so on, avoiding labels like Greek or Roman. On one level this is understandable: Roman London and the Danubian gateway site of Magdalensburg occupied similar surface areas (albeit at different intensities); the former has received much more attention because it is 'Roman'. Yet the Romans are in danger of becoming the 'elephants in the room' of northern Europe, the big factor about which no one wants to talk. The decline in the knowledge of classical languages, when compared to the position a generation ago, has, reasonably enough, encouraged the adoption of this partial engagement within university curricula. Equally, despite many pious words about interdisciplinarity (and some examples of this rare beast in action), many ancient history courses have traditionally engaged with archaeological evidence in the most trivial way. The marginality (in traditional curricular terms) of the textual evidence for the European areas of the empire, when compared to the main focus of, say, Livy or Sallust, compounds the situation. The egregious examples must be the older ancient history courses, like the one I studied as an undergraduate at Oxford: Roman history began in 264 BC and ended with the death of Trajan ('ancient history' is somewhat more generously defined now): history is textual or it is nothing at all, on this view. Things are changing, but paradoxically, as history moves closer to archaeology, archaeology's sympathies tend to move further away from the Graeco-Roman historical core.

The post-colonial view of the history of the north-western provinces has advantages over what it replaced. It also has drawbacks: too much talk of 'negotiation' in Roman–native interactions threatens to sanitize what was often a brutal encounter at first, and remained subject to the dynamics of an asymmetrical power relationship. The post-colonial emphasis on native elites also threatens to write the Romans out of the picture, and reduce historical and cultural change to a woolly process played out in the *longue durée*, with limited importance attributed to human agency, and little which is distinctive in any period: leaving a homogeneous sea of 'social complexity' which washes in and out between high- and low-water marks every few hundred years. The Romans may be hard to love—indeed, if I may be allowed another crude generalization, they are not very nice. Yet it will not do to efface entirely their role in change, which is the logical conclusion of the direction some scholarly and curricular trends are pursuing (a direction wildly at odds with popular enthusiasm, if television schedules are any guide). We must learn to think reflectively about the Roman era, and not idolize it; but equally, we do not need to be embarrassed about it. Apologizing for the Roman Empire can be left to politicians who prefer saying sorry for the deeds of our ancestors to admitting present mistakes.

This book is a history of the Roman Empire, but one which retains a European perspective throughout. To this end, the African and Asian thirds of the empire receive limited mention, although we do not pretend that they did not exist. Events, phenomena, and trends deriving from, or involving, these parts of the empire are discussed, and noted in the Chronology at the end of the book. This leaves us with a Roman Empire shorn of its richest and most culturally sophisticated areas (and by extension allows no discussion of important phenomena like trade with Arabia, India, and China: Pliny, *Natural History* 6. 101; 12. 83–4). Moreover, it is a Roman Empire framed on a very modern definition: the Romans understood where Europe was in geographical terms, but they attached no meaning to it as a concept in the way that we do. Defining Europe is a tricky issue today: the positive achievement of Rome in creating an empire which embraced the different cultures of Europe, Asia, and Africa is overlooked, it seems, in politicians' reluctance to allow Turkey into the European Union. The Champions' League and the Eurovision Song Contest operate on different criteria, admitting Turkey and Israel to the European club, without obvious ill-effects on either institution. Given the lack of cohesion in modern EU thinking about what Europe is, or might be, it may well seem absurd to put the Roman Empire into the Eurocrats' procrustean bed.

We hope, however, that this approach will not only allow us to look from the centre outwards, whether the centre be Rome or Constantinople, in constructing an overall narrative of the Roman Empire. It will also allow the European provinces to step out from the shadow of their African and Asian cousins in a way which histories of Rome, as we have seen, do not normally encourage. Inevitably in a work like this, complete coverage is unobtainable (readers will probably find the Iberian peninsula, for example, underrepresented); but by taking 'Rome and the European provinces' as the object of our story, we hope to employ a useful heuristic category. The study of this third of the empire should suggest what is unique about it, throw into relief its particular characteristics, and by implication allow us to isolate more clearly what were the developments which it held in common with the rest of the empire.

Such an ideologically motivated approach, stressing Europe to the exclusion of the rest, allows, it seems, a more serious consideration of the *context* of the Roman Empire, rather than simply treating it as the Romans did, as an inevitable, predestined given. In Europe, Rome stepped into a moving stream as the empire expanded, and expansion cannot be considered in isolation from that stream. Equally, that same watercourse in flood was later to overwhelm the levees of the Roman frontiers: we need to understand the fall of the empire in terms of outside pressures in a more sophisticated way than by simply invoking 'barbarians'. Consequently the chapters which narrate the political and military history of the Republic, the early and late empire, and the thematic studies of Roman society, war, the economy, and religions, are deliberately framed by two chapters on Europe before, and outside, the Roman conquest. These give the empire in its European context, and encourage new reflections on Roman imperialism, and the changes wrought by Roman domination.

These changes were until relatively recently described by the term Romanization. As we have seen, scholarship has moved away from talking of a simple top-down transfer of Roman culture to previously benighted barbarians. This Introduction apart, the present volume uses the term Romanization sparingly, on only three occasions outside Chapter 8 and its Further Reading (which have another half-dozen instances). We have found the term insufficiently helpful as a description of cultural change, except at the highest level of generality. Yet the fact of cultural change in Europe as a result of the Roman conquest cannot be denied. Let us take the case of Roman Germany. The associations of the cover image to this volume have been discussed. Another emblematic image is a detail from a third-century AD mosaic signed by one Monnus from Trier showing, amid images of the nine Muses, and assorted greats of Graeco-Roman literature, the Muse Urania and the Hellenistic poet Aratus of Soli. Aratus was perhaps the most-read poet in antiquity after Homer; his fame rested on his Stoicizing poem on constellations and weather signs, the *Phaenomena*. In the West his popularity was spread through translations by Cicero, Tiberius' nephew Germanicus, and Avienus. The appeal lay not only in the quality of the poetry, but in the ideal of an ordered universe, which might be taken as paradigmatic of the good government of the empire as a whole. Do these two images, one of systematic education, the other a testimony to the popularity of Aratus on the banks of the Moselle half-a-millennium after his death, not speak of the success of Graeco-Roman culture in capturing the minds of the provincials?

Yes and no. Trier was a Roman colony, founded by imperial mandate, and settled by legionary veterans from the Rhine garrisons. We should not be surprised to find here plentiful evidence of Graeco-Roman literary and visual culture. What is perhaps striking is the globalized nature of that culture: urban society and culture operate in such a way that the Greek figures of the *grammaticus* (teacher of literature) and the Hellenistic Stoic poet can move seamlessly within its fabric, wherever that fabric is. This is also the result of aspiration, a wanting to belong, on the part of the communities concerned. On the other hand, Trier's religious activity was, as the Altbach complex excavated before the Second World War shows, distinctively Romano-Celtic. Furthermore, this is not a manifestation of religion which one would expect to find outside the north-western provinces. The balance of religious trade was in favour of the Mediterranean and the East: Mithras was heavily 'exported', but there was little or no corresponding 'import' of, say, the Celtic goddess Epona. Moreover, once we move out of the major towns and away from the legionary fortresses, what kind of cultural impact did the Roman conquest make? Was it more than a change of masters for the rural peasantry? In view of these problems we have devoted a separate chapter (Chapter 8) to the historiography of 'Romanization', and to a provocative reconsideration of the nature, scale, and intensity of cultural change in the European provinces.

This volume begins c.1000 BC. This needs no justification: Rome was one society among many in the European Iron Age. But what is the justification for ending in AD 400, at which point the Roman Empire in the West still had three-quarters of a century to run? This terminal date was imposed by the organization of the series to which this volume belongs. Yet two points might be made in its favour. First, the essential processes which brought down the western empire were all being clearly manifested by 400: barbarian incursions and internal weakness had already fatally weakened the western empire; the emperors of the fifth century were increasingly figureheads, with real power lying with barbarian generals. Secondly, AD 400 marks a watershed, after which the Roman aristocracy can be said to have been predominantly Christian in a way in which it quite clearly had not been a century earlier; from this point paganism, its temples now closed and sacrifices banned, slips into a gradual but ineluctable decline—in the sixth century even the pagan philosophical schools in Athens closed. From 400 the holding of ecclesiastical positions began to be a really attractive alternative to the holding of secular and civic ones for the ambitious.

Constantine's conversion to Christianity, and the foundation of Constantinople, saw a shift in the sacred geography of empire. Besides Rome and Constantinople, the Holy Land saw a major ecclesiastical building programme funded by Constantine; it was there that the chief sacred focus of the empire now came to lie. Pilgrimage now became a major preoccupation of Roman Christendom, linking the furthest parts of Europe to the Levant: our earliest account of a Christian pilgrimage is the *Bordeaux Journey*, recording a trip from the Gironde to Palestine in AD 333. One of the other well-known accounts from the fourth century is that of the Spanish aristocratic lady Egeria, who travelled to the Holy Land in *c.*380—looking for holy men and women, drawn by the same religious gravity. While pilgrimage had an authoritative guidebook only for the Holy Land, in Rome the tombs of Peter and Paul offered a template for a sacred topography which could attract pilgrims—the development of the tombs of saints and martyrs as cult sites transformed Roman topography under Pope Damasus (AD 366 onwards). From here it was only a short step to the association of churches with saints' names, a phenomenon which began in the fifth century.

These changes in sacred geography, Roman and Mediterranean, in the late fourth century illustrate how Christianization was already placing 'clear blue water' between the Christian and pagan worlds by the end of that century; with the fifth century we do begin to look into a very different world. It is salutary to remember, in view of the warnings given above about the artificiality of the concept of Roman Europe, that the centre of the world at the end of our period lay not in Europe (no more than it had done in 1000 BC), but in the Holy Land.

1

Peoples of temperate Europe before the Roman conquest

Peter S. Wells

Introduction

THE Roman conquest, leading to the incorporation of half of temperate Europe into the Roman Empire for five centuries, can be understood best not as an event or series of events, as many investigators interpret the textual sources, but rather as part of centuries-long processes. As a number of ancient historians have emphasized recently, the relevant texts are biased in many ways, and in order to interpret them usefully we need to examine those biases. Texts represent what struck the writers as significant and worthy of mention at the particular time that they were writing. Ancient authors often present information in ways that are intentionally slanted for political purposes. For the most part, Greek and Roman authors did not know much about the peoples beyond the Alps. The image we get from the texts of contacts with these peoples—one that prevails in many accounts today—is of discrete violent episodes in which bands of warriors from the north suddenly appeared to terrorize peoples of the Mediterranean world. Then, beginning with Caesar's campaigns in Gaul, the image becomes one of Roman legions marching to conquest of the lands west of the Rhine, south of the Danube, and across the English Channel into Britain. But archaeology shows that contact between northern and southern regions of Europe had existed for millennia. During the prehistoric Iron Age (c.800 BC to the Roman conquest), such contact played significant roles in linking peoples north of the Alps with the societies of the Mediterranean basin, with important effects on all of the parties concerned. The Roman history of Europe needs to be understood in the context of these long-established, consequential interrelations.

The European Iron Age is an immensely complex subject. Archaeologists in all parts of the continent investigate the diverse cultural developments that took place during the eight centuries of this period (Kristiansen 1998 is a recent synthesis). In this chapter I highlight topics that are especially important for understanding the subsequent developments during the Roman period. One is interactions between peoples north of the Alps and those of the Mediterranean basin, from the Early Iron Age onwards. A second is the formation of increasingly large and complex communities, with the associated emergence of social and political identities on ever-larger scales. A third is the creation of distinctive ways of representing elite social and political status, through specific kinds of funerary ceremony and public rituals that involved feasting and military symbolism. These two themes are represented materially by objects that were placed in burials and deposited in the earth and in water at sites that were used for ritual activity. I use selected sites as examples to illustrate the patterns under discussion.

Geography

In order to give coherence to my treatment, I concentrate on the central regions of the continent, from the Pyrenees and southern Britain in the west to the Dniester river in the east, from the Alps and the Balkan mountains in the south, to the North and Baltic Seas in the north. After the Roman conquests, the frontier of the empire ran, more or less, diagonally from north-west to south-east through the centre of this region. For our purposes this part of Europe can be understood in terms of two major topographic zones.

The southern zone consists of hilly uplands. These extend from south-central France in the west, to Cologne on the lower Rhine river, to just south of Hanover in northern Germany, and through southern Poland in the east, and to the Alps in the south. The hilly uplands are characterized by low hills, often highly eroded, and valleys of some major rivers, such as the Rhine, Danube, and Rhône, as well as many smaller rivers and streams. A few low mountains include the Vosges and the Black Forest on either side of the upper Rhine, the Ore mountains and the Bavarian and Bohemian forests between Germany and the Czech Republic, and the Carpathians. The generally hilly character of the landscape is interrupted by the Hungarian Plain and by smaller plains in places along the Danube.

North of this hilly region of continental Europe is the North European Plain. This flat, low-lying, generally sandy landscape extends from the Atlantic coast of south-west France in the west, across western and northern France, south-eastern Britain, the Low Countries, Denmark and southern Sweden, and across northern Germany into Poland and beyond. There are few appreciable hills in this region. Many major rivers flow through the North European Plain, including the Garonne, Loire, Seine, Thames, Rhine, Weser, Elbe, Oder, and Vistula.

These two zones of temperate Europe offer different kinds of resources. Parts of the hilly uplands include fertile soils, and provided ideal situations for farming communities from the beginning of the Neolithic period (about 5500 BC in this region) onwards. The more mountainous areas often yield valuable minerals such as copper, gold, and salt. Iron ore was abundant, often available on or near the surface in hilly areas. The rivers offered routes for communication and for commerce.

The soils of the North European Plain are generally not as rich as those of the hilly uplands, but tend to be sandy and often boggy. Much of the environment is, however, ideal for livestock. Communities in these northerly regions have traditionally emphasized the raising of cattle and sheep in the abundant natural meadows. Metals such as copper and gold were not available in this region, but iron, in the form of bog ore, was. The rivers flowing through the North European Plain into the Atlantic, the English Channel, the North Sea, and the Baltic Sea, important routes of communication from early times, were by the Iron Age heavily used in commerce.

The Late Bronze Age background

By the Late Bronze Age (1200–800 BC), the fundamental economic and social structures that lay at the base of developments in the Iron Age and Roman period had been established (Harding 2000). Communities were small, rarely more than fifty persons, and nearly all people were primary food producers. Settlements ranged in size from individual farmsteads inhabited by a single family to what we might call hamlets, several households occupying a common settlement area. Subsistence economy was based on cereal cultivation, with several varieties of wheat, barley, and millet the predominant crops, supplemented by lentils, peas, and beans. Domestic livestock included cattle, pigs, sheep, and goats, as well as dogs and in some cases horses. Most excavated settlement sites yield evidence that wild plants and animals were exploited to supplement the diet. Berries, fruits, and nuts are commonly represented; it is unclear to what extent, if any, they were domesticated at this time. Hunted animals, especially deer and boar, as well as birds and fish, are indicated by their bones. Often around 10 per cent of the animal bones from a Late Bronze Age settlement are of wild animals. This diversity of domestic and wild plants and animals shows that communities had developed a system of exploiting a wide range of resources, providing protection against potential disasters created by drought, blight, flood, and other threats to the food supply. Earlier tendencies in agricultural regimes persist: a general emphasis on cereal cultivation among communities in the hilly upland regions, and an emphasis on livestock, especially cattle and sheep, on the North European Plain.

Bronze was widely available, not only in the mountainous regions near the sources of copper and tin, but across the whole of temperate Europe. Its widespread use indicates that extensive circulation systems had developed through which metals were transported. At the same time many other goods entered into circulation; this growth in trade is one of the principal characteristics of the Bronze Age. Particularly abundant as trade goods were amber, primarily from the south coasts of the Baltic Sea; glass beads from southern Europe; and graphite, used to decorate pottery, mainly from deposits in Bohemia and along the Danube near Passau on the German–Austrian border. Production debris shows that bronze was worked—cast and hammered—in many communities, but that items that required knowledge of the properties of bronze and of metalworking techniques, such as swords and vessels, were made by specialists. In contrast to the Iron Age, we have no evidence for manufacturing or trading centres during the Bronze Age in temperate Europe.

The widespread distribution of the materials of limited natural occurrence just mentioned indicates that communities throughout the continent were linked together in a complex network of inter-relationships. Along with the materials recovered archaeologically, information also passed between communities. The sharing of ideas, through interaction between farming settlements and travelling merchants, between family members who resided in different areas, and between neighbouring hamlets, resulted in the spread and adoption of similar architectural techniques, craft methods, design styles, and ritual practices among communities throughout Europe.

The predominant burial practice in most of temperate Europe during the Late Bronze Age was cremation, with the burned bones and ashes placed in an urn, accompanied by modest grave goods such as items of personal ornament or small ceramic vessels, all placed into a hole in the ground. During this period a special practice developed of burying some individuals with lavish funerary ritual. The specific elements of this ritual became a tradition that was maintained throughout the Iron Age and into Roman and early medieval times. A grave at Hart an der Alz in Upper Bavaria is an example of these elite burials. The grave had been arranged in a wooden chamber, the whole covered with a mound of earth and stone. Associated with the cremated man was a four-wheeled wagon with bronze attachments, a set of ornate pottery of types associated with feasting, three bronze vessels, also components of the feasting paraphernalia, a sword and several arrowheads, and a gold finger-ring. Such graves show that a few individuals were emerging with special status and wealth, displayed through the manipulation of material culture in lavish funerary ceremonies. In most cases, as at Hart, the archaeologist is able to investigate directly only the burial itself, not other aspects of the funerary ceremony.

Towns, trade, and status in the Early Iron Age (800–450 BC)

Between 800 and 500 BC centres of population, manufacturing, and trade activity developed in several regions in the hilly upland part of temperate Europe. Among the earliest are those that emerged in the south-east Alpine area of what is today Slovenia, where the site of Stična is the best documented. Characteristic of the ten or fifteen centres known in this region are hilltop settlements, fortified by earth and stone walls, and extensive tumulus cemeteries (during the Early Iron Age a gradual shift from cremation burial to inhumation as the dominant practice is evident in most of Europe). The evidence does not yet allow us to make confident estimates of population, but around 500–1,000 people might be reasonable for the population at sites such as Stična at their peak, between 700 and 500 BC. These centres were places of unusually active production of iron, glass, and finished bronze items. Large quantities of amber from the Baltic region, and imports from the Greek and Etruscan worlds, as well as some objects from east Mediterranean lands, attest to the long-distance connections of these centres. Burial patterns indicate significant differences in wealth and status between individual members of the communities.

Similar centres emerged during the seventh century BC in other regions. Among the best-documented is Závist in Bohemia, a fortified hilltop settlement with evidence of significant workshop production in both local materials and imported goods, including amber and glass. In western Slovakia, Smolenice-Molpír was the site of an important fortified centre, associated with extensive cemeteries of often well-outfitted burials. At Biskupin in south-west Poland, a walled settlement comprised of 102 houses yielded evidence for a substantial population and a variety of manufacturing activities. Recent research at Belsk on the Dnieper river in Ukraine has uncovered a fortified complex with extensive evidence for manufacturing in a wide range of materials and for lively trade with the Greek world from the sixth century BC. In Britain, important settlement centres were established on hilltops, with substantial defensive walls, during the fifth and fourth centuries BC. Settlements excavated at Danebury and Maiden Castle show sizeable populations and intensive manufacturing activity.

Among the most thoroughly studied Early Iron Age centres are those in western central Europe. Characteristic are fortified hilltop settlements, with extensive tumulus cemeteries around them. The most fully investigated centre is the Heuneburg on the upper Danube river in south-west Germany; similar sites have been identified at Mont Lassois and the Britzgyberg in France, Châtillon-sur-Glâne in Switzerland, and the Hohenasperg and Marienberg in southern Germany. Where excavations have explored settlement remains, archaeologists have uncovered extensive evidence for manufacturing in iron, bronze, gold, lignite and jet, amber, coral, and other substances. Interaction with the Greek world is evident in the presence of fine pottery from Athens, Greek wine amphorae, Greek and Etruscan bronze vessels, Mediterranean coral, ornaments of amber, probably from the Baltic region but carved in Mediterranean workshops, and other foreign materials.

The Heuneburg has a wall constructed of clay bricks, which is of special importance because it is modelled on Greek walls in the Mediterranean region. This structure is particularly significant because it indicates consequential interaction between individuals, not just trade of goods, which could take place indirectly between the Mediterranean coasts and south-west Germany. The architect of the brick wall—whoever he or she may have been—must have learned the technique of clay-brick architecture in the Mediterranean region and brought it to the Heuneburg. The wall is indicative of what we might call technology transfer between representatives of two different societies.

A unique indication of the significance of these interactions for commercial interests in the Mediterranean region is the Vix *krater*. This enormous bronze vessel—1.64 m tall, 204 kg in weight, and with a capacity of 1,100 litres—was recovered in the richly outfitted burial of a woman next to the settlement at Mont Lassois (other goods in the grave included an ornate four-wheeled wagon, a neck-ring fashioned from 480 g of gold, two Attic wine cups, an Etruscan bronze jug, two Etruscan bronze basins, and numerous pieces of bronze and iron jewellery, some ornamented with coral and gold). The enormous and finely crafted *krater* (mixing bowl), believed to have been manufactured in a Greek workshop in southern Italy around 530 BC, was almost certainly a 'political gift'—a specially made, extravagant, object for presentation to a potentate with whom the donor wished to establish favourable relations, for political or economic purposes. Recent excavations near the grave have uncovered a ritual complex that included a near life-size stone statue of a seated woman wearing a neck-ring very like that in the rich grave. This monumental representation adds support to the idea that the woman buried at Vix was a person of significant political authority who was important to the commercial interests of Greek merchants.

The goods that Greek merchants might have procured from the centres in temperate Europe have been much discussed. In contrast to the finished Greek and Etruscan objects that loom so large in the archaeological material—ornate painted pottery, bronze vessels, and exotic ornaments—the materials traded from interior Europe to the Mediterranean ports were raw materials that do not survive archaeologically, and were subsequently further worked in any case: foodstuffs such as grain and perhaps preserved meats, metals, fur, leather, textiles, timber, tar, pitch, resin, and honey can be plausibly suggested.

There has been much debate about the connection between the rise of the Early Iron Age centres in west-central Europe and their commerce with the Greek world. In the 1950s and 1960s, when for the first time Greek and Etruscan objects were being recovered in quantities on Early Iron Age sites, these imports were interpreted to indicate substantial, intensive commercial relations between the trade centres north of the Alps and commercial communities in the Mediterranean world. Since then, the quantities and variety of such imports have grown immensely. In some cases Greek and Etruscan products are recovered on newly identified centres. In other instances such imports are turning up on smaller settlements that are more representative of Iron Age communities throughout temperate Europe. It is now apparent that objects from the Mediterranean region were not uncommon in Early Iron Age Europe, and that their distribution is by no means restricted to the major centres. The great increase in the number and variety of Mediterranean imports that have been recovered in the past four decades has necessitated a re-evaluation of earlier understandings of the role of this particular trade in the rise of centres and in the emergence of elites in Early Iron Age Europe. Now the best approach seems to be to consider temperate European and Mediterranean societies as parts of a single complex network, in which all communities were linked together through systems of goods circulation and of interpersonal interactions.

In the richly outfitted burials associated with the Early Iron Age centres we can trace the development of the signs of status and power that were already apparent in the Late Bronze Age, as in the grave at Hart an der Alz. In west-central Europe, where these burials have been most intensively investigated, around fifty have been studied, including the Vix grave mentioned above. These rich burials are typically in chambers constructed of hewn timbers, covered by substantial mounds of stone and earth. The individuals interred in such graves typically wore gold neck-rings and other ring jewellery (bracelets, finger-rings, earrings), and they were buried with sets of feasting vessels of bronze and pottery, often of Greek or Etruscan manufacture, with four-wheeled wagons, and, in the case of men, with weapons.

The best-documented of this series of richly outfitted burials is that at Hochdorf, just west of the Early Iron Age fortified settlement on the Hohenasperg, north of Stuttgart in south-west Germany. While most of the richest burials had been looted in antiquity, the Hochdorf grave, dated at around 550 BC, was intact when it was excavated by archaeologists in the late 1970s and early 1980s. The investigation was conducted in unusually precise fashion, with the central portion of the burial removed intact from the site for excavation in the laboratory (Biel 1985).

The deceased, a male of about 40 years of age, had been laid on a bronze couch 2.75 m long supported by eight cast bronze figurines of women, inlaid with coral, each mounted on a wheel. The Hochdorf man had not only the typical gold neck-ring and a gold bracelet, but also two gold *fibulae* (brooches), a gold belt plate, a dagger with hilt and scabbard covered with ornate gold, and large bands of ornamental gold on his shoes. All of the gold that this man wore in the funerary ceremony was intended to display his status, and was placed where it was highly visible to onlookers. From the Neolithic period on, gold had been employed as a sign of status, and the unusual quantity of gold arranged for display with the man buried at Hochdorf makes it apparent that he was a person of the highest status in his society. The weapons in the grave—the gold-decorated dagger at his belt and the quiver of arrows—indicate his role as a warrior. As in later times, gold (or silver) ornament on weapons was a sign of special status within a military hierarchy.

The man's role within ritual feasting is also represented in the grave. At his feet was a bronze cauldron 1.04 m in diameter, manufactured in a Greek workshop, capable of holding about 400 litres of liquid and containing the residue of a beverage similar to mead. With it was a gold bowl, apparently for use as a dipper. Arranged on the wagon in the grave were nine bronze dishes and three bronze basins, and hanging on one wall of the chamber were nine drinking-horns. The largest, 1.23 m long, was made of iron and had gold bands decorating it, the other eight were fashioned from aurochs' horns and outfitted with bronze attachments. The nine sets of dishes and drinking-horns, together with the large cauldron and bowl, have been interpreted as material representations of the buried individual's role as a host of feasts, leader of a band of warriors, represented by the eight smaller drinking-horns, and chief of the community that resided in and around the fortress on the Hohenasperg.

The wealth of special objects in the Hochdorf grave has led to discussion of the buried man's status in Early Iron Age society as a whole. Some investigators argue that the objects buried with him indicate that he was not merely the chief of a local community, but instead a potentate of regional significance. While variation in burial structures and contents provides good data regarding social statuses at the centres and in the countryside of Early Iron Age Europe, larger-scale political organization is not yet well understood for this period, and hence such a political role for the Hochdorf man must remain hypothetical.

New styles and changing relationships (450–400 BC)

During the fifth century BC the Early Iron Age centres in much of Europe declined in importance. In most cases there is no evidence for large-scale destruction, but rather for gradual abandonment of the centres and movement of the occupants into the countryside. A new series of richly outfitted burials dating to the second half of the fifth century BC appeared slightly to the north of those of the Early Iron Age. Those rich graves are also characterized by gold-ring jewellery and other ornaments, wheeled vehicles, feasting gear, and Mediterranean imports, but they are not associated with manufacturing and commercial centres in the way that the rich graves of the Early Iron Age are.

The most apparent difference between these and the earlier series of wealthy burials is in the style of ornament applied to objects in the graves. The change in style is part of a profound change in attitudes and values on the part of elites in temperate Europe (Wells 2001: 54–73). The new style is known as La Tène, after a lakeshore site in western Switzerland that has been designated as the 'type site' of the Late Iron Age, and it is characterized, not by the geometrical patterns of Early Iron Age design, but by floral motifs and stylized representations of human faces and of animals. The elements of this style were created through adapting ornament from a variety of sources to the south and east, including the decorative traditions associated with Etruscan Italy, Greece, and the Scythian lands north of the Black Sea.

Evidence from the rich burials indicates that significant changes were taking place in the attitudes of members of the elite groups toward the Mediterranean societies from which exotic imports were being acquired. One indication of this change is the frequent modification of Mediterranean imports. The Greek and Etruscan objects found in Early Iron Age graves were for the most part unaltered. They were used, presumably by the individual with whom they were buried, were employed in the funerary ceremony, and finally were placed in the grave, all with little or no modification to their shape or decoration subsequent to their arrival in temperate Europe from Greece or Etruria. But many of the imported vessels placed in graves of the later series, together with objects decorated in the La Tène style, were transformed by local craft-workers. The two Attic wine cups from the grave at Kleinaspergle, for example, were outfitted with thin gold appliques decorated in La Tène style, attached to the ceramic vessels with tiny rivets. Several bronze jugs from Etruscan Italy recovered in other graves had been reshaped by local metal-smiths. Furthermore, just as motifs from Mediterranean decorative traditions were transformed to create the new style, so new forms of bronze vessels were developed through transforming the shapes of jugs imported from Etruscan Italy. For example, local adaptations of the 'beak-spouted' jug, and the newly created cylinder-spouted jug, occur in many of the rich burials of this period.

By the end of the fifth century BC many richly outfitted graves did not contain Mediterranean imports at all. Apparently the elites no longer felt it necessary to display and use objects imported from Greece and Etruria to make the statements about status that were a principal purpose of the funerary rituals. A striking example is the recently excavated grave at the Glauberg near Frankfurt. It contained lavish gold jewellery, ornate weapons, and decorated bronze vessels, and the burial structure included monumental sculpture and the creation of an entire funerary landscape of which the burial mound was the focal point. But no Mediterranean imports were included in the assemblage.

Among the objects most commonly ornamented with the La Tène style were weapons. Especially common is linear decoration on sword scabbards, but ornament was also applied to helmets, and to spear- and lance-heads. This close association between the new style and weaponry in the rich burials illustrates the continued importance of military symbolism in the acquisition and maintenance of status and wealth during this dynamic period of European prehistory. In the lands north of the Black Sea, the tradition known as Scythian art incorporates many of the same elements as early La Tène decoration, and there too weapons were often highly ornamented. In northern parts of continental Europe, however, the style known as Jastorf (ornament on metal objects and on pottery that was distinct from the La Tène style, without the floral motifs of the latter) did not incorporate lavish ornamentation, or the use of gold, to any appreciable extent, either on weaponry or on personal ornaments.

Larger communities and public ritual (400–150 BC)

The series of richly outfitted burials associated with the early La Tène style and with Etruscan imports, concentrated in the middle Rhineland but also well represented in eastern France, Bohemia, and Austria, ended at the start of the fourth century BC. Around this time all over temperate Europe the practice of burying the dead in large flat-grave cemeteries was adopted. Graves with gold ornaments and with Mediterranean imports are rare during this period, but distinctions can be recognized in wealth and status nonetheless. Women were buried with bronze ring jewellery, including neck-rings, bracelets, sometimes leg-rings, finger-rings, and earrings; glass bracelets; *fibulae*; and belts made of bronze links, often with enamel inlay. Some male graves (on average about half of male burials in a given cemetery) contained iron weapons, such as swords, spears, and shields. Male graves had few personal ornaments. One or two ceramic vessels are common in both women's and men's graves.

After the fifth century BC evidence of iron-smelting, forging, and of abundant iron objects in cemeteries and on settlements makes it clear that ironworking technology was expanding rapidly. Much more iron was being produced and fashioned into tools, weapons, and ornaments, and it was of increasingly fine quality. As metallographic studies have shown, already in the Early Iron Age some smiths had mastered the technique of alloying iron with carbon to produce fine steel cutting-edges on tools and weapons, but not until this later period was fine steel being produced consistently by large numbers of smiths.

During the fourth and third centuries BC the La Tène style spread widely from the region in which it first appeared—the middle Rhine valley and southern Germany—throughout temperate Europe, west-ward through France to Iberia, north-west to Britain, eastward into Poland and beyond, south-eastward into the Balkans, and even across the Alps into Italy. The character of this spread has been a source of controversy. In essence, the debate is whether the spread of the La Tène style was the result of migration of peoples, or rather of the adoption of a new fashion by communities throughout Europe who became familiar with it through trade and other kinds of interaction.

Greek and Roman texts mention movement of groups at this time. Livy's history recounts the migration of peoples he calls Gauls (*Galli*) across the Alps into northern Italy, then southward down the peninsula. Several Greek writers mention Celtic mercenaries serving in armies in Greece, Sicily, Asia Minor and Egypt during the fourth and third centuries BC, asserting that Celts were favoured because of their supposed ferocity in battle. Such texts, together with the spread of the La Tène style, have led many investigators to consider this a time of 'great Celtic migrations'.

As with so many cultural changes that have been ascribed to migrations, perspectives on this phenomenon are changing. While there was always some movement of individuals and of groups, many now question whether migration is necessary as an explanation for the spread of the La Tène style. The texts that refer to migrations and mercenary service are among the earliest that concern peoples north of the Mediterranean basin, and there is no reason to think that conditions of movement and interaction were any different when Greek writers became aware of peoples in temperate Europe from what they had been before. The texts may tell us more about what was in the minds of the Greek writers, or about the events or rumours that reached their attention and that they felt were worthy of recording, than about the historical reality of the peoples described. Except in a few limited instances, there is no archaeological evidence for substantial migration at this time, while there is considerable indication that the new style was eagerly taken up by peoples all over temperate Europe and beyond.

The issue of mercenary service in Mediterranean armies requires special attention. We must be cautious in accepting Greek and Roman writers' assertions regarding Celtic mercenaries in the service of armies of Mediterranean potentates. It is not clear what the writers meant when they used the names 'Celts' (Greek *Keltoi*) or 'Gauls' (Latin *Galli*), nor is it evident how much they knew about the origins of the peoples they mentioned. Still, there can be no doubt that the overwhelming textual evidence, as well as some archaeological, attests to instances of service by young men from temperate Europe in military contexts in the Mediterranean region. The significance of such service lies in what the individuals involved experienced and what they brought back with them by way of knowledge of Mediterranean peoples and life-styles and desires to change their ways of life in their homelands. As happens so often in world events, the military experience of young men from temperate Europe in the Mediterranean world, and their gain in wealth through such service, probably served as stimuli to social and economic change in temperate Europe. The first coinage minted north of the Alps dates to the late fourth and early third centuries BC. The earliest locally minted coins were of gold and were modelled on Greek prototypes, which were most likely to have been brought home by returning mercenaries (see Chapter 6).

A major change evident in temperate Europe during the third and second centuries BC is the much larger, communal scale on which ritual is practised. Rectangular enclosures were constructed, with substantial ditches and walls, altering the landscape to create special places for the practice of ritual (see also Chapter 7). Among the best-researched are Libenice in Bohemia and Gournay-sur-Aronde and Ribemont in north-eastern France. At Gournay excavators have found about 2,000 iron weapons, including swords, scabbards, shields, and lance- and spear-points, many of them purposely bent or broken, deposited in the enclosing ditches and in pits within the enclosed area. At Ribemont large numbers of human bones have been found, including one deposit that contained the skeletons of eighty persons, accompanied by weapons, but without skulls. The major role of weapons in these deposits is of particular significance. The architecture and positioning of these sites place emphasis on public accessibility and visibility, indicating that they were intended to be places where large numbers of people could gather to observe and participate in the rituals. At La Tène on the shore of Lake Neuchâtel in Switzerland, many hundreds of weapons, many of them elaborately decorated, were deposited by being dropped into shallow water. This place also was a highly visible one that probably involved large numbers of observers in the ceremonies.

During the second and first centuries BC rectangular enclosures defined by banks and ditches, not unlike the earlier sites at Libenice and Gournay, known as *Viereckschanzen* ('rectangular enclosures'), became standardized features of the landscape over much of temperate Europe. Evidence from excavation suggests that these enclosures served largely, though not exclusively, ritual purposes. Since a primary function of ritual is to create and reaffirm feelings of community and group identity, the construction of many large, public ritual sites in the third and second centuries BC is an important indicator of major social and political changes in Late Iron Age society. Specifically, this seems to manifest itself in the formation of larger communities in Late Iron Age Europe, a phenomenon supported not only by this evidence pertaining specifically to ritual activity, but also by other kinds of evidence.

Urban centres of the Late Iron Age

During the first half of the second century BC a new form of settlement began to appear in temperate Europe. Settlements much larger in area than any earlier ones were enclosed by massive walls built of earth, with outer faces constructed of cut stone and timber. These settlements are known as *oppida*, after Julius Caesar's use of that term in reference to the centres which he encountered in Gaul (Collis 1995). Around 150 of these sites have been identified across the whole of the hilly upland regions of Europe, from central France in the west to Slovakia in the east. The majority is located on hilltops, but some are situated in well-protected lowland locations. What distinguishes the *oppida* from all earlier settlements in temperate Europe, and from the majority of contemporary settlements, is both their size and the density of habitation and manufacturing debris that excavations have uncovered at many of them.

In Gaul (west of the Rhine river), *oppidum* walls enclose settlements several tens of hectares in area, only a portion of which had been built up with structures. In some places east of the Rhine sizes can be much greater. At Manching, the most thoroughly investigated *oppidum*, the walls enclose 380 ha, at Kelheim 600 ha. Most of the *oppida* that have been objects of systematic excavation, such as Bibracte, Hrazany, Kelheim, Manching, Staré Hradisko, Stradonice, the Titelberg, Trisov, and Závist, have yielded evidence of intensive occupation, along with substantial remains of manufacturing and commerce. But some sites, such as Zarten, have produced very little by way of settlement material, leading to the hypothesis that some of the *oppida* were constructed as refuges, for protection in times of danger, but were never permanently inhabited by any substantial community.

Excavation results show that the centres of the major *oppidum* settlements were organized with streets as open passageways, substantial post-built houses and workshops, and large numbers of pits for the storage of grain and other commodities (Sievers 2003). Ironworking was carried out intensively at the *oppida*, and a variety of new types of iron implements were made and used, including ploughshares, coulters, scythes, and nails. In many of the crafts represented at the *oppida*, a new level of mass-production is evident, consistent with the much larger scale of population, manufacturing, and trade at these centres. Most pottery at the major *oppida* was made on the fast-turning potter's wheel. Personal ornaments such as *fibulae* were designed to be mass-produced, rather than hand-crafted as they had been previously. About the time that the *oppida* were first established, coinage in silver and bronze was introduced, and minting of gold coins increased. Numismatists believe that a money-based economy emerged at the *oppida*, based on the coinage in three metals of different values. Since each *oppidum* minted distinctive coins, coins recovered through excavation provide important evidence for trade. Sizeable quantities of Mediterranean imports are evident at the *oppida*, indicating a resurgence in commerce between communities in temperate Europe and the Mediterranean world early in the second century BC. Goods imported from the Roman world include ceramic amphorae for transporting wine and perhaps olive oil, fine pottery, bronze vessels, medical instruments, coins, jewellery, glass ornaments, and writing implements. Similar Roman imports have been recovered at the trade centre of Hengistbury Head on the south-central coast of Britain, especially from the end of the second and the first centuries BC. Writing appears at the *oppida*, for example Greek letters that seem to spell personal names, incised on sherds of pottery at Manching, suggesting that merchants who were engaged in trade with Mediterranean societies learned that medium of communication in the course of their transactions.

The population size of *oppida* is difficult to estimate. During the second century BC the practice of burying the dead with grave goods declined, and as a result we have relatively few cemeteries that provide the kinds of demographic data that we need to estimate the sizes of the communities. For most of the *oppida* no sizeable cemeteries contemporary with the major period of occupation have been found. Based on quantities of habitation and manufacturing debris, numbers of structures on the sites, and other considerations, estimates of 3,000–5,000 inhabitants for the largest of the *oppida*, such as Bibracte, Manching, and Stradonice, are reasonable. The often dense occupational debris at these centres represents only a relatively brief period of use—most of the *oppida* were inhabited for not more than 100 years.

The reasons behind the establishment of the *oppida* during the second century BC are not well understood. The common situation of these sites in locations that offer good natural defence, and the massive enclosing walls, suggest that protection from attack was a primary consideration. Textual sources indicate that during the second century BC movement of peoples, and warfare, were increasingly common. Recent survey research suggests that at the time that the *oppida* were founded, rural settlement in their vicinities declined substantially. These results support the idea that people moved from small undefended settlements into the newly established fortified *oppida* for protection. On the other hand, for sites such as Heidengraben and Kelheim, with their enormous enclosed areas, investigators have argued that the walls were much too long to be defended by members of the community that resided at the sites, even taking into account the participation, in times of danger, of smaller communities in the vicinity. Such considerations support the idea that the *oppidum* walls were in large part boundary markers, intended to impress and perhaps intimidate, rather than strictly military in function.

When Julius Caesar campaigned with his conquering legions in Gaul between 58 and 51 BC, his written account (*The Gallic War*) describes the *oppida* as tribal capitals, political, economic, and religious centres of the indigenous peoples. Although some of the *oppida* inhabited by groups allied with Rome remained occupied for a time after the conquest, the majority of the sites were abandoned by their substantial populations at the time of the Roman conquest, and their former occupants moved down into lowland locations. East of the Rhine, in southern Germany, the Czech Republic, Austria, and elsewhere, *oppida* were also abandoned around the middle of the first century BC, for reasons that are not well understood.

Many smaller settlements, not enclosed by walls such as those at the *oppida*, were inhabited by communities that performed many of the same economic functions as the *oppida*. These included not only making pottery, but also smelting iron ore, and casting bronze ornaments for local use. Some small communities produced iron for export, processed precious metals, cast luxury ornaments for elite consumption, and minted coins. Examples of settlements at which such unexpectedly complex economic processes were carried out are Gussage All Saints in southern Britain and Leonberg in southern Germany.

The native peoples and Rome

Military symbolism in ritual

Symbols of military activity, specifically weapons manipulated in ritual activities, played significant roles in later European prehistory, from the Late Bronze Age onwards. As noted above of the Late Bronze Age burial at Hart and the Early Iron Age grave at Hochdorf, weaponry was an important aspect of burial ritual for elite males. Much early La Tène ornament occurs on weapons. From the third century BC on, weapons played a major role in the large public ritual-offering places, such as Gournay and Ribemont in France and La Tène in Switzerland.

In the final two centuries BC a new degree of uniformity throughout temperate Europe can be recognized in graves that contain sets of weapons, in the southern regions where the La Tène style was dominant, in the northern parts of the continent characterized by the Jastorf style (above), and in southern Britain. This phenomenon represents what can be called an international warrior aristocracy, and it is characterized by full sets of weapons that include long swords with scabbards, spears and lances, and shields. Not only did the practice of burying this standard 'set' become common across Europe, but the specific types of weapons were often very similar. The emergence of this pattern suggests both that warfare was becoming an increasingly important activity during the final two centuries BC, and thus ever-more often represented in graves, and that elites throughout Europe were engaged in ever-more frequent interaction through the networks that linked their communities together.

The spread of this relative homogeneity in weapon sets in well-outfitted men's graves took place at the same time that Rome was becoming increasingly involved in temperate Europe, with its political and military interventions in southern Gaul and the intensification of commerce northward. Rather than suggesting that the increasing indications of militarism throughout temperate Europe mark the beginnings of direct responses on the part of native societies to Rome's imperial ambitions and military plans, I would argue instead that Rome's expansion during this period, and the growing importance of military symbolism in the north, were interrelated aspects of widespread changes taking place throughout the networks that linked the societies of Mediterranean and temperate Europe.

Roman texts and the threat from the north

From the middle of the second century BC on, the interplay between archaeological evidence in Late Iron Age Europe and information in textual sources becomes particularly complex and problematic. Consideration of this interplay is essential for understanding the processes of change associated with the Roman conquest and subsequent developments. In Greek and Roman accounts of the migrations of the Cimbri, Teutoni, and groups that allegedly joined them in the final two decades of the second century BC, we have accounts of population movements that threatened Roman Italy and neighbouring lands under Rome's sphere of influence. We do not know whether such movements were unusual, and thus merited commentary, or whether such migrations were common, and for some reason only these happened to be mentioned. If the latter, then the origins of the *oppida* could be understood in the context of such increased mobility on the part of sizeable groups of peoples moving through the countryside. Yet neither the specific movements of the Cimbri and their allies, as described in the texts, nor other movements on such a scale, are evident in the archaeological record.

Whatever the reality may have been, these migrations recorded between 113 and 101 BC had a profound impact on Roman thinking about peoples north of the Alps, as had the sacking of Rome in 390 BC, in creating an image of dangerous, warlike peoples to the north, always representing a threat to Roman Italy. In his *Gallic War*, Caesar made specific reference to these migrations described by his predecessors. He wrote: 'Nor did he suppose that barbarians so fierce would stop short after seizing the whole of Gaul; but rather, like the Cimbri and Teutoni before them, they would break forth into the Province [*i.e.* Gallia Transalpina, modern Provence], and push on thence into Italy, especially as there was but the Rhône to separate the Sequani from the Roman Province' (*Gallic War* 1. 33). Whether Caesar was motivated by the threat of the aggressive Gauls of his time to view them as similar to the earlier Cimbri and Teutoni, or simply used this familiar threat as a way of justifying his actions in Gaul to his fellow Romans, the significance of this disposition in the Roman mind is clear as regards Rome's perception of the peoples beyond the Alps.

Texts, archaeology, and cultural identity

We first encounter names associated with the peoples of prehistoric Europe in textual sources from the Mediterranean world dating to the Iron Age. The question of identities among the indigenous peoples with whom the Greek and Roman worlds came into contact has been much discussed recently (James 1999; Wells 2001). I shall review briefly the problem of distinguishing between Celts and Germans in what became the Roman frontier zone along the Rhine and Danube rivers; similar issues pertain to other named groups, such as Dacians and Illyrians.

The name Celts, in the form *Keltoi*, first appears in Greek sources of the sixth and fifth centuries BC, in reference to peoples inhabiting western regions of Europe. Hecataeus notes that the Greek colonial city of Massalia (Marseilles) was situated in a region inhabited by Celts, and Herodotus tells us that the Danube originates in the land of the Celts. The principal problem with using such information, aside from the fact that those writers do not provide any description of the people so designated, is that they do not name any other peoples in western Europe with whom the named group could be compared. It is unclear whether they meant that Celts were a specific people, or they were using that designation to refer to all non-Greek peoples of that part of the continent. Later, in the fourth and third centuries BC, more Greek references to Celts seem to build upon those earlier usages. Romans called the peoples north of the Alps, and some settled in the Po plain just south of the Alps, *Galli* (Gauls). Several ancient writers inform us that the people the Romans called Gauls were the same as those the Greeks called Celts. But the very general way in which those names are used makes it difficult to link them with any specific archaeological sites or regions. When Greek writers tell of Celtic mercenaries in the eastern Mediterranean region, it is not clear where such Celts came from. According to what we are told elsewhere by Greek writers, they could have come from the Lower Danube region, southern Germany, central France, or other parts of temperate Europe.

The earliest surviving use of the name Germans (*Germani*) is in Caesar's account of his campaigns in Gaul. Caesar informs us that Gauls live west of the Rhine, Germans (for the most part) live east of it. He characterizes the Germans as very different from the Gauls in having no towns, practising much less elaborate rituals, and pursuing a simpler way of life with respect to subsistence and other activities.

The archaeology suggests a different situation. The *oppida* of the final two centuries BC occur both west and east of the Rhine, and the material culture—wall structures, domestic architecture, pottery, jewellery, coins—west and east of the Rhine are very similar, indicating no such significant difference between the peoples as Caesar's distinction between Gauls and Germans implies. But east of the lower

Rhine, on the North European Plain to the north of the region in which *oppida* occur (that is, north of a line from the mouth of the Rhine east through Cologne, north-east to Hanover, and south-east to Dresden and on to Krakow), communities were different from those in the hilly uplands. On the one hand, the rituals and subsistence practices do not correspond to the simple character attributed to the Germans by Caesar; on the other, the Germans did not live in towns similar to the *oppida,* something which correlates with Caesar's description.

Today many historians approach Caesar's statements from the perspective of his political interests. In ancient concepts of geography, rivers frequently formed boundaries between peoples. In his quest for support from Rome for his campaigns in Gaul, Caesar may have been trying to portray the Rhine as a major cultural frontier and thus as a natural goal for his conquests. In this sense, perhaps he intentionally overdrew the differences between the peoples west of the Rhine and those to the east of it. We also need to ask how much Caesar knew about the peoples east of the Rhine. Although he made two forays across the river, in 55 and 53 BC, he did not engage any troops there, let alone become familiar with the inhabitants of the region and their way of life. Caesar's account of the peoples he called Germans may have been largely constructed from Romans' general ideas about barbarians, along with some information from merchants who had travelled in the lands east of the Rhine and possibly from literary predecessors such as Posidonius.

Approaches to understanding changes at the end of the Iron Age

Process versus events

The textual sources that pertain to interactions between representatives of Rome and the native peoples of temperate Europe represent those interactions largely in terms of specific events. These include the sacking of Rome in 390 BC, the migrations of the Cimbri and Teutoni between 113 and 101 BC, Caesar's campaigns in Gaul between 58 and 51 BC, Augustus' construction of military bases on the west bank of the Rhine between 16 and 13 BC, and the loss of Varus' legions in the Teutoburg Forest in AD 9. The written sources that survive tell us very little about economic, social, and political conditions in the native societies, let alone about ongoing changes in those societies, apparently because the Roman authors neither knew nor cared about those subjects; some information is available in texts about trade in Gaul, a matter of direct concern to Rome.

The archaeological evidence, on the other hand, does not generally tell us about events (the evidence at Kalkriese for the 'Battle of the Teutoburg Forest' seems to be a significant exception—Wells 2003), but it does provide evidence concerning processes of change in the native societies of temperate Europe, before and during engagement between native peoples and the Roman world. For example, in considering the impact of growing Roman influence in temperate Europe during the second and first centuries BC, it is important to consider the long history of interactions between communities north of the Alps and the societies of the Mediterranean basin. The important point is that the Roman conquest, and even the intensification of trade during the second and first centuries BC, did not constitute the sudden appearance of new Mediterranean cultural elements or ideas in temperate Europe. These were aspects of processes that had been operating for centuries.

The development and practice of rituals that involved military symbolism, in burials and in offering deposits, indicate that elite groups in temperate Europe had created a special role for military activity by the Bronze Age. The set of symbols representing this activity played major roles in ceremonial activity throughout the Iron Age. When Roman armies encountered forces of native warriors, those groups had a long tradition of military preparedness and planning. Understanding the chronological depth of this tradition and the pervasiveness of military ritual in Late Iron Age societies helps us to understand the character of the societies that Rome faced in the course of its military campaigns north of the Alps and then across the frontiers during the first five centuries AD.

Networks of interaction

Instead of thinking of the Roman world and the peoples of temperate Europe as two fundamentally separate political and cultural entities, we need to be aware of the long history of interaction between communities north of the Alps and societies of the Mediterranean basin. Interaction between communities within temperate Europe was more intensive than long-distance contacts, but the Greek and Etruscan imports at the early Iron Age centres, the Etruscan bronze vessels in burials associated with early La Tène ornament, and the masses of Roman goods at the *oppida* and at other sites of the Late Iron Age all make clear that contacts and commerce between north and south were regular throughout later prehistory. If we think of these interactions in terms of networks, and of the communities involved as nodes on those networks, we shall be able to understand better the processes of change that accompanied the Roman conquest and the dynamic relations between the Roman provinces and the peoples beyond the frontier.

2

The Roman Republic: political history

G. J. Bradley

THIS chapter links together the most important events in the history of the Roman Republic into an explanatory narrative, describing the dynamic changes in Roman politics, society, and culture over a period of some five hundred years (509–31; all dates are BC). Writing such an account presents several challenges. The most obvious is that the literary sources for the early and middle Republic are very late. The first Roman histories of the city were not compiled until the late third century, and most of these early works are lost. The earliest to survive is the Greek history of Polybius, from the mid-second century; most were written a hundred years or more after that. This shortcoming is not fatal, however. Greek historians had begun to notice Rome in the fourth century, and the Sicilian Timaeus wrote at considerable length about the history of Rome down to 264, that is, his own time. We have some idea of his work through citations in later authors. In addition, the Romans were keenly aware of their history well before there was a literary tradition. Documents recording treaties, magistrates, priests, temple foundations, and colonies existed from at least the early years of the Republic. These records were not always accurate, and were rudimentary until the late fourth century. It is from that point onwards that the narrative of Livy, the early Augustan writer who is our most important historical source for the early Republic, becomes more factual and detailed. The earliest Roman historians could also draw on popular stories associated with monuments or place-names, on drama, poetry, and family records. This rich historical tradition was certainly more malleable and unreliable than literary histories, but the obviously 'oral' character of much of what we find in histories of early Rome shows that these memories had always been a vibrant part of Roman ideology and political discourse.

Besides the basic problem of the origin of our information for the first centuries of the Republic, ancient accounts have some misleading tendencies. Most of our evidence shares a 'Rome-centred' perspective, presenting the peoples with whom the Romans came into contact, and eventually conquered, in a stereotypical and often unsympathetic fashion. Most of our sources also exaggerate the poverty and austerity of early Rome, because they share a pervasive ideology of its early history as a 'golden age', in contrast to their own milieu, the late Republic and early empire.

From monarchy to Republic

There are signs of settlement on the site of Rome from the late Bronze Age (*c.*1000). Rome's location was central to its subsequent domination of Italy. Here, 25 km from the sea, the Tiber could first be forded (just downstream from the Tiber island), as for example by the route of the ancient *via Salaria* ('salt road'), which linked the summer pastures of the Apennine mountains to the coastal salt-pans at the mouth of the river. The seasonal transfer of animals between the mountains and plains (transhumance) was of great antiquity. The Tiber itself was navigable. The Forum Boarium below the Capitol served as a river port; here was an extremely ancient cult of Hercules, which followed rites regarded by the Romans as Greek. Finds of Greek pottery suggest a strong Greek presence, probably of traders, in this area. Forum Boarium means 'the *forum* for cattle', suggesting that there was a livestock market here, linked to transhumance. Rome was at the centre of one of the largest plains in central Italy, and thus ideally suited to become a major market for agricultural produce.

Rome was traditionally regarded as having been ruled by kings from its foundataion in 753 until 509. The evidence for the reigns of the first four kings, beginning with Romulus, is uncertain and controversial, but archaeological excavations show that Rome had become a powerful and sophisticated state under the later monarchs. By the end of the sixth century Rome was a major urban centre, with many monumental buildings. These included the temple of Jupiter Optimus Maximus, Juno, and Minerva on the Capitoline hill, a project of the last king, Tarquinius Superbus, in the late sixth century. The outline of the massive podium on which the temple stood, measuring around 62 by 53 m, recently revealed to its full height by new excavations, shows this to have been one of the largest temples in mainland Italy at that time. The political heart of the city was the large Forum Romanum with its *comitium* (assembly-place), which had been laid out by c.650–625. This was the main public meeting-place of the city, demonstrating the existence of a political community. Here the people could be addressed by the king, who might be acclaimed in the same way as Homeric princes (e.g. Homer, *Iliad* 2. 390–5). Religious pronouncements could also be made here by priests. At the other end of the Forum from the *comitium*, in the shadow of the Palatine hill where Romulus was thought to have established the first settlement, lay the sanctuary of Vesta, closely associated with the *regia*, the house of the *rex* (king). There was also probably a complete circuit of walls around the city by the late sixth century.

The city already had complex political and religious institutions by the fall of the monarchy. The citizen body was arranged in *curiae*, supra-family groups reputedly established by Romulus; in tribes, arranged geographically and attributed to the penultimate king, Servius Tullius; and in the military *classis*, a wealth-class of those who could afford to equip themselves for army service. These groups formed the basis of the political assemblies, which probably met in the *comitium*, and the army, which could only meet outside the *pomoerium* (the sacred boundary of the city). The groupings by tribe and *classis*, though progressively elaborated, continued to be the fundamental means of articulating the citizen body for various purposes until the end of the Republic. The monarchical period also saw the establishment of a sophisticated religious system, with a complex calendar and a wide range of priesthoods.

These developments reflect the close contact with the developing city-states of Etruria and Campania, which shared with Rome a strongly hellenized culture. Greek influence came from settlements on the coasts of southern Italy and Sicily, regarded by later sources as colonies of the Greek mainland and Aegean. Contact with Greek states was intense because cities settled by Greeks dominated the coasts of southern Italy and Sicily in the archaic period, and Rome was a stopping-point on the way to the mineral-rich region of Etruria. This trade in raw materials was enticed up the Tiber and fostered at the Forum Boarium. Similar *emporia* (markets), like Minturnae, Pyrgi, and Gravisca, served shipborne merchants along Italy's Tyrrhenian coast. The intense mercantile interchange which resulted promoted the distribution throughout Etruria and Latium of prestige items such as Greek (especially Athenian) pottery, and of customs such as ostentatious burial practices. Traders, craftsmen, and other travellers also stimulated the exchange of political ideas and institutions, and of gods like Apollo and Hercules.

By the time of the last king, Tarquinius Superbus, Rome controlled much of the surrounding region of Latium. The Romans themselves thought certain festivals preserved the record of the primordial city's boundaries, no more than a few miles from the centre (Strabo 5. 3. 2, 230C). Literary sources recount the progressive conquest of Rome's immediate hinterland under consecutive kings. The historicity of the early conquests is uncertain. For example, a sweeping victory over Etruscan forces attributed to Servius Tullius is also questionable, although some sort of Roman hegemony over southern Etruscan cities seems to be implied independently in Hesiod's *Theogony* (1011–16; Cornell 1995: 210). To the south, Rome's control of Latium as far as Ardea and Lavinium by the end of the monarchy is directly confirmed by Polybius (3. 22, 26), drawing on a treaty struck in 509 between Rome and the great Phoenician city of Carthage.

Tarquinius Superbus is said to have been a tyrant. This is not implausible in the context of the close links between Rome and Greek cities, many of which were governed by tyrants in the seventh and sixth centuries. The revolution that overthrew him and set up the Republic was led, according to tradition, by a few heroic individuals. Several were closely related to the king: L. Junius Brutus (his nephew) and L. Tarquinius Collatinus (a cousin). The events supposed to have instigated the revolt, the rape of the Roman matron Lucretia by the king's son, Sextus, and her subsequent suicide, echo stories about archaic Greek tyrants, whose downfall was often attributed to the abuse of their subjects. But the existence of dictators in Latin cities, and of Etruscan kings whose office is described in terms of magisterial years (as at Caere), suggest that republics were also developing in neighbouring cities (Cornell 1995: 230 f.). That the monarchy did end in 509 or thereabouts is supported by the existence of the *Fasti Consulares*, the official list of consuls. Although our versions of this document are no earlier than the Augustan period, it is widely accepted to be an authentic record of magistrates going back to the start of the Republic. The traditional date of the foundation of the Republic is also supported by independent Greek accounts of two contemporary events linked to the fall of the monarchy: the formation of the first Romano-Carthaginian treaty, and the battle of Aristodemus of Cumae with the Etruscan forces of Porsenna in Latium (Dionysius of Halicarnassus 7. 5–6).

The early Republic (*c.*509–338)

The novelty of the new Republic was the way that the power of the king, *imperium*, was shared between two consuls (perhaps originally called praetors), who had a term of office limited to one year. *imperium* was required to lead the army, and conveyed the power of life and death over subordinates both in military and civilian contexts. Subsequently, in the later fifth and early fourth centuries, there were more than two supreme magistrates, known as military tribunes. These magistracies came to be dominated by patricians, members of favoured *gentes* (clans) who monopolized the priesthoods and claimed sole right of interpreting the will of the gods through 'holding the auspices' (*auspicia*; see Chapter 7). The clan of the Claudii was added to the patriciate after its leader Attus Clausus emigrated to Rome from the neighbouring region of Sabinum with his relatives and followers, traditionally in 504 (Livy 2. 16. 4–5). The Fasti Consulares show that some non-patricians gained the consulate before *c.*450, but hardly any in the second half of the century. This 'closing of the patriciate' was challenged by the plebeian movement, which was probably an alliance of the oppressed poor and the richer non-patricians (Raaflaub 2005).

Social strife developed in the early Republic hand in hand with a deterioration in economic conditions. Rome suffered a series of military setbacks at the hands of enemies such as the Volsci and Aequi; trade was probably affected by the wider geopolitical situation, which saw old links between southern Etruria and Campania (north and south of Rome respectively) imperilled by an Etruscan naval defeat to Syracuse in 474. The scarcity of Roman funerary evidence in the early Republic probably reflects customary restraint more than economic downturn, but the virtual ending of public building in the early fifth century speaks eloquently of a more uncertain climate. It is thus plausible that, according to our sources, major plebeian concerns included the burden of debt, the lack of land, and the distribution of food.

Other factors gave impetus to the plebeian movement. First, the masses had probably become more important in the latter stages of the monarchy: the last kings are said to have sought popular support for their rule; Servius Tullius exemplifies this trend. The new Republican magistrates must have relied for legitimation on the assemblies (already present under the monarchy). The assemblies were weighted in favour of the rich (and excluded the poorest) through the unequal distribution of voting groups (tribes and centuries; further below). Yet the very fact of annual election must have encouraged aspirations towards more representative government. Secondly, the Romans were well acquainted with contemporary Greek states in south Italy and Sicily, where popular sovereignty was frequently championed if often not fully realised.

Matters came to a head with the 'First Secession' in 494. This saw the withdrawal of part of the population to the Sacred Mount (a short distance to the north of Rome), and the creation of a plebeian organization. Almost an alternative state in Rome, the *plebs* created their own assembly (*concilium plebis*) and magistrates (plebeian tribunes and aediles). The tribunes were protected by their sacrosanctity, the result of an oath sworn by all plebeians to protect them, and came to exercise a power of *veto* (literally, 'I forbid') against magistrates and the Senate, the body of elders which advised the consuls (below). They also had a guardian cult of three deities (Ceres, Liber, and Libera), which echoed the Capitoline triad (Jupiter, Juno, and Minerva), the supreme state cult. The plebeian triad derived from the Greek triad Demeter, Kore, and Dionysus, and was worshipped at a temple on the Aventine hill. This became a great plebeian centre, acting as an archive and a treasury. Religious, cultural, and political ideas travelled together; the plebeians' choice of deities suggests a Greek political inspiration.

The plebeian movement pursued a share in political opportunity and alleviation of oppression for the poor through further secessions (in 450 and c.287). The *plebs* demanded the establishment of a decemvirate (board of ten), to publish a code of laws, in 451. In 450 a second such decemvirate was deposed after the Second Secession. The text of its laws survives in part as the Twelve Tables, widely quoted by later authors. They reveal a society with predominantly agricultural concerns, already familiar with slavery. A law prohibiting intermarriage between patricians and plebeians shows that social conflict between the two groups was a critical feature of the period; it was repealed five years later.

The most important achievements of the plebeian movement were yet to come. The Licinio-Sextian laws of 367 opened the consulship to plebeians, and restricted holdings of *ager publicus* (state-owned land, which could be rented for farming or pasture). In 342 one consulship was reserved annually for a plebeian, and by 300 the most important priesthoods, previously key sources of patrician authority, had become accessible. In about 287 the Hortensian law gave plebiscites (decrees of the plebeian assembly) the force of law over the whole population, not just plebeians. This law effectively made the plebeian assembly a regular institution of state. The result of all these measures was the formation of a new mixed patricio-plebeian nobility: the wealthiest plebeian families joined the Senate, and to some extent the poor lost their political champions. But the movement had also been successful to a degree in alleviating poverty and exploitation. In 326 *nexum*, the debt-bondage of Roman citizens, was outlawed (Livy 8. 28: overly dramatic). This legislation may also suggest that the rich already had an alternative labour-source in slaves. Land distribution, especially through the foundation of Latin colonies, beginning with that of Cales in Campania in 334, now became extensive, and was followed by some two-dozen more colonies over the next century and a half. Latin colonies had been founded before by the Latins, acting in concert with Rome, on land recovered from the Volsci and Aequi. They now became fortified cities of regular size and plan, protecting Roman control in Italy.

Movement of aristocrats between city-states was easy in archaic Tyrrhenian Italy, and state barriers correspondingly were comparatively weak. Many aristocrats and their followers migrated into Rome in the archaic period. The best known examples are Tarquinius Priscus moving from Tarquinii to become king of Rome (Livy 1. 34), and Attius Clausus (above). There must have been others: several names in the Fasti suggest a non-Roman origin. This may imply an underdeveloped communal identity; but the partial resolution of early social struggles must have compensated. This may be reflected in the changing focus of Rome's historical tradition, clear from Livy's first ten books. His history is initially dominated by great individuals: the kings, and generals such as Coriolanus and Camillus. By the middle Republic his focus has shifted to the community as a whole.

The middle Republic (c.338–218): formalization of the state

Two critical features of Rome in the decades around 300 are worth noting: its oligarchic constitution, and its openness to outsiders. The close connection between openness and oligarchy is clear from the diametrically opposed case of classical Athens, where a closed citizenship was the logical outcome of democratic politics. Put simply, the greater the power of the individual voter, the less he was willing to share his privileges.

In Rome the new patricio-plebeian nobility, which would dominate the religious and civic offices of the state for 300 years, was bound together by a powerful collective ideology that expressed competition and its limits. Competitive instincts were manifested in funeral orations praising the deceased, family records of great achievements, public monuments to military successes (especially temples, vowed in thanks for divine assistance in battle), and—from the second century—coinage (Flower 1996). Other ideological attitudes helped to tie this new nobility together, stressing that no one figure should become too successful. This principle underlies the cautionary tales in our sources of men aspiring to be king, such as Spurius Cassius (486), Spurius Maelius (439), and Manlius Capitolinus (385), all regarded as legitimately killed. Kingship was built up into a great evil which the aristocracy had to resist at all costs.

The historical traditions also preserve some striking stories of Republican heroes, which clearly played a central part in defining Roman virtues from an early period. These stories promoted ideals of sacrifice for the state (e.g. Horatius, Mucius Scaevola, Verginia, the Decii), and emphasized the austerity and humility of generals like

Cincinnatus and Curius Dentatus. Their memory was often preserved by monuments, which linked their deeds to topographic features of the city (e.g. Livy 2. 13. 5; Dionysius of Halicarnassus 5. 35, on the Mucian meadows).

Despite the success of the wealthier plebeians in gaining access to magistracies, the poor had little say in political affairs. Inequality was institutionalized in the *comitia centuriata* (centuriate assembly), which elected the most important magistracies (praetor, consul, censor). A complex group-voting system, probably introduced alongside or soon after army pay in 406, ensured that the votes of the rich counted for more. In the final form of this assembly adult males were divided into five wealth classes: each class was divided into centuries (voting units). There were more centuries in the higher classes (voting first) than in the lower. There were also equal numbers of centuries of *seniores* (men over 45) and *iuniores* (men of military age), although the latter were far more numerous: this gave the old more voting power than the young. By contrast, the *proletarii*, too poor for even the lowest of the five classes, were all lumped into a single century, voting last, and so had little say. Cicero, in the first century BC, thought it ideal that 'the preponderance of votes should be in the hands ... of the wealthy ... [with the masses] neither excluded from the right to vote (for that would have been high-handed), nor given too much power, which would have been dangerous' (*On the Republic* 2. 39, trans. Rudd).

The other important assembly, based on voting tribes, was the *comitia tributa*, which reputedly went back to Servius Tullius. The number of tribes increased as Rome expanded (see below), until by 241 there were thirty-five. This assembly elected the lesser magistracies (like aediles and quaestors) and passed legislation. Since rural districts were divided into thirty-one tribes, and the city into four, with each tribe casting one vote, the rural tribes were more important. They tended to be dominated by those wealthy enough to make the trip into Rome to vote, although issues of particular relevance to the rural poor might encourage great crowds to attend.

Populist leaders were still to be found. Appius Claudius Caecus, censor in 312, commissioned public works including the famous Via Appia, Rome's first public road, leading to Capua in Campania, overhauled the Senate (seen by the rest of the aristocracy as an attempt to introduce his own supporters), and instituted voting reform in favour of freedmen. These last two measures were, however, rapidly overturned. In 304 his protégé Gnaeus Flavius, as aedile (a magistrate responsible for the care of the *plebs*), published the procedures of civil law and the calendar (which governed the days on which action could be taken). This was a significant populist move: such information had previously been the preserve of patrician priests; it broke their monopoly on legal activity. In 232 the tribune Gaius Flaminius, to the annoyance of the conservative elements in the nobility, distributed the extensive lands of the *ager Gallicus* on the Adriatic coast to needy plebeians. Land distributions such as this helped to mollify the grievances of the poorer plebeians, and diffuse social tension.

A small band of families in the upper ranks of the aristocracy, the *nobilitas* (nobility), now dominated the highest offices of state. But the senatorial elite was continually rejuvenated by a regular turnover of members in its lower ranks (Hopkins 1983). Nobility was defined by descent from office-holders: the need to be elected to be ennobled, along with the broader patricio-plebeian field of candidates, led to intense competition for office. This in turn drove the expansion of the Roman state, through conquest, incorporation of defeated peoples, and colonization (below), all of which benefited the consuls responsible. The higher magisterial offices were carefully shared amongst the nobility (repeated tenure was rare for the consulship after 300), but rarely available to a *novus homo* (new man), someone without a senatorial family background.

The representative body of this new elite was the Senate, which became the primary governing institution. The Ovinian law, passed in the late fourth century, was an important stage in the definition of the Senate: it required the censors (in charge of the five-yearly census) to choose senators formally on the basis of their economic worth and qualifications, rather than leave it to the consuls to pick their friends (Festus, p. 290L). The Senate thus became a prestigious body, whose members normally had tenure for life; it developed a corporate ethos. By the time of Polybius it had firm control over finances and foreign relations, including the administration of Italy, as well as the security of the state (Polybius 6. 13). It decided where to send the consuls in time of war and received foreign delegations. It had few formal powers, but its advice, particularly in the form of decrees (*senatus consulta*), was rarely ignored. There were some limits to the Senate's influence in foreign policy. Magistrates in the field often had to act quickly, and were unable (or unwilling) to consult it, a problem that became more acute as Rome's empire grew. The consuls and people could combine against the majority opinion of the Senate (as with the help sent to the Mamertines in Sicily: see below). But such episodes are unusual. Magistrates held office for only a year, yet would sit in the Senate for life: individuals were thus loath to ignore its huge authority at the risk of limiting their own influence later. Debates within the Senate, however, would often show up divisions and conflicts within the ruling class, and it should not be assumed always to have worked as a unified body acting, for example, against the plebeians; the latter often found senatorial champions.

Rome was already a cosmopolitan city by the mid-Republic. Continued Greek influence is evident in many spheres of Roman culture. Statues of Alcibiades and Pythagoras (the wisest and most famous of the Greeks) were set up in the *comitium* in the late fourth or early third century (Pliny, *Natural History* 34. 26). The Romans first issued coinage, produced on Greek lines in Neapolis (Naples), in 326 on the occasion of a treaty with the city, again around 310 when the Via Appia was constructed, and as regular issues from 270, linked to the war with Pyrrhus (below). Rome also accommodated at this period a series of Greek cults. Aesculapius, the Greek god of healing, for instance, was introduced onto the Tiber island in 291 in response to a plague (Livy, *epitome* 11), and temples were erected by successful generals to Greek-style personifications like Bellona (War), in 296, and Victoria (Victory), in 294.

Foreign relations to the end of the Hannibalic War

The major changes which we have been considering in the internal organization of the Roman state went hand in hand with the rapid conquest of Italy between 338 and 264. Perpetual war clarified the militaristic institutions that underlay Roman imperialism (see also Chapter 5); greatly expanded colonization solved social pressures and contributed towards the openness of Roman society; the mass importation of slaves replaced earlier forms of dependent labour, and their supply became an integral part, perhaps even an aim, of Roman warmongering.

The constituent elements of Roman imperialism had existed from the early Republic. The late sixth century, when the first Romano-Carthaginian treaty was struck, was an early high point of Roman power, and for the next hundred years Rome was apparently on the defensive. First the Latins revolted, but were defeated at Lake Regillus in 496. A new League of Latin states, with Rome as the most powerful partner, was established by the Cassian treaty of 493, which probably provided a blueprint for later bilateral alliances. The cities of the League shared rights of *conubium* (intermarriage), *commercium* (the right to contract legally binding business deals), and *migratio* (movement to another city and adoption of its citizen status). The League's main activities were fighting against hill-tribes who threatened Latium (Volsci, Aequi, and Sabines). The Volsci had captured most of the Pomptine Plain in southern Latium, which had been under Roman control by the terms of the Carthaginian treaty of 509. This plain was famously rich: Rome sought grain here in time of famine in the fifth century; the Capitoline temple at Rome had traditionally been built in the sixth century out of the spoils of Pometia (the greatest city in the area). The most famous advance of the Volsci was immortalized by the story of Coriolanus, a Roman renegade who led them to the gates of the city. This story has many poetic details, such as Coriolanus being persuaded to withdraw from a final assault on Rome only by the entreaties of his mother. But in essence it is another case of the social mobility of the archaic period (above). At the same time, the Aequi and Sabines attacked the northern areas of Roman and Latin territory.

Our sources represent such attacks as plundering raids by rustic uplanders on the wealthy city-states of the Tyrrhenian coast. This depiction probably draws on the Greek characterization of the Lucanians and Bruttians, who pressured their cities in southern Italy, as barbarians. Interaction with the peoples of the mountainous Apennine interior was not a novelty. The Sabines were thought by the Romans to have provided two kings, Titus Tatius and Numa, and, with the rape of the Sabine women, the original female element in the city of Romulus. Mediterranean ecology enforced interaction between the peoples of the plains and of the mountain areas, given that both were essential for the seasonal grazing of animals, and there was mutual dependence on resources like timber (a mountain product) and salt (from the pans by the sea) (Horden and Purcell

2000). But the clash of hill-tribes and lowlanders in the fifth century demonstrated the critical need for the Romans to cooperate with their Latin neighbours. Unlike the Etruscans of Capua (in Campania) and the Greeks of Poseidonia (in Lucania), Rome never fell prey to raiding groups from the mountains. One of the characteristic features of later Roman expansion is their openness to offers of alliance from virtually any source (including Gauls), and their willingness to intervene on their allies' behalf, which led to repeated, and to our eyes often unnecessary, wars. This Roman enthusiasm for gaining and keeping allies must stem from the fifth century.

Rome also fought a series of wars in the fifth century with its nearest Etruscan neighbour, Veii, over control of minor strongholds in the Tiber valley. By 400 Rome had gained the upper hand, and began a long-drawn-out siege of Veii. It was another formative experience for the Republic, as *stipendium* (army pay) was first introduced, and *tributum* (a property tax) instituted to pay for it. Veii was captured in 396, after its tutelary deity, Juno, was 'called out' of the city and persuaded to come to Rome (the ritual of *evocatio*). Veii was one of the largest Etruscan cities: its incorporation increased Roman territory by some 50 per cent to around 1600 km². Much of the population was enslaved, its land taken by Roman settlers. The survivors were incorporated into the Roman state. Four new tribes were added to the Roman citizen body, making a total of twenty-five, further augmenting its manpower (Livy 6. 4. 4, 5. 8). The two principles of settling captured territory, and incorporating the conquered population into the Roman citizen body, illustrate the flexibility of the Roman state and its potential for expansion. These policies do not, as scholars sometimes suggest, reflect Roman generosity. Citizenship brought burdens not yet matched by equivalent rights, and the creation of new citizens benefited both Rome (through manpower) and the leaders in charge of that extension (through new dependent clients; see Chapter 4).

Just as Rome was gaining a more substantial footing in Latium, it was sacked by Gauls in 390. Later Romans considered this to have been the city's most serious reverse, the only time when the city was conquered by a foreign power before the Goth Alaric in AD 410; it is the most calamitous episode in Livy's first ten books. Rome was probably completely captured, although tradition maintained that the Capitol held out. The physical trauma was not lasting, as the Gauls were more an ephemeral raiding group than an occupying army, and although they are said to have burnt the city, there is no archaeological evidence for this. The impact of the sack on the Roman psyche was more lasting. The anniversary of the defeat at the River Allia, which preceded the sack, was preserved as a *dies atra* (a 'black day', that is, ill-omened) in the Roman calendar. In later history a *tumultus Gallicus* ('Gallic invasion') called for a mass levy of troops, in which not even priests were exempt from military service. The Gallic sack was used by the Romans to justify their harsh treatment of the Gauls in northern Italy in the first decades of the second century (below), after the Gauls had allied with Rome's enemy Hannibal.

A period of limited expansion followed; the 'Servian' wall of some 11 km was built around the city in 378, probably replacing an earlier circuit. Rome's wide interests remained evident, with the establishment of links with foreign states across the Tyrrhenian Sea. Treaties were struck with Massilia (Marseilles) in 389, and renewed with Carthage in 348. The text of the latter treaty, reported by Polybius (2. 24), reveals an expectation that the Romans would trade with Sicily and Carthage, and shows that the Carthaginians were very concerned to prohibit Roman contact with Africa and Sardinia. In fact, Rome had already undertaken expeditions to Sardinia and Corsica in the early fourth century, although they were not successful in establishing long-lived settlements.

Relations with Carthage indicate a recovery of Roman power, and a renewed phase of expansion from this point on led into new spheres of activity, and contact with new enemies. The first struggle with the Samnites, Rome's most resilient opponents in Italy, began when they attacked Capua in 343. The Campanians (citizens of Capua) appealed to Rome, surrendering their city in exchange for assistance against the Samnites. In answering their appeal the Romans became involved in the complexities of Campanian politics, and broke an existing treaty with the Samnites for mutual aid and defence. Nevertheless, once the Samnites had been driven off, their alliance with Rome was renewed. Events took another twist in 341, when Capua joined with the Latins in breaking from Rome. The Latins resented Roman domination of Latium, and were aiming to establish themselves as an independent force. Instead they were defeated by 338, and the Latin League was dissolved.

In 338 Rome organized the whole area as far south as Capua in a complex settlement, partly based on earlier arrangements, and partly an exercise in divide and rule. Some cities were directly incorporated into the Roman state as *municipia* (self-governing cities). Some of the more distant communities, including Capua and Cumae, were given the innovative status of Roman citizenship without the vote. A few other cities continued to have Latin status as allies of Rome, such as Praeneste and Tibur. They retained the rights of *conubium, commercium*, and *migratio* (above) which had characterized Romano-Latin relations since the Cassian treaty.

In practical terms this gave Rome firm control over two of the richest and most densely populated regions of Italy (Latium and Campania). From now on, Rome probably had a larger citizen body (estimated at around 350,000) and more troops available (citizen and allied) than any other state in Italy. Rome was poised to expand out of this power-base to control all of Italy. It was symbolically important that Roman citizenship had been imposed on *municipia* well away from the capital city, whose inhabitants now had Roman in addition to local citizenship. The divorce of citizen status from ethnic or geographical origins allowed Roman citizenship to be limitlessly extended. The complex pattern of hierarchical statuses created here—citizen, Latin, ally—would be replicated throughout Italy, the Mediterranean, and ultimately the rest of western Europe.

By 264 Rome had subjugated all the other peoples of Italy south of the Po valley. Our sources provide us with a narrative detailing and glorifying the extension of Roman control through military triumphs, intimidation, and alliance-building (see particularly Livy 8–10, covering the years 341–292). This final phase of the Roman conquest of Italy was dominated by the struggle with the Samnites, conventionally divided into three 'Samnite Wars' (343–341, 327–304, and 298–290). But the conflict with the Samnites was not confined to these wars, as it continued later and involved other theatres beyond Samnium. The 'Second Samnite War' was sparked by Roman encroachment, with the foundation by Rome of the Latin colony of Fregellae on the Samnite bank of the River Liris. Rome suffered a great setback at the Caudine Forks in 321, when a Roman army was trapped and forced into a humiliating surrender; but in the end Roman armies were triumphant. The 'Third Samnite War' was characterized by a broad alliance of anti-Roman forces, which was finally defeated at Sentinum in Umbria (295), after being divided by Roman diversionary tactics. The greatest battle seen in Italy up to that point, it was decisive for the peninsula's destiny. It was recorded by a Greek contemporary, Duris of Samos, although his figure of 100,000 dead is implausible.

Domination of Samnium led Rome into conflict with the Greek cities of southern Italy. Some acquiesced in Roman expansion. But when threatened by Rome in 281, Taras called in Pyrrhus, king of Epirus (a powerful confederation in north-west Greece). The Greek colonies in southern Italy had a long tradition of requesting the aid of commanders from mainland Greece. This offered figures like Pyrrhus the chance to extend their influence in the area whilst championing the 'freedom' of the Greek cities. The war with Pyrrhus, the first time the Romans had faced an opponent from outside Italy, lasted for five years. Pyrrhus' well-honed Hellenistic army, complete with war-elephants, twice defeated the Romans. He advanced as far up the Adriatic side of Italy as Asculum, but suffered so many casualties that he is said to have remarked that after one more victory like that, they would be completely lost (the proverbial 'Pyrrhic victory': Plutarch, *Pyrrhus* 21). Pyrrhus was worn down by the Roman capacity to field new armies drawn from their vast pool of citizens and allies, and withdrew to Greece after the Battle of Beneventum in 275, abandoning southern Italy to the Romans. This victory put Rome firmly on the map of Mediterranean powers, and further demonstrated to Greek observers her growing might.

Rome had come to be in full control of the other cities and peoples of the Italian peninsula south of the Apennines between Ariminum (modern Rimini) and Pisa. The Gauls, Ligurians, and other tribes of the Po valley, were as yet undisturbed, though their time would come. Was Rome aiming to conquer Italy? Polybius thought that she had conceived this ambition in the early third century, after successes against the Etruscans, Samnites and Gauls (Polybius 1 .6. 6). Some strategic planning in Roman policy is evident from the way that roads were quickly built linking new colonies to Rome; many scholars have discerned a deliberate scheme to hem in and dismember Samnium with Latin colonies. But it is easy to overemphasize global strategic thinking with hindsight.

Structural pressures of which the Romans will have scarcely been aware played a very significant part in Roman decisions to go to war. As defeated enemies were either incorporated into the Roman state as citizens, or forced into alliances which required them to contribute troops to Roman armies, success in war provided resources for further campaigns. A similar pressure towards expansion was exerted by the need for slaves in the Roman economy (see further Chapter 6). More slaves benefited all owners; the numbers of enslavements noted by Livy for the 290s imply that the Roman authorities were for the first time keeping accurate records of captives sold, whose revenue enriched the treasury. Competition amongst the nobles encouraged risk-taking and provocation of enemies, but rivalry often inhibited ambition, and not all chances to expand were taken. These sorts of structural factors, and the Roman system of collective leadership, pushed territorial expansion along in a piecemeal way, rather than as part of an overarching master plan (Rich 1993).

In 264, with barely a pause, Rome moved from mopping-up operations in Italy to the first of many wars abroad: the First Punic War. It began when the Mamertines, Campanian mercenaries who had taken over Messana in north-east Sicily, requested Roman aid against Syracuse and Carthage. The Senate was reluctant to intervene, because it would be inconsistent with their brutal punishment some six years earlier of a Romano-Campanian garrison which had seized the city of Rhegion, just over the straits from Messana. But the consuls won over the people with warnings about Carthage's threat to Italy and promises of plunder (Polybius 1. 10 f.). The war rapidly escalated into a grim struggle with Carthage for supremacy in Sicily. In 256 the consul Regulus even mounted an aggressive, but ultimately unsuccessful, expedition into North Africa itself.

The Romans were required for the first time to build navies, as without a counter to the Carthaginian naval threat, or the ability to blockade the almost impregnable Sicilian coastal cities, there would be no chance of victory. Although their assimilation of naval warfare was presented by Polybius (1. 20. 8–16) as a complete innovation, the Romans must have had some familiarity with the sea. The Rome–Carthage treaties envisage Romans sailing to Africa and Sicily; fourth-century expeditions reached to Sardinia and Corsica; in 313 Rome colonized the Pontine islands off the Tyrrhenian coast; and two fleet officers (*duumuiri nauales*) were appointed in 311. The real innovation was the creation of full-scale naval forces, manned by enormous numbers of men. After a series of mishaps, defeats, and victories, the Roman navy wore down the more experienced Carthaginian navy by attrition. Carthage was forced to evacuate Sicily; in 237 Rome took advantage of Carthage's preoccupation with a local mercenary war to seize Sardinia and Corsica as well. According to Polybius, this was a major cause of the Second Punic War (3. 30. 4). The conquered portion of Sicily, about two-thirds of the island, became the first Roman province.

In the 230s and 220s Carthage brought the southern Iberian peninsula, where there had long been a substantial Phoenician presence, firmly under its control. Our sources claim that the Carthaginian general Hamilcar Barca was bent on revenge against Rome after the humiliation of the First Punic War. Yet it would in any case have been prudent for Carthage to rebuild after the loss of Corsica and Sardinia, with their associated timber and grain supplies, and to look to the mineral and manpower resources of Spain as an insurance against a future war with Rome. That war eventually came when Hamilcar's son Hannibal took over the Carthaginian command, and laid siege to the coastal city of Saguntum. It had been designated an independent city in an agreement between Rome and Carthage in 226 (Livy 21. 2. 7, the Roman perspective). But by this same agreement the River Ebro had been fixed as the boundary between the two powers, and Saguntum lay well to the south, within the Carthaginian zone of control.

After capturing Saguntum, despite Roman protests, Hannibal mounted his audacious invasion of Italy (218), crossing the Alps with a force of mercenaries, allies, and elephants. This battle-hardened army, despite being heavily outnumbered, inflicted defeats of increasing severity on Roman forces at the River Trebbia in northern Italy (218), Lake Trasimene in Etruria (217), and Cannae in Apulia (216). Cannae was another 'black day' for Rome, and helped bring many of Rome's allies in southern Italy over to Hannibal. But a wholesale defection was not forthcoming, and central Italy remained securely garrisoned by a network of Latin colonies. Capua, the second city in Italy, was the most significant defector, but the Romans recaptured the city in 211 after a siege. From this point Hannibal became confined to an ever-smaller area of southern Italy, eventually occupying just Bruttium (the toe of the 'boot'). In 204 he was recalled by the Carthaginian senate to defend against a Roman invasion of Africa. The victory of Scipio Africanus at Zama in 202 destroyed Carthaginian dominance, and established Rome as an unrivalled power in the western Mediterranean.

The key to the strength of resistance to Pyrrhus and Hannibal, and the reason why Rome went on to conquer the Mediterranean world so rapidly, was the effective mobilization of conquered Italians in the

Roman army. The intensity of Roman warfare in this period is clear from various indices: the regularity of triumphs was very high, and the number of legions, when compared with the Roman census figures (the Romans' own figures for their total population), suggests that between 9 and 16 per cent of Roman adult males were regularly under arms, rising to 25 per cent in times of crisis. These are proportions unmatched by any other pre-industrial state. Part of the explanation for this extraordinary bellicosity must lie in early Roman history, when Rome had formed the habit of alliance-building. In the case of most allies, the Roman consuls probably had the power to call out all their manpower if they so wished (Brunt 1971: 545–8). A record of the manpower resources of each ally was kept by Rome; Polybius (2. 24) invokes manpower to explain why Hannibal found himself confronted by freshly raised Roman armies after each defeat, like ' "waging war against a hydra" ' (Appian, *Samnite Wars* 3. 24).

There were three important consequences of this system. First, the Romans usually won because they were always supported in battle by their allies, and so simply outnumbered their opponents. Even when defeated they could come back for more, demoralizing the enemy with their inexorable resistance. A tightly controlled oligarchic society, with a pervasive militaristic ideology, Rome was capable of greater sacrifice of its citizens than most of its rivals. The Roman peasantry also benefited from war, and did not often need to be forcibly levied. There is a striking contrast with the endemic warfare between classical Greek city-states, where manpower resources had to be more carefully husbanded. Secondly, if Rome was to benefit from previous conquests she had to continue to employ the manpower that her allies were obliged to supply. Thirdly, the allies also gained from the system: being on the winning side, they could share in the booty. This system, with its own self-reinforcing logic, and reliant on a central military role from Rome's Italian allies, interlinked the fortunes of all the peninsula's inhabitants. Although beneficial to Rome, it also led in the second century to the allies demanding political parity with Roman citizens, to reflect their military contribution, demands which would eventually lead to the conflagration of the Social War (91).

On land which had been confiscated from defeated communities, Rome founded colonies. Roman colonies tended to be small coastal forts until the early second century. Latin colonies were fortified cities, either newly built or pre-existing. They were of 'Latin' status because they had originally been foundations of the Latin League, a practice continued by Rome alone after the dissolution of the League in 338. Colonies formed vital strongholds for Rome, and all were strategically placed, usually on powerful hilltop sites commanding communication routes. Crucial in holding down conquered territory, their role was also (and perhaps more importantly) socio-economic. Between 2,500 and 6,000 adult male settlers were sent to each, and while they could be readily called upon for military service, they were allotted farming land to which they might not otherwise have had access in Rome. Latin colonies were independent cities, and although borrowing or being assigned certain distinctly Roman or Latin features, such as their (diverse) magistracies, they also showed contact with their local surroundings in terms of cults and weight standards, and had some political buildings modelled on contemporary Greek lines (such as their *comitia*). In fact, although the majority of settlers was Roman in origin, many colonies probably included substantial numbers of indigenous inhabitants, as at Paestum (founded 273), sometimes amongst the colony's aristocracy but often as dependent labour. Colonies became more standardized in the early second century, when each was assigned a capitolium and other Roman features. Thus they propagated the spread of Roman culture in surrounding areas, especially urban models in the un-urbanized Apennine areas, even if this was probably incidental to their primary functions (see further Chapter 8).

World domination, political strife

In 200 Rome was poised for a decisive move eastwards. Roman involvement across the Adriatic had begun earlier, with a war against the Illyrians undertaken in the name of suppressing piracy (229–228). During the Second Punic War, King Philip V of Macedon had allied with Hannibal, and fought Rome in Greece between 212/11–205 (the First Macedonian War). Revenge was clearly called for, and the Senate urged war on the war-weary people under the pretext of a Macedonian invasion. That the Senate was not restrained by the depleted state of Rome's resources, especially manpower, after the Second Punic War, is testimony to the strong pressures favouring military intervention. The Second Macedonian War began in 200, and was ended by

T. Quinctius Flamininus at the Battle of Cynoscephalae (197). At the Isthmian Games in 196 Flamininus proclaimed that the Greek cities previously controlled by Philip would be free of garrisons and able to govern themselves by their own laws (Polybius 18. 46). This famous proclamation of the 'Freedom of the Greeks' was met with rapturous acclaim on the part of most, if not all, Greek states. But it by no means entailed a return to full independence, and should be seen in the context of a long tradition of Hellenistic kings (the successors of Alexander the Great) posing as champions of the freedom of Greek cities. An appearance of freedom suited Rome, as it restricted the room for manoeuvre of the Hellenistic monarchs. In particular, in asserting the 'freedom' of Greek cities in Asia Minor as well as in mainland Greece, Rome was encroaching on an area that the Seleucid kings had a historic claim to control.

In 194 the Roman army was withdrawn from Greece, but it was called back in 191 to counter the invasion of Greece by the Seleucid monarch Antiochus III Megas (the Great), who ruled over an area stretching from Anatolia to Syria and Iran. His defeat by Rome at Magnesia (189), and the subsequent peace of Apamea (188), confined Antiochus to the south and east of the Taurus range, stripping him of his Anatolian possessions, and imposing a vast indemnity. Further major intervention came with the Third Macedonian War (171–168), and the defeat of Perseus, son of Philip V, at Pydna (168) by Aemilius Paullus. Macedonia was split into four republics, rather than directly annexed, but both Macedonia and Illyria were made subject to Roman taxation at this point, as if under direct Roman control. The booty from Aemilius Paullus' triumph amounted to 300 million sesterces, which allowed direct taxes to be suspended in Italy until the very last years of the Republic. It was only after rebellions had broken out in Greece and Macedon in 148, and had been brutally suppressed, that a province was created out of the old Macedonian kingdom, and Greece was subjected to the authority of the Roman governor. The sack of the ancient city of Corinth by L. Mummius in 146 demonstrated that Roman generals were now willing to assert their domination through naked force.

In the course of their involvement in Greece and the East, Roman generals had manipulated prevailing ideologies and rapidly assimilated new ideas. This was an era in which Roman nobles were eagerly taking on board Greek cultural practices and norms (see further Chapter 8). The significance of Rome's apparent reluctance to annex Macedonia in 167 should not be exaggerated. In their diplomacy the Senate and its generals were continually careful not to upset the Greeks as a whole, which would have made their position vulnerable and difficult. The Senate had probably learnt from mistakes in the First Macedonian War, when Rome's alliance with Aetolia (211), which reserved all booty for herself, gave the impression that this was all that they cared about. Rome may also have been unable to put a permanent standing army in Macedon just then. But it was already quite apparent to the Greeks how dominant Rome was. Polybius, for instance, originally intended his history to go down to 167, at which point he considered Rome to have won control of the 'whole world' (*oikoumenē*—1. 1. 5). After Pydna, no Greek state or monarch could contemplate independent action without consulting Rome.

The Roman provincial system was quicker to evolve where Roman policy was less constrained. Sicily had come under Roman control according to the terms of the treaty imposed on Carthage at the end of the First Punic War. From 227 the number of praetors was doubled to four, to administer the new holdings here and in Sardinia and Corsica (praetors were the most senior magistrates after the consuls). Politicians normally held such offices in a regular order (the *cursus honorum*): quaestorship, aedileship (or tribunate), praetorship, and consulship. This allowed for permanent Roman garrisons and governors in Sicily and Sardinia/Corsica. In Sicily the pre-existing system of taxation was maintained.

Roman armies and commanders were continuously present in Spain from 218 onwards. Gnaeus and Publius Cornelius Scipio were sent to Spain at the start of the Second Punic War to cut off possible reinforcements for Hannibal. From around 206 two Roman governors were appointed to the Spanish command each year, and in 197 two provinces were demarcated. The number of praetors was increased to six, with two of these serving in the Spanish provinces. Rome had thus quickly adjusted to the idea of a permanent presence here, and Cato the Elder, consul in 195, was quick to exploit the iron- and silver-mines. The imposition of Roman control over this less-developed region was much harder than in Greece, mainly because the political situation, with its shifting tribal alliances, more often required crude military means than the sensitive diplomacy characteristic of Roman operations in Greece. Particularly hard-fought were the wars against the Lusitani, led by Viriathus (defeated in 139) and against the Celtiberi, culminating in the destruction, after many attempts, of their stronghold Numantia (133). The difficulties faced by the Romans here caused many of the military problems that would come to a head with the Gracchi in the 130s and 120s.

The notion of a province in the territorial sense of the word (see further Chapter 3) develops in this period. The Latin word *provincia* originally denoted the task or area of duty assigned to a magistrate; only gradually did it assume the meaning of an administrative area within the empire. As *provinciae* denoted tasks given to holders of *imperium*, the change in the application of *provinciae* to fixed geographical areas involved a reformulation of what the concept of an empire was for the Romans. In parallel to the emergence of the Roman provinces, Italy was separated from overseas territorial possessions. Outside Italy, Rome more commonly formed friendships with other states than alliances, unless they made a *deditio*, an unconditional surrender, to Rome.

The other great area of Roman military activity in the first half of the second century was northern Italy. The Gauls of the Po valley had allied with Hannibal when he invaded, and were feared because of their own attacks on Rome and its territory in the past, both in the Gallic sack (above) and later. The 190s and 180s saw the Romans regaining control of the region, re-establishing colonies that had been sacked, and founding new ones along the newly established Via Aemilia, such as Bononia (modern Bologna). Liguria, where the Alps and the Apennines converged, was another area of heavy fighting in the first three decades of the century; some Ligurians were transplanted south to Samnium in central Italy in the wake of Roman victory.

In 149, after long agitation by Cato the Elder in the Senate, the Third Punic War was declared on the weakened remnants of the Carthaginian empire. The war had come about just after the expiration of the indemnity Carthage paid annually to Rome after the Second Punic War. Carthage had attacked Masinissa, the neighbouring Numidian king, after long provocation, but in violation of the treaty with Rome. A Roman army was sent, and its commander made the impossible demand that the city be resited at least 10 miles inland. War followed; Carthage held out for three years, but in 146 was finally captured by Scipio Aemilianus (grandson by adoption of Scipio Africanus). The great city was utterly destroyed, and its population, though not that of other Punic cities, enslaved. Its territory became the province of Africa. Further additions to the empire in the next fifty years included various territories in the East: the central coastal district of western Asia Minor, which was bequeathed to Rome in 133 by the last king of the ruling Attalid dynasty, and made the province of Asia in 129–6; Cilicia (south-western Asia Minor) in 101; and Cyrene in Libya in 96.

In the West, Rome established the province of Gallia Narbonensis (modern Provence, from the Latin *prouincia*) in 125–121. Roman forces had intervened in 125 to protect Massilia, a Greek city long allied to Rome, against a hostile Gallic tribe, the Salluvii. The Salluvii were crushed in 123, and a Roman fort built in their territory at Aquae Sextiae (Aix-en-Provence). In 121 Rome answered an appeal from the Aedui, in the area of modern Burgundy, against neighbouring tribes, the Allobroges and Arverni. Both were defeated, and a province formed in 120 from the territory gained, encompassing most of southern France; Massilia remained an independent ally. Immediately following the creation of the province the Via Domitia, the critical link between Italy and Spain, was laid out, and the colony of Narbo Martius (Narbonne) set up on it as the province's capital.

These external developments deeply affected life in Rome. Politics in the early second century, at least as far as we can follow until the narrative of Livy breaks off in 167, was characterized by fierce competition, and increasingly desperate attempts to restrain it. The increase in junior magistracies, including the praetorship (see above), had opened up more competition for the consulship. Competition was particularly evident in the feuds pursued by Cato against his enemies, and in the prosecution of the Scipiones. Scipio Africanus, the hero of Zama, and his brother Lucius, consul in 190, were attacked in 187 and 184 for embezzlement of public funds after defeating Antiochus III at Magnesia, and ended their careers under a cloud.

Senatorial concern about competition is evident from contemporary legislation. There was a series of laws regulating the *cursus honorum* (stages in the career ladder), such as the *lex Villia annalis* (180), which laid down minimum ages for each office and was probably intended to limit the number of candidates at elections. Sumptuary legislation controlling spending on banquets was passed in 182 (*lex Orchia sumptuaria*), 163 (*lex Fannia*), and 143 (*lex Didia* and *lex Licinia sumptuaria*). The laws on the *cursus* could, however, be disregarded when the military situation was thought to require it.

Thus Scipio Aemilianus was elected to the consulship and command against Carthage, having stood for the more junior post of aedile in 147. As future events would show, laws were not enough to prevent youthful generals gaining a dangerous position of pre-eminence.

The period of the Roman conquest of Greece was marked by an increasing cultural Hellenization of Rome. There had long been Greek influence on Rome, and although the directness of contacts with Greek traders and cities waxed and waned, the connection was never really lost. From the late fourth century, the Via Appia directly linked Rome to Campania, with its ancient Greek cities such as Cumae and Naples (partially Oscanized from the late fifth century). But the conquest of the Greek East accelerated the movement of goods (such as plundered works of art, and even libraries), people (free and enslaved), and ideas from the Greek mainland to Rome (see also Chapter 8). This was not just an elite phenomenon. Many legionaries served on eastern campaigns. Livy reports the speech of an experienced centurion, Spurius Ligustinus, in 171, who had previously served in the wars against Philip II and Antiochus III during his twenty-two years in the army, and was now advocating service against Perseus of Macedon. Familiarity with Greek mythology is evident from Plautus' plays, written around 200 for an audience of ordinary Romans. The format and plot of these plays was adapted from the Greek by Plautus, although made distinctively Roman in character and humour.

Plautus is part of another important trend in these years, the development of literature at Rome. This began with the work of Livius Andronicus (240 onwards), and saw the first history of Rome, written in Greek by Fabius Pictor around 200. Fabius' history is a clear manifestation of a new sense of who the Romans were and why Rome was important. As Roman horizons expanded, Roman identity became more self-conscious and clearly defined. Equivalent changes in religious attitudes are evident from the Senate's suppression of the Bacchanalia, the cult of Dionysus. The Bacchanalia was another product of the Hellenization of Italy, and whilst it caused alarm primarily through its autonomous cultic organization, which cut across traditional social boundaries, the very fact that it was suppressed, an unprecedented step, shows that the authorities were more willing to police what was, and was not, Roman.

Italy in the second century was rapidly changing. The most intense phase of Roman Republican colonization was in the 190s and 180s. New colonies were concentrated in the Po valley, to hold down the Gauls and exploit the agricultural potential of the region, and in southern Italy, where cities and peoples were punished for joining Hannibal. The territory of each colony was divided by surveyors into regularly sized parcels of land, a process known as centuriation; the land was then distributed on hierarchical lines, with larger plots of land for the wealthy and smaller plots for ordinary settlers. Along with army service, colonization in this period promoted the diffusion of Roman culture through Italy (see Chapter 8), although this was never official Roman policy. The colonies had a majority of settlers from Rome and Latium, used Latin as their official language, and were equipped with Roman constitutional elements (magistracies, assemblies, senate). From the 180s the colonists in most of the new towns were given citizen status, as Latin status had become less attractive. But the foundation of new colonies slowed, if it did not halt altogether, between the establishment of Aquileia at the head of the Adriatic in 181 (the last certainly recorded Latin colony) and Luna in 177 (a citizen colony). The only colony recorded for the mid-second century is Auximum in 157 (Velleius Paterculus 1. 15). The social and economic role that colonization had played since the early Republic thus came to an end.

Two other developments had significant long-term implications. First, as the victors in the Hannibalic War the Romans became more willing to interfere in the affairs of their Italian allies, building roads, suppressing undesirable religious cults (notably the Bacchanalia), and closing down avenues to Roman and Latin status (by returning migrants to their place of origin and winding down the foundation of Latin colonies). At the same time, Romans and allied Italians were sharing in the conquest and exploitation of the provinces, and were treated as equals by provincials. The most famous example comes from Delos, whose massive slave-market was dominated by Roman and Italian traders. Thus the Romans were becoming more overbearing just as their allies were becoming wealthier and identifying more closely with them (Brunt 1988). This partly reflects a change in Roman identity, as the old practice of liberality with citizenship ended. Tension between Rome and the allies gradually increased through the second century, as the Italians had little way of expressing their grievances. The elite had Roman patrons, but no direct political representation; they did, however, possess enormous military power. Their resentment built in the period 125–91, and exploded into the Social War.

The other major development of the second century was the changing agrarian situation. Our literary sources present a picture of free farmers declining as the slaves of the rich increased, but the situation is likely to be more complex than the replacement of one by the other. Archaeological surveys have mapped the remains of farms and villas in various regions of Italy, particularly south Etruria (just to the north of Rome), and the Biferno valley in Samnium (Barker 1995). The distribution of larger villas, where slave labour will have been most extensively employed, seems to have been more common near Rome and along the western coast, and much sparser in the hilly territory of inland zones. It is clear from Cato's mid-second-century work *On Agriculture* that the estates of the rich were usually fragmented into many medium-sized farms, and not yet amalgamated into the enormous *latifundia* (broad estates) of the imperial era (see Chapter 6). Slave-owning probably extended quite far down the social scale, with even comparatively modest farmers able to afford slave help, given the mass of cheap slaves produced by Roman conquest in the second century.

In the last third of the second century violent conflict erupted within the Roman ruling class. Tiberius Gracchus, tribune in 133, proposed agrarian legislation to address the perceived decline in the numbers of citizen farmers able to serve in the army. This was a traditional issue, although the last distribution of public land to individual settlers, by Gaius Flaminius in 232, had proved extremely controversial. Tiberius proposed the reapplication of a law of 367 limiting holdings of public land (see above), seizure of holdings in excess of this limit, and their redistribution to the landless poor. But his primary belief that Rome's manpower was being eroded by the import of slaves misread the changes in Italy, and reveals more about contemporary Roman preconceptions than it does about the reality of the agrarian situation in Italy. He was followed in the tribunate by his brother Gaius (tribune 123/2), who attempted to reform many areas of Roman administration and government, as well as reopening the agrarian question, subsidizing the price of corn for the *plebs*, and proposing to extend Roman citizenship to the Latins. Both attempts at reform met with senatorial intransigence. Tiberius was forced to seek the deposition of his fellow tribune Octavius, who, in league with Tiberius' opponents in the Senate, had vetoed his legislation. Against Gaius a rival tribune, Livius Drusus, came forward, who trumped his proposals in order to undermine his support. Gaius' proposals show him to be a genuine reformer, with a clear vision of eliminating corruption and improving the lot of the *plebs*, the soldiers, and the provincial subjects of the empire. Most of his legislation was successful, with the exception of his colonial proposals (abandoned) and his franchise bill (rejected). It set the political agenda for the first century, particularly over the extension of the citizenship, corn distributions for the *plebs*, and political control of the extortion courts. To hardliners in the Senate, the Gracchi were characterized by their own ambition and lack of restraint, an attitude adopted by most of our sources (Velleius Paterculus 2. 6: 'Ten years later Gaius Gracchus fell victim to the same madness as had gripped his brother Tiberius'). They were therefore held responsible for the violent confrontations which ended in their deaths (133 and 121 respectively) and the deaths of many of their supporters. But these events exposed serious flaws in the consensus that underlay senatorial authority; the Gracchi created a template for ambitious politicians willing to respond to the latent disaffection amongst Rome's lower orders, a stance known in the first century as *popularis*.

The issue of citizenship for the allies had first been raised in the Gracchan period, when it was probably mooted as compensation for the loss of their holdings of Roman public land, confiscated to resettle the Roman poor (Appian, *Civil Wars* 1. 21). Italian aristocrats probably saw Roman citizenship as a way of improving their status without compromising their existing traditions and identities. Their political autonomy would inevitably be ended, but in an Italy dominated by Rome this autonomy counted for little. They would have to adopt Latin as an official language of business and law and Roman-style constitutions, but many had already made moves in this direction in the second century. In return they would gain a share in the status of the ruling power, and eligibility for holding office at Rome. For the Italian masses the appeal of Roman citizenship must have been more straightforward. They saw the citizens of the Roman legions, their comrades in arms, receive more reward for facing the same dangers (e.g. Livy 41. 13. 6–8). Citizenship of Rome would entitle them to share in distributions of land provided for the Roman *plebs* (from which they had probably been excluded since the ending of Latin colonization in the 170s). They would gain the protection of *prouocatio* (the right of appeal) against the arbitrary abuse of Roman magistrates. Voting rights in the Roman assemblies, a privilege which might require a journey to Rome to exercise, were probably less important.

The Senate was largely unreceptive to Italian desires. The Licinian–Mucian law in 95 to root out usurpers of Roman citizenship was particularly badly received, and was 'perhaps the chief cause' (Asconius 67C) of the allies deciding to prepare for full-scale military revolt. This eventually led to the Social War (91–c.87), precipitated by the failure of the proposals of Livius Drusus (the younger) to extend Roman citizenship to the allies, and by the discovery of allied plans for rebellion in Asculum. When it became clear to the allies that the Senate would never as a body voluntarily consent to their incorporation, their aims probably shifted to independence and the defeat of Rome, as we can see from the allies' coinage and from their call to Mithridates of Pontus (on the southern Black Sea coast) to join their cause. Mithridates was an avowed enemy of the Romans, held responsible for the massacre of 80,000 Romans and Italians in Asia, when he invaded the province in 88.

The Social War was a titanic struggle between the legions and the other main component of the Roman army, the allied contingents. The Romans suffered severe defeats and lost two consuls in battle. Two of the Latin colonies in the south, Aesernia and Venusia, were lost to the rebels (something not even Hannibal had been able to bring about). The issue was only resolved by the enfranchisement of allies who had not participated or had laid down their arms (the historic Julian law of 90), and by the adherence to the Roman cause of the vast majority of the Latins. The last stages of the war were superseded by Roman civil strife, in which all the defeated rebels were enfranchised. All of Italy south of the Po river had become part of the Roman state. But this was at a huge cost to Rome and to the Italians, and, in illuminating the intransigence of a Senate dominated by its conservative elements, foreshadowed the conflicts that would erupt when further challenges to senatorial authority arose.

The end of the Republic

Politics in the last century were characterized by the rise of 'dynasts', great figures who achieved unprecedented dominance over Roman political life, and whose rivalry ended the Republic. The most important are Marius, Sulla, Pompey, Caesar, Antony, and Octavian. Their conquests determined the shape of the Roman Empire. The precedent was set in the late second century by Marius, a new man who held seven consulships, a record for the Republic. He rose to power on the back of popular and equestrian support in the *comitia centuriata*, which awarded him key commands against Jugurtha, king of Numidia, in 107, and against the Germanic tribes of the Cimbri and Teutoni, involving four continuous consulships from 104 to 101. After defeating the Germanic invaders at Aquae Sextiae in southern Gaul (102) and at Vercellae in the Po valley (101), he used his military prestige to provide land for his veterans. He needed a political ally in a position to propose the necessary legislation, and turned to Appuleius Saturninus, tribune in 103 and 100. Saturninus secured the provision of farms for Marius' veterans, but sought to extend his power through the violent intimidation of opponents. In late 100, under pressure from the Senate, Marius apparently abandoned Saturninus and his supporters, who were killed by a mob. His prestige seriously damaged, Marius withdrew from public life.

He did not return until the Social War, when he played a major role in defeating the allies, alongside his great rival Lucius Sulla. While Sulla, as consul in 88, was in Campania besieging Social War extremists, the tribune Sulpicius engineered the transfer of the lucrative command against Mithridates from Sulla to Marius. In response Sulla marched against Rome, the first Roman general to lead an army against the Republic. Sulpicius was killed, but Marius escaped to Africa to regroup. Once Sulla had left for the East, Marius and his supporters re-entered Rome and took control, enacting summary judgement on their opponents. Marius died in 86, but his supporters remained in control of Rome. Sulla returned in 83, bent on vengeance. He won the ensuing civil war, established himself as dictator, and had his opponents systematically hunted down (the infamous 'proscriptions', or posting of death warrants), 'filling the city with more murders than anyone could count or determine' (Plutarch, *Sulla* 31) (82–81). As dictator he passed a wide range of reforms, in part reactionary (curbing the power of tribunes, abolishing the corn dole), and in part far-sighted (enlarging the Senate, invigorating regulations concerning the *cursus honorum*). He also raised the number of praetors to eight to cope with the demands of administering the empire, but thereby increased the number of candidates seeking the next rung on the career ladder, the consulship, and so aggravated political competition. The anti-tribunician legislation was repealed by two of his former lieutenants, Pompey and Crassus, when they gained the consulship for 70. Sulla succeeded in stabilizing his control of Italy by placing colonies of his veterans in towns that had opposed him. His predominance re-established political peace after the turmoil of civil war. But his settlement proved short-lived and was achieved at a terrible price; the march on Rome, the proscriptions, and his dictatorship set three catastrophic precedents.

In the 70s and early 60s the Roman state was beset by military problems. Sertorius continued the struggle of Sulla's enemies in Spain, carving out a quasi-independent state until his eventual betrayal and death. Spartacus' slave revolt ravaged Italy from 73 to 71, and piracy ran unchecked in the Mediterranean. The rise of Pompey was closely connected to the Senate's inability to solve these problems efficiently. Pompey had gained his reputation as a supporter of Sulla when the latter returned from the East, and then by regaining Spain from Sertorius (or at least claiming most of the credit for doing so). Laws passed by friendly tribunes appointed him to two unprecedented commands, although he held no magistracy: in 67 (to curb piracy) and in 66 (against Mithridates, again resurgent). He rapidly crushed the pirates, based in Cilicia. Keeping his massive forces from that campaign, and adding to them the legions of Lucullus (who had succeeded Sulla in the eastern command), Pompey defeated Mithridates and suppressed further threats to Roman power in the East. He then reorganized Asia Minor and Syria as Roman dominions and vastly enriched the Roman treasury.

While Pompey was away in the East, the legacy of Sulla was also evident in an attempted conspiracy by the renegade senator Catiline, thwarted by the consul Cicero in 63. Catiline was able to draw for support on a wide range of people disaffected with the status quo, including indebted aristocrats, failed veteran farmers, and victims of land confiscation. After the conspiracy was exposed in Rome, Catiline was utterly defeated in a military engagement in Etruria. When Pompey returned to Rome in 62, his senatorial opponents, jealous and fearful of his success, frustrated attempts to reward his veterans with land and to ratify his settlement of the East. By the end of the 60s Pompey's difficulties had forced

THE ROMAN REPUBLIC | 63

him into a loose alliance with two other pre-eminent figures, the wealthy Crassus and hugely ambitious Caesar. Their agreement, often misleadingly called the First Triumvirate (it had no constitutional basis), ensured that Caesar was elected consul for 59. Despite fierce opposition, he succeeded in fulfilling Pompey's aims, and secured himself a potentially lucrative command in Gaul. Whilst Caesar was campaigning in Gaul, Pompey gained a five-year post supervising the corn supply in 57, and the consulship, with Crassus, for 55. Each was then assigned a five-year command, Pompey taking the two provinces of Spain, and Crassus Syria. Pompey exercised his commands through legates, setting a precedent that the emperors would later follow (Chapter 3). In 52 political chaos and the desperation of the *optimates* (conservative members of the Senate) led to Pompey's appointment as sole consul. The constitutional anomaly of a single supreme magistracy, whose power had hitherto always been divided, was compounded by its means of election: senatorial decree, rather than a popular vote—another innovation with a future.

The agreement between Caesar, Pompey, and Crassus had been renewed in 56 at Luca, but Crassus was defeated and killed in an opportunistic expedition into Parthia in 53. Between 58 and 52 Caesar subdued all of Gaul north of Narbonensis, adding an enormous area to the Roman Empire. Caesar himself is our main source, his *Commentaries* imposing his perspective on events and conveying his achievements to the Senate. The *optimates* had wanted to give him the *siluae callesque*, the woods and mountain pastures of Italy as his proconsular province (Suetonius, *Divus Julius* 19. 2), but he was assigned Cisalpine Gaul and Illyria instead by popular vote. Transalpine Gaul was added at Pompey's initiative when the designated proconsul died. Caesar rapidly extended his involvement beyond the boundaries of Narbonensis, first moving up towards the Rhine to repel the Helvetii, who had started to move into Gaul to find land to settle in 58. He then turned against their Germanic enemies the Suebi, who had been occupying Gallic land at the expense of the Aedui (now Roman allies). Caesar ended 58 occupying the strategic site of Vesontio (Besançon), and looking to the north. In 57 he was attacked by the more northerly Belgae and Nervii, whose territory he was clearly threatening, and subdued them. His forces then moved west through Normandy, subduing the Veneti (southern Brittany) and the Aquitani on the Atlantic coast (56). After his command was extended for five years at Luca, he carried on his campaign into Germany and Britain in 55 and 54, only to be faced with revolt of Vercingetorix, a noble of the Arverni, involving a massive coalition of central Gallic peoples (52). The rebels were overcome in the siege of Alesia, where Caesar used a double fortification to resist a relieving Gallic force; in 51 his forces were devoted to pacifying the newly conquered territory. It was a formidable and devastating campaign, driven more by Caesar's desire for personal aggrandizement than any strategic need, and causing, by one ancient estimate, around a million Gallic dead.

The conquest of Gaul left Caesar enormously wealthy, and in a powerful position, immediately to the north-west of Italy with a battle-hardened army. Crassus' death had left the field open for the two remaining dynasts to dispute control of Rome, and while their fatal disagreement was not necessarily inevitable, it was stoked by the *optimates*, determined to cut Caesar down to size. The years from 49 to 45 saw a series of civil wars between Caesar and Pompey, his sons, and followers. The *optimates* had largely chosen Pompey as their champion, and made it clear to Caesar that he would suffer politically once he lost the protection of his proconsular *imperium* in Gaul—for this reason Caesar sought, but was denied, a seamless transition to a consulship in 49 or 48. When Caesar crossed the boundary between his province and Italy (January 49), at the Rubicon, near Ariminum, he was illegally leaving the area of his command and in effect declaring war. Pompey, whose new recruits were no match for Caesar's legions, decided to withdraw to Greece, and was accompanied by much of the Senate. But he was defeated at Pharsalus in August 48, and fled to Egypt, where he was killed. Further campaigns in Africa (46) and Spain, including a difficult battle against Pompey's sons at Munda (March 45), saw Caesar eliminate all military opposition to his rule. In contrast to Sulla, Caesar did not use his position of unopposed domination to proscribe, instead pursuing a policy of *clementia* (clemency) to his defeated enemies.

At Rome he was made dictator, initially as a temporary measure (as was traditional), then in 46 with a term of ten years, and finally in February 44 becoming perpetual dictator. This last and most unconstitutional step, combined with his evident desire to be worshipped as a god, led to his assassination on the Ides of March, 44. At the head of the conspiracy were Brutus and Cassius. In aiming to eliminate a tyrant and restore the Republic, the former was echoing the legendary actions of his ancestor L. Junius Brutus, regarded as the chief mover in the expulsion of the last king.

Although they had succeeded in eliminating the dictator, the assassins failed to win over the Roman *plebs*, who held Caesar in great esteem, and quickly lost control of the city to Antony, Caesar's lieutenant. Under pressure from a resurgent Senate led by the elder statesman Cicero, Antony allied with the two other military leaders who had emerged in the aftermath of Caesar's assassination, Octavian, the great-nephew and heir of Caesar, who had briefly supported the senatorial opposition to Antony, and Lepidus, Caesar's official deputy or Master of the Horse. Together they defeated Brutus and Cassius at Philippi (42) and carved up the empire as a legally constituted 'triumvirate' (board of three; Chapter 3) (43–33). More powerful than consuls or provincial governors, they enacted savage proscriptions of their opponents. In the 30s Octavian, against the odds, consolidated his power in Italy, arresting Lepidus in 36 and placing him under permanent house arrest. In the East Antony unsuccessfully attacked the Parthians. He acted as a quasi-Hellenistic prince, with his wife the Ptolemaic queen Cleopatra, last of the descendants of Alexander's successors; in the inevitable showdown at Actium (31) Octavian defeated Antony and Cleopatra, and pursued them to Egypt, where they committed suicide (30). In 29 Octavian returned to Rome to hold a threefold triumph, rewriting Actium as a victory over foreign powers. He went on to transform the city through a building programme, already begun in the 30s, and to legitimize his power in the constitutional arrangements of 28–27 and 23. The imperial era was inaugurated.

Individuals came to dominate late Republican history, and whilst their characters and actions were often of vital importance, the opportunities available to them cannot be explained without an examination of some wider trends. These include the rise of the *populares* after the example set by Tiberius Gracchus, and the polarization of the Roman elite into conservative and radical camps. The role of radical *populares* such as Caesar was only possible through the exploitation of the democratic element in Roman politics, which had been built up by a series of measures championing popular sovereignty in the second century. Four measures introduced secret ballots in elections (139), judicial assemblies (137), legislative assemblies (129), and treason trials (107); as Cicero reflected, 'who does not realise that the ballot-law has removed all the influence (*auctoritas*) of the *optimates*' (*On the Laws* 3. 34; see Millar 1998: 2, Morstein-Marx 2004; a different view in Mouritsen 2001). A vital role in the downfall of the Republic was played by its own tribunes, some of whom promoted political violence and the interruption of civic institutions as a means to achieving personal ends (even if also acting in the interests of the masses): such were Clodius and Milo, and others who throughout the late Republic proposed special commands for individual dynasts.

The late Republican Roman elite was also divided in another way, between senators and *equites* (equestrians). The equestrian order, like the senatorial, was reputedly as old as Rome itself, the earliest cavalry of the Romulean state. Servius Tullius supposedly raised their numbers to 1,800, making up eighteen centuries in the *comitia centuriata*. They were provided with a 'public horse' (paid for by the state), and had to present themselves at the census every five years. From 304 they took part in a grand procession to the Capitol (the *equitum transuectio*) on 15 July every year. By the late Republic the military role of the equestrian order had become unimportant, and instead they had become a wealth class, second only to the senatorial order, and far more numerous. In the Gracchan period several measures separated the equestrian from the senatorial order, and made them into a political interest-group. Senators were excluded from the equestrian order in 129, and in 123 Gaius Gracchus transferred control of the courts trying provincial governors for *repetundae* (extortion) away from the Senate to the *equites*. Gracchus aimed to discourage provincial corruption by preventing senators passing judgement on their peers (all governors were senators); but he merely created an alternative source of corruption. Tax-raising in the provinces from Gracchus onwards lay in the hands of *publicani*, companies of equestrians who bid for collection contracts. They could only be reined in by provincial governors, but equestrian control over the extortion courts meant that conscientious governors were vulnerable to conviction by equestrian colleagues of the *publicani*.

The *equites* were not a completely different class to the Senate, and were often their financial peers; after all, the Senate drew its (numerous) new members from the equestrian order, and senators will have had equestrian relatives. In the late Republic the *equites* strove to defend their interests. Their aims were the same as the Senate's, in that they desired the continued success of Rome and its domination of the empire, but there were also increasingly frequent conflicts between the two orders, especially over control of the courts. The latter was ended only in 70, by recruiting jurors equally from the Senate, *equites*, and *tribuni aerarii* (an obscure group similar in background to *equites*). The *equites* sought to protect the collection of taxes by *publicani*, which were especially lucrative in Asia, as well as traders in vulnerable provinces; for instance, playing a critical role in obtaining for Marius his command in the Jugurthine War.

We also have to reckon with the increasing role of the army in politics. Military leaders established themselves in dominant political positions in 88, 82, and 49, and the Senate was often menaced by armies at other times. This was owing at least in part to the ultimate failure of the state to provide for Rome's soldiery through land distributions. Chronic instability was the result, as the allegiance of soldiers shifted from an abstracted notion of Rome as a state—expressed by phrases such as *senatus populusque Romanus* (*SPQR*), or *res publica*, the Republic—to the dynastic generals who would secure their future (see Chapter 5).

These political and military developments were linked to deeper changes in Roman society. Primary amongst these was social differentiation (the growth of specialist roles; Hopkins 1978: 74–96). Greater social complexity led to a more diverse citizen body and, inevitably, greater ideological conflict. These shifts also affected the changing rhythms of Roman life, which had in the early Republic revolved around annual cycles of warfare and agriculture governing the lives of all Rome's citizens. They were also connected to the openness and the inevitable growth of Rome as an imperial capital. Rome became a far more cosmopolitan society in the late Republic, and inevitably more difficult for the elite to control. The massive population of the city increasingly depended on a fragile corn supply, which the state was very slow to secure in a systematic way. Any politician who could improve this situation was guaranteed political influence; hence the tribunician measures of C. Gracchus (123), Saturninus (100), and Clodius (58), by which a corn ration was subsidized and then made free. The issue was never far from the minds of Roman emperors.

Changes in Roman society were exacerbated by shifts in Roman culture and ideology under the impact of Hellenistic ideas. Many of the old orthodoxies and values (particularly religious conservatism, social hierarchies, and militarism) began to be challenged in the late

Republic, as a complex intellectual life involving dispute, choice, and the invention of traditions developed. As these traditional values underlay the elite consensus that was the mainstay of the Republican form of government, their erosion fatally undermined the ability of the Republic to operate. The rise to power of Octavian was in part due to his skill in asserting control over all the new sources of power within Roman society, such as the soldiery, religious groups, antiquarians and other writers, and collegial organizations. The imposition of his largely conservative values and interpretations on Roman religion, literature, art, and history created an 'official' culture into which all aspiring members of the empire could buy. Many vibrant forms of Roman political and intellectual activity were stifled, but for its new citizens, especially those from the provinces, fresh cultural fields and opportunities were opened up by the empire.

3

The Roman Empire from Augustus to Diocletian

Benet Salway

SUPERFICIAL comparison of the political structure and geographical extent of the Roman Empire at the death of Augustus (AD 14) and at the accession of Diocletian (AD 284) gives an impression of remarkable stability. This is in striking contrast to the great changes in the Roman state over the equivalent span of time from the First Punic War to Augustus' acquisition of unchallenged control. The foundation of this relative stability was laid in a fifty-year period of rapid transformation in Rome's political, administrative, and social structures between the assassination of Julius Caesar and the death of his adopted son, Augustus. This phase of radical change was followed by two-and-a-half centuries during which developments were generally more gradual, even if the system was periodically convulsed by political crisis and stretched almost to collapse over the last half-century before the reign of Diocletian.

Much of the initial success of the Augustan political 'settlement' as a system of government can be attributed to the continued representation of the Roman state as a republic rather than the personal fiefdom of a monarch. This stance is reflected in the complexity of the nomenclature used to describe the emperor's position. We might call Augustus and his successors simply 'emperors'; but when Gaius Aurelius Diocles was elevated to the throne at Nicomedia in November 284 he adopted an elaborate string of names, titles, and powers

(*Imperator Caesar, Augustus, pontifex maximus, tribunicia potestas, proconsul, pater patriae*) to signify the imperial office, most of which had been developed or gradually acquired by Augustus as part of the establishment of a monarchy that dared not speak its name. On the surface the behaviour expected of an emperor also remained similar across the period. Diocletian assumed Rome's chief magistracy, the consulship, just as Augustus and most intervening emperors had done, and even went as far as adjusting his own name to make it sound more noble and 'Roman' (appending the Latin suffix '-ianus' to his Greek personal name). Nevertheless, the imperial 'office' he assumed had developed considerably from the special personal position occupied by Augustus. For, as the position of the emperor had become increasingly embedded in the structures of civil and military society, it had also become much more like a constitutional office. This development was in fact taken to its logical extreme by Diocletian's own eventual innovation—the termination of his reign by voluntary resignation so as to end his life in retirement, a private citizen once again.

The political balance between the elements that comprised the state ruled by Augustus was also quite different from the balance in that ruled by Diocletian. Augustus' chief political constituencies were, in the city of Rome, the senatorial aristocracy and urban plebs and, largely in the provinces, the now fully professionalized armed forces. He derived no small part of the authority that facilitated his rule from his connections by birth, adoption, and marriage alliance with two families of long-established nobility (the Julii and the Claudii). In addition, despite his accumulation of powers, the Senate as a body, the traditional magistracies, and most particularly the senators as individuals fulfilled significant roles in the government of the empire. Diocletian inaugurated his reign by taking as his partner in the consulship a Roman senatorial aristocrat, but he himself was of non-senatorial, provincial origin, and elevated to the throne directly from professional, full-time military service. For, by the later third century, credible candidates for the throne no longer needed to have been born into the senatorial class or to have progressed through the magistracies of the city of Rome. Nor did senators any longer enjoy a near-monopoly of the most important positions in the government of the empire. Moreover, with the military exigencies and political fragmentation of much of the third century making emperors a rare sight in the city of Rome, the political voice of its masses ceased to be heard. The same pressures had further concentrated political power into the hands of the army, which made it ever more necessary for an emperor to be, above all else, a credible military leader in order to establish and maintain legitimacy (Chapter 5). Not that this transformation had taken place without resistance; the tensions caused by these developments had come to a head violently nearly half a century before Diocletian, in AD 238, a year of no less than six emperors, as provincial landowners, the Senate, and the urban populace promoted different candidates in turn against the incumbent supported by the Rhine legions.

In terms of geography, the empire that Diocletian came to rule over had recognizably the same shape as that bequeathed by Augustus to Tiberius, and was slightly larger, although not quite matching up to the territorial high point reached at the death of the emperor Trajan in AD 117. For this entire period the Romans could claim that their empire stretched from the North Sea, in the north-west, to Aswan in Egypt, in the south-east. For the most part this huge territory was subdivided into a tessellation of provinces, each commanded by a governor answerable to the central government. Although very hard to estimate, the empire's population was almost certainly higher under Diocletian than it had been under Augustus, but perhaps still lower than the peak reached in the second century before successive plagues swept across the Mediterranean world (see also Chapter 6). However, the populations ruled over by Augustus and Diocletian were quite dissimilar in terms of composition. The slave population, whose size at any time is difficult to estimate, remained a consistent feature; it was amongst the free inhabitants of the empire that there had been the most significant changes. Under Augustus, aside from the Italian peninsula itself where most freeborn people had full citizen status, Roman citizens had existed as a privileged minority. Moreover, under Augustus Italy as a whole had enjoyed freedom from submission to provincial governors. In contrast, most of the free inhabitants of Rome's provinces were merely subjects, classed in the eyes of Roman law as 'foreigners' (*peregrini*). By Diocletian's reign, however, these inequalities had largely disappeared. The vast majority of the free population was now of citizen status and, conversely, Italy had ceased to be accorded a special status within the empire, as its regions began to be organized into provinces. Certainly some of the expansion in provincial citizen numbers between Augustus and Diocletian was the result of incremental growth in the first two centuries AD. This was achieved through a number of relatively controlled mechanisms, such as the freeing of slaves by Roman citizens or the enfranchisement of non-citizen veteran soldiers. Nevertheless, most of the increase is to be accounted for by the extension of citizenship to almost all free subjects by the emperor M. Aurelius Antoninus (Caracalla) in AD 212 (the *Constitutio Antoniniana*). Yet the political privileges of citizenship had long been rendered meaningless by the demise of the free Republic. For, although certain types of election continued on at least into the early third century, the emperors effectively controlled both legislation and choice of magistrates. Even those judicial privileges that attached to citizen status had been largely whittled away before Caracalla's dramatic gesture. Despite this devaluation of the citizenship, the emperor's action still had profound consequences in the longer term for the way the descendants of the newly enfranchised perceived their Roman identity. These were really only just beginning to be felt by the time of Diocletian's accession.

Europe in the empire

'Europe', as a label for the area that we would understand by the term, certainly featured in the Romans' geographical vocabulary. The Roman view of their world (the *orbis terrarum*) was ultimately derived from the Greek notion of the *oikoumenē* (habitable world) as defined by Eratosthenes in the third century BC. According to this view the habitable world was divided into three continents, Europe, Asia, and Africa (*Libyē* in Greek), surrounding the Mediterranean Sea, and in turn surrounded by the outer ocean (*Oceanus*). By the end of Augustus' reign Roman power had encompassed the entire Mediterranean world, to the extent that it was easy enough for Romans to pretend that their empire was synonymous with the *orbis terrarum*. Of the three names of the continents, both Asia and Africa also served emblematically as labels for the provinces occupying the portions of those two continents nearest Rome, where her first footholds had been gained in the second century BC (Chapter 2). Despite the currency of 'Europe' as a geographical concept, however, the term did not generally feature in the Romans' political geography (at least not until after our period) as either a provincial or regional designation.

After all, given the physical location of Rome and Italy on the European continent, Europe could not usefully serve to distinguish any provincial territory from the empire's 'home counties'. It is no surprise, then, that there is no evidence for any consciousness of a common European identity amongst Rome's subjects on the continent.

Nor did the geographical concept of Europe coincide with any significant contemporary cultural or economic fault-lines. Rather, two significant lines of distinction bisected the European portion of the empire, one horizontally, so to speak, the other vertically. Culturally, the most significant distinction was between the Latin-speaking West and Greek-speaking East or, to be more precise, between those areas in which the language of Roman government was Latin and those in which it was Greek. On the North African coast this divide separated the eastern and western arms of the Gulf of Sidra (modern Libya) dividing Greek Cyrenaica from Latin Tripolitania. On the northern shore of the Mediterranean the Latin–Greek divide ran roughly east–north-east through south-eastern Europe from the Adriatic to the Black Sea, dividing the Latin provinces of Dalmatia, Moesia, and Dacia from Greek Epirus, Macedonia, and Thrace.

The second major divide in the Roman Empire was that between the provinces of the Mediterranean littoral and those provinces orientated towards the great rivers of mainland Europe, the Rhine and the Danube. The fundamental basis of this divide was ecological. It distinguished those provinces whose agricultural system comprised to a significant extent the classic Mediterranean polyculture of wheat, vines, and olives, and those whose climate meant that beer and butter took the place of the latter two crops (also Chapter 6). The Romans' own perception of the centrality of wheat, wine, and olive oil to Mediterranean life achieves no more eloquent expression than in Diocletian's famous Edict on Maximum Prices of AD 301, in which these products comprise the first three categories listed. The wine–beer and olive oil–butter divide also had important cultural resonances; it largely coincided with the distinction between those areas that had a civilization comprising urban communities, literate culture, and coined money long before the imposition of Roman authority, on the one hand, and those where these Mediterranean-style features were a direct result of the impact of Rome, on the other (see also Chapter 8). In Europe this broadly distinguished most of the Iberian peninsula, Gallia Narbonensis (modern Provence), Italy, Dalmatia, Greece,

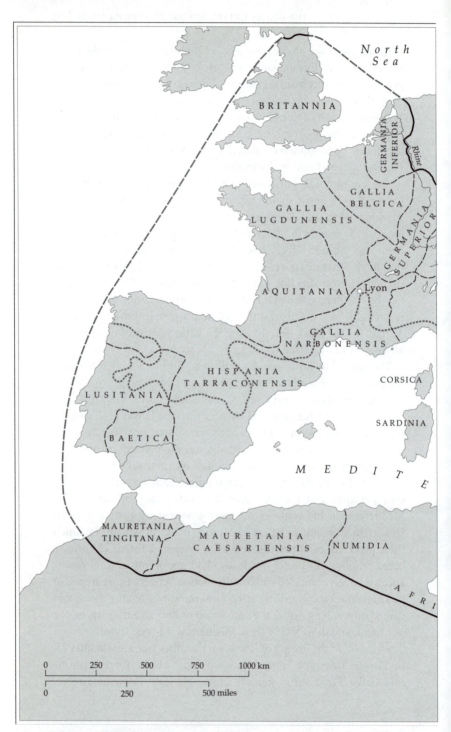

Fig. 3.1. Significant ecological and cultural divisions within the Roman Empire's European provinces (c. AD 117)

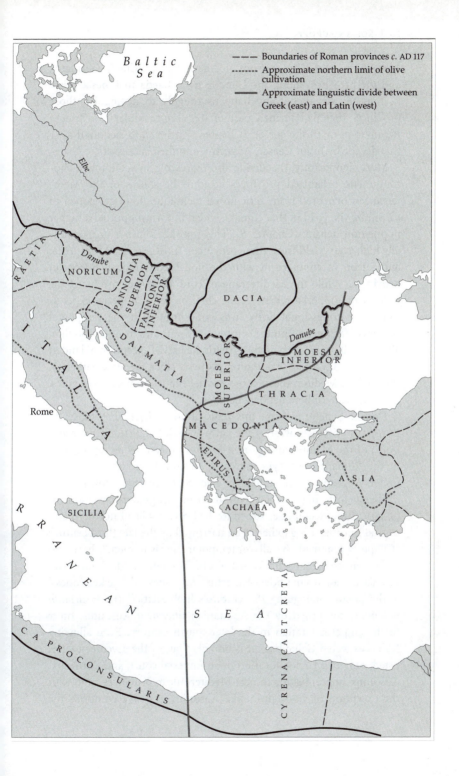

Baltic Sea

Elbe

- – – – Boundaries of Roman provinces *c.* AD 117
- ·········· Approximate northern limit of olive cultivation
- ——— Approximate linguistic divide between Greek (east) and Latin (west)

RAETIA

Danube

NORICUM

PANNONIA SUPERIOR

PANNONIA INFERIOR

DACIA

I T A L I A

DALMATIA

Danube

MOESIA SUPERIOR

MOESIA INFERIOR

Rome

THRACIA

MACEDONIA

EPIRUS

ASIA

ACHAEA

SICILIA

M E D I T E R R A N E A N   S E A

CYRENAICA ET CRETA

CA PROCONSULARIS

Macedonia, and Thrace from northern Gaul, Britain, Germany, and the provinces along the Danube from Raetia to Moesia. Also, in Europe, this dichotomy happens roughly to distinguish those provinces that had formed part of the empire under the Roman Republic prior to the 50s BC (Chapter 2) from those acquired after that decade by Julius Caesar, Augustus, and their successors.

More significantly, this divide also represents an economic dichotomy. The urbanized provinces around the shores of the Mediterranean benefited from agricultural techniques long developed to maximize the yield in that climate, which in turn supported a higher population density (Chapter 6). This translated into a proportionally higher tax-yield from these provinces, most notably Africa, Asia, and Egypt, in comparison with the non-Mediterranean European provinces. While the Mediterranean 'core' provinces produced the bulk of the imperial revenues, the chief object of imperial expenditure, the professional army, was concentrated in the peripheral provinces facing the Rhine, Danube, and Euphrates frontiers. So that, although all provinces paid taxes (with the partial exception of land in Italy, free from direct taxation on property since 167 BC: Chapter 2), those of the Mediterranean core were net exporters of state revenues, those of the periphery net beneficiaries.

Despite benefiting from this redistributive effect, that subset of European provinces west of the Latin–Greek linguistic frontier and north of the Mediterranean–non-Mediterranean divide represented in the Romans' own eyes the most backward area of the empire under Augustus, both culturally and economically. Through the deliberate fostering of urban civilization and the gradual development of agricultural techniques suited to the heavier soils of northern and central Europe, this gap had been narrowed by the late third century (Chapters 6 and 8). By all contemporary measurements, however, this remained the most backward area of the empire under Diocletian, just as it had been under Augustus. An index of 'backwardness' is the poem cataloguing the empire's 'noble cities' (*Ordo urbium nobilium*) composed by the Aquitanian *littérateur* Ausonius, tutor to the emperor Gratian in the later fourth century. Even allowing for an expected Gallic bias, it is notable that, of the seventeen cities listed, only two (Trier, location of an imperial court, and Bordeaux, Ausonius' home) belong to non-Mediterranean provinces, and, with the exception of Constantinople, Ausonius' top five comprise the same names that one would have expected in a poem written 400 years earlier: Rome, Carthage, Antioch, and Alexandria. The first 300 years of the empire did witness a flourishing of Latin literary culture outside Italy, latterly and most notably in North Africa, but the cultural level of the non-Mediterranean provinces of the Latin West continued to be scorned by the aristocracy of the city of Rome. The noble Symmachus (*Letters* 1. 14) mocked Ausonius' attempt to dignify the Gallic River Moselle in Latin poetry, insincerely praising him for having rendered it more noble than the Tiber itself. In terms of cultural production, Symmachus' view is to some extent justified by the fact that, archaeology aside, very little of the material used to write the political history of the Roman Empire originates in the non-Mediterranean provinces of Europe. Symmachus' snobbery is, however, revealing of the author's deeper anxiety that the traditional political order had been upset, inverting the proper priority of Italy over her transalpine provinces.

For, despite the cultural and economic handicap under which Europe's non-Mediterranean provinces laboured, by the reign of Diocletian there had been a decisive shift, whereby political initiative had moved from the empire's Mediterranean heartland to its traditional periphery. A combination of factors explains this development, above all the gradual specialization in the organs of imperial government and the shift in the balance of priorities that pushed military considerations to the fore. Accordingly, a distinct military cadre emerged that largely dominated the selection of emperors from the third quarter of the third century onwards (see Chapter 5). This favoured imperial candidates from the provinces of the Rhine–Danube frontier, which served as both principal military recruiting-ground and launch-pad for imperial power, thanks to the concentration of military deployment along that line and the relative proximity of these forces to Italy. So the story of Europe in the political history of the Roman imperial period does have its own particular trajectory, although it is not in any way sensibly separable from the mainstream narrative of Roman history. The European provinces, both Mediterranean and non-Mediterranean, performed different roles as part of an integrated political system within the Roman Empire. Nevertheless, even though the European provinces did not have a recognized common identity distinct from the rest of the empire, the story of Europe *is* distinctive as the arena in which the inversion of the balance of political power between the empire's traditional core and periphery was largely played out.

The sources

We are not able to write a political history of the entire period from Augustus to Diocletian in a uniformly detailed manner or from a consistent perspective. There is no unbroken sequence of comprehensive chronological narrative accounts in either Latin or Greek. This is in part owing to the accidents of survival, but in part also to changes that eventually made the centres of political decision-making and court intrigue remote from the kind of people minded to write histories in the mould of Sallust or Livy. Moreover, only a small proportion of the surviving accounts covers contemporary affairs or is written from an eyewitness perspective. In the imperial period writing about the past was politically less risky as an occupation than writing about the present; the historian Tacitus flattered Trajan by claiming that his reign provided an atmosphere without danger for the writer of contemporary history (*Histories* 1. 1). Nevertheless he, like others, took the precaution of terminating his narrative before Trajan's accession.

The fullest surviving account of the transition from republic to empire is actually provided by an early third-century source. Cassius Dio, a Roman senator from Nicaea in Bithynia (modern İznik in Turkey), wrote a history in Greek of Rome from its origins to his own day, rather immodestly culminating in AD 229 when he was consul for the second time along with the emperor Severus Alexander. Although some parts remain only as Byzantine abridgements, most of Augustus' reign survives in Dio's original text. It is to be remembered, however, that it was written with 200 years of hindsight and is occasionally demonstrably anachronistic on minor details. For most of the first century AD our prime source is the Latin writings of Cornelius Tacitus, a Roman senator probably from Gallia Narbonensis. Besides a biography of his father-in-law Agricola, a successful general, Tacitus wrote two historical works at the end of the first and the beginning of the second century: the *Histories*, originally running from the civil wars of AD 68–69 to the death of the emperor Domitian (AD 96); and the *Annals*, covering the Julio-Claudian emperors from Tiberius to Nero (AD 14 to 68). Neither, however, survived intact. Tacitus' account is complemented by the work of his younger contemporary Suetonius Tranquillus. He was also a provincial, probably from Hippo Regius (modern Annaba) in Africa, and although not a senator, still very much part of the Roman social elite as a member of the equestrian order (see Chapter 2), and an insider on the corridors of power as a secretary to the emperor Hadrian. This position allowed Suetonius to exploit the imperial archives in writing a series of biographies of the 'Caesars' from Julius Caesar to Domitian. Because the style is very much more 'lifestyle' than 'lives' of the Caesars, however, it is of limited utility for reconstructing a political narrative. These sources generally comment on the imperial system from the slightly jaded perspective of the inhabitants of the gilded cage of Roman elite society. This perspective is generally urban, aristocratic, and infused with elements of nostalgic republicanism: it is a powerful lens, through which we receive our image of the early imperial system. We should remember that it is not necessarily representative of contemporary non-elite and provincial opinions.

Parallel with Dio's account for the period from Commodus (AD 180) to the 220s, the Greek history of Herodian is our main guide to political history from Severus Alexander to the end of AD 238. Little is known about Herodian's background, except that his name suggests an origin somewhere in the Levant; the partiality of some of his comments suggests that he worked in a provincial tax-collection department. Often ill-informed and confused compared with Dio, Herodian certainly was not close to the centre of events. Thereafter, apart from a few fragments of Greek histories and traces of contemporary accounts in later potted imperial biographies in Latin, there is little evidence of much historical writing in either language until the later fourth century. The gap was filled retrospectively by the anonymous *Historia Augusta*. Although written by a single author in the late fourth century, this work purports to be a set of biographies for emperors up to 285, by a series of authors writing soon after that date. The author's deliberate mischievousness aside, the fact that for the middle decades of the third century its factual content scarcely extends beyond the emperors' last names is testimony to how little could be recovered in the next century.

Other than the legends on imperial coinage, the survival of overtly political material issued by the organs of Roman central government is a rare occurrence. The emperor Trajan's replies, preserved in the correspondence of the younger Pliny, sometimes reveal general principles of his administration, but most such material survives in the documentary rather than the literary record. The prime example is Augustus' political testament, his *Achievements* (*Res Gestae*), published posthumously on bronze plaques outside his mausoleum in Rome, but surviving today only in copies inscribed on stone in the province of Galatia (central Turkey). Other significant surviving inscriptions are the text of the Senate's decision in the trial of Cn. Calpurnius Piso, who stood accused of treason and murdering the heir to the throne in AD 19, and Claudius' speech of AD 48 to the Senate arguing for the recruitment of senators from the provinces of Gallia Comata ('long-haired' Gaul). Both serve as complement and corrective to the relevant accounts by Tacitus.

Inscriptions add to our knowledge in other ways too. A genre that became increasingly common in the first two centuries of the empire is the honorific text, often inscribed on the base of a statue, listing an individual's public offices and achievements, a fashion previously confined to epitaphs (funerary texts). Analysed en masse, these texts allow modern scholars to perceive patterns of office-holding amongst the Roman elite. This invaluable category of evidence suffers a catastrophic downturn in the political and economic turmoil of the mid-third century, unfortunately coinciding with the hiatus in our reliable narrative histories.

The acquisition of Egypt as a Roman province generated a significant further category of evidence: documents on papyrus. This was the 'paper' of the ancient world, made from the reed-like papyrus plant native to Egypt; papyrus documents survive in large quantities because of the extremely dry conditions of the Egyptian desert. Amongst these papyri, just as significant as the remnants of the provincial administration's paperwork, are the scores of humble customs receipts and donkey-drivers' contracts, whose dating clauses can provide precious nuggets of information on who was in power for otherwise poorly documented periods.

In all these categories of evidence the viewpoint is predominantly a male one (see also Chapter 4). Those writing political history were men, writing for a male audience and treating a sphere of life they considered ought to be a male preserve—hence the generally hostile representation of women when they appear as actors on the political stage.

From *triumvir* to *princeps*

Through a series of shrewd manoeuvres, the once obscure 19-year-old Gaius Octavius adopted as his heir by Julius Caesar, and now going under the novel name of *Imperator Caesar Diui filius* ('Commander Caesar, son of the deified [Julius]' but generally referred to in modern literature as Octavian), had by 36 BC made himself the dominant player in the western Mediterranean. Meanwhile, Mark Antony, his colleague as *triumuir rei publicae constituendae* ('one of the three men charged with the establishment of public affairs') had been focusing his efforts on avenging Crassus' defeat by the Parthians (Chapter 2). Antony's political alliance and personal liaison with Cleopatra was a propaganda gift to the young Caesar, allowing him to present the final showdown between him and Antony in 31 BC as a patriotic war against a traitor allied to a foreign queen. The naval victory won at Actium on the west coast of Greece left Caesar undisputed master of the Roman state, after which Antony and Cleopatra were hunted down in Egypt, itself then transformed into a Roman province. So by 30 BC he had not only re-established his adoptive father's monopolization of political power within the Roman state, but also extended Rome's empire significantly by the absorption of the last serious independent power in the Mediterranean. The acquisition of Egypt also further reinforced the identity of the empire as just as much an Asian and African as a European power.

Although the normal process of election to high office had been supplanted by appointment under the triumvirs, the politically ambitious nevertheless could still choose between alternative patrons. The cementing of sole rule meant a further narrowing of the field of traditional politics. Now that there was only one patron, competition for office effectively meant competing for his favour; political opposition focused on his removal, or on deliberate refusal to participate in the regime. Tacitus lamented the stultifying effect this change was to have on the production of political oratory (*Dialogue on Famous Orators* 36 f.). The young Caesar's political dominance was guaranteed by his monopolization of military command (Chapter 5). Nevertheless, his adoptive father's fate was sufficient demonstration that Roman aristocratic culture would not tolerate overtly monarchic tendencies for long. The young Caesar was not about to throw away his hard-won political dominance, but he could not rule alone: for the sake of long-term political stability a semblance of power-sharing was desirable. Accordingly he effectively wrong-footed critics of his regime by a well-choreographed piece of political theatre acted out in 28–27 BC. As Cassius Dio relates it, Caesar stunned the Senate by renouncing his command over the provinces and handing them all over to its care, though this was not a complete abdication of power, since he remained consul. The senators' response was to urge him to reconsider, and a compromise was reached. The near-contemporary account of the Greek Strabo (*Geography* 17. 3. 25) summarizes the outcome as the granting to Caesar of the 'foremost position of leadership' and the 'responsibility for war and peace for life', and his division of the empire into two portions, one remaining in his care, the other allotted to the people. Transfer to the public domain of the most peaceful and prosperous provinces (with the significant exception of Egypt) satisfied senatorial honour. The political risk of this arrangement was mitigated by the fact that Caesar retained command of the vast majority of the armed forces, since his portion comprised those provinces (initially Gaul, Spain, and Syria) requiring garrisoning because of their frontier location or potential rebelliousness. In any event, Caesar and his successors reserved the right to redistribute provinces between the two shares as necessity demanded. Elections for magistracies were also reinstituted. In the words of the inscribed calendar set up in the *forum* of the Italian town of Praeneste, the settlement marked the 'restoration of the *res publica* (public affairs) to the Roman people' or, as a contemporary coin legend puts it, 'he [Caesar] restored the laws and rights to (*or* of) the Roman people' (British Museum, Department of Coins and Medals, accession no. 1995.4-1.1).

In recognition of this benefaction, amongst other honours, some senators suggested that Caesar be called 'Romulus', but, preferring to avoid a title with such openly monarchic connotations, he accepted instead the epithet 'Augustus'. The word was appropriately evocative of respect and religious sacrosanctity, because the connotation of the straightforward meaning 'majestic' was compounded by a supposed etymological link with augury (Chapter 7); the Greek translation of the title, *sebastos* ('worshipped'), was less subtle. None of this fundamentally altered the basis of Augustus' power, which remained his control of the legions. Nor was the settlement of 27 BC the end of the process of negotiating a constitutional definition of his position. Nevertheless, the whole charade symbolized the striking of a tacit bargain between Augustus and the senatorial aristocracy, whereby the senators would not challenge the emperor's authority as long as he used his military power to provide security, agreed to mask the monarchic nature of his position, preserved their privileges and opportunities, and maintained the prestige of their social status. Thus was born the 'principate'—that is, a political system dominated by one pre-eminent individual (*princeps*).

The fact that Augustus managed to die in his bed peacefully at the age of 76 is testament to the success of his political arrangements. In formal constitutional terms, between 31 and 23 BC his executive power rested in his tenure of a continuous series of consulships. Yet his annual occupation of this magistracy frustrated the ambitions of others. So in 23 BC Augustus arranged that he be made a personal grant of enhanced proconsular power (*imperium proconsulare maius*), which allowed him to intervene in the public provinces as well as his own, and the power of the tribunate of the plebs (*tribunicia potestas*), with its right of veto over other magistrates and legislation, and ability to summon the Senate and assembly of the *plebs*. The annual renewal of this power became a way in which emperors measured the length of their reigns. On the death of his erstwhile triumviral colleague Lepidus, in 12 BC, Augustus was able also to step into the chief religious office of state, that of *pontifex maximus*. He seems to have been proudest, however, of the honorific title *pater patriae* ('father of the homeland') bestowed on him by the Senate and people in 2 BC, perhaps because he felt that it acknowledged his transformation from party politician to statesman.

Government: city and empire

The establishment of the Augustan principate provided Rome with a head of state whose political horizon was considerably wider than that of the elected magistrates who enjoyed their offices for only a year at a time. The extended time-frame of the rule of the *princeps* allowed solutions to be evolved for some long-standing systemic shortcomings in the running of the Roman state. Although essential symbols of the continuity of the *res publica* under the emperors, Senate and magistrates found their roles profoundly altered as part of the process of organizational reform. Under the republic the provinces of the empire had continued to be administered through the organs of city-state government. The growth in the size of subject territory had put increasing strains on the system, to the detriment of the proper administration of both Rome and the provinces. Augustus maintained the basic sequence of magistracies (*cursus honorum*; Chapter 2), progression through which augmented a senator's standing (*dignitas*). Many senators may have been satisfied that the restoration of the regular schedule of elections and observation of the established intervals between offices constituted sufficient evidence of the proper working of the *res publica*. In the highly rhetorical preface of Justinian's law of December AD 537, redefining senatorial membership, the emperor's chief legal officer, Tribonian, reflected on the role of the Senate under the principate:

Indeed, after the rights of the people and Senate of Rome had by the republic's good fortune been transferred to the emperor's majesty, it came about that those, whom they [the senators] themselves chose and appointed to administrative posts, did everything that the imperial voice enjoined upon them. Provincial commands were placed under them and everything else made subject to their ordinances; while the remaining senators passed the time at rest. And after the administrators laid down the tasks entrusted to them it was reserved to the emperor's will whether he wished to free them from the burdensome belt of office and send them back to the security of the Senate, or to assign them to other tasks.

(Justinian, *Novel* 62)

Although an oversimplification, Tribonian's description encapsulates some of the key features of the Augustan system in a recognizable manner. As he implies, most public posts remained in the hands of senators, whether occupying their positions in their own right as traditional magistrates and pro-magistrates, or acting as imperial deputies. For, in appointing subordinates to represent him in his provinces, Augustus was in general careful to respect existing conventions. Accordingly, he appointed his deputies (*legati*) in the provinces from amongst those senators who had reached the upper echelons of the hierarchy of public magistracies (the praetorship and consulship). Just as tenure of the consulship was the qualification for entering the lottery for the proconsular command of one of the two great public provinces (Africa and Asia), so the emperors also reserved their senior legateships for ex-consuls. In fact, the most significant innovation of the Augustan regime was to have the 'ordinary' consuls step down during the year and be replaced by sequences of extra pairs of consuls (*suffecti*), precisely in order to create sufficient candidates for these legateships.

Mindful of the well-being of the urban populace, Augustus also created new positions devoted to the everyday administration of the city, many of which were linked to stages in the traditional *cursus*. These included curatorships for Rome's infrastructure and amenities (for example, public buildings, riverbanks, and drainage), held at praetorian or consular level, and the post of urban prefect (*praefectus urbi*), the head of Rome's civic government, to which the emperor appointed only the most senior consulars. So, while the traditional public magistracies were deprived of much of their effective power by the development of an alternative administration for the city, and by the emperor's monopolization of both executive authority and legislative initiative, they nevertheless retained their desirability because their tenure remained an essential prerequisite for appointment to positions of real responsibility in the city or the empire.

The Augustan system preserved a number of principles of Republican government. First, a public career was not intended to be a full-time profession. It was understood that public service was simultaneously a privilege of, and a duty incumbent upon, the socio-economic elite. The *cursus honorum* was not a seamless sequence of positions of responsibility: it entailed a considerable number of fallow years, time to be devoted to cultured leisure (*otium*). Second, provincial governorships combined both civil and military responsibilities, so it was appropriate that a young senator's training should include experience of both spheres. The aristocratic ideal esteemed the gentleman all-rounder above the technical expert. To this end, for the aspiring senator, the nursery slopes of a public career comprised a stint as one of the twenty junior magistrates (*uigintiuiri*) and service in the legions as a military tribune, before election at age 25 or above to the quaestorship, which afforded a seat in the Senate for life. As Tribonian mentions, however, the imperial appointments were not constrained by defined periods of office. The emperor might extend or curtail the tenure of the urban prefect or one of his legates as he wished. An extreme example is C. Poppaeus Sabinus, who served as legate of Moesia (including Achaea and Macedonia) for twenty-four years under Augustus and Tiberius (AD 11–34). Only death finally released him from his responsibilities.

The career of any one senator would typically involve a mixture of posts in the direct service of the state as well as in the service of the emperor, both in the city and abroad, and it was marked out by progression through the urban magistracies. The career of the historian Tacitus can be taken as a fairly representative (if above averagely successful) example. As we now know from fragments of the epitaph from Rome (*Corpus Inscriptionum Latinarum* 6. 41106), he began his career in the 70s AD in the vigintivirate as one of the ten men assigned to judging civil cases (*decemuir stlitibus iudicandis*). A spell as tribune of the soldiers in one of the legions probably followed. He entered the Senate proper in 81, in the especially honoured position of quaestor to the emperor Titus. Under Domitian he went on to serve as one of the now purely decorative tribunes of the plebs, and then, in 88, became praetor and member of the college of fifteen priests for the performance of sacred rites (*quindecimuir sacris faciundis*; Chapter 7). Between 90 and 97 Tacitus spent most of his time away from Rome again, probably serving as legate of a legion and then governing a province as an imperial legate. Under Nerva, Tacitus was back in Rome as one of the suffect consuls of 97, before leaving again to serve Trajan as legate of a strategically significant province (perhaps Lower Germany) for some years up to *c.*105. His known public career culminated in his being allotted the prestigious proconsulship of Asia *c.*112–13. Tacitus' career illustrates how, as long as senators were able to convince themselves that they were free agents serving the *res publica* rather than subjects of a monarch, it was possible to reconcile nostalgia for the Republic with active participation in the imperial regime.

The role of senators as administrators may have been easily accommodated to the imperial system, but the Senate as an institution was a different matter. As an authority for the conferment of titles, renewal of *imperium*, and the passing of judgement on whether an emperor was worthy of posthumous deification, the Senate helped maintain the pretence of the independent existence of the *res publica*. The position of the Senate as an active deliberative body, however, posed more of a dilemma. While the emperor was expected to consult, the expression of genuinely independent opinion could be problematic, as epitomized by an exchange between Vespasian and a dissident senator. Epictetus reports (*Discourses* 1. 20) that, when asked to be less outspoken, Helvidius Priscus retorted: 'Don't ask me my opinion and I'll keep quiet.' To this the emperor responded: 'But I must ask you your opinion;' 'And I must say what appears just,' Priscus replied. Ironically, with the authority of the emperor behind them the Senate's decrees (*senatus consulta*) became unchallenged sources of law, even if in reality they might amount to no more than the verbatim repetition of an imperial proposal. The Senate also conveniently functioned as the supposedly impartial venue for political show trials, such as that of Cn. Piso in AD 20, whose proceedings were then published in major cities and military camps throughout the empire.

Here the Senate was essential in providing the appearance of open government. It was imperative that the emperor Tiberius be seen to be doing something to satisfy the outpouring of public emotion at the death of his nephew Germanicus and dispel the popular conspiracy theory that he had engineered it. Not only the soldiers but also the general populace in Rome lamented the charismatic prince's death. For, although effectively politically disenfranchised, through sheer weight of numbers the urban populace could make life very uncomfortable for an emperor in Rome, menacing him, for instance, with hostile chanting at public gatherings. After all, the armed forces immediately available to restore order were limited to the praetorian guard, and the cohorts of the urban prefect and of the night-watch (*uigiles*), a considerable concentration of troops, but still small in relation to the urban population.

The governing class

Julius Caesar had presided over an influx of Italians into the Senate. Augustus' reign saw a further widening of the net, but at the same time the Senate itself, which had expanded to about a thousand members, was pruned to 600. Augustus also changed the economic definition of the highest class of Roman society. Hitherto a property qualification threshold of 400,000 *sestertii* had defined membership of the class of *equites*, and was a prerequisite for standing for political office. Augustus created a separate senatorial class as a subset of this equestrian class by introducing a higher threshold of 1 million *sestertii* for office-holding. By a combination of censorial powers and targeted endowments, Augustus and his successors were subsequently able to control entry to the senatorial order to some extent. Within a century the families of republican nobility, other than those who had been absorbed into the imperial family, had almost entirely died out in the male line or dropped out of the senatorial order. As a result, the senatorial class became almost entirely a creation of the imperial regime. Nevertheless, as the example of Tacitus illustrates, the ethos of the Senate survived the change of personnel. Indeed, the widening geographical origins of senators should not be taken to imply any real change in the cultural outlook of that body. By AD 48 the political and cultural identification of the Gallic elite with Rome was sufficient that the emperor Claudius might appeal for the Senate's approval for recruitment of its members from beyond Provence. The emperor prevailed despite the strong prejudices of the existing senators. The bronze tablet that preserves the text of Claudius' speech (*Corpus Inscriptionum Latinarum* 13. 1668) was probably originally displayed at the national altar of the imperial cult outside Lyon, the meeting-place of the Council of the Gauls (the annual assembly of the provinces of Gallia Comata).

The changing geographical origins of the emperors themselves can be taken as one barometer of assimilation. The Flavians (AD 69–96), the dynasty established after the demise of the Julio-Claudians, came from central Italy; Trajan and Hadrian (98–138) originated from southern Spain, the Antonines (138–92) from Narbonensis—all, no doubt, of émigré Italian ancestry. So the European provinces were in the vanguard, but with the Severans (193–235) the baton passed to families of indigenous origin from Africa and Syria, not European—but still Mediterranean. It was not until Decius (249–51) that a senator from a province of the northern frontier (Pannonia Inferior) acceded to the throne. Britain, even more remote from the Mediterranean core, is never known to have provided even senators. All the while Italians certainly remained the single biggest element in the Senate, and a common identification with Italy was encouraged by Trajan's ruling that provincial senators should invest a third of their wealth in Italian land. Moreover, it was considered better that men did not govern their province of origin after the usurpation of Avidius Cassius in Syria in 175. On the other hand, there is little evidence of senators (as opposed to armies) banding together on the basis of a shared provincial or regional origin in our period. In the civil war of AD 193–4 the Numidian Ti. Claudius Candidus, legate to the proconsul of Asia, did opt to support his fellow African Septimius Severus, then governor of Pannonia Superior, while his superior declared for Pescennius Niger in Syria. Candidus' decision, however, might equally have been motivated by the calculation that Severus not only had more legions at his disposal than Niger but was also closer to Rome.

The corollary to Augustus' creation of a separate senatorial order was the redefinition of the equestrian order as a second tier in economic and political terms. As well as continuing to supply the commanders of the auxiliary troops and subordinate officers of the legions, members of this order found employment in new prefectures (posts in public service as appointees of the emperor), all of which were open-ended positions without formally defined powers and not governed by traditional rules. They were used for key, politically sensitive positions that, if occupied by a senator, might form a basis for challenging imperial authority. The first to be established was the prefecture of Egypt, strategically significant as the source of grain for distribution to the citizens of Rome. This post was complemented at the Roman end by the prefect of the grain supply (*annona*). Augustus considered the command of the emperor's 'military headquarters' (*praetorium*) too sensitive to entrust to a single individual, so established it as a collegiate office to be shared by two praetorian prefects. The general principle enshrined in these arrangements is that the political risk associated with the effective power of these posts was offset by appointing to them men whose social dignity ought to disqualify them from seeking political power for themselves. Nevertheless, the praetorians and their commanders were frequently to exercise their political muscles in making or breaking emperors. Along with the prefecture of the *uigiles*, these posts gradually coalesced into the top rungs of a hierarchy of equestrian offices on the model of the senatorial *cursus honorum*.

The third significant group in imperial government was the emperor's own private household staff, comprising slaves and freedmen who acted as the secretarial support staff in the administration of the empire, and as overseers of the emperor's assets. Although in essence no different from the staff of any aristocratic household (Chapter 4), the emperor's slaves and freedmen came to exercise quasi-public roles because of the extraordinary economic and political influence of his household. In Rome imperial secretaries might use their special access to the emperor to wield political influence, a fact resented by the senatorial aristocracy when their de facto power was acknowledged with public honours, as happened most notably under Claudius. In the imperial provinces the emperor's procurators not only collected rents from the tenants of imperial estates but also the public taxes. Given the procurators' direct connection with the emperors, the provincials often treated them as representatives of the Roman state, and in some cases they were appointed to the command of provinces. Moreover, the taxes from all the imperial provinces were centrally pooled in a holding account (*fiscus*), from which any surplus, minus necessary expenditure, ought technically to have been transferred to the public treasury. In reality, the extent of the emperor's private income, combined with control of the *fiscus*, enabled him to dispose of financial resources that far outstripped those of the state itself. Another formidable element within the imperial household was the emperor's womenfolk. Removal of politics to the private arena of the imperial household gave the women of the family an influence in political affairs that the chauvinist Republican political tradition would not allow them.

Together these elements formed, already at the beginning of the principate, the nucleus for an alternative to the traditional system of senatorial government. This position was tolerable to senatorial opinion as long as the social conventions that guaranteed their privileged status were not transgressed. As early as the reign of Tiberius, the limits of acceptable behaviour were being explored. With Tiberius in retreat on the island of Capri, Seianus, having established himself as sole praetorian prefect and conduit between Senate and emperor, had received honorific senatorial titles and forged a marriage alliance with the emperor, before gaining election to the consulship for AD 31, despite his equestrian status and continued occupation of the prefecture. This last promotion was too much, and a whispering campaign convinced Tiberius to engineer his downfall within the year. No equivalent transgression of convention was attempted until Plautianus under Septimius Severus over 170 years later (below). The socially offensive character of the powers of imperial procurators and secretaries was mitigated by the gradual transfer of these posts to freeborn *equites*, so assigning the posts to men of a dignity appropriate to their quasi-public role. By the early second century the senator Pliny the Younger found the honours that had been offered to Claudius' freedman Pallas incredible (*Letters* 7. 29, 8. 6).

Nevertheless, although highly stratified, it is wrong to think of Roman political society as divided horizontally into impermeable layers. In fact, with sufficient resources and the right connections, remarkable social mobility was possible. At the death of Commodus on 31 December 192, that the throne should fall to P. Helvius Pertinax—as one of the most senior senators around—seems unremarkable until one considers that he was the son of a freedman. This origin did not prevent him from rising from the local municipal elite, through lengthy public service: first he spent fifteen years as an equestrian officer; then, co-opted into the Senate, he rose eventually, over twenty years and a long string of provincial commands, to the urban prefecture and a prestigious second consulship (with Commodus) for 192. The uncontroversial nature of his ascent contrasts with Seianus' attempt to leapfrog the entire *cursus honorum* in one jump.

The emperor and the army

A key factor in providing stability, both financial and political, was Augustus' reorganization of the Roman army, by which he managed an awkward transition from the ad hoc professionalized army of the civil wars to a permanent professional standing army see further reading Chapter 5. Since soldiers' wages were always the biggest item of the state's budget, the demobilization of superfluous forces after Actium permitted a reduction in expenditure of about 50 per cent. Still, the extended commands of the 50s, and the emergency situations of the 40s and 30s BC, had meant unpredictably prolonged periods of service and an increasing reliance on recruitment from the landless peasantry and urban poor. The need of commanders to reward these soldiers on demobilization had been a significant feature in the political landscape of the last decades of the Republic (Chapter 2). Traditionally they had been rewarded with parcels of farmland. In Italy, however, this became increasingly scarce and politically difficult to acquire, and the veterans' need could only be partly satisfied by the planting of colonies in the provinces; a sustainable solution was required. A regular fixed term of service was eventually established for legionaries, completion of which was rewarded by a cash lump-sum retirement bonus (*praemium militiae*). This scheme was funded not from regular provincial taxation but from indirect taxes for which only Roman citizens were liable, perhaps to remind them that they were the chief beneficiaries of the move from legions of conscripts to professional volunteers. Of course, as Tacitus tells us (*Annals* 4. 5), the citizen legions only accounted for about half of the armed forces, the rest being composed of units of non-citizens (the auxiliaries). These too were given an incentive for long-term loyalty to the imperial regime. A tradition inherited from the late Republic, whereby commanders might reward the service of non-citizen soldiers with Roman citizenship, was developed by Augustus' Julio-Claudian successors into a regular system of awarding the citizenship to auxiliaries after twenty-five years' service.

The changes in military organization wrought by Augustus transformed the relationship of the soldiers to political affairs, but certainly did not reduce their political significance. Mutual self-interest bound the soldier and the emperor together. Professionalization engendered a heightened group identity in the soldiery as against the empire's civilian subjects, and they perceived their loyalty to lie in the first instance with that man whom they acknowledged as their supreme commander. As a creation of the imperial system, it is scarcely surprising that the professional army was not a hotbed of republican sentiment. An emperor might lose the respect of the Senate and people of Rome and of his provincial subjects but, as was to be repeatedly demonstrated, gaining and maintaining the respect of a sufficient proportion of the army was a crucial factor in keeping him on his throne. Since the vast majority of the army was posted in the provinces far from Rome, it was clearly the case that an emperor might be made or broken outside the capital. Still, it would be wrong to make an artificial distinction between the army's respect for the emperor and that of the Roman senatorial and equestrian elite, since these two classes supplied its senior officer grades, a group significant in the formation of opinion.

Augustus certainly justified his retention of the vast majority of the armed forces by living up to the role of defender of the state in the years after 27 BC. Following the pattern of the pro-magistrates of the late Republic, he sought to build up his political capital through military glory. Indeed, after 19 BC the honour of a triumph was reserved to members of the imperial family alone. Augustus personally commanded campaigns of conquest in north-western Spain and, through subordinates, extended the frontiers of Roman power elsewhere in Europe (in Germany and along the Danube) as well as in North Africa and Egypt. He even managed to negotiate a favourable peace-deal with the Parthians, Rome's rivals to the east of the Euphrates, involving the return of the standards lost by Crassus. Augustus' success in delivering peace, both internal and external, was trumpeted by the dedication in 9 BC of the Altar of Augustan Peace (*Ara Pacis Augustae*) on the Campus Martius at Rome. The centrality of this function in justifying the emperor's place in the political system is illustrated by one of the sculpted relief scenes decorating the ceremonial approach to the imperial cult building at Aphrodisias in Caria (south-western Turkey). It suggests the superhuman accomplishments of the emperor in the military sphere by depicting him as a heroic nude, one hand resting on a trophy of victory beneath which crouches a female figure personifying a subdued province. That this does not symbolize the selfish pursuit of glory but a service rendered to the Roman state is indicated by the fact the emperor is himself crowned by a male figure in a toga, perhaps representing the Roman people or the Senate.

By the end of the first century BC Roman power in Germany had been extended far to the east of the Rhine. The extent to which this area was being transformed into a normal province was doubted until the archaeological discovery of a Roman town at Waldgirmes confirmed Cassius Dio's account (56. 18. 1) of the founding of cities beyond the Rhine (von Schnurbein 2003). The loss of this territory in AD 9, after Augustus' legate, P. Quinctilius Varus, perished in an ambush along with three legions, seems to have been a psychological blow from which the emperor never fully recovered. In Lower Germany Roman forces fell back permanently to the line of the Rhine. By contrast, in Upper Germany the frontier was eventually extended under Domitian to close off the angle between the Rhine and Danube (Chapter 10). Nevertheless, the Varian disaster did spell the end of continuous expansion, and according to Tacitus (*Annals* 1. 11), Tiberius claimed that Augustus had left him with the advice not to extend the empire beyond its current limits. Over the course of the first century AD there was a general consolidation of vassal states (for example, the kingdoms of Mauretania, Judaea, and Thrace) into Roman provinces, but significant territorial extensions of Roman power were limited: Britain under Claudius, Dacia under Trajan, Mesopotamia under Septimius Severus. In Europe there is some evidence to suggest that the line along which the Roman frontier came to rest approximated more or less to that dividing those pre-Roman Iron Age societies organized into units with fixed central administrative places from those without such structures (see Chapter 10). The former provided a foundation on which Rome was able to encourage the development of its city-based administrative system. The latter required the permanent attention of the armies in their forward positions along the Rhine and Danube, taking an overtly aggressive stance as much for internal political consumption as to ward off external enemies. To judge by the balance of legionary deployment along the frontiers, the primary threat was perceived as coming from across the Danube. By the reign of Septimius Severus twelve of the empire's thirty-three legions were stationed in the Danubian provinces, as opposed to ten in the eastern provinces facing Rome's sophisticated Parthian rivals, only one in Egypt, and a further one facing the Sahara in Numidia. A solitary legion garrisoned the mountains of north-western Spain and Severus placed another to overlook Rome from the Alban hills. When the four Rhine legions, backed by three in Britain, are taken into consideration, it is clear that the European frontier accounted for nearly half of all Rome's military forces. This distribution helps to explain the tendency for the allegiance of the European frontier forces to dictate the outcome of civil wars.

Despite the essentially static pattern of the army's deployment from Augustus onwards, the emperors of the first and second centuries maintained an ideological commitment to the idea of the reassignment of military units at short notice through a ban on soldiers marrying. By the second century, however, resistance to upheaval was such that recourse was increasingly had to forces composed of detachments (*uexillationes*) from disparate units in order to meet new demands. By the time Septimius Severus conceded the right to legal marriage, the integration of the soldiery with the local population of the areas in which they had been stationed for decades or centuries was far advanced thanks to generations of local recruitment and the formation of de facto families. The strength of these regional loyalties was an important factor behind the fissiparous tendencies of the later third century.

The transmission of power: Tiberius to the Antonines

By the late 20s BC it was abundantly clear that Augustus was not intending his political dominance to remain simply personal; that is, he was not going to emulate Sulla's retirement once the job of reform was done (Chapter 2). But how was his delicately constructed position to be transmitted? The self-representation of the regime as the restoration of a republican system of government made it impossible explicitly to legitimize hereditary succession as the exclusive means of transmitting imperial power. In default of natural sons, candidates were singled out by adoption as heir to Augustus' not inconsiderable personal fortune, and by early advancement to public offices. When premature death deprived him of his grandsons, he was compelled to fall back on his stepson Tiberius. Nevertheless the army was regularly to remind Augustus' successors of the fundamental underpinning of their power. When Augustus' arrangements were put to the test in AD 14, the legions in Pannonia and Lower Germany flexed their political muscles by mutinying in the hope of extracting better pay and conditions. The eccentricity of Tiberius' successor Gaius (Caligula) provoked his assassination, and the senators were debating the restoration of the republic when Claudius' acclamation by the praetorian guard decided the issue (Chapter 5). Their mutually beneficial deal was commemorated in two coin types: one showing Claudius' entry into the camp, the other the emperor shaking hands with a guardsman. Again, it was the declaration of the praetorian prefect for Galba more than the fact of provincial rebellion itself that prompted Nero's suicide. Galba in turn succumbed to the praetorians' suborning by Otho. The provincial armies, however, were not going to let the praetorians in Rome dictate the entire course of events. The

Rhine legions descended on Italy to impose Vitellius on the Senate, swiftly followed by their colleagues on the Danube fighting on behalf of Vespasian, who remained out in the East. Nero's death had brought an end to simple family succession to the principate. The law passed to ratify Vespasian's powers (the so-called *lex de imperio Vespasiani*) marks an important stage in the formalization of the principate as defined office, a process exemplified by the definitive transformation at this stage of Augustus' personal names—*Imperator Caesar Augustus*—into titles of office. The surviving clauses of the law show it to be an enabling rather than a limiting act, simply establishing a baseline for the emperor's powers with reference to those held by his respectable predecessors: Augustus, Tiberius, and Claudius.

Vespasian's own dynasty came to an end with the assassination of Domitian in 96: his paranoid tyranny was too much for the senators. There was, however, no talk of a return to a republic, and the elevation of the venerable and childless Nerva looks like a stopgap measure, designed to buy breathing-space in which a consensus candidate with a longer-term future could emerge. But again the praetorian guard forced the pace by bullying Nerva into adopting an heir. His choice of the militarily experienced Trajan proved a wise one. It also inaugurated a series of successions by adoption (those of Hadrian, Antoninus Pius, Marcus Aurelius, and Lucius Verus). This provided Rome with its greatest period of political stability and economic prosperity, the golden age of the Antonines that Gibbon took as the high point from which to trace the empire's decline and fall (see further Chapter 9). This succession policy, however, was forced by the accident of childlessness, not the triumph of meritocracy over heredity; and, when opportunity afforded, the hereditary principle reasserted itself. In 180, since Commodus was already co-Augustus with his father Marcus Aurelius, his accession to sole rule was a smooth transition. As with Caligula and Domitian before, so Commodus' erratic conduct led to his assassination at the end of 192. Again, as in 96, the praetorians seem to have resented being cut out of the selection process by the Senate's choice of Pertinax. The largesse promised by Didius Julianus persuaded the guard of the rightness of his cause but, as in 69, the provincial armies threw up their own candidates, this time simultaneously: the legions of Britain and the Rhine, Clodius Albinus; the Danube legions,

Septimius Severus; and the Syrian legions, Pescennius Niger. Once again the Danube legions' candidate was triumphant. Geographical position and superior numbers favoured Severus, who first made common cause with Albinus while his 'Balkan army' picked off Niger, before turning on his erstwhile ally. In both cases the 'showdowns' came on European soil, at Byzantium and Lyon. This three-way split and subsequent reunification also prefigures the course of events of the 260s and 270s.

Centre and periphery

The provincial units into which the subject territory of the empire was divided generally had some ethnic or cultural rationale. In some cases these preserved the identities of pre-existing entities subsumed into the Roman system, most famously the kingdom of Egypt or, in Europe, the kingdoms of Thrace and Noricum, for example. Nevertheless, in the empire's Mediterranean core the city-state rather than the province remained the primary unit of political organization and interaction with the ruling power. The self-governing nature of these communities meant that the Roman government could focus on two tasks: the maintenance of order and the collection of taxes. Accordingly, Rome exported this model of political organization to its non-Mediterranean territories, frequently mapping it onto indigenous tribal units (Chapter 8). The limited aims of central government allowed the number of administrative personnel (and therefore costs) to be kept low. Indeed, in its small scale and limited ambition the Roman government of the principate has been likened to the Thatcherite ideal of 'government without bureaucracy'. As the surviving correspondence of the Younger Pliny with Trajan demonstrates, this did not translate into administration without paperwork. The simple existence of the emperor's overarching authority encouraged a tendency on the part of governors to refer anything that might conceivably be considered a policy decision to the emperor. Judicial matters might also be referred up to the emperor's hearing. Add to this the petitions from communities and individuals seeking some special grant or privilege, and it is easy to see how the emperor came to be besieged by people and letters demanding a share of his attention.

During the first two centuries of the imperial regime, when emperors spent most of their time based in Rome, this traffic ended up there. Under an emperor with a taste for travel, however, such as Hadrian, or when military campaigning demanded the emperor's presence on the frontier, then the imperial court might present a moving target. For those areas where the court came to rest, its presence could be something of a mixed blessing. On the one hand it offered the opportunity of direct access to the emperor and profits to be made from servicing the needs of his entourage; on the other, the commandeering of lodgings and the requisitioning of supplies might put a considerable strain on the hosts. For petitioners chasing the imperial whirlwind, considerable time and expense might be involved in tracking down the eye of the storm. For example, the city of Ephesus in Asia honoured one of its citizens for winning the city's case (for primacy in the province over its rival Smyrna) before the emperor Macrinus in Syria, and for having previously been its ambassador and advocate before Severus and Caracalla in Rome many times, in Britain, in Upper Germany, at the sanctuary of Apollo Grannus in Gaul, Sirmium, Nicomedia, Antioch, and Mesopotamia (*Inschriften von Ephesos* 802 = *Supplementum Epigraphicum Graecum* 17. 505). The envoy's journeys demonstrate how from the 170s onwards heightened levels of military activity, both aggressive and defensive, turned the political geography of the empire inside-out. The emperor was increasingly likely to be found not in Rome but in one of the frontier provinces. So it was that Marcus Aurelius came to spend the last years of his life at Carnuntum on the Danube, and Septimius Severus his last months at York.

Not all areas of the empire were of equal status in the eyes of the Roman government. Italy was not a province, and was subject neither to governors nor, as previously mentioned, to the payment of direct taxation, a status briefly extended to the province of Achaea (southern Greece) under Nero. This grant of freedom reflects Nero's special relationship with Greek culture, held—unlike those of other peoples—in unquestioned esteem by the Romans. Thus, while the Roman government communicated with its subjects in the western Mediterranean provinces and those of the Rhine and Danube frontiers in Latin, Hellenophone communities across the Greek East corresponded with Roman authorities (both central and provincial) in their own language. The anonymous Ephesian no doubt delivered his petitions and gave his speeches in Greek, even when appearing before the emperor in faraway Britain. The reasons for this differential treatment were both historical and cultural. The Greek East comprised the native and long-established Greek-speaking areas of Greece and the Aegean rim, as well as those Hellenized territories in the Levant and Egypt that Rome inherited from the Seleucid and Ptolemaic kingdoms which had succeeded to the break-up of Alexander the Great's empire. Although the region was home to some far more venerable literate cultures, across this area as a whole Greek had become the lingua franca and language of government and administration before the arrival of Rome. Its position was maintained and even reinforced because of the perception of the cultural superiority of the Hellenic over barbarian tongues (including Latin), a perception shared equally by the Romans and the Hellenophone provincial elites. The Latin West too contained some ancient literate cultures, notably Punic in North Africa, but Romans did not hold them in the same regard. Thus, while Neo-Punic might remain a language of local civic government (as, for instance, at Lepcis Magna in Tripolitania), there was never any question of central government communicating with, or accepting communications from, such communities in anything other than Latin. For provincials in the West acquisition of Latin culture was an acceptable marker of civilization in Roman eyes, but those who aspired to the highest cultural status needed also to gain a familiarity with Greek literature. The position of Greek at the acknowledged pinnacle of the cultural hierarchy of the Roman world had some advantages for Rome's Greek subjects. Numbers of Greek-speaking provincials did gain Roman citizenship and enter the equestrian and senatorial orders, reaching the consulship by the early second century. At the same time, however, the relative disdain for Latin felt by the Hellenophone elites of the cities of the Greek East did create a barrier that prevented a political involvement on their part in the running of the empire fully commensurate with their cultural and economic potential.

Indeed, it was the historical glory of Greece rather than the achievements of the contemporary Greek world that were prized by the Romans. Accordingly, when Hadrian established a supra-provincial league of Greek cities, the Panhellenion, not only was it centred on Attica, but the admissions criteria included foundation by one of the cities of Old Greece. This effectively limited membership to cities in the provinces of the Aegean rim: Crete with Cyrenaica, Achaea, Macedonia, Thrace, and Asia. In excluding Macedonian and later Hellenistic foundations, Hadrian's vision of Greekness left out some of the most significant Greek centres of the time, including Antioch and Alexandria.

One Hellenistic phenomenon that the Romans did adopt was ruler cult (Chapter 7). Its role in the trials of Christian martyrs, however, has perhaps tended to exaggerate its centrality to assuring loyalty and to providing religious and ideological underpinning to the principate. After all, when faced with a cash crisis in the mid-230s the emperor Maximinus confiscated the endowments of the temples of the deified emperors in Rome, no doubt because there was no popular attachment to them, making them politically expendable. Although it was acceptable to honour only deceased emperors as gods in Roman state cult, worship of emperors both living and dead was tolerated in other contexts. The phenomenon of the 'imperial cult' was transplanted to the West and made the focus of national or provincial shrines, for instance, at Lyon (above). The imperial government fostered the creation in the West of provincial assemblies, on the model of Greek federal leagues, which met at the annual festivals of the provincial cult of the emperor. These meetings became the opportunity for the gathered delegates to pass judgement on the conduct of outgoing governors, who might receive honorific decrees or alternatively be indicted for maladministration. In fact, the ending of costly competition for magisterial offices had reduced the necessity for systematic extortion by governors. So, while this mechanism might not have secured many convictions, it may nevertheless have offered sufficient appearance of accountability to serve as a safety-valve for the release of feelings of discontent. In fact, taxation was the chief cause of unrest; its imposition and unwarrantedly harsh exaction were common factors in the provincial revolts that occasionally erupted in the north-western provinces in the first century of the empire. Despite the singular success of the German revolt of AD 9, however, the European provinces remained quiescent after AD 70, in contrast with the Jews of the Greek East, whose opposition to Roman rule was not finally crushed until the 130s.

The Augustan settlement renegotiated

After the defeat of Albinus, Severus did not display the magnanimity or clemency of Augustus after Actium towards the supporters of his erstwhile colleague. The legacy of distrust was compounded by a second major purge of the Senate fifteen years later by his son Caracalla, anxious to root out any who lamented his assassination of his brother and co-Augustus Geta. Dio's version (77 [76]. 15. 2) of Severus' deathbed advice to his sons—to care only for each other and the soldiers—reflects how little valued the Senate felt itself to be in the Severan monarchy. The soldiery certainly benefited from bonuses and pay-rises, rewarding their loyalty in the civil wars of 193–7, and again on Geta's death in 211; on top of which Severus also added three extra legions to the military establishment (Chapter 5). It seems that the imperial budget of the first and second centuries had been finely balanced, because these extra costs could not be borne by existing revenues. One solution employed was debasement of the currency in order to make the amount of silver available to the imperial government go further (Chapter 6). This measure, which brought only short-term benefit, was resorted to repeatedly during the rest of the third century, and eventually rendered the silver *denarii* effectively a bronze coinage. Moreover, Dio claims (78 [77]. 9. 4 f.) that Caracalla's grant of citizenship to most free subjects (above) was a direct response to the increased level of military overheads, since it spread the net of liability for the indirect taxes that flowed into the military treasury. Several structural changes were also made: the large military provinces that had produced Severus' rivals (Britain and Syria) were subdivided, the praetorian guard that had elevated Julianus disbanded, and its traditional recruitment from Italy ended. Instead, it was now selected from veterans of the Danube legions, presumably to encourage common interest between the two groups. At the same time one of the newly raised legions was stationed at Albanum overlooking Rome, perhaps as much to act as a counterbalance to the praetorians as to increase imperial security in the capital. The other two legions garrisoned territory newly conquered from the Parthians. All three new legions, and the new provinces of Osrhoene and Mesopotamia, were put under equestrian prefects rather than senatorial legates.

In fact the Severan age witnessed a general advance in the profile of the senior equestrian officers, spearheaded by Severus' fellow townsman Fulvius Plautianus. He surpassed the infamous example of Seianus, combining sole prefecture, consulship, and being father-in-law to Caracalla, before similarly falling from grace. Plautianus even had the unprecedented honour of having his first consulship in 203 considered a second tenure on the basis of previously conferred consular insignia—an infringement of protocol that outraged Dio (79 [78]. 13. 1); generally, the senior equestrian prefects were awarded honorary senatorial rank. More significantly, the seeds of the destruction of traditional senatorial government were sown by the occasional employment of provincial equestrian procurators (technically only as stand-ins) in place of senatorial legates. Each such appointment had a ripple effect: social etiquette would not contemplate the appointment of senatorial legionary legates and military tribunes in the province of an equestrian governor. Deprived of such military experience, a senator would cease to be a credible candidate for the command of a military province later in his career, entailing further reliance on equestrian substitutes.

These policies suggest some distancing between Senate and imperial court. Indeed, the accession of the praetorian prefect Macrinus, after Caracalla's assassination near Carrhae (Harran in south-eastern Turkey) in 217, may reflect a dearth of suitable senatorial candidates on the spot in the imperial entourage. Not only did Macrinus' elevation offend senatorial opinion, but he exacerbated the offence by assuming various titles without waiting for the traditional senatorial confirmation. Questionable legitimacy in the eyes of the Senate was one thing, but his rule was fatally undermined by the machinations of Caracalla's Syrian-born aunt and her daughters, who were able to pull the rug of legionary support out from under him by winning over the Syrian army to a local candidate tangentially related to the Severan dynasty—M. Aurelius Antoninus (Elagabalus). His eccentricity proved a liability, but the dynasty achieved stability with his cousin, Severus Alexander. Senatorial opinion was mollified by discontinuance of the granting of senatorial honours to serving equestrian prefects, but the precedent of Macrinus could not be completely undone.

Despite some success on the eastern front, the Rhine legions were less impressed by Alexander's reputation as a 'mother's boy'. When he was deposed and killed at Moguntiacum (Mainz) in 235, an equestrian officer from the lower Danube, C. Iulius Maximinus, was elevated in his place. That Maximinus stuck to the job of defending the northern frontier ought to have been to his credit, but this was offset by the negative publicity of the tax increases needed to fund his doubling of the soldiers' pay. Indeed, it was an uprising instigated by disgruntled landowners in Africa that triggered the dramatic sequence of events of 238, narrated by Herodian (7. 4. 1–8. 8. 8), that led to his downfall. Lacking troops and faced with an improvised army of tenants, the octagenarian proconsul and his son (Gordian I and II) took the path of least resistance in accepting acclamation as emperors, which gave them the authority to remit taxes. Although swift, their suppression by the governor of Numidia and his legion did not take place before they had been acknowledged as legitimate by the Senate at Rome. Once galvanized, the opposition to Maximinus gained its own momentum, and the Senate put up two of its own senior members as co-emperors, Pupienus Maximus and Caelius Balbinus. This hour of glory was tempered by the fact that the Roman populace, preferring the hereditary principle, menaced them into associating the 13-year-old grandson of Gordian I with them as Caesar. Meanwhile Maximinus, marching south to quash this rebellion and meeting tough resistance at Aquileia, seems to have lost his nerve. Detachments of the second Parthian legion with Maximinus calculated that his assassination was preferable to risking the lives of their families at Albanum in fighting their way through to Rome. The praetorians, loyal to their Danubian colleague but until now penned into their camp by the Roman populace, took their revenge by assassinating Pupienus and Balbinus. Thus, quite unusually, all three elements—army, Senate, and people—played their part in putting Gordian III in power. Although Gordian's praetorian prefect and father-in-law, Timesitheus, was the power behind the throne, he courted no extraordinary public honours. Consensus appeared to have been rebuilt on the understanding that the senators would not complain about the ceding of increasingly large areas of government to equestrian officials as long as traditional differentiations of social status were maintained. Indeed, despite the examples of Macrinus and Maximinus, the Augustan vision of senatorial government was far from dead. Gordian may have been replaced on the throne by one of his later praetorian prefects, Philip, but he in turn was to be replaced by the senator Decius. For the time being, senatorial and equestrian careers had been established as alternative pathways to the imperial throne.

The principate in crisis

Had the problems of the empire been entirely governed by internal factors, then perhaps the political instability of the 240s to 280s might have been averted. As Alexander's and Maximinus' almost continuous preoccupation with frontier warfare from 230 onwards shows, however, external pressures were a factor of growing significance. The supplanting of the Parthians by an aggressive and ambitious Persian dynasty, the Sassanians, shattered Rome's relative security on the eastern front. At the same time, the advantages that Rome had enjoyed over the barbarians in Europe had been eroded by three centuries of close contact. The fragmented German tribes had coalesced into larger confederations and, as a result partly of this process and partly of migration, Rome was faced with increasingly sophisticated groups along its Rhine and Danube frontier: the Franks, Alamans, and Goths (Chapter 10). Given the slowness of communications, the centralization of executive decision-making in the hands of one emperor proved a liability. The military situation continually required the personal attention of the emperor. If he was preoccupied on another front or his reaction was deemed too slow or ineffective, the frontier armies were liable to put decision-making powers into the hands of their local commander by acclaiming him emperor. Treating such acts as rebellion involved distracting and costly civil conflicts that only exacerbated the financial and military problems of the state. Such already was the nature of the gathering clouds that overshadowed the celebration of Rome's millennium in AD 248. His role in staging this event as urban prefect had perhaps led Q. Decius Valerinus to muse on the possible cause of the systemic malaise. He diagnosed a collapse in traditional piety and, when thrust to the fore himself by the Danube legions in 249, he decreed an unprecedented universal order for sacrifice to the traditional gods. Their goodwill towards the Roman state could only be assured if all its citizens—now, of course, the vast majority of the empire's population—participated. Although the policy died with the emperor, it did focus particular attention on the Christians as a nonconformist group within society, who would be singled out again under Valerian. Decius' order put the Christian church and Roman state on a collision course that culminated in the Great Persecution under Diocletian, from which both sides were eventually to emerge fundamentally transformed (Chapter 7). Decius' death in battle (in 251) against the Goths in Lower Moesia marks one of the low points in Roman fortunes, and was followed by a couple of years of extreme instability. While attentions in Europe were split between internecine conflict and stabilizing the situation on the Danube, the Sassanian Persians took advantage to ravage the eastern provinces.

The joint reign of the father–son duo Valerian and Gallienus (253–60) provided an interlude of relative political stability, as they took separate responsibility for the European and eastern frontiers respectively. However, the capture of Valerian by the Persians in 260 was a major blow to Roman morale, and in the ensuing political crisis the empire fractured into three sections: the eastern provinces looked to the dynasts of the frontier city of Palmyra to contain the Persians; Gallienus retained control of the Danube legions and the central portion of the empire, including Africa; to his rear, the legions of Britain and the Rhine pledged their support to the governor of Lower Germany, M. Cassianius Latinius Postumus, whose names suggest an origin in the Gallic provinces. The background to this latter event has been recently illuminated by the discovery of an altar erected to Victory at Augusta Vindelicorum (Augsburg) in Raetia. This celebrates the vanquishing of the Iuthungi, a Germanic tribe, by an ad hoc force comprising the provincial garrison, reinforced by detachments from the Rhine armies and, significantly, Italian prisoners liberated from the barbarians (*Année épigraphique* 1993: 1231b). That the troops involved recognized Postumus' authority suggests that his usurpation may have resulted from a perception that Gallienus was unable to respond adequately to emergencies on this front. Still, the interception of the Iuthungi on their way back out of the empire would have been cold comfort to the victims of their raiding in Italy. That this was cause for celebration says a lot about the changed circumstances. Moreover, this was but an isolated victory in a litany of defensive failures throughout the European provinces. Even core areas such as Italy, Greece, and Asia Minor were now vulnerable to external attack. Many cities received new walled circuits, including eventually Rome itself (Chapter 9).

In conditions where the military initiative had passed to Rome's enemies, its armed forces were required to be more mobile than the traditional model of static forces and local provincial military command permitted. Gallienus and others assembled more or less permanent mobile forces ready to react to threats wherever they might present themselves. These were commanded not by provincial governors but specialized military commanders (*duces*) with spheres of responsibility that might extend across several civil provinces (Chapter 5). This gradually put an end to the republican tradition of combined military and civil authority, and led to increasingly divergent civil and military career paths for equestrian officers; it had the advantage of putting military operations in the hands of professional soldiers. The deposition of Gallienus in 268 by his cavalry commander marks the beginning of the domination of the throne by these equestrian military officers, predominantly of Balkan origin. One of these, Aurelian, was between 272 and 274 able to restore the political integrity of the empire by a mixture of military force and diplomacy. The reintegrated empire was not quite what it had been before 260. The Persians had retaken part of Mesopotamia, but the difference was most apparent in the European provinces. Having become the front line between the realms of Postumus and Gallienus, the Agri Decumates had been abandoned as the opposing forces fell back to the older Rhine–Danube lines. Aurelian now took the difficult decision to withdraw from Dacia in order to shorten the defensive line on the lower Danube. He was not successful in restoring political stability, however, and he succumbed to assassination by the soldiers in 275. Despite Aurelian's efforts to restore the silver coinage, pay concerns may be at the root of his downfall. The fact that by the 270s retail price inflation had finally taken off, in response to the long-term debasement of the silver coinage, eroded the purchasing power of the soldiers' pay. This was compensated for by free rations of basic food and personal equipment extracted by new requisitions, and an increasing reliance upon special bonuses to celebrate accessions and significant anniversaries as a regular part of the soldiers' income. Although costly, an emperor could not afford to forgo such generosity. Intended as a measure to secure and reward loyalty, these payments became a perverse incentive for the soldiers to increase the rhythm of imperial events. The hiatus that followed Aurelian's murder suggests that many, not unreasonably, perceived imperial office as a poisoned chalice. The rapid succession of emperors over the next decade proved them right. There was nothing in the circumstances of Diocletian's elevation to indicate any prospect for improvement in this situation. Indeed, the Dalmatian army officer Diocletian, having being raised as a usurper in Asia, secured his unchallenged tenure of the imperial throne only after he had defeated the emperor Carinus on European soil, in the strategically important Danubian arena.

The empire at the accession of Diocletian

Chronic political instability suggested that the structures of the Roman state required some fundamental reconfiguration to take account of changed circumstances. Clearly, the continual cycle of assassinations and usurpations driven by the soldiery needed to be broken. In the second half of the third century, however, emperors scarcely ruled long enough to engage in anything but crisis management. Nevertheless, structural changes had taken place. A significant legacy of the 260s and 270s was that the political partition of the empire had necessitated regional fiscal independence. In this situation the privileged status of Italy was no longer sustainable. The peninsula was progressively normalized by the imposition of direct taxation and provincial governors. Political fragmentation and defensive priorities had led to the eclipse of Rome as the regular base of imperial operations, in favour of other centres strategically positioned within striking-distance of the frontiers: Trier in Gaul, Milan in Italy, Sirmium in the middle Danube region, and Antioch in Syria (Chapter 9). The three-way split of the 260s also suggested that even two simultaneous emperors might not be sufficient at times of particular crisis. Conversely, this fragmentation actually demonstrated the durability of the Roman empire as a concept. Despite the breakdown of central political control, each of the separate regimes had prioritized external defence above elimination of internal rivals, and no region attempted to liberate itself from Roman rule. In the West the 'Gallic' empire of Postumus never represented itself as anything other than Roman, and in the East the Palmyrenes positioned themselves as representatives of Roman authority.

In some respects the elements of the Augustan principate had survived to a surprising extent. In outward form the imperial office was no more explicitly a monarchy than it ever had been, even if the Senate no longer played any real role in conferring the apparatus of titulature developed by Augustus; and, despite a tendency to prefer hereditary succession, legitimacy did not require it. Institutional continuity with the Republic was still demonstrated by the annual succession of ordinary consuls giving their names to the years. The senatorial aristocracy still occupied the pinnacle of the social hierarchy and, even if reduced to little more than the proconsulships of Africa and Asia, the public provinces still existed. It was from the increased imperial portion that the senators had been displaced; though the provincialization of Italy under senatorial governors was to compensate for this to some extent. The starkest change was in the background of the dominant ruling group that provided candidates for the throne. Under the Julio-Claudians this still comprised the noble families of the Republic; by the 280s the high commands were dominated by military officers of no long-standing social eminence from some of the empire's most economically backward provinces. Some might lament the passing of possession of the throne from those steeped in the gentlemanly ethos of the cultured aristocrat, but the commitment of the career soldiers to public service cannot be doubted. There was no longer any scope for the self-indulgence of a Gaius, Nero, Commodus, or Elagabalus.

4

Roman society

Mary Harlow

Let me turn to the question of your sister, which you added in the margin of your last note. This is the position. When I returned to Arpinum, my brother came to see me. First we spoke about you for some considerable time. Then I mentioned the conversation we had about your sister when we were at my estate at Tusculum. On that occasion no one could have been nicer and more conciliatory than my brother was about your sister; if there was a grudge for any reason, it did not surface. So much for that day. Then on the next day we set off for Arpinum. I was on my way to Aquinum; because of the festival, Quintus had to stay the villa at Arx for the night, and we stopped there for lunch (you know the estate). When we arrived, Quintus said in a perfectly nice way, 'you call the women, Pomponia, and I'll deal with the lads.' To me at least, it seemed totally agreeable—the words, the intention, the manner. She said—in our hearing—'I myself am just a guest in this house.' Perhaps the real reason why she was upset was that Statius had been sent on ahead to get the meal ready. Quintus said to me: 'You see what I have to put up with all the time?' 'Why did it matter?' you may ask. A lot—I was greatly upset myself. Her words and behaviour were uncalled for and rude. I did not show how annoyed I was. We all reclined at lunch, except for her; when Quintus nevertheless had something sent out to her, she sent it back. In sum I have never seen anyone as restrained as my brother, or as impossible as your sister. I omit several things that upset me more than Quintus at the time. I continued to Aquinum; Quintus stayed at the estate at Arx and came to see me the next morning. He told me that Pomponia had refused to let him sleep with her that night, and that when he left she had behaved just in the way I had seen myself. You may

tell her to her face that I think her behaviour that day was
unacceptable.

(Cicero, *Letters to Atticus* 5, 1. 3 f. May, 51 BC; trans. Gardner
and Wiedemann 1991: 55–6)

THIS extract from a letter of Cicero to his friend Pomponius Atticus
may strike chords of recognition in a twenty-first-century western
audience, with its tale of a rather tense matrimonial relationship. It
also highlights, however, distinct differences between Roman family
relationships and modern western comparisons, and the problems
inherent in the nature of the ancient evidence. We must avoid
assuming that the Romans shared modern western values in terms
of affective relationships and family aspirations. The letter gives us
only a single point of view, that of an elite male. Cicero complains
about his sister-in-law's behaviour towards his brother and looks to
Atticus, as her eldest surviving male relative, to admonish Pomponia
(although he seems to expect that Atticus may not automatically
find Pomponia's behaviour reprehensible). He particularly disap-
proves of the open nature of her behaviour towards her husband.
Cicero assumes his brother is in the right and behaving as a good
husband should.

We have no idea what Pomponia herself thought or what her own
justifications might have been for her behaviour. Cicero suggests that
she might have been upset that Statius, one of Quintus's former slaves,
was sent on ahead to prepare the meal. Roman social and family
life took place within a slave-owning society. The ubiquity of slaves
within the Roman household has ramifications for all levels of social
relationships, and significantly affects the interaction of public and
private domains. This letter reminds us that within a marriage husband
and wife did not legally hold goods or—as in this case—slaves in
common. It is also a rare example of reportage of family life which is
not in line with the idealized marital relationship normally depicted
in the majority of ancient literary and visual sources.

The place of a Roman in society was a product of birth, rank,
status, gender, and citizenship. As in most pre-industrial societies,
the family group was central to the life of the individual and the
community. The household was the centre of a network of social
relations that extended outwards to embrace both wider kin-groups
and non-related individuals. This chapter examines the dynamics

of Roman family life and the place of the household in the social networks of the individual Roman man and woman. Given the nature of the evidence, the discussion will be centred almost entirely on the urban upper classes living in Italy: those who left marks of their existence in the literary or archaeological record. They (mostly men) wrote the literature of the Roman Empire, and could afford to express their achievements both in the houses they occupied and the funerary monuments they left behind. A huge percentage of the population of the Roman Empire left virtually no record of its existence at all, and our view of Roman society is thus primarily that of the dominant group, the upper-class heads of households (*patres familiae*). Even those with whom these men interacted on a daily basis—women, children, slaves, the lower classes in general—left little of their own view of the world, and what is known about them comes through the prism of aristocratic writings. Yet one way in which we can begin to understand more of the lives of these 'muted groups', especially women, children, and domestic slaves, is to examine the milieu in which they lived: the Roman household.

Until the 1980s the Roman family and household were of interest primarily to historians concerned with the law and 'daily life'. Roman law codes, such as the *Digest*, compiled in the sixth century AD but containing rulings by many much earlier jurists (lawyers), offer a large body of evidence about the family, kinship relations, inheritance, and marriage practices. Roman civil law presents an image that stresses the patriarchal nature of Roman social relations and the importance of legitimacy and inheritance within the structure of the Roman family. This reflects the fact that law was of most interest to the propertied classes, and betrays their concerns and anxieties. To take a solely legalistic view of the family would, therefore, produce a very one-dimensional vision: the traditional image of the patriarchal household ruled by an authoritarian *paterfamilias*, wherein affection came low on the list of priorities. Law, however, tends to reflect life as precept rather than mirror social practice, and its evidence needs to be tempered by that of other writings, which offer a 'more personal' view of the world. Even here, however, the way is not straightforward: there are problems with using any literary text, even Cicero's letters, to access the real feelings of the author. Upper-class writers reflect the preoccupations and interests of their class; they were not, for the most part, interested in descriptions of social or family life per se; their writings, nonetheless, offer some insight into social norms and ideals. Tacitus and Seneca, for instance, though not personally involved in childcare, were happy to express opinions on the subject (Tacitus, *Dialogue on Famous Orators* 29. 1, on nurses; Seneca, *On Anger* 2. 21. 1–6, a philosophical treatise on child behaviour; Gardner and Wiedemann 1991: 112). We cannot know how far their comments reflected actual practice, but by taking a 'broad-brush' view we can exploit the information imparted from the full range of literary and sub-literary genres and archaeology to gain a more nuanced view of the family and society that balances the overbearing notion of patriarchy offered by the legal sources.

The Roman household

In a discussion on the nature of human society written for the edification of his son Marcus, Cicero claimed 'the first association is that of marriage itself; the next is with one's children; then the household unit (*domus*) within which everything is shared; that is the element from which a city is made, so to speak the seed-bed of the state' (*On Duties* 1. 54, drawing on Aristotle, *Politics* 1; Gardner and Wiedemann 1991: 2). The association of marriage and children may be familiar, but the extension to the household highlights one of the significant differences between the Roman family and any modern western conception of 'family'. This difference needs to be understood from the outset. The Romans had two words that encompassed the family/household unit: *familia* and *domus*. The definitions of these words overlap and the context in which each is used normally defines its meaning. *familia*, the word most likely to be 'familiar' to English speaking readers, rarely has the meaning 'family' in current use in western societies. It is best translated as 'household', as it encompasses a far wider group than we would normally denote as family. It is the legal definition of *familia* as the group of persons and property in the power (*potestas*) of one man (*paterfamilias*) that reflects the idea of the Roman family as a highly controlled patriarchal unit. *familia* is also used of the wider kinship group of 'agnates', who are descended from a common male ancestor and share the same name. In terms of the household, *familia* also encompassed all the slaves owned by the *paterfamilias*, and, outside strictly legal usage, this was the normal meaning of *familia* in Latin social discourse (*Digest* 50. 16. 195: Ulpian).

In the quotation above from *On Duties*, Cicero uses the word *domus* to denote the family (that is, wife and children) and household. *domus* was more commonly used to describe the biological and/or adoptive group to whom an individual owed a primary sense of loyalty, but, like *familia*, it could also encompass a wider grouping. Thus it expresses the conjugal group of husband, wife, and children, but also slaves who lived within the same household. It was also used to describe the physical house, the home. *domus* could also be used, like *familia*, to refer to a wider kinship group, but where *familia* stressed agnate relationships, *domus* referred to kinship links through women as well (cognates) (Saller 1994). Romans knew instinctively which group was being referred to by each term, and understood their associated nuances, which are far more difficult for modern historians to read.

The power (*potestas*) of the Roman father is almost proverbial; it gave him the power of life and death over all those in the *familia*, and only ended at his death. This power was enshrined in law and considered by lawmakers to be one of the defining characteristics of power dynamics within the household, and of Roman society itself (Gaius, *Institutes* 1. 55; Gardner and Wiedemann 1991: 5). It was held by the eldest living male in a family, usually the father, occasionally the grandfather, and very rarely a great-grandfather. Those in the *potestas* of the father comprised all his children (biological and adopted), his grandchildren by his sons, and slaves. A wife could leave the power of her own father and enter that of her husband (*manus* marriage, below), and indeed routinely did so in the early Roman period. By the first century BC this custom had been superseded, and a wife remained in the power of her own *paterfamilias* (usually her father). The ramifications of this change in practice are discussed below. The *paterfamilias* also had economic control of the *familia*. Children, even when they became adults, could not own property or receive inheritances in their own right before their father's death, unless legally 'emancipated'. As there was no age of legal majority in Rome, this meant that, in theory, a grown man with children of his own might still be dependent on his father for all income. In reality, demographic and social trends mitigated this outcome. Saller has shown that less than half the population would have had a living father by the time they came to marry (Saller 1994: 121).

Within the context of the household, power operated on a number of levels. Members of the conjugal group could, if they wished, deal with *potestas* in ways that were mutually advantageous to both sides, and there was strong social pressure to do so. Husbands, wives, and children ideally treated each other with mutual respect (*pietas*: see below; Saller 1994: ch. 5). Slaves, on the other hand, were completely under the control of their master or mistress, without any legal recourse to obtain redress for cruel behaviour towards them; but here again, how this power might be expressed was dependent on the personality of a master.

The typical household was not a static entity, and was subject to change throughout the life-course of the inhabitants. The arrival of children would enlarge it, and as they grew up and moved out to create households of their own, it would shrink again. Sons tended to leave home at some time in their youth, and to set up new households when they married. On their wedding day daughters departed to the houses of their husbands. The death or divorce of a spouse could also change the composition of the core conjugal unit, and might result in introduction of a step-parent and step-siblings, or the return of a daughter to her father's house. Elderly female relatives, once widowed, might gravitate to the home of a married adult child. Some widowed mothers who had raised their children alone, such as Aurelia, mother of Julius Caesar, remained in the household once their sons married (Plutarch, *Caesar* 9–10). Slaves also grew old and were given jobs more suited to their age, or were simply sold on. Slaves who were given their freedom might move away, but might also remain within the household and continue their duties in their new status. The household was thus a flexible unit, expanding and contracting over time. On the death of the head of a household all children became legally independent (*sui iuris*), and all sons became *patres familiae* in their own right, regardless of age or marital status. Daughters became legally independent too, unless they had married into the husband's power (see below). Fatherless children would be appointed a *curator/tutor* to look after their interests and maintain their patrimony.

Marriage was regarded as a social duty and expected of both men and women; indeed, it was the only 'career path' available to most women. As most of the marriages that we know about occurred within the upper classes, and are recorded by men, they tend to look like a series of political alliances between males and little else. Marriage certainly did play a central part in maintaining social, economic, and political networks in upper-class society, but this did not preclude it from also fulfilling an emotional role. It was one of the duties of the *paterfamilias* to find suitable marriage partners for his children. In reality this seems to have been very much a decision made by the whole family in consultation with particular friends. Pliny the Younger was flattered to assist a friend in seeking a groom for a young niece (*Letters* 1.14; Gardner and Wiedemann 1991: 110). Pliny's candidate, Minicius Acilianus, is recommended for the virtues of humility, honesty, wisdom, integrity, and propriety, which he inherited from his father, maternal grandmother, and paternal uncle. His good looks and, in Pliny's view, his natural nobility are fair exchange for the bride's virginity. He is also independently wealthy and has already held the praetorship, so will not require too much in the way of resources from his prospective father-in-law in order to advance his career. He will also be able to support his offspring in the appropriate style.

This letter highlights some typical factors in Roman marriage. As the unnamed girl is still a virgin, we can assume that this is her first marriage. The age difference between husband and wife at first marriage was usually between eight and ten years. A survey of epigraphic evidence suggests that men were marrying for the first time in their late twenties or early thirties, while women were more likely to be in their late teens and early twenties (Saller 1994: 12–69). The age differential remained the same among the upper classes, although they tended to marry at a slightly earlier age. The youngest legal age for marriage was 12 for girls and 14 for boys. Pliny's letter also stresses the desire for heirs. Women were prized for their fertility; motherhood was a role a young girl was schooled to expect from an early age. Her virginity is emphasized, as the need for specifically legitimate heirs was felt by the families of both partners in order to maintain the family name and transmission of property. For the potential husband the marriage offered links that would extend his social and political networks, and presumably enhance his social status. It is very easy to view Roman marriage as a purely mechanistic process of alliances between men, in which women were merely pawns and there was little room for emotion, but that is to misunderstand the social realities of the relationship. Roman marriage was structured in a way that is culturally unfamiliar by western standards.

In the Roman era marriage took two forms. In the older version (with *manus*, lit. 'hand'), which had all but gone out of fashion by the late Republic, the wife left the power of her father and entered that of her husband, or his *paterfamilias*. She entered the inheritance networks of her new family, and on her husband's death stood in the line of succession alongside their mutual offspring. Any property or goods she brought to the marriage or might acquire during it were passed to her husband. By the first century BC marriage without *manus* was far more common. In this form the wife lived and shared a life with her husband, but remained in the power of her father and the inheritance networks of her natal family.

Under this system the dowry was owned by the husband only for the duration of the marriage, and the property of husband and wife was kept separate. They could not even give each other gifts of property. On the death of her father the wife became *sui iuris* (above), and inherited her father's estate equally with other siblings under the Roman practice of partible inheritance. This had the potential to create economic asymmetry between the couple, especially if the husband was still in the power of his father and financially dependent on him. This form of marriage also meant that a mother was in a different *familia* from that of her children, who belonged to the *familia* of their father.

Legalistic views of Roman marriage, and the fact that marriages were arranged rather than arising from personal choice, have led to the assumption that such unions lacked affection. Marrying for love was considered aberrant in Roman eyes. The Romans rather valued the virtue of *concordia* (harmony) between a married couple. To describe a good marriage was to comment on the *concordia* between husband and wife, but the same term carried overtones from the public sphere, as it also described political alliances and the harmonious operation of civic society (Bradley 1992: 7–9). Affective relations are notoriously hard to quantify in any culture, let alone in past societies. It is almost impossible to see the inner workings of a Roman marriage, but anecdotal evidence from biographies, letters, and poems suggests we should not be too swift to write all marriages off as purely 'business arrangements'. Inscriptions to devoted wives illustrate a number of idealized attributes: modesty, fidelity, chastity, thrift, bearing of children, loyalty, wool-working, being happy at home (e.g. *Corpus Inscriptionum Latinarum* 1. 1007 (= *Inscriptiones Latinae*

Selectae 8403); 6. 11062 (= *ILS* 8402; Gardner and Wiedemann 1991: 52); 1. 2. 1211 (= *ILS* 8403; Shelton 1998: 44); 1. 2. 1221 (= *ILS* 7472; Shelton 1998: 47)). Inscriptions are, of course, private monuments displayed in the public sphere with a tendency to be formulaic; but similar virtues can be seen in Pliny's description of his young wife Calpurnia. Pliny married for the third time, at the age of 40, to a young girl of 15. In a letter to the aunt who raised Calpurnia, Pliny described her as follows:

My wife is sensible and careful with our money. She also loves me, a sign of her virtue. Because of her love for me, she has even gone so far as to take an interest in literature; she possesses copies of my writings, reads them repeatedly and even memorises them. When I am preparing to speak in a lawsuit, she is anxious on my behalf; when I have completed a case she is relieved. She sends out slave messengers to tell her whether I am getting the sympathy and applause of the jury, and whether the verdict goes my way. When I recite from my works, she will sit nearby, behind a curtain, eager to share the praise I receive. She has even set some of my poems to music, and chants them to the accompaniment of a lyre, untaught by any music-teacher, but rather by the best of teachers, love. All this gives me the highest reason to hope that our mutual happiness (*concordia*) will last for ever and go on increasing day by day, for she does not love me for my present age nor my person, which must surely grow old and decay, but for my aspirations to fame.

(Pliny, *Letters* 4. 19. 2–6; Gardner and Wiedemann 1991: 62, with additions)

Calpurnia's virtues are those of the ideal *matrona* who is loyal to her husband and subordinates her interests to his. In this letter Pliny is complimenting both his wife, for her talents, and her aunt, for her upbringing. His expression of affection is framed within the cultural norms of his society. Calpurnia is willing to defer to her husband and to centre her life on his interests. Her character is reticent and respectful. In other letters Pliny expresses similar sentiments: writing to Calpurnia herself at a time when they are apart, he talks about how much he misses her and, during the time of day he usually spent with her, wanders to her rooms only to be left sick at heart by their emptiness (*Letters* 7. 5; Shelton 1998: 46). Similar expressions of affection and sense of loss are found in the letters of Cicero concerning his wife and children while he is in exile, and by Ovid, also exiled, to his wife (Cicero, *Letters to Friends* 6. 3; *Letters to Quintus* 3. 3;

Ovid, *Tristia* 3. 3. 24, 55). However, even here we have to be cautious about the 'authentic' voice of such apparently loving husbands. These letters are all highly stylized expressions of idealized cultural and social norms, and often meant for publication. This is not to deny the presence of affection or emotion, but these are mediated through a degree of literary and social construction. What we lack any sense of here, constructed or otherwise, are the opinions of the women themselves. Can we imagine that Calpurnia shared her husband's feelings (constructed as they might be)? Or did the fact that she had been married off to someone old enough to be her father destroy any potential for affection on her side? We cannot know. Equally, we cannot assume that she did not absorb the dominant values and ideals of her society and class and aspire to them. Literate Romans did not expect affection to be a criterion for arranging a marriage, but they did expect it to grow during the partnership. Of course, not all marriages were successful, as we have seen in the example of Quintus Cicero and Pomponia. Affective and emotional relationships within the family have to be understood within the context of other defining factors.

The age difference between husband and wife reflected very different life experiences. Girls were raised to expect marriage, motherhood, and the running of a household as the successful outcomes of their lives, and prepared for the role from an early age. Their education was essentially down to parental choice, but could include a high degree of literacy and numeracy (Hemelrijk 1999). Skills that were essential to the successful overseeing of a large household and accomplished social life, such as those exhibited by Calpurnia (see above), enhanced the standing of a young woman. Social skills and etiquette were presumably inculcated from an early age by imitation of female family members. It was considered the duty of a good husband to continue his wife's education and teach her the skills she lacked in terms of household management (Plutarch, *Moralia* 145b–146). However, before her marriage the life experience of a daughter of the upper classes would have been limited primarily to contact with her family, close friends and slaves/freedwomen. A father was expected to protect his daughters from potentially dangerous outside influences. Boys, on the other hand were expected to have had a relatively wide life experience by the time they married. Male youths were traditionally regarded as unstable, easily led, and unable to control their youthful passions. They were thought to need a period in which to exorcise these less desirable traits, to shape their physical bodies, and prepare themselves for adult life. The transition from boyhood to youth was marked by the assumption of the *toga virilis*. At a ceremony that usually took place some time prior to his seventeenth birthday, a boy would lay aside the markers of childhood—the *toga praetexta* and the *bulla* (an amulet worn by Roman girls (until their wedding) and boys (until they became legally adult) to bring good fortune)—and take up the toga of manhood.

This ritual marked the beginning of a process that would hopefully end, after a period of training, with full incorporation into the adult male world. In their late teens young men might perhaps have a period of study abroad, as Cicero's son Marcus did in Athens; have undertaken a period of military service or been on a governor's staff; have been in training under a master jurist; and have taken their first steps on the public career ladder. Cicero undertook the training of young men (as he had himself been trained), one of whom was Marcus Caelius Rufus. At 19 Caelius spent time on the staff of the governor of Africa, returning to Rome in his early twenties. In the following few years he successfully prosecuted his first case, took a central role in the religious festival of Lupercalia, and lived an unchaperoned life in a rented house away from his father (Cicero, *Pro Caelio* 17 f.; Harlow and Laurence 2002: 71 f.). Caelius had begun to live his life independently of his family, and with the stereotypical rashness of youth had got himself into bad company. In 56 BC he ended up in court, accused of a number of charges which included borrowing money from the notorious aristocratic lady Clodia and then attempting to murder her. He was successfully defended by Cicero, who used Caelius' youth as mitigating circumstances: 'When he has listened to the voice of pleasure and given some time to love affairs and these empty desires of youth, let him at length turn to the interests of a more domestic life, to the activities of the *forum* and public life' (Cicero, *Pro Caelio* 42; Harlow and Laurence 2002: 72). The final end of youth, for a boy, was marked by the holding of first public office and by marriage. Asymmetrical life experiences and difference in ages between bride and groom gave the husband the upper hand in dealing with matters of socializing, and household and family finance, and buttressed the paternalistic slant which underlay marital relationships.

The view of Roman marriage given in the ancient sources is very much that of the husband/father, but we should not overlook the women in these relationships. Women were perceived to be 'naturally' inferior to men in terms of physical and mental capacity. They were considered as the weaker sex, easily influenced, with a tendency to emotional rather than rational response. Women were thought to be inherently vulnerable and in need of protection by a father, husband, or guardian. The image of the modest, chaste, pious, stay-at-home wife recorded on epitaphs is at odds with the social authority that an upper-class married woman, and certainly a mother, might wield: the lived reality of women's lives presents a very different picture. Roman history is full of powerful and influential women. Despite having no political rights and relatively limited legal rights, upper-class Roman women could be highly influential within the domestic sphere and, via husbands, fathers, and brothers, in the public and political arena. Motherhood enhanced a woman's status: she was no longer simply a wife, but a provider of legitimate heirs and a mother with direct influence over her children. A mother had no legal power (*potestas*) over her children, but she certainly had social power. Giving birth increased a woman's standing in society, but also highlighted her ambiguous positions within the *familia*. She and her husband shared responsibility for children and the reflected glory of their successes (and vice versa). One of the first women to have a statue erected to her in the Forum Romanum was known primarily for her maternity. Cornelia, mother of famous sons, Tiberius and Gaius Gracchus, was praised for raising them to high achievement and for remaining loyal to her deceased husband and refusing offers of remarriage (Plutarch, *Tiberius Gracchus* 1). Highly educated and able to pass her talents onto her sons, she was thought to embody ideal qualities: she remained in the domestic sphere and did not presume to enter that of politics, except by pressuring her sons to ever greater achievements. Cornelia is also a prime example of the Roman ideal of *uniuira* (a woman who married only once and remained faithful to her husband's memory after his death).

A woman's children might be considered primarily as assets to her husband's family (their agnate relations), but their mother was expected to pass her wealth on to them. Now, *sine manu* (without *manus*) marriage gave women the right to dispose of their property as they wished. Nevertheless, while in legal terms a mother in this form of marriage remained in the inheritance networks of her natal family, it was expected that she would leave her children as her heirs. Law was here slow to keep pace with social practice, which had clearly been established by the late Republic but was not legally recognized until the late second century AD. The separation of husband's and wife's property also gave the woman a certain amount of potential freedom in the arrangement of domestic affairs. A wife could also divorce her husband if she wished, and take her dowry with her. Potentially, therefore, a wife could hold a very powerful position. Despite this, customary ideals are very powerful tools of social control, and the inferior position of a young bride with respect to her husband's age and experience may have inhibited any move to independence, particularly by young wives. Divorce may have been an option, but for women it could mean a loss of contact with her children, who normally remained with the father; it would certainly mean the loss of the home she shared with her husband, and probably a return to her father's house. Parents and associates would then set about finding a new partner for her: as a result of Augustus's social legislation (*leges Iuliae*, 18 BC; *lex Papia Poppaea*, AD 9) members of the upper classes were expected to remarry. This was in conflict with the ideal of *uniuira* mentioned above. For an older woman remarriage might have advantages, and offer her more say in the choice of partner. Cicero's daughter Tullia chose her third husband with the support of her mother Terentia, in the face of disapproval from her father. In the end Cicero had to accept the situation, as he was presented with a fait accompli.

Among the upper classes there was a limited number of available marriage partners, and a woman might find herself married again and in the role of stepmother to her new husband's offspring by a previous marriage. Remarriage was not uncommon, but the myth of step-parents being more interested in their own children, and even perhaps actively hostile to stepchildren, thrived in Roman literature. This idea was so pervasive that it was addressed by jurists, who assumed a father might be swayed by the charms of a new wife and privilege children of a second marriage over those of the first (*Digest* 5. 2. 3, 4), or a wife might subvert the inheritance prospects of her husband's children by earlier marriages in favour of her own or 'forget' the duty owed to her own children of a previous partnership. Agrippina the Younger is a prime example of such behaviour. To further the interests of her own son, Nero, she married her third husband, her uncle the emperor Claudius, and is accused, by Tacitus (*Annals* 12. 5–66), who clearly indulges in the literary stereotype, of getting rid of both him and his biological son, Britannicus, to clear the way for Nero's accession. Given the pressure for remarriage, step-parenting must have been common, and not all stepmothers conformed to the negative stereotype. An inscription put up by a son for his mother, Murdia, commemorates her for doing the right thing (*Corpus Inscriptionum Latinarum* 6.10230 = *ILS* 8394; Gardner and Wiedemann 1991: 132; Shelton 1998: 291). Murdia appears to have married twice and had children by both marriages. She left all her children as heirs to her property, but also returned to the son of the first marriage that share of his father's patrimony she had been granted for her upkeep. On the death of a husband, wives were not legally allowed to undertake the role of *tutor* for their children but would often be granted part of the patrimony to hold in trust for them, from which they were granted the profits (*usufructus*).

The marriages in Cicero's family are instructive as a warning against taking ideals as normal behaviour. His daughter Tullia's persistence in her own choice of partner is an interesting comment on the limits of *patria potestas*. At the age of 60 Cicero divorced Terentia, his wife of over thirty years, to marry his young, 15-year-old ward Publilia, who became stepmother to his children, who were older than her. The wealth and connections of Cicero's first wife, Terentia, had helped his early career; she had borne him two children and carefully guarded his finances during his exile in 58–7 BC. Their relationship in this period appears to embody the essence of partnership and *concordia*. The reasons for the divorce are unclear. Cicero claimed he had need of new alliances; Tiro, his secretary, said he had need of money to pay off his debts; Terentia accused him of succumbing to Publilia's youthful charms (Plutarch, *Cicero* 41). Whatever the reasons, this second marriage also ended in divorce after a very short duration.

Women like Pomponia, in the extract which opened this chapter, who acted against the dominant stereotype or trespassed into the male domain, risked getting a very bad press from male writers. The young Caelius Rufus, for instance, was allegedly led astray by an older widow, Clodia, who was vilified by Cicero when he defended Caelius. The same Clodia has often been thought to be Lesbia, the subject of a series of love poems by Catullus (see most recently Dixon 2001: 134–45). Livia, the wife of Augustus, and Agrippina, wife of Claudius and mother of Nero, were also given damning reputations by historians. Their movements in the political arena were frowned upon, both because political manipulation was considered an unsuitable role for women, and also because their power reflected a weakness on the part of their menfolk in failing to control them.

As a woman aged and her fertility diminished, her chances in the marriage market decreased. Divorced and widowed men, on the other hand, could take younger and younger brides. Pompey the Great married five times. His fourth wife, Julia, was the daughter of Julius Caesar, and the marriage was arranged to cement the political alliance between the two men in 59 BC. At age 16 this was Julia's first marriage. Her husband was aged 46, an older contemporary of her father. Pompey had three children from an earlier marriage, and thus Julia became stepmother to 'children' of her own age. Pompey remarried for a fifth time in his late fifties to another young woman, Cornelia. Cornelia became step-grandmother to Pompey's grandchildren before she could become a mother herself. This sort of extreme disparity in ages in marriage was frowned upon in society. While all of Pompey's marriages improved his standing in the political scene of the day, interestingly the last two are characterized by Plutarch as being very affectionate, again reminding us that we should be careful about any generalized expectations of social behaviour (Plutarch, *Pompey* 53, 55, 74).

The aim of marriage was the production of legitimate children who would be subject to the power of the *paterfamilias*. We have seen that the power of the father was mitigated by demographic factors: many men would not have a living father by the time they reached adulthood. There was also social pressure on both fathers and children to behave in a good fashion towards each other. *pietas* was a cardinal Roman virtue. It encompassed respect for the gods, for the state, and also for the family (Chapter 7). The most enduring image of *pietas*, especially in Augustan imagery and mythology of the 'golden age', was that of the Trojan hero Aeneas, fleeing the burning Troy, carrying his aged father and leading his son. *pietas* required a reciprocal respect between children and parents. Parents provided sustenance and education and raised the child to the correct station in life, while in return children were supposed to respect and obey their parents, and look after them in their old age. Each had a duty to bury the other in the event of death. It was considered a travesty of fate if the child died before the parent, but this was not an unusual occurrence in the ancient world. Model life tables and demographic simulations suggest that up to 39 per cent of the population would die before the age of 10 (Saller 1994: 21–5). The power of life and death that epitomized *potestas* was rarely invoked. Its most obvious use came in the decision whether to let a newborn infant live or die. A father was supposed to formally accept a child into his family shortly after birth. If the child was disabled in any way, or there was any suspicion about its parenthood, it might be abandoned. Abandonment did not entail infanticide, although death was an obvious risk: exposed infants were often claimed and raised by others. Indeed, the foundation myth of Rome is based on the exposure of Romulus and Remus. The practice of exposing children carried little moral stigma. For the vast majority of the population it was presumably a pragmatic decision based on economic constraints and basic survival instincts.

Once a child was accepted by the father it entered his *potestas* and the inheritance networks of his family. The father accepted the obligation of raising and educating the child. He would be involved in arranging a marriage, for which his consent was required. He also had considerable leverage in instigating divorce for his children, although both these powers were inhibited by social custom, which frowned upon a father marrying off, or enforcing divorce on, his children against their will. As we have seen, however, in considering paternal power we must remember that only about a fifth of Roman men would have a living father by the time they came to marry. We should not overstate the constraints of *potestas* for adult sons (Saller 1994: 114–30). The most potent aspect to *potestas* must surely have been the economic control it gave fathers over their children. Offspring, even once adult and living away from the family home, were financially dependent on their fathers, who controlled any property or money accruing to them. Daughters escaped this to some extent by being given a dowry and moving to another household on marriage, but this advantage could be tempered if they made a bad marriage. Sons were usually granted an allowance (*peculium*), but the extent of this was subject to the father's whim. Cicero, complained about the amount of money his son ran through while studying in Athens, but does not seem to have cut his allowance; nevertheless, the threat of disinheritance must have been a powerful tool for a father. If he died intestate all his legitimate children, daughters as well as sons, were entitled to equal shares of the patrimony. However, a father could explicitly disinherit a child in his will. The child had the right to counter-claim through a charge of unduteous will (*Digest* 5. 2. 24; *Code of Justinian* 3. 28. 3, 6; Gardner and Wiedemann 1991: 142–6). The relative age difference at marriage would mean that adult males were likely to have a much longer relationship with their mothers than their fathers. While mothers did not have *potestas*, they did require respect and obedience from their children, and could also use the threat of disinheritance if not treated with due deference.

The experience of the young child at Rome is very difficult to ascertain. Like women and slaves, children leave no direct literary record of their lives, and what we see of them is filtered through the prism of elite adult fathers. As the children grew they would come into contact with a number of adult carers. They might stay with their own parents or, through the death or divorce of a parent, they may find themselves with a step-parent and step-siblings. Within an upper-class house a child would certainly have experienced a number of slave carers, some of whom assumed duties we would today consider the proper role of parents. A case in point is wet-nursing. It was accepted practice for most classes to employ wet-nurses for their offspring (some masters also employed them to nourish slave infants; see below). The relationship between nurses and their charges could develop as the child grew, and the latter often expressed their loyalty and gratitude with gifts in later life: Pliny, (*Letters* 6. 3; Gardner and Wiedemann 1991: 93–4) left his nurse a farm, and the testator of the so-called 'Will of Dasumius' (*Corpus Inscriptionum Latinarum* 6. 10229; Gardner and Wiedemann 1991: 134–9) left the nurse, Dasumia Syche, silverware and a sum of money. In such cases the relationship between child and carer could be a very close one. It was this potential for closeness that caused anxiety among some male commentators. Tacitus worried that Roman children would be imbibing servile or foreign habits with breast-milk (*Dialogue on Famous Orators* 29. 1). Aulus Gellius, on the other hand, criticized women for 'abandoning' their children to wet-nurses for the sake of their figures (*Attic Nights* 12. 1; Gardner and Wiedemann 1991: 104). Wet-nursing may have been common for a number of reasons: it would be necessary if a mother died in childbirth; if she needed to return to work soon after the birth; or, according to ancient understanding, if she wished to conceive again in the near future (for full discussion see Bradley 1992; Garnsey 1991).

Practices such as the farming out of children to nurses, exposure, and a very legalistic view of *potestas* have led in the past to the idea that Romans related very remotely to their children. While it is true that the use of wet-nurses might create an emotional distance between mother and infant, in a time of high infant mortality the distancing may also be seen as an emotional protection for a new mother. The issue of how we interpret wet-nursing merely serves to highlight the fact that, as with affective relations between husband and wife, we cannot judge parent–child relations outside their chronological and cultural context (Garnsey 1991). Romans who employed wet-nurses could easily have been following social custom, what was believed to be best practice in child welfare and maternal health. The relationship between children and slaves also highlights the social ambiguity of these cross-status links. Children often had pedagogues who, despite their lowly social position, were there to accompany their charges outside the home and to instruct them in social etiquette. These relationships changed over time. Martial complained about the control which his pedagogue, Charidemus, thought he could retain, even though now Martial was greasing his hair and chasing girls (*Epigrams* 11. 39; Shelton 1998: 34). Cicero too felt that the intimacy that might characterize these relationships in childhood should not be extended into adult life (*On Friendship* 74).

Children were generally considered a desirable asset in the Roman world, but the care they received depended on their status, rank, and economic position and, ultimately, on the whim of their parents and carers. Children whose parents had sufficient economic resources could expect a reasonable period of childhood, when they could be admired and indulged for their childish behaviour and exploits. Those in less-well-off families could expect to work in some form or another from an early age, with a very limited period in which they lacked some form of responsibility. Children no doubt helped in family businesses or on farms as soon as they were capable. Apprenticeships, for instance, were common, and evidence shows children contracted to work in various trades from about the age of 12 (Bradley 1992: 108).

The position of slaves within the *familia*, and in wider society, is complex. As we have seen, this is an area where legal status could have widely varying relevance to social relationships. Slaves should not simply be quantified as a single social class of unfree. Within the slave population there were some who were both better-off and had a greater chance of achieving freedom than others. Some slaves, probably the majority, lived short, brutal lives, doing hard manual labour. Others, however, particularly those employed in urban households, may have had a much better life. Slaves did not have any legal rights, but there were unwritten rules about how they should be treated. Masters such as Vedius Pollio, who would happily have thrown his servant into a pool of lampreys for breaking a crystal goblet had not Augustus intervened (Cassius Dio 54. 23), may or may not have been common, but physical punishment, and whipping in particular, was closely associated with slavery. Excessive physical punishment was, however, frowned upon. It was thought that a good master should not have to resort to extreme measures, but this is an attitude that presupposes that slaves behaved in an appropriately servile manner. Pliny the Younger expressed anxiety about the state of health of the slaves in his *familia*. He consoled himself, and in his eyes his slaves as well, by granting freedom to those who were ill, and by allowing them to make bequests of their belongings which he respected (*Letters* 8. 16; Gardner and Wiedemann 1991: 39). In this case slaves were expected to identify with the interests of their owner's *familia*.

Pliny also claims that the household is a substitute community for slaves, and indeed it could act as such. In some households slaves do appear to share a sense of community. Funerary commemorations show slaves putting up memorials to *conservi*, fellow slaves with whom they worked, sometimes in the same occupation: thus Eros and Felix, bakers from the same *familia* who were buried together (*Corpus Inscriptionum Latinarum* 6. 6687). More intimate ties also appear to have been tolerated in some *familiae*. Legally slaves were not allowed to marry, but they could form unions that were, to all intents and purposes, marriages. These unions usually took place within a single household. This would be to the owner's advantage, as any offspring would belong to him. For the slave partners the advantage of being in the same household presumably meant they had more chance of a 'family life'. Slave children might enjoy a period of childhood shared with their master's children, but their lives were by no means guaranteed. They would be lucky if they stayed with their birth mother or even within the *familia*. Seneca was horrified when, later in life, he met a slave playmate and failed to recognize him because of his physical degeneration (*Moral Letters* 12; Gardner and Wiedemann 1991: 95). Clearly, as slave and free child grew up, their life courses diverged dramatically. Children born of slave mothers within the *familia* were known as *uernae*. *uernae* could hold privileged positions within the household, especially if they were thought to be the master's own child. Attractive little child-slaves could also function as fashion accessories. *deliciae*, as they were known, were enjoyed for their charming qualities: Martial mourned the death of his slave Erotion, who died before her sixth birthday (*Epigrams* 5. 34; 10. 61; Gardner and Wiedemann 1991: 106).

As with all slave relationships there was the potential for sexual involvement, and some *deliciae* were doubtless so used. The constant presence of slaves in the household had obvious ramifications for ideas of 'private' life. The actions and behaviour of both the free and unfree members of the household were under scrutiny at all times. Sexual relationships with slaves were relatively unproblematic, so long as they were not considered a threat to the legal union of husband and wife. In Petronius' novel *Satyrica*, the buffoonish ex-slave Trimalchio had earned his freedom through sexual favours performed for both his former master and mistress (*Sat.* 75). On the other hand, male citizens, outside the senatorial order could free their female slaves if they wished to marry them.

As with other social relationships in the Roman world, we have to be careful to balance the evidence with regard to slaves within the *familia*. As a counter to any idea that slaves might on the whole have had a comfortable life, it is salutary to remember that if a master died in suspicious circumstances his entire slave household could be put to death. Tacitus recalls a debate in the Senate from AD 61 when a city official, Pedanius Secundus, had been murdered by one of his slaves. Although there was some dissension against what was seen as excessive cruelty, the Senate voted to uphold the law, that all 400 of Secundus' slaves be put to death. This reflects the pervasive anxiety of slave-owners in daily contact with a numerous oppressed underclass (Tacitus, *Annals* 14. 42–5; Shelton 1998: 175 f.).

familia, domus and social networks

Visitors to the remains of Pompeii or Herculaneum cannot fail to be struck by the seeming openness of the Roman house. From the street it is possible to see through the open entrance, across the courtyard (*atrium*), to the room at the far end (*tablinum*), and catch a glimpse into rooms opening off the atrium (*alae*). A colonnaded area (the peristyle) beyond the *tablinum* is often visible through a window. This architectural structure is a product of, and a response to, the demands of the Roman social system of the early empire. Those lower down the social scale lived in a variety of dwellings, from the one-room house shops, also common at Pompeii, to the apartment blocks which predominated later in large cities, and whose remains can be explored at Ostia. *domus*, as we have seen, referred both to the family and to the physical house. It was here that the private domestic world of the family interacted with the public, civic world of the male citizen. The family and home were the core of the social and political networks an upper-class male needed in order to be successful throughout his life. Some of these links would be made through his own marriage and those of his children. The *domus*, in both its physical and social form, was the backdrop against which an upper-class male lived his life. In the early stages of his career he would attend on those further up the social scale in their homes, and, as his own career advanced, others would attend on him (see below, on the *salutatio*).

Rome was a hierarchical society, but one also notable for its social mobility. The Roman social system was based on a network of personal relationships in which favours and services were given and received. Reciprocity was the key to these relationships: a favour given had to be both acknowledged and returned, according to the ability and resources of the recipient. This system is broadly defined by the term 'patronage'; as with familial relationships, its actual mechanics are often hidden from us. While reciprocity was essential, patronage also implies an unequal relationship between the benefactor and the recipient. This inequality is sometimes obvious, as between freed slave and ex-master/mistress. Elsewhere, as between those of equal social status but dissimilar rank (for example, between senior and junior senators), it is less clear. The Romans themselves sometimes obscured the relationship out of courtesy. They tended to refer to all those of the same class with whom they shared obligations as friends (*amici*); friends, however, could fall into a number of categories: superior, equal, or inferior (full discussion: Saller 1982; Wallace-Hadrill 1989).

Wealth, as well as status, was essential to success in Roman life, and the judicious expression of material success was expected in the layout and decoration of the home. Those in public life were expected to have domiciles commensurate with their status and office. By the second century BC the architecture of the public world had begun to invade domestic space. Towards the end of the first century BC Vitruvius expressed the Roman ideology of space in his treatise *On Architecture*: those engaged in oratory, the struggle for office, politics, and public life required houses that had high entrance halls, wide courtyards, and porticoes to show off their importance. These structures should emulate the grandeur of public architecture, as their owners often needed to preside over public meetings, or cases that required adjudication, in their homes. Vitruvius also claimed that these areas were spaces which people had a right to enter without being invited (*On Architecture* 6. 5. 1 f.; Gardner and Wiedemann 1991: 9). Entry may not have been as free as Vitruvius implies, as access to the house was often controlled by a heavy door, a slave doorkeeper, or a guard dog (real or mosaic).

This central area of this 'public space'—entrance, *atrium, tablinum, alae*—hosted the institution of the *salutatio*, which was re-enacted daily in the households of the upper classes, as they opened at dawn to receive clients and *amici*. Close friends and important individuals were identified by being admitted first, and perhaps even to areas of the *domus* where most clients were not permitted (Wallace-Hadrill 1994; Hales 2003). Lesser friends and clients would be met in the *atrium*, in strict order of social standing. Household slaves would control access to the house and its master. Roman social hierarchy was on view during the *salutatio*, and each participant recognized his own and others' places. It is a common subject of complaint in Roman satire that the client has to get up early and rush through the streets to attend on a patron who might keep him waiting for ages, and then reward him with only a small handout of food or money (the *sportula*: Horace, *Epodes* 2. 1. 104; Martial, *Epigrams* 5. 22; 6. 88; Shelton 1998: 14). Juvenal also complained that after waiting all morning, someone he considered his social inferior, or a Johnny-come-lately foreigner, would be received ahead of him, a Roman citizen (*Satire* 1. 95–112)! The social flow of the *salutatio* also illustrated one of the paradoxes of Roman society: within the household some slaves might find themselves controlling the movements of their social superiors. In this context, those with no legal status in the Roman world could exercise some degree of social power by permitting or preventing access to those over whom, in the normal course of life, they would have absolutely no rights. Outside the *domus*, slaves reverted to status-less beings, and could not presume to such behaviour.

It was a mark of a successful man for his house to be full of callers at this time of day. The openness of the house also made his prestige visible to passers-by. For his part, the patron would dispense favours. The nature of these benefactions would vary depending on the status and power of the patron and the nature of the request of the friend or client. During the Republic friends could offer political support in the form of canvassing and votes. Others might come seeking business advice, loans, or legal opinions. Those who merited the title 'friend' might also solicit favours. Ambitious men who wanted to succeed in the arena of public life needed supporters and influential individuals to recommend them for office or provide letters of introduction. In the absence of any formal training, the network of personal relationships was essential to the success of a political career. Even when highest offices became the preserve of the imperial benefaction, an ambitious young man would still need someone close to the seat of power to speak for him. Even if they were of the same social class, it was essential for a junior (usually younger or holding a lower office) man to behave with deference and respect towards his senior, and to advertise the fact that he had been given support. While the family and wider kin-group was one of the first places young men might seek support, for many it was also necessary to look outside the family. As we have seen, many young men would be without a father at the age they began their political careers; others—'new men' (those who were the first of their family to attain political office) like Cicero and even the Younger Pliny—needed the support of established patrons to help them advance their careers. Once established, a man might enhance his own client base as the types of favour he could offer increased. Both Pliny and Cicero, for instance, would defend their friends and clients in court. Pliny owed his start in political life to the senior senator Corellius Rufus, and while the senior man paid Pliny the compliment of treating him as a friend, the asymmetry of the relationship is illustrated by the way Pliny frequently sought his advice (*Letters* 4. 17; 9. 13; for further discussion see Saller 1982; Garnsey and Saller 1987: 153).

Among the range of clients a patron might have was one clearly identified group—his former slaves (*liberti*). The Romans are remarkable among slave-owning societies for the fact that they not only freed many of their slaves, but also granted the freed slave citizenship (albeit with some restrictions in the first generation: see below). Some who had learned a trade or skill might continue these occupations as freedmen, and remained dependent on their former owners or were set up in business with their *peculium*. Others, like Tiro, Cicero's secretary, earned their freedom through long and loyal service, and continued in the same position under their newly acquired status. A very few became extremely wealthy. A freed slave took his master's name (thus Tiro becomes M. Tullius M. l. Tiro—'Marcus Tullius, freedman of Marcus, Tiro', Tullius being Cicero's clan name), and became his client. He owed his former owner a series of obligations, and these set him apart from the freeborn. The freedman was expected to show respect (*obsequium*) to his patron, who also had a right to demand the performance of *operae* or duties. Freedmen and freedwomen undertook all types of occupations: tradesmen; artisans; businessmen, bankers, and financiers; shopkeepers; doctors and midwives; teachers. They interacted on a daily basis with both the free and slave populations. Relations with patrons could be loyal and long-lasting. The epitaph inscribed on the tombstone of Marcus Aurelius Zosimus praises his former master and now patron, Marcus Aurelius Cotta Maximus, for offering him a fortune equivalent to that of equestrian status, helping him raise his children, and providing dowries for the daughters. Zosimus' son Cotta obtained a commission as military tribune, and finally paid for Zosimus' tombstone (*Corpus Inscriptionum Latinarum* 14. 2298, from the Via Appia outside Rome; Gardner and Wiedemann 1991: 40–1). Zosimus acted as business agent for his patron, and they clearly had an enduring relationship. The epitaph also demonstrates the generosity of the patron, which the client was expected to acknowledge. It also illustrates the social mobility of the freedman family. While the first generation might not be allowed to forget their servile origins, their children and grandchildren could progress in traditional society, as Zosimus' son did. Horace, whose father was a freedman, praises him for investing in his son's education, in order that he could improve his position in society (*Satires* 1. 6). Some freedmen did become very wealthy, but they could not, at least in the first generation, join the ranks of the upper classes. The wealth and social power of some freedmen, especially those of the imperial household, created a great deal of tension among the upper classes (Chapter 3). Even among the lower classes resentment could be expressed, if freedmen were seen to be more successful than their freeborn contemporaries. Martial complained that while the poor Roman-born poet, Maevius, shivered in a thin cloak, a former slave mule-driver was resplendent in scarlet (*Epigrams* 10. 76).

Conclusion

The Roman family and household were, as Cicero, claimed, a microcosm of the state. The success of his family and the decoration of his splendid home were the backgrounds against which a successful upper-class male showed himself off to the world. Within the *domus* a child would learn from an early age how to negotiate the power dynamics of society: between husband and wife; parents and children; master and slave; patron and client. The elite males who recorded their lives and their milieu in various ways present a particular view of the world, one which we have to 'unpick' in order to understand something of the lives of the quieter majority. The ideals of Roman society as promulgated by the upper classes were pervasive: ideals are influential in shaping the lived experiences of individuals. We cannot know to what extent women, slaves, and freedmen and -women bought into the dominant ideologies of Roman society. Familial bonds, however, could be particularly strong among all social groups, even those who could not form legal unions. Among ex-slaves, who could legally marry, the desire to emulate the family life of patrons is striking. As well as influencing social behaviour, ideals also mask some of the 'murkier' realities of life. Some marriages were doubtless made entirely for the convenience of male alliances; some were unhappy; wives, husbands, and children could suffer abuse, as did many slaves. Life for the majority of the population of the Roman Empire was short and brutal. A lucky minority lived productive lives, during which they formed a series of intimate relationships that ranged from lover to parent to friend. The upper classes judged the success of these relationships on criteria that privileged the political and economic outcomes, but they also recognized the value of emotional support and social harmony.

5

Warfare and the Army

Edward Bispham

For the modern reader the Romans are imperial conquerors par excellence: their military symbolism—above all the eagle and the triumphal arch—has been appropriated by many empires and would-be emperors in history. The Roman military machine has become a byword for ruthless efficiency—a trope subverted in most *Asterix* adventures, which often end with a legion advancing in a geometrical, tightly disciplined, and heavily armoured formation to (as the reader knows) certain defeat at the hands of our indomitable Gauls. Yet this is only part of the story. Long periods of undisturbed garrison duty saw the army engaged in non-military activities. Some, like road-building, are predictable. Others are not: the Elder Pliny (*Natural History* 10. 54) records how some auxiliary commanders in Germany got into trouble for sending detachments away from sentry duty to capture geese, whose feathers were in demand to make luxury pillows in Rome.

Warfare was central to Roman life; it was, under the Republic, expected almost every year. Wars were fought ostensibly to avenge wrongs done to Rome or her allies, but in reality from a complex mixture of fear, self-interest, greed, and strategic considerations. Roman society was shaped by an aggressive militaristic ideology, enriched by the economic and cultural consequences of conquest, and finally placed under enormous strain both by the demands of constant warfare and the growing power of the generals who fought ever more spectacular wars of conquest. The narratives of imperial expansion and contraction are told elsewhere in this book (Chapters 2, 3, 9).

Here I will focus on developments in warfare and fighting, and the socio-cultural impact of war. Above all, four interwoven questions will be considered. Who desired and promoted wars? Who fought them? What was the impact of war and the army on Roman politics and society? And what was the impact on the empire at large? The army of the Caesars comprised a quarter of a million men, and as such formed not only the largest unified, professional body in the empire, but also the largest 'single issue' sociological group ever known in antiquity. Its impact on diet, dress, economy, infrastructure, and linguistic development in Roman Europe was very significant.

Our sources for the army and warfare are heterogeneous and frustratingly incomplete; the gaps in our evidence will often be obscured by the synthetic treatment which follows. We do not know, for example, the full strength of the Roman legion under Augustus: 4,800 or 5,000 men? It is symptomatic of our evidence that our two best descriptions were written by non-Romans: Polybius under the Republic and Josephus under the empire—both at one time judged enemies of Rome. The details of the early Roman army were already obscure by the late Republic: even Varro knew little about the cavalry called *ferentarii*, apparently depicted *and named* in a painting in the temple of Aesculapius (*On the Latin Language* 7. 57f.). With the Hannibalic War our sources improve. War was a pervasive cultural preoccupation in this period, to judge by the frequency of military metaphors in Plautus. Slightly later, Polybius gave a detailed description of the mobilization and encampment of a Roman army, in his exploration in book 6 of the strength of the Roman people, both in its civic institutions and under arms. He had seen Roman armies in battle and sacking cities; he also had an officer's interest in strategy, and used autopsy where possible for description of battlefields (9. 20. 4). Historical writers, despite (or perhaps because of) striving after *enargeia* (vividness), often add little to our understanding of the battles and sieges which they describe as set pieces, or of military technicalities. Sometimes they are downright confusing (Sallust's battle narratives in the *Jugurthine War*, for example).

Julius Caesar, Velleius Paterculus, and Ammianus Marcellinus, military officers and often eyewitnesses, are more valuable, but still employ rhetorical tropes and exaggeration. Nor do they tell us what to them was obvious: readers interested in the armour worn by

Caesar's Gallic armies will search his text in vain for a description. All ancient writers represent an elite viewpoint: warfare through the eyes of emperors and officers. The poor common soldier was either idealized or seen as disobedient and grasping, potentially the agent of revolution. Military treatises were often addressed to would-be generals, as with the Elder Cato's (now lost) *On Military Practice*. His influence can probably be traced through to the fourth-century *Epitome on Military Practice* of Vegetius. His subject-matter epitomizes the two main themes of military treatises: technical advice on weapons (for example, the discussion of artillery and siege engines in the last book of Vitruvius' *On Architecture*) and strategy (as in Frontinus' *Stratagems*). In a class by itself is the *Notitia Dignitatum* (*List of Offices*), an illustrated list of the imperial bases, military commands, and the units attached to them, of the late fourth century AD.

We also have a wide range of documentary evidence, mainly from the imperial era, from soldiers' epitaphs to commemorations of victories inscribed on stone. These inscriptions offer an enormous amount of repeated routine detail on individual units and careers, and on the religious activities of soldiers; there are also commemorations of building projects, from roads to aqueducts. Of particular interest are the hundreds of *diplomata*, bronze tablets certifying the honourable discharge and grants of citizenship to auxiliaries (collected in volume 16 of the *Corpus Inscriptionum Latinarum*); and the series of wooden tablets produced by an auxiliary unit at Vindolanda on Hadrian's Wall, recording everything from unit strengths to petitions and personal letters: these provide a remarkable flavour of garrison life.

Material culture is a particularly rich (but uneven) source for the army. Some physical traces of the Roman army's presence are very substantial: as well as marching camps and fortresses (known in quantity through aerial photography, but rarely systematically excavated), we have the remains of vast siege works like those around Numantia in Spain (later second-century BC), or Caesar's at Alesia. Perhaps most famous of all, Hadrian's Wall and its forts offer a salutary lesson: had the wall perished utterly, we would know next to nothing about its location, nature, or course from literary evidence. Artistic commemorations of military success have given us representations of moments from triumphal processions and campaigns. Trajan's Column, commemorating his Dacian victories, is an outstanding example of the latter, its narrative frieze containing accurate depictions of armour and engineering works. Yet it is sobering to compare it with the monument to the same campaign at Adamklissi in Romania, very different in style and content: this was the one put up by the soldiers. The arches of Titus and Septimius Severus also provide valuable iconographic evidence; and the frieze from the Arch of Constantine is exceptional in portraying scenes from a *civil* war (that between Maxentius and Constantine: Chapter 9; Fig. 5. 1). Military gravestones from all over the empire provide us with a wide variety of portraits of soldiers and junior officers in uniform.

Bringing us closer to the thoughts and words of 'squaddies' in combat are a number of (often scabrously) inscribed sling-bullets: well-known examples derive from Italy and the civil conflicts of the first century BC: 'I'm aiming for Octavian's arse' is an example from the siege of Perusia (41–40 BC; *Inscriptiones Latinae Liberae Rei Publicae* 1108). Examples of everything from swords to horse-harnesses have survived in the archaeological record. Their contexts are very diverse, from dedications in sanctuaries and rivers, to grave

Fig. 5.1. The Arch of Constantine, Rome (north side). Dedicated by the Senate and People of Rome in AD 315, following Constantine's defeat of Maxentius at the Milvian Bridge in 312.

goods and accidental losses, from Pompeii to the furthest reaches of gift-exchange networks, often travelling with returning auxiliaries (Chapter 10). But by far the most common is the mass dumping of apparently unwanted metal items when a Roman base was abandoned. Widespread types often bear the name of the site at which they were first recorded: thus we have the 'Montefortino' and 'Intercisa' helmets, and the 'Mainz' and 'Pompeii' swords. The arms and armour of the Republican period are seriously under-represented in finds to date—the paucity of permanent forts at this period must be part of the explanation.

War: what is it good for?

Archaic warlords

One benchmark of the emergence of states out of family or tribal groupings is the creation of a monopoly on the use of legitimate violence on the part of the community, both internally and against outsiders. This channels the efforts of aristocratic warlords towards the common good, rather than into familial aggrandizement. The community takes responsibility for the raising, payment, leadership, and discharge of troops, who in turn submit to the discipline of the collective, for which they fight.

Roman writers present a story of expansion beginning under Romulus, who celebrated the first triumph, continuing under the subsequent kings and into the Republic, despite setbacks such as the sack of Rome by the Gauls in 387/6 BC (Chapters 1, 2), to the present day. Yet this seems to obscure the considerable complexities of the archaic period. Italy was then characterized by 'horizontal social mobility' (Cornell 1995: 133–40, 143–50, 156–9), by which, amid a weaker conception of citizenship and state than those obtaining later, warlords and their followers moved easily between communities. Examples are the story of the immigration of the Claudii under Attus Clausus (Chapter 2); and the emperor Claudius' account in a speech to the Senate in AD 48 (*Inscriptiones Latinae Selectae* 212; see further Chapter 3), which equated King Servius Tullius with an Etruscan warlord called Mastarna, who seized Rome by force. Most striking, however, is a late sixth-century (?) inscription found at Satricum near

Rome, a dedication by the *suodales* of one Poplios Valesios to the god Mamars (that is, Mars). Valesios may well be one of the aristocratic Roman Valerii; the *suodales* are almost certainly to be understood as his companions and retainers, the core of a 'private army'. This evidence suggests that the power of the kings was to a degree constrained by the power of individual lineages and their private resources. The problem seems to have persisted after the fall of the monarchy. At the Cremera river in 477 BC 300 members of the Fabian *gens* (clan) were annihilated, apparently while conducting operations against Rome's neighbour and rival Veii: the Republic seems still not to have had a complete monopoly on legitimate violence, and was either unable to restrain forces composed of the dependants and clansmen of leading families, or needed them to supplement its own militia. This situation was, ironically, to recur in late antiquity, as the Roman state tried to harness to the needs of imperial defence the groups of barbarians coming into the empire, and local landowners took their defence into their own hands with the decline of the central authority (see Chapter 9).

The Roman commonwealth probably obtained a complete monopoly on the use of legitimate violence from the middle of the fifth century BC (the date, we may note, of the Twelve Tables: Chapter 2). And when the change came, it came with a vengeance. One of the most striking things about Republican citizen armies and their imperial successors is the severity of the discipline to which the soldiers submitted themselves on campaign, meted out through the enhanced *imperium* (power of command) which magistrates could wield outside the *pomoerium* or sacred boundary of Rome.

Aristocrats to Dynasts

Just as the common soldiers submitted to harsh discipline, the Roman elite adopted a rhetoric which publicized an ethic of service to the commonwealth in war. Thus, to make up losses in the Hannibalic War, for example, the Senate supplemented its numbers from various sources, including 'those who had not been magistrates, but had spoils captured from the enemy affixed to their houses [a significant practice] or who had been awarded the civic crown [for saving a fellow-citizen's life]' (Livy 23. 23. 6). Yet the growth of communal power did not efface the ambitions or the competition of the great aristocratic families: in one sense Roman history is the sum of their glorious deeds. Indeed, the Republican aristocracy was driven by an overriding militaristic ethos, in which success in war was for a very long time the only serious way for an aristocrat to win *gloria* (glory) for himself, live up to his successful ancestors' deeds, and accumulate symbolic capital, both for his own political struggles with competitors and for his descendants to draw upon (Harris 1992). Imperial conquest brought increasingly large amounts of wealth from war booty (*manubiae*); various forms of ephemeral and permanent commemoration of victors were funded by this means, including the dedication of a temple. Indeed, for the very successful it was possible to get, even if only momentarily, closer still to the divine, by celebrating a triumph, dressed like the cult statue of Jupiter Optimus Maximus (Greatest and Best). Many manubial temples overlooked the route of the triumph, and their presence created a dialogue between past, present, and future military success. They were also permanent reminders for the Roman populace of the narrative of conquest, marking the subjection of a wider world which many of them would never see; the use, under the empire, of exotic foreign marbles in building programmes added symbolism, a visual metaphor for empire.

As the scale, and the material benefits, of military victory and foreign conquest increased, manubial monuments broke new ground in scale and complexity: a crucial moment was the erection of the theatre and portico of Pompey the Great on the Campus Martius. The erection of a permanent stone theatre was an affront to senatorial conservatism, but Pompey claimed that the theatre was merely an elaborate flight of steps leading up to a shrine to his protecting deity, Venus Victrix (Tertullian, *On Spectacles* 10; Aulus Gellius, *Attic Nights* 10. 1). Subsequently such monuments became the prerogative of the emperors: examples are as typologically diverse as the Colosseum and the Forum of Trajan (built from *manubiae* from the Jewish and Dacian wars respectively).

Rome's higher magistracies (consulship and praetorship) entailed not only military *imperium* (the right to command armies) but also regular campaigns in which it could be exercised. The consulship was thus the object of fierce competition (Chapter 2). Traditionally the Roman elite was able to limit competition within its ranks, sustained by its power-sharing, pluralist outlook. As the trials of the over-mighty Scipiones show, the power (and jealousy) of the collective could still, in the early second century BC, restrain the ambitious. Subsequently, however, it proved increasingly difficult to deflect the impetus, or match the new means, for increased competition for office by individuals. By the end of the century the Senate had to live with the extraordinary pre-eminence of a Scipio Aemilianus or a Marius.

By the end of the second century BC successful generals were likely to make provision after discharge for an increasingly proletarian army; often this meant grants of land. The Senate, opposed on principle to anything which might threaten the principle of (unequal) private property ownership, obstructed such proposals, as for example with Pompey's proposed settlement of the veterans of his eastern campaigns. Individual generals would, it was feared, become dangerously popular by pandering to their troops: and so they did. By the end of the Republic the loyalty of many soldiers lay with their commanders, not the commonwealth. The ambitions of the generals, and their perceived ability to take care of their troops where the commonwealth—or the Senate—could not or would not, led inexorably to the ending of the state's monopoly on legitimate violence, and in the late 50s BC the Senate was forced to ally with one of the two great military dynasts (Pompey) in order to have a chance of suppressing his less palatable rival, Caesar. Both men commanded what were in effect private client armies. Crassus' well-known remark that no one could be considered wealthy unless he could support an army from his annual income (Pliny the Elder, *Natural History* 33. 134; cf. Cicero, *On Duties* 1. 25; Plutarch, *Crassus* 2) made all too clear the cachet of military power, and the close ties which could subsist between general and army, when the former substituted his own resources for those of the commonwealth.

Sulla's soldiers (unlike the majority of his officers) had no scruples in following him against Rome (88 BC) in defence of his right to lead them to sack the historic cities of the Greek East. The careerist of the Civil War years was not unlikely to see himself as a 'soldier of Pompey' or a 'soldier of Caesar', rather than a soldier of the Roman people: 'would that the immortal gods had made me your soldier (*miles tuus*) rather than Pompey's', laments a captured officer to Caesar in Spain ([Caesar], *Spanish War* 17). All the same, opposing forces often saw themselves as the 'legitimate' Roman people under arms. When Caesar reminded his troops of their motivation before crossing the Rubicon in 49 BC, he recounted not only the affront offered to his own standing (*dignitas*), but also the arrogance of the clique of oligarchs who had corrupted Pompey and ridden roughshod over the freedom (*libertas*) of the Roman people, by expelling their tribunes (*Civil War* 1. 9). We believe Caesar's own account of his injuries at our peril; but this blend of motivations is picked up later by the veteran centurion Crastinus, who before leading the charge in battle tells Caesar, 'I shall do things for you today which will make you remember me; and at the same time we shall recover our *libertas*' (*Civil War* 3. 91). Nevertheless, the phenomenon of the client army created a deep-seated distrust of common soldiers. Cornelius Nepos (8. 2) wrote bitterly in his biography of Eumenes (Alexander the Great's secretary, and would-be dynast after his master's death, who was sold to his rival Antigonus the One-Eyed by his own men): 'that phalanx of Alexander the Great, very experienced in both glory and licence, demanded not to obey its leaders, but to give the orders, as our veterans do now [30s BC].' Civil wars were seen as not just power-struggles between leaders, but as the brutal self-indulgence of their men: leaders might be reconciled, but how would the cycle of rank-and-file greed be broken?

Imperial legitimation

The Latin for 'emperor' is *imperator*, originally the acclamation accorded a victorious commander by his troops. The leaders of the Civil War years (49–30 BC) depended on maintaining the loyalty of their subordinates and their soldiers in what could all too easily become a free market. The power of the emperors was, in the final analysis, no different; a situation ironically underscored by the remark of the rhetorician and philosopher Favorinus, yielding to Hadrian in an intellectual debate: who could gainsay the master of thirty legions? Conversely, when coups removed emperors, it was sometimes only the troops who regretted their demise (Suetonius, *Domitian* 23). It has even been argued that the size of the Augustan military establishment was aimed not so much at countering external threats as at deterring potentially dangerous rivals from among the ranks of provincial governors. Indeed, the relative infrequency of major wars fought beyond the frontiers after the Augustan conquests had doubled the size of the empire between 26 BC and AD 6 is very striking, given the scale of imperial military resources.

The relationship between emperor and army has already been lucidly discussed (Chapter 3). Here I will restrict myself to commenting on some aspects of the role of a credible military persona in legitimating imperial rule and the formation of dynasties. Augustus (who carried Alexander the Great's image on his seal ring: Suetonius, *Deified Augustus* 50; Pliny the Elder, *Natural History* 37. 10) sent his grandsons, his heirs-apparent, around the 'armies and provinces' (Suetonius, *Deified Augustus* 64. 1) even before they were old enough to hold commands; some of Gaius Caligula's initial popularity, and even his nickname ('little boot'), derived from his time spent as a boy on campaign with his father Germanicus, where he wore a miniature uniform (Suetonius, *Gaius* 9). Tiberius was, by a country mile, Rome's greatest living general when he came to the throne, a reputation won in wars of conquest and the suppression of serious revolts; this in no small measure contributed to his rehabilitation in AD 4 (after a period of self-imposed exile—or sulking) and subsequent accession. His rapport with the troops emerges clearly from Velleius Paterculus' eulogistic, but nonetheless plausible, account for AD 5. It is a remarkable testimony to the bonds which could exist between a prince of the imperial house and his men, built on the shared hardships of conflict:

Indeed the tears of joy drawn from the soldiers when they caught sight of him, their enthusiasm, their almost unprecedented elation at greeting him and their eagerness to touch his hand, their failure to restrain themselves from at once blurting out 'Is it you whom we see, general? Have we got you back safe and sound?'—and the shouts of 'I was with you in Armenia, general!', 'And I in Raetia!', 'I was decorated by you amongst the Vindelici!', 'And I in Pannonia', 'And I in Germany': all this cannot be expressed in words, and perhaps can hardly be believed.

(2. 104. 4)

Claudius, on the other hand, had only the reflected glory of his brother Germanicus (whose name he, like Gaius and Nero, included in his own titulature), and the support of the praetorian guard (Chapter 3), to sustain his transition from relative obscurity to the throne. The governor of Dalmatia did not win the support of his two legions for an abortive revolt in AD 42. Claudius rewarded them with the titles 'Claudian, Dutiful and Faithful'; but how long would mere titles like these justify blind loyalty to an unknown quantity with no military record, and enemies amongst the senatorial elite whence governors were drawn? Claudius needed good old-fashioned republican *gloria*. No ordinary cross-border raid would do: conquest was required. Britain was selected as the objective: it was exotic (lying at the edge of the world), and unbowed (even Julius Caesar managed only brief invasions). Like George W. Bush landing on the USS *Abraham Lincoln* to declare an end to major hostilities in Iraq, Claudius appeared from Gaul with a retinue, and even elephants, to take the victory salute in front of assembled Roman troops and British rulers at Camolodunum (Colchester).

As we have seen, the social status and relationship to the army of the emperors during the 'third-century crisis' (Chapter 3) were sometimes very different from those of earlier dynasties, especially in the case of those who excluded senators from major military commands. The increasingly thin veil which had concealed the military basis of the principate (what Tacitus had referred to as the *arcanum imperii*— 'the secret of empire, that emperors could be made elsewhere than at Rome: *Histories* 1. 4) was now ripped aside, and the power of an emperor was openly measured by how tightly, and for how long, he retained control of his troops; although at points in the third century one is left wondering who controlled whom. The standard male dress of the north-western provinces (breeches, long-sleeved tunics, and cloaks) had, by the Severan period, become the predominant military uniform in this part of the empire. Septimius Severus had advised his sons to pay attention to the soldiery above all; at the end of the civil wars in 197 he also extended the equestrian privilege of wearing a gold ring to soldiers (*Digest* 40. 10. 6, Herodian, 3. 8. 5). Thus, it should not come as a surprise to find emperors at this period adopting this military dress, followed by their courtiers, functionaries, and other elites across the empire. This intensification of relationships between emperor and army, and the worsening barbarian threat, itself inextricably linked to the internecine conflict between rivals for the purple, provoked a correspondingly greater presence of the emperor in the field than had been the case previously, despite the obvious risks. Taken prisoner while trying to negotiate his way out of a tight spot (AD 260), Valerian ended his days as the footstool of the Sassanid emperor Sapor I. Ancient writers also stress how movement of the emperor and armies from their regular positions could be an invitation to invasion (Ammianus Marcellinus 20. 8. 15f., 21. 4. 6, 31. 7. 4, 31. 10. 4–10; Zosimus 4. 24).

'Good emperors' often campaigned, and sometimes took the field in person. Conversely, it is notable how many 'bad emperors' did not, or did so only in the most inconsequential way: Gaius, Nero, Commodus, and Elagabulus. Nero attempted to hybridize Greek and Roman customs to celebrate his Greek athletic victories (AD 66–7), fusing the traditional honours paid to Olympic victors with a Roman triumphal procession. Like his grant of citizenship via military-style *diplomata* to dancers after a performance (Suetonius, *Nero* 12. 1), this was taken by aristocratic writers as emblematic of his failure to comprehend the seriousness of a *princeps'* responsibilities. Yet a different, and importantly *non-senatorial*, light can be shone on military reputations from the *Sibylline Oracles*, where we find judgments passed on emperors in part on the basis of whether their reigns saw either war against barbarians and peace at home (positive), or war within the empire (negative). Even Gaius, Nero, and Domitian do well on these criteria; it is the third century which presents the gloomiest picture (12. 551–3, 78–94, 127 f., 172 f.).

The imperial monopoly on legitimate violence

Even a martial *princeps* could not be everywhere at once. The majority of fighting in any reign was undertaken by the emperor's deputies. These were the legates of the *princeps* in his own provinces, and senatorial governors in the public provinces (most of the legions being, by design, in the former: Chapter 3). In special cases (like Egypt), and in smaller provinces, we find equestrian prefects with military forces at their disposal (such as, famously, Pontius Pilate in Judaea).

Success in war had always fuelled competition; under the empire, however, it could lead to fatal jealousies, even within the imperial house. Examples of cooperation, as in the cases of Augustus and Agrippa (Dio praised Augustus' equanimity: 56. 38. 2), or Marcus Aurelius and Lucius Verus, are rare. Tiberius was probably not jealous of his dashing adopted son Germanicus, but the first three books of Tacitus' *Annals* depend on just this assumption, and his audience was not meant to find it implausible. A successful senatorial commander might find that victories were ultimately rewarded with disgrace and death, as did Corbulo in the reign of Nero, or Stilicho under Honorius (early fifth century AD). Tacitus' account of Domitian's jealousy of Agricola (*Agricola* 39–42), and the latter's refusal to press for the proconsulship which was his due because of the emperor's resentment, is only the most famous account of such distrust: Septimius Severus appropriated his subordinates' glory (Dio 75. 2. 3 f.; cf. 77. 11. 5 on Caracalla).

Augustus appreciated as well as anyone the effect that military glory might have on the ambitious. Soon after Actium (29 BC) he was faced with the legitimate request of a loyal general, M. Licinius Crassus, to dedicate the 'rich spoils' (*spolia opima*) to Jupiter Feretrius on the Capitol, something permitted only to a Roman commander who had killed the enemy commander in single combat (in this case Deldo, king of the Bastarnae, a Balkan tribe). Tradition made Romulus the first to achieve this; only two men had emulated him, Cornelius Cossus (437 BC) and M. Claudius Marcellus (222 BC). Augustus' role at Actium had been, it was rumoured, unspectacular; Crassus now looked, probably without malice, to overshadow completely his leader. Augustus was unable to brook even friendly competition at this level; Crassus probably aimed at no more than restoring his family's *gloria*, left in tatters after his grandfather's defeat at Carrhae. Augustus refused the request (it is not clear that he was entitled to do so). He argued that only he, as commander-in-chief and thus holder of the auspices (Chapter 7), could make the dedication; a linen corslet dedicated by Cossus now came to light, which bore a handy inscription testifying to his rank. Crassus was allowed a triumph, and vanished into obscurity. The moral of the story was that the *princeps* needed to outshine all competition, and thus to monopolize military success. The right to triumph became restricted to the *princeps* and members of his immediate family: the last triumph by a man outside the imperial house was in 19 BC, significantly not for a scion of the Roman nobility but for L. Cornelius Balbus, a second-generation Roman from the Hispano-Punic city of Gades (Cadiz), who had defeated the Libyan Garamantes. It was Balbus whose name closed out the Triumphal Fasti (the record of triumphators) set up in the Forum Romanum on or near Augustus' own triumphal arch, filling the last available space; thereafter victorious generals had to be content with triumphal regalia (*ornamenta*) without the procession and celebrations.

Commanders and commands

A practical need for tried and tested commanders was often balanced by a temptation for emperors to appoint men without real military credentials, often loyal supporters or marriage connections. Quinctilius Varus, who in AD 9 lost the Seventeenth, Eighteenth, and Nineteenth legions in Germany, is a prime example of the latter (Chapter 10). Already in the late Republic, the ten seasons' campaigning (*decem stipendia*) which had previously been essential for candidates for magistracies was rarely served in full. By the early empire the military tribunate (below), at one time the preserve of men of five or more years' service, was being held, if at all, for a year at most, and ceased to be necessary for a senatorial career. Even an 'experienced' military man might boast no more than a year as a tribune 'of the broad stripe', and later a year commanding a legion, normally after the praetorship (*Inscriptiones Latinae Selectae* 1066, for a typical career). Rome produced no specialized 'military men' until the third century AD 'soldier emperors'—to speak of Roman commanders as 'generals' is thus somewhat misleading.

This tradition of gentleman amateurs had deep roots: under the Republic consular and proconsular commanders could prove disastrous. Postumius Albinus and Calpurnius Bestia, humiliated by the Numidian king Jugurtha (111–110 BC), were then savaged as arrogant armchair generals by the bluff careerist Marius, whose scars recorded his courage (Sallust, *Jugurthine War* 85. 16). Rome sometimes suffered 'mission creep', for example at the start of the Second and Third Macedonian Wars, and against Viriathus in Spain. In all these cases new commanders had to be appointed to regain the initiative, sometimes emerging from youthful obscurity to attain *gloria*, like Flamininus against Philip V or Scipio Aemilianus in the Third Punic War.

Competent or not, Republican commanders were not always able to prosecute campaigns unconstrained by political considerations. A consul's *imperium* was often prorogued (extended when his year of office expired); but the military situation which required his continued attention was also attractive to the serving consuls, who often sought to supersede their predecessors. Commanders anxious not to yield lucrative opportunities to potential successors often, like Flamininus, devoted much of their energy to political machinations, mobilizing both contacts and public opinion in Rome and, where possible, in the theatre of combat itself. Equally, jealous rivals worked to replace field commanders, sometimes irrespective of, or to the detriment of, the situation 'on the ground'.

Below the magistrates or pro-magistrates with *imperium* there was a range of junior officers. These too had reason to seek, and to expect to profit from, the opportunities which war brought. Most important were the commanders of the individual legions, the *tribuni militum* (tribunes of the soldiers). They were often equestrians, sometimes senators' sons; even ex-consuls are known to have served. From the second century BC we begin to find legates (*legati*) being appointed as pro-magistrates' delegates, especially in campaigns fought over large areas. Military tribunes were less useful, being too tied to their legions, and their importance now began to decline as that of the legates grew, in administrative as well as military roles. By the empire the legionary legate had become the legion's commanding officer. Of Caesar's *tribuni* and legates in the Gallic Wars, the former were senators and equestrians, the latter were senators alone. Some were senior figures, others were clearly inexperienced; their quality ranges from the dependable, through the unexpectedly capable (like Cicero's brother Quintus), to the irresolute, and those who, as Keppie puts it, were 'on the make' (1984: 98), with an eye to profit and socially advantageous contacts.

Who did the fighting?

The characteristics of the Roman militia

In antiquity fighting was done either by citizen-farmers during a short campaigning season (pay recompensed absence from their farms), or by mercenaries (as at Carthage or in the Hellenistic East). Rome took the former course: the peasant character of the Roman militia is reflected in archaic religious festivals marking the start and the end of the campaigning season. Yet Roman armies were unlike those of other city-states. We have already noted the fierce discipline to which citizen-soldiers were subjected while under arms. Military service was a duty owed to the community, but also a privilege: only those able to afford their own weapons (the *assidui*) were enrolled in the legions, and they were rewarded with political power in the *comitia centuriata*, according to the ranking of their property in the five-yearly census (Chapter 2). Those below a minimum property threshold were simply referred to as *capite censi* (those numbered in a head-count); they were effectively disenfranchised in the *comitia centuriata*, and could not serve in the legions. Military service and citizen status were thus intimately linked via the census, more so than in any other ancient state's timocratic system (Nicolet 1992).

Another peculiarity is the persistent extension of the Roman citizen body by the absorption of conquered peoples (Chapters 2, 3). This created an increasingly vast manpower reserve, which allowed Rome to absorb defeats that would have crippled other powers, and to undertake ever more distant campaigns, simultaneously in multiple theatres. This citizen resource was supplemented by Rome's unique taxation of her Italian allies (*socii*), using their manpower to augment hers, according to a specific formula. Failure to meet the demands of the levy was severely punished by an increase in the military quotas of defaulters (e.g. Livy 27. 9). The structural implications of this dependence are significant. It determined the perpetuation of Roman aggression, since (as with modern institutional budgets) failure to use up the available resources for one year might make it harder to exact the same manpower in the next. Rome's war machine underpinned her hegemony; but the retention of that same hegemony required the continuous running of the machine. And allies might learn from enforced campaigning with Romans: earlier experience of service with Rome allowed the rebel leader Viriathus to turn from gamekeeper to poacher in Spain; Arminius (Chapter 10) in early imperial Germany turned similar experience to deadly advantage.

Unlike Greek equivalents, the Roman citizen militia underwent a gradual quasi-professionalization under the pressure of changing circumstances, one which gathered speed with the Spanish campaigns of the second century BC (Gabba 1976: 23), and culminated in Augustus' reforms of 13 BC, which regularized pay and conditions and created a professional career structure. It was only at that point that the archaic city-state template on which Roman armies had been predicated for six centuries was definitively abandoned.

The legions: beginnings to the Hannibalic Wars (500–218 BC)

Throughout Roman history the army remained essentially a heavy infantry force, augmented at different times by varying proportions of cavalry and light-armed specialists. Originally the levy (*legio*) was organized in a single *classis*, with a distinction being made from the start between the younger fighting men (*iuniores*) and the older men who formed the reserves (the *seniores*). Later the *classis* was split into five, each class now representing a differing wealth-band in the census rating, distinguished by their armour and weapons: *classes* I–III were more heavily armed than *classes* IV and V, and only *classis* I was fully armed. There were also eighteen centuries of cavalry, with horses provided at the public expense. This differential structure certainly reflects growing complexity within Roman society; it may also signal a lowering (or creation) of the minimum census rating in order to tap new reserves of manpower.

Early weapons and tactics were those of Greek-style hoplite warfare. Over time two important changes occurred. One was the substitution of a *manipular* structure for the hoplite phalanx. Maniples were small units, 120-strong in Polybius' day, which formed up in three lines (the *hastati*, *principes*, and *triarii*) to constitute the legion. The second change concerned equipment: the *pilum* (a javelin for throwing) replaced the hoplite thrusting-spear (still used, however, in the late third century by the *triarii*: Polybius 2. 33), and the *gladius* or stabbing-sword (derived from an Iberian type) replaced shorter swords of the Halstatt II type. At the same time the long *scutum*, or Italic shield, ousted the round hoplite shield; it was better adapted to fighting in more open formations, and had superior resistance to slashing-swords. The central Italic 'button' or 'Montefortino' helmet (also sometimes called the 'jockey-cap') became the dominant type, although the older hoplite types might be retained as status symbols; so too the anatomically moulded cuirasses of the fifth and fourth centuries were generally replaced by leather tunics augmented by chest-protectors, and for soldiers in the first class chain-mail (Polybius 6. 23. 15; perhaps borrowed from Gallic armour). This willingness to borrow superior weaponry or armour from their enemies is part of a wider Roman cultural mentality.

These changes perhaps began as early as the fourth century (Livy 8. 8–10), and by the Hannibalic War the last pieces of the mid-Republican package, such as the Iberian *gladius*, were being adopted. Heavy infantry were now complemented by lightly armoured *uelites* (Polybius 6. 19 ff.; Livy 26. 4. 9; Valerius Maximus 2. 3. 3; Frontinus, *Stratagems* 4. 7. 29). They represented a last vestige of the archaic wealth-based distinctions in military role and weaponry, which had otherwise yielded to a system of more homogeneously armed units grouped by age. Now the cavalry too became more heavily armed (as represented on Aemilius Paullus' victory monument at Delphi), probably in order to combat Hannibal's cavalry.

The manipular legion, unlike the cumbersome hoplite phalanx, did not need to remain tightly knitted, but could operate in an open formation. Its front line was able to withdraw through gaps in the lines behind, and fresh troops could join the fray by the same route. The adoption of manipular tactics thus brought unprecedented agility; furthermore, the adoption of the *pilum* gave the Romans a 'first strike' technology which many opponents lacked. The superiority of the manipular legion over the phalanx was established by Flamininus' victory at Cynoscephale in 197 BC over the army of Philip V (Polybius 18. 18–32). Conversely, the Roman defeat at Cannae has been blamed in part on abandonment of manipular tactics on the day; yet these tactics had already been tried against Pyrrhus with mixed results (and even Cynoscephale was not a one-sided engagement). It seems that the manipular legion was not effectively exploited against Hannibal until Zama; and it may have been Roman *discipline*, not manipular tactics, which had provided the edge until that engagement.

The armies of conquest (218–108 BC)

The consular levy was still subdivided into four legions in the latter part of the third century BC. Thereafter the pressures of war with Carthage rapidly increased the numbers of legions raised each year. Casualties in the first three battles of the Hannibalic Wars were very heavy; in addition Rome conducted operations in Sicily and Spain, and supported the Aetolians in the First Macedonian War against Philip V. The years 214–203 BC saw twenty legions in the field annually; and even when the worst was clearly over, sixteen legions were still being levied. Six legions constituted the routine levy thereafter, although as many as ten might be raised: this meant, allies included, between 60,000 and 120,000 men under arms each year.

Most of the theatres in which these large numbers of Roman legionaries saw action in the Hannibalic War were outside Italy. Overseas warfare quickly became a defining feature of military service. Tours of up to six years became regular after the Hannibalic War, and others were longer. One of the legions sent to the Iberian peninsula in 196 BC was not relieved until 180; its replacement remained for another dozen years; this theatre, which also offered harsh combat conditions, quickly became unpopular (Appian, *Iberikē* 78. 334, on recruitment difficulties in 140 BC). Again, some of the men who mutinied in the East under Lucullus had left Italy in 85 BC to fight whichever of Sulla or Mithridates they encountered first; they then served with Lucullus, and finally enlisted with Pompey, probably returning to Italy with him in 62 BC. Extended foreign service was an essential condition of gaining and holding empire, and remained a structural feature of Roman warfare.

Marius and after (107–49 BC)

Marius (Chapter 2) has been credited with some of the most profound changes to the Roman army. Above all, attention focuses on three interrelated changes for which he has been made responsible: the 'professionalization' of the army; its 'proletarianization'; and its transformation into a 'client army'. His novel levy of 107 BC, which enabled him to raise a 'somewhat larger number' (Sallust, *Jugurthine War* 86. 4) of troops for his Numidian campaign than the Senate had decreed, is widely seen as crucial. Marius was later thought to have changed the composition of Roman armies, recruiting men whose loyalty generals could easily suborn with promises of land on discharge, and use to their own ends. Thus the armies which followed Sulla, Pompey, and Caesar, and overthrew the Republic, came to be.

Far from being responsible for a revolutionary abolition of the ancient timocratic basis of the Roman army, all Marius did was to ask for volunteers, irrespective of their census rating: as a result, *capite censi* as well as *assidui* presented themselves at the levy. Marius did not *abolish* anything, or *legislate* for reform; he simply acted unconventionally, and shocking as breach of *mos maiorum* (ancestral custom) was, it was also true that *capite censi* had been recruited in past crises. Poor soldiers were, as Sulla realised in 88 BC, likely to back a general unreservedly if they believed that he was devoted to their welfare. Marius, it is true, sought land on discharge for his veterans, through the radical tribune Saturninus, but not until 103 BC. Nor is there any evidence that he realized the implications of changing the sociology of the legions; if he did, he did not act on them, and displayed remarkable naivety in not foreseeing that others might. Those men who marched on Rome with Sulla found their rewards in the fleshpots of Asia in the winter of 85–84 BC, and in generous veteran settlement programmes after the Civil War, which dwarfed Saturninus' schemes. And in a sense the client army was not new: Scipio Aemilianus had taken some 3,000 of his provincial clients as volunteers to Numantia (Appian, *Iberikē* 84. 365).

Other factors suggest that Marius' levy needs to be seen in the context of longer-term socio-economic changes in Italy. The *capite censi* might have nothing to go back to after a campaign, and thus come to regard long-term service as their best bet economically; but the same could equally be said of poor *assidui*. For them the century since the Hannibalic War had been one of increased frequency and length of service. They probably regarded military service as a source of financial compensation for their inability to work on their farms—after all, military pay was traditionally introduced to offset soldiers' expenditure. Changing conditions had already built up a hard core of serially enlisted men during the Hannibalic Wars (Livy 28. 46. 1; Gabba 1976: 10–12); this in turn led to the beginnings of a distinct military ethos, which had become particularly strong by the first century BC, and is well illustrated by Caesar's quelling of a mutiny with the single word *Quirites*—'civilians' (Suetonius, *Deified Julius* 70). As well as developing their own outlook, the legions enjoyed greater standardization of equipment and tactics. But none of this made soldiering into a profession. Nor is it even clear how large a proportion of the total number of recruits the *capite censi* constituted in the century after Marius (some scholars have denied them any significant role).

The legions, indeed, continued almost obstinately to retain characteristics of a citizen militia long after professional attitudes had begun to make an impact. The legions were reconstituted each year as if they were new formations, often with new numbers, even when in winter quarters overseas, with new tribunes and centurions enrolled; the military oath (*sacramentum*) was taken again at the start of the year by all ranks (and again when new commanders were appointed). In the time of Cato the Elder only the soldier who had sworn the military oath (*sacramentum*), and not been discharged, had the right to fight the enemy (Cicero, *On Duties* 1. 37; Plutarch, *Roman Questions* 39; Livy 8. 34. 10). Legionary commanders were magistrates of the Roman people, whose year-long commands, when not prorogued, mirrored the annuality of civic institutions. The highest decoration available to soldiers was the oak-leaf *corona ciuica* (the citizen's crown), for saving the life of a fellow citizen (i.e. not a fellow soldier). And, as we have seen, freedmen, not full citizens and of suspect servile origins, did not normally fight except in emergencies, for example, in AD 6–9 (Suetonius, *Deified Augustus* 25. 2; it seems that they were not debarred by *law*). Freedmen, and even slaves, were employed in the fleet (Livy 22. 11. 8, 24. 11. 7; cf. Polybius 6. 19. 3 and Livy 42. 27. 3: 217 and 214 BC, revealingly, on the former occasion, with *capite censi*).

Finally, the property threshold for the *assiduus* class may have been progressively reduced over the course of the second century in order to widen the recruitment pool (classic statement: Gabba 1976: 1–69). On this theory (which depends on an ingenious, but by no means inevitable, reading of scrappy and heterogeneous evidence), *capite censi* were being drawn into the *assiduus* class for a century before Marius. What is certain is that C. Gracchus passed a law in 123/2 BC requiring the state to pay for soldiers' equipment and clothing. This points to the impoverishment of many *assidui* during the second century, although there had been occasional state subsidies for arms, armour, and even rations since the third century (Livy 22. 57. 11, and Gabba 1976: 5, n. 28, 20; Festus, p. 406L; Cicero, *In Defence of Rabirius on the Charge of Treason* 20). In 109 BC deductions from pay to cover equipment and clothing may have been reintroduced; they were still an object of resentment in the mutinies of AD 14 (Tacitus, *Annals* 1. 17. 6).

What of Marius' other reforms? He is sometimes credited with replacing the manipular legion with one organized around cohorts (larger units, typically of 480 men, divided into six centuries). The maniple is not certainly attested after the late second century (Sallust, *Jugurthine War* 49. 6); Marius, however, probably did not abolish it, nor did he introduce the cohort, which already existed (Cato the Elder, in *Oratorum Romanorum Fragmenta*[4], frag. 35). The post-Marian legion remained a three-line formation; the cohort was no less flexible than a manipular formation, but packed a bigger punch. Its gradual adoption entailed a full standardization of equipment throughout the legion.

The Cimbri and Teutoni (Chapters 1, 2) did not, as expected, enter Italy immediately after their crushing victory over a Roman army at Aix-en-Provence in 105 BC, but ravaged the Iberian peninsula instead. Marius profited from the reprieve to train his troops, and this training may have been predicated on greater use of the cohort, and perhaps the new prominence of the famous 'eagles' as standards. Incidentally, the 'eagle' implies a corporate existence for each legion which transcended their archaic annual life-cycle. A new *pilum*, more likely to break on impact and thus not suitable for reuse by the enemy, is probably also a Marian innovation (Plutarch, *Marius* 25).

Marius also pared down the presence of camp-followers, and made soldiers carry their own equipment. Marius' former patron Metellus Numidicus had been one of the few recent commanders to encourage such self-sufficiency, and Marius probably copied the idea from him; but ironically, the heavily laden legionaries who defeated the Cimbri and Teutoni became known as Marius' 'mules' (Festus, p. 135L; Frontinus, *Stratagems* 4. 1. 7). Earlier training regimes may also have influenced Marius: in the Second Punic War, Scipio Africanus had subjected his legions to cross-country marches in full kit, as well as weapons practice (Polybius 10. 20; Livy 26. 51). Appian (*Iberikē* 90) states that Scipio Aemilianus at Numantia made his men dig practice earthworks, and then fill in the ditches, flatten the ramparts, and start again. Marius' legacy in this area is clear too: Julius Caesar, whose aunt was Marius' wife, and whose politics were superficially similar, reputedly had his troops primed to follow him out of camp for a forced march at the drop of a helmet, especially in bad weather or on public holidays (Suetonius, *Deified Julius* 65).

Disciplina

Discipline was a crucial part of the idealized self-image of the Romans, on and off the battlefield. It was explicitly required of recruits: Livy purports to give the contents of the military oath from the time of the Hannibalic War (22. 38), in which soldiers promised that 'they would not depart because of rout or fear, and would not withdraw from their position in the line, unless it was to look for or pick up a weapon, or to strike the enemy or to save a citizen'. It is thus unsurprising to find 'improving' stories like that of Manlius Torquatus, who executed his son for disobeying orders to win an impromptu victory (Livy 8. 7; two types of *pietas* in tension here, and contrast 8. 30–5). In book 6, Polybius' interest in military discipline and punishments, from decimation downwards, is evident; it seems that his contemporary Cato had similar concerns in his *On Military Practice*. Nor is this simply ideology: in 167 BC, after the Third Macedonian War, Aemilius Paullus' own soldiers lobbied against his being granted a triumph, because his discipline was felt to be too harsh and booty too slender (Plutarch, *Aemilius Paullus* 31; Livy 45. 35–9).

And discipline was needed: the Roman military machine was not always the well-oiled killing-machine we tend to imagine! After defeats, or periods when focus had been lost, new commanders often introduced new training and revived discipline. Marius' contribution we have noted; Rutilius Rufus in Gaul in 105 BC is another example. Rutilius prescribed remedial killing tuition from gladiators (for connections between gladiatorial games/wild-beast hunts and military training: Cicero, *Tusculan Disputations* 2. 41; Suetonius, *Deified Claudius* 21; Pliny the Elder, *Natural History* 9. 14 f.; Pliny the Younger, *Panegyric* 33; Dio, 61. 9. 1; Ammianus Marcellinus 24. 5. 2; *Inscriptiones Latinae Selectae* 2091). Again, sent in after the defeat of consular armies in 72 BC, Crassus decimated some of the defeated units, raising and training new ones.

Why fight?

Repeated campaigning brought opportunities for enrichment and promotion. It might even bring personal acquaintance with the commander, and men who had distinguished themselves previously might be sought out to form the backbone of a new army. Commanders were also a valuable source of patronage: the speech put into the mouth of the centurion Spurius Ligistinus during sluggish recruiting for the Third Macedonian War in 171 BC is a case in point (Livy 42. 34. 5–11). The speech might be a Livian invention—its emphasis on exemplary bravery and duty would not be lost on an Augustan audience; but Ligustinus' record is not implausible. At over 50 years of age he had already served for twenty-two years. His recorded interactions with his commanders are arresting: he received thirty-four awards for bravery, including six *coronae ciuicae* (but note Cato, *Oratorum Romanorum*

Fragmenta[4], frag. 148 on 'inflation' in military decorations). He was repeatedly entrusted with positions of responsibility, and eventually became *primus pilus* (chief centurion). One of his commanders also led him back to march in a triumph. He had, at the least, been twice to Greece and twice to Spain.

Promotion, as in the case of Ligustinus, led eventually to the centurionate, prominent in every military narrative and well represented by military tombstones. Cicero claims centurions in his day had rural origins (perhaps meaning only that they came from Italian country towns: *Philippics* 10. 22). Competition for places as centurions on new expeditions was probably fiercer than that which Livy has Ligustinus address, and reputation was clearly important in getting a posting. Publius Considius had served with Sulla in the East and then against Spartacus, before joining Caesar in Gaul; Caesar found the man less impressive than his CV (*Gallic War* 1. 21 f.).

The spoils of empire also lay open to the allied contingents, as did the chance to attract the notice of the imperial power (as Jugurtha did at Numantia in the 130s). Thus, allies did not necessarily begrudge their service to Rome. Yet by the second century BC they were doing more of the fighting for less of the reward: in 170 allies marched in the triumph of C. Claudius in curmudgeonly silence to advertise their displeasure at a smaller share of booty than their Roman counterparts. A tendency to spare Roman blood if non-Roman troops could be used reappears in the imperial period: Tacitus could praise his father-in-law Julius Agricola for defeating the Caledonians at Mons Graupius using auxiliaries alone (*Agricola* 35). Italians in the second century BC were perceived as part of an undifferentiated master race in the Mediterranean, and referred to as 'Romans' by Greek-speakers; on active service they made contacts subsequently used in business (especially on Delos, centre of the Aegean slave trade), and accumulated cultural capital. Experiences such as this repeatedly emphasized their discrepant status in Italy, where increasing Roman exclusiveness manifested itself in unwillingness to share the citizenship and its benefits (Chapter 2).

The Social War and the end of the Republic

The Social War marked an important turning-point. With the extension of the citizenship to her allies, Rome's available manpower increased, and we now see more than a dozen legions in the field annually. The cost of these was of course borne by the Roman treasury; the wave of building in former allied communities in the last generation of the Republic may reflect the liberation of Italian cities' funds from payment for their own military contingents. The levy now became decentralized, carried out through recruiting officers each acting in a specific district of Italy (Gabba 1976: 24 f.). Soldiers, as before, came from predominantly rural backgrounds (Sallust, *Jugurthine War* 73. 6). They thus came from backgrounds where, in practice, distance from Rome made any exercise of political rights impossible. Increasingly divorced from the institutional fabric and political life of the commonwealth, soldiers were, paradoxically, driven to politicize their support for the military dynasts in their own (economic) interests, gaining a political importance which they would not otherwise have had (Appian, *Civil Wars* 2. 92–4; Dio 42. 52–5; Gabba 1976: 25, 28).

The effect of the enfranchisements was, however, a zero-sum game. The growth in the number of potential legionaries was offset by a drop in the number of available allied troops. This meant, in particular, the loss of the cavalry which allied elites had supplied; and this in turn was matched by the decline of the Roman cavalry. After the Social War, Roman equestrians probably no longer undertook cavalry service in a systematic way (last mention of Roman and allied cavalry: Sallust, *Jugurthine War* 95), until the Augustan reforms which saw them reappear as commanders of auxiliary cavalry units. Cavalry now had to be drawn from elsewhere: Caesar employed Germans and Iberians; a lack of cavalry was a major weakness in Crassus' army at Carrhae. As well as Numidian horsemen, other 'specialists', such as Balearic slingers and Cretan archers, now became staples of Roman recruitment. These were to be reorganized under Augustus; at that time a small cavalry force was added to each legion.

The Augustan reforms and the imperial army

Julius Caesar's close relationship with the legions which had swept him to power was clearly expressed by his doubling of army pay; it was also based on mutual respect. His heir, the young Octavian, was able to use his talismanic inheritance—the name Caesar—to attract many veterans to his cause in the months after the Ides of March, despite being a 19-year-old unknown. Yet the future survival of the empire depended on the ending of such unhealthily close relations. Exclusion of the legions from politics, into which they had marched with disastrous consequences, was vital, as well as a renewal of their loyalty to the Senate and People of Rome. Augustus was able to combine in his own person the roles of supreme commander, patron of the army, object of veneration and embodiment of the commonwealth. From the end of the Civil Wars he ceased to use the term 'fellow soldier' (*commilitio*), which evoked a familiarity incompatible both with military discipline and Augustus' own position (Suetonius, *Deified Augustus* 25. 1).

Ironically, discipline was restored by one of those responsible for undermining it: Suetonius (*Deified Augustus* 24) details the restoration of discipline for officers and men, including a range of traditionally humiliating punishments which would have pleased Cato and Polybius (cf. Dio, 51. 3. 1–5; 56. 13. 1 f. on Tiberius). More importantly, in 13 BC Augustus introduced new, normative conditions of pay and service, as well as fixing cash payments on discharge instead of politically unacceptable grants of land (Suetonius, *Deified Augustus* 49; Dio 55. 25. 6). Dio specifies the introduction of a sixteen-year term of service (53. 27, 54. 25. 5; cf. 55. 23. 1, 55. 23. 2–7, 24. 5–8); there were also to be four years as a reservist, with liability for recall in an emergency (a provision with Republican precedents: Polybius 6. 19. 2). New periods of service and sums for pay-off on discharge were agreed in AD 6; at this point Augustus introduced an inheritance tax (5 per cent) to fund these payments (*Achievements of the Deified Augustus* 17; Suetonius, *Deified Augustus* 49; Dio, 55. 24. 9). Three prefects of praetorian rank were instituted to manage the new military treasury, a further link between the commonwealth and the army.

Long service nevertheless remained a major complaint, as in Germany and Pannonia on the accession of Tiberius. What had changed were expectations consequent on demobilization. For their forebears like Spurius Ligustinus, the end of a campaign meant return to Italy, to settle down or await the next war. For imperial legions, release from service often meant settlement in the province where they had served, in veteran colonies. It is notable that few Italian legionaries returned to the peninsula.

Over 400,000 Italians enlisted during the two decades of the Civil Wars. Yet Italians were soon to become a minority in the legions. Caesar had, quite illegally, recruited non-Romans for his Gallic campaigns: his Fifth legion, the 'Larks', was recruited from Transalpine

Gaul (Suetonius, *Deified Julius* 24—Caesar had to pay for them himself, in the absence of senatorial recognition). From the time of the Civil Wars non-Italians were volunteering for the legions in significant numbers, attracted by regular pay and opportunities for advancement, and the troops of the Galatian king Deiotarus, who had been trained and equipped in the latest Roman style in the middle of the first century BC, were incorporated into a regular legion. Under the Flavians only half of all legionaries were Italian recruits, and by the Antonine period almost none; Trajan even forbade the levying of troops in Italy (*Historia Augusta: Marcus* 11. 7, perhaps making a virtue of necessity; Aelius Aristides, *To Rome* 26, 74, 86, noted the Roman habit of leaving newer subjects to do the fighting). By contrast, the praetorian guard, an elite force based in Rome for the protection of the emperors, recruited heavily in Italy (Dio 74/5. 2. 4). These old-fashioned, chain-mail clad troops were the soldiers whom Italian civilians would have been most likely to see in the early empire, except during civil wars.

As Keppie (1997) points out, contemporary writers saw the Vitellian army which marched into Italy from Germany as hairy and barbaric; note too the 'Syrian' religious habit of saluting the rising sun practised by the Third ('Gallic') legion (Tacitus, *Histories* 3. 24). These writers did not, however, seek an ethnic explanation for the Civil War itself, but preferred the moral one typical of Roman historical writing. Roman soldiers were wicked and indisciplined, but were still Roman soldiers. Indeed, the existence of auxiliary units, for whose soldiers citizenship on discharge was a fundamental attraction under the empire, acted as a touchstone for the essential Romanness of the legionary army, an ideological package and identity which persisted, at least as an aspiration, into late antiquity. In *Latin Panegyric* 24, for example, we find the 'savage Frank' contrasted with the disciplined Roman soldier (certainly a provincial, and probably of barbarian origin); and according to Zosimus (4. 30), Egyptian soldiers (but Roman citizens) serving beside barbarian levies under Theodosius attempted to prevent the latter from maltreating the cities they passed through, citing the barbarians' professed willingness to live according to Roman laws.

In one area Augustus' reforms had precisely the opposite effect to that which he had intended. So effectively were the legions depoliticized, and so distant was the professional army that he created from the idea of a citizen militia, that a dichotomy gradually grew up within

Roman society, between the army and everyone else. Paradoxically, this special status only encouraged more self-indulgence on the part of this cosseted special-interest group, who eventually ceased to care about the commonwealth and the fellow citizens from whom they had been so effectively divided.

The late imperial army

Under Septimius Severus some thirty-three legions were under arms, an increase of five from the Augustan total; of these, nineteen were survivors from the Augustan military establishment. Severan military discipline (or the lack of it) was savaged by Dio Cassius; his reputation as a disciplinarian gained while governor of Pannonia (80. 4. 2–5. 1) so incensed the praetorian guard against him that he had to spend part of his consulship of 229 outside Rome—indeed, their hostility nearly cost him his life (Dio 73. 8. 1–4, 11. 2–12. 1, 75. 12. 3–5, 78. 3. 4 f., 80. 2. 2 f., 4. 1 f.). Both the cost of paying these legions and supplementary purchases of soldiers' loyalties were seen as driving increases in taxation and confiscations of property (Dio 74. 2. 2 f., 74. 8. 4 f., 9. 4, 76. 16. 1–4—Severus; 77. 3. 1 f., 78. 36. 1–3—Caracalla).

The Severan army was still in many respects close in character and appearance to Augustus'. With the Tetrarchs we see very substantial changes to the Roman army, which rendered some aspects of its organization and deployment largely unrecognizable when compared to the Augustan template. As well as changes in military units and structures, Diocletian's reforms separated out military from civil roles in the wider Roman administration, increasing size and cost in both areas (Chapter 9).

The major reform, spread across the reigns of Diocletian and Constantine, was the division of the military into mobile field armies (*comitatenses*) and static frontier defence forces. The field armies served with the emperors, whence their name in the eastern empire of 'praesental': in the imperial presence. They included crack infantry troops (the *palatina*), and were supported by the heavy cavalry (*uexillationes*) and sometimes the *scholae* of the imperial guard. Commanded now by equestrian rather than senatorial officers, and based further inside the empire than the imperial legions had been, they could be moved around to where they were needed without unbalancing the frontier defences. They could also be more quickly deployed by the emperors against rivals than legions on the frontiers. Legionary fortresses on the frontiers now became smaller, reflecting the reduction in size of the forces they housed. These, from at least the late fourth century, were the *limitanei*, under their commander the *dux*; they are often blamed in the written sources for failure to resist barbarian incursions. By the late fourth century the gradual consequences of all these changes were beginning to be seen in increasingly permeable and unstable frontiers.

The major transformations of this period were not always appreciated by historians, who saw, with hindsight, that the reforms had not arrested Rome's military decline. For many the Roman army was over-reliant on barbarians (below), and was itself weak, effete, and unmanly, lacking in *disciplina* (above). Not recognizing, or not being willing to recognize, that the military response was only part of a wider imperial strategy, they blamed various emperors not simply for the loss of discipline, but for failing to win battles and for weakening the frontier (so *De Rebus Bellicis* 5, noting also the financial drain caused by army pay). The laying of blame is couched in colourful, and often predictable, rhetoric: the pagan Zosimus, for example, saw the rot setting in with the Christian Constantine. As a result of the reforms of the Tetrarchy, army pay was partly made up in supplies, including the *annona* (Chapter 6). As a consequence, troops were often billeted in towns, where this pay could be collected and distributed more easily. It was widely felt that the armies were not where they ought to be, and that urban living would undermine discipline, as well as exacerbating the already tense relations between soldier and civilian (MacMullan 1963).

Barbarian settlement, sanctioned or otherwise, was a fact of life in the empire, increasing in scale from the time of Marcus Aurelius onwards (Chapters 9 and 10). In the final analysis it was beyond the power of the state to contain the phenomenon by force or negotiation; and such settlements often ended up creating new stable populations. A pivotal moment came in AD 376. Pressure from nomadic Huns forced the Gothic Tervingi across the Danube; they were settled in the Balkans by the emperor Valens. The Goths were themselves an organized military force, as the defeat inflicted on the Roman field army at Adrianople two years later made painfully clear: this is where Ammianus Marcellinus' history ended, and it ranked as one of the great defeats of Roman history, beside those at the Allia, Cannae, and the slaughter of Varus' legions in the Teutoburgerwald (Chapters 2, 3, 10);

not even Valens' body survived. The defeat allowed the Goths free rein to roam and pillage, and fired the starting-gun for other incursions.

Barbarian newcomers also served in the Roman army. Some, known as *laeti* or *gentiles*, were allowed to settle within the empire on the specific condition that they undertook some military service. Germanic graves from Gaul suggest that this process was under way already before the end of the fourth century (Chapter 10). These troops are often referred to as 'federates' (although *foederati* seems strictly to mean barbarians recruited on an individual basis). By the end of our period they had become a major, and very expensive, feature of the Roman military establishment, found across the empire whether as ethnic units or as mercenaries: by the fifth century the Roman army had effectively been transformed into an army of barbarian mercenaries. In the civil wars of the 40s and 30s BC, non-Italians in the legions had stimulated anxieties: where would the loyalties of recruits from conquered peoples lie? By the fourth century AD anxieties had become nightmares: Roman armies were composed not of the conquered, but of invaders.

Literary sources like Vegetius are generally contemptuous of federates, who were seen as at best an unpleasant symptom of Roman military weakness; the *Notitia Dignitatium* ignores them completely. Instead, stress is laid on the army's Romanness (above). It was the Gallic army's consciousness of its Roman identity which prompted its distrust of the association of emperors with barbarian incomers: Zosimus (4. 35) on the army's dislike of Gratian consorting with the Alani is a case in point, and may have contributed to his overthrow in 383. Certainly, Maximus' coinage features legends advertising the restoration of the commonwealth (*res publica*), the army, and the combination of 'courage of the Romans' and 'the army' (Maximus: *Roman Imperial Coinage* 9. 2, nos. 1, 2a, 2b; 9. 49, no. 31, 32; 9. 28, no. 70, 75; 9. 29, no. 84a, b, c, d; similar issues by Theodosius: 9. 233, nos. 83a, b, c, d).

Yet it is hard to prove that barbarian mercenaries were less loyal than their Roman counterparts. Barbarians had the advantage that their deployment meant fielding armies without taking a tied peasantry away from the fields of increasingly powerful landowners. They were also plentiful, although almost certainly not as numerous as ancient writers imply; and many were clearly good fighters. Ammianus Marcellinus' narrative mentions barbarian officers in positions of trust; and some, like Stilicho, saved Rome, at least in the short term.

War and society: Rome and Italy

Rome's militaristic culture fuelled a constant fighting, but war shaped society in other ways. It has, for example, been argued that the strict discipline expected in war rubbed off in domestic politics, where the Roman people showed a remarkable willingness to be led by a relatively closed hereditary aristocracy for several centuries, without asserting its sovereignty to any notable extent (Chapter 2). War and religion were intimately linked too: war could not be declared nor battle joined without a magistrate holding *imperium* seeking to know the will of the gods through taking the auspices, and favourable omens being reported after sacrifice (Chapter 7). Wars also had to be just to meet with the approval of the community's gods: in other words, for self-protection or reparations.

The high percentage of Roman youth regularly under arms (Chapter 2) had serious effects on politics and on agriculture. For the predominantly agrarian population of Italy, the balance between labour needs and hours available was already delicate enough in the fragile Mediterranean environment without persistent exogenous demands for manpower. There were not a few reluctant recruits, especially for what promised to be hard campaigns, such as those in Spain in the second century BC. The effects of recruitment on the *assidui* have been much discussed. A generation ago scholars accepted a picture of a free peasantry declining after the devastating Hannibalic invasions and in the face of large-scale capitalist, slave-run agriculture; this situation, exacerbated by aggressive conscription, resulted in the Gracchan 'agrarian crisis' (Chapter 2). Today we tend to play down 'Hannibal's legacy' and the crisis of peasant farming, and even the effects of conscription. The evidence, literary and archaeological, admits of no clear interpretation: *perceived* decline in the total number of *assidui* in the mid-second century was perhaps sufficient to generate a mood of crisis; it is also true that the acquisition of empire was directly responsible for the enrichment of many landowners, and for a large rise in the number of slaves in Italy (Hopkins 1978). Tiberius Gracchus was undoubtedly concerned about the impact of slaves on the numbers of *assidui*.

Romans and Italians had fought together in Rome's great wars of conquest. The implications of this interaction for the Hellenization of the peninsula were profound, as they were for the spread of Latin. In this context the Social War was profoundly shocking, fought between men who, like their fathers and grandfathers, had been levied together, and had marched and bled side by side; it was (as Appian saw) effectively a civil war, and in terms of willingness to fight former friends, and of general brutalization, it anticipated the Civil Wars proper. Veteran colonization in Italy after the Social War contributed to the final eradication of regional cultural distinctiveness in Italy, as groups of ex-soldiers moved into, and disrupted, existing social structures. As well as 'horizontal' geographical mobility, the army was also a vehicle for 'vertical' social mobility. Caesar's Gallic wealth is well known; as revealing is his ability to borrow from his centurions and tribunes on the eve of the Civil War, with the former offering to pay for a cavalryman each. Former centurions often appear as local magistrates in Italian townships, as do aides-de-camp (*praefecti fabrum*). For the more ambitious or better connected, routes on into the Senate and the consulship might offer (as for Pompey's supporter Lucius Afranius, who combined skill on the battlefield with grace on the dancefloor).

The impact of war: the empire

The political fallout from the confiscations made veteran settlement, whether in individual plots or in colonies, politically impossible in Italy with the return of orderly government. Yet there was ample room for colonization in the provinces, an opportunity taken up on a large scale by Caesar and Augustus. Such settlement was sometimes controversial: the colony at Camolodunum, and especially its cult of the Deified Claudius, the 'citadel of repression', was a factor in pushing the Iceni to rebel in Britain in AD 60, according to Tacitus (*Annals* 14. 30). The veteran colonies certainly had a primary function in underpinning Roman power in the provinces. They were definitely not *intended* to spread Roman culture to the 'benighted natives' (Chapter 8); yet they necessarily represented intense concentrations of spoken and written Latin, Graeco-Roman architecture, Roman political practices, law, diet, and sexuality. These colonial social dispositions did present an attractive package (associated with the power of Rome and the emperors) to some natives, above all elites, who adopted and adapted elements as and where they could. Colonization did lead to socio-cultural change, but the evidence for this becomes weaker the further one moves from the colonies and military bases.

Let us take the example of diet. Analysis of discarded butchered animal bones shows clearly that the traditional pork-rich diet of west-central Italy was deliberately replicated in some Augustan legionary camps, for example those in Germany, which probably had Italian garrisons. Yet even military meat-consumption did not consistently follow the Roman model: from Britain to Switzerland we find a pre-dominantly *beef*-based diet, with variations by region (more mutton in Britain) and status (legionaries ate more pork than auxiliaries). The legions did not, then, effect a Romanization of diet: interestingly, the predominant beef-based diet just described was probably imported to (parts of) Britain by troops redeployed from the German provinces. It must reflect the dietary preferences of the legionaries recruited there, and demonstrates the *globalizing* nature of Roman culture: being Roman meant doing things which were perceived to belong to a wider 'Roman' cultural sphere, but which might not actually replicate Roman practice as found in Italy.

Discharged and enfranchised auxiliaries were similarly influential. It was probably Claudius who regularized grants of citizenship on discharge for them, and gave them the privileges accorded to husbands in Augustan social legislation, in order to compensate for their being unable to marry (Suetonius, *Deified Claudius* 25. 1; Dio 60. 24. 3). Their role in the spread of Latin was important: the military has throughout history been important in spreading the dominant language of the state into heteroglot areas, as Dr Johnson noted in Gaelic-speaking Scotland. In the Roman Empire this is particularly well exemplified by archaeological evidence from the territory of the Batavians in the Rhineland. They provided large numbers of auxiliaries, whom we know from the Vindolanda tablets to have used Latin with considerable facility in all areas of military life (Bowman 2003).

Interactions between soldiers and civilians were conditioned by the fundamental separation between the two groups which we have already noted. This is well illustrated by an inscription from the mining community at Vipasca in Portugal (*Corpus Inscriptionum Latinarum* 2. 5181); it preserves the terms on which a bath-building is to be leased out. It concludes with the entry fees to be charged: women pay twice as much as men; the emperor's freedmen and the staff of the imperial procurator running the mine are to have free access; so too minors and soldiers. The last two are significant: just like children who are below the age of majority, soldiers are not treated as members of the *community*. Even veterans occupied an ambiguous status: various imperial edicts exempted them from civic duties, but not honours, in communities in which they settled.

Nevertheless, soldiers could not do without the communities around them, not least for obtaining food and other consumer products: indeed, Hopkins (1980) argued that the taxation which in large part supported the military establishment was a stimulus to economic development in the provinces. There were other types of interaction too. Relations between soldiers and (non-Roman) local women were common, but were officially frowned upon. It was not until the reign of Hadrian that what were effectively family units were treated as such in the eyes of the law, in matters such as inheritance. After AD 139 emperors ceased to grant citizenship retrospectively to soldiers' offspring from their years of service—for these too military service was now required, and it was not until Septimius Severus (significantly) that soldiers' unions were regarded as legal marriages.

Relations between soldier and civilian could also be brutal. Random acts of overweening violence at the hands of troops on the move feature in Apuleius' *Golden Ass*, and we may note the petition found at Vindolanda (probably from a trader from another province, not one of 'Brittunculi'—'wretched Britons'—mentioned in another tablet), complaining at rough treatment from soldiers (Bowman 2003: no. 43):

he punished (?) me all the more until I should declare my goods to be worthless or pour them down the drain. As befits an honest man I implore your majesty [here a senior official, not the emperor] not to allow me, an innocent man, to have been beaten with rods, and, my lord Proclus, I was unable to complain to the prefect because he was detained by ill-health and I have complained in vain to the *beneficiarius* [military aide] and the (?) rest of the centurions of (?) his unit, I accordingly implore your mercifulness not to allow me, a man from overseas and an innocent one ... to have been bloodied by rods as if I had in some way committed crimes.

A range of other texts stresses the perennial friction generated by military requisitions in the provinces, and by billeting soldiers on civilians.

In the world of Asterix and Obelix, violence is spectacular but sanitized: no one is killed, and the injured recover (just in time to be beaten up again!). The reality of Roman warfare was altogether bleaker. The Roman army knew a thing or two about what Donald Rumsfeld called 'Shock and Awe'. Its discipline whilst inflicting damage is perhaps most strikingly seen in the employment of systematic ritualized brutality, on the battlefield and in the terrorizing of hostile, or potentially hostile, populations. Polybius famously noted how the Romans, when they sacked cities, even cut the dogs in half (10. 15. 4 f., a passage which may overplay the discipline of a Roman sack). During Caesar's campaigns in Gaul the male inhabitants of Uxellodunum, treated as 'enemy combatants', had their hands cut off; the vision of the vanquished in the Roman world was often gruesome and brief. Nor were these tactics reserved for Rome's enemies. Pompeian troops fired some 30,000 arrows into Caesar's camp at Dyrrhacium in 48 BC (Caesar's men counted them after the engagement); and Florus (2. 13. 50) records Caesar's chilling instructions to his troops before Pharsalus in the same year: 'faciem feri' — 'strike to the face' (tellingly coupled with an injunction to spare fellow citizens!).

Recent work on the Roman Empire has stressed how cultural change happened by 'negotiation', with the complicity of local elites, rather than against their will or beyond their comprehension. This has proven a useful approach, but it runs the risk of sanitizing what were often violent encounters, and were followed by dynamics of clear inequality between Roman and non-Roman. Our own politically correct preoccupations must not blind us to the fact that the Romans had no Citizens' Charter, no Human Rights Act: in short, almost no reason to fear the consequences of brutality—and many reasons to feel satisfied with them. It is curious that a recent (and stimulating) essay on Romanization in Britain devotes less than a page to the role of violence in cultural change. Negotiation is hard with a sword at one's jugular, or from any other position of inferiority: Prasutagus tried it, leaving half of his kingdom to Nero and half to his wife Boudicca; much good it did her. Dr Johnson's judgement on Cromwell has the measure of the Romans too (however much we may baulk at the criterion of *utility*): 'he introduced by useful violence the arts of peace.'

6

Economy and trade

Andrew Wilson

Introduction

IN 200 BC there were no towns in Europe, except in Italy and Greece, further than thirty miles from the Mediterranean coast. Nearly all of the population of north-west Europe away from the Mediterranean lived in scattered homesteads, small villages, or hillforts, and was involved in agriculture or tending livestock, the products of which were consumed locally. There were skilled specialist metalworkers and carpenters, some of whose products were traded on a regional scale; but while there was trading contact between temperate Europe and the Mediterranean, it was not intensive and the imports were available primarily to the tribal elites (Chapter 1). Coins, if used at all, were portable units of gold and silver wealth, not money for ordinary purchases. Three hundred years later, by AD 100, towns and urban lifestyles had spread extensively throughout north-west Europe, as far north as York in Britain. Increased specialization of labour boosted craft production, and even farmers on small rural sites used pottery, drank wine, and cooked with olive oil from different provinces hundreds of miles away. Coinage was used for everyday transactions, even on rural sites. By AD 500, however, north of the Alps there was, once again, only a handful of towns worthy of the name, and those were shadows of their former selves. Few new buildings were constructed in stone, and exchange networks had shrunk, often to no more than a day's walking distance (Chapter 9). Money, in the sense of coins used for everyday purchases, had largely disappeared.

Things were different in Mediterranean Europe, especially Greece and Italy, where urbanism, intensive long-distance trade, and coinage began earlier, and never disappeared. But the parabolic trajectory for northern Europe is striking, and illustrates how cultural and economic change are intertwined. Economic growth can transform society—but so, drastically, does economic decline.

Agricultural production is fundamental to any pre-industrial society. Its efficiency is critical to the first stages of economic growth. The size of the agricultural surplus determines the proportion of the population which can be engaged in sectors other than food production, and thus constrains the level of urban development and of craft specialization that can be achieved. Arguably, in the Roman period, this agricultural surplus enabled a far greater degree of urbanization than had ever been achieved in Europe before, or was to be again until the later Middle Ages. This in turn facilitated the expansion of craft industries and the formation of larger urban markets, while political unity, hithero unprecedented techniques of metal extraction, and extensive monetization contributed to a huge expansion in the trade both of foodstuffs and of manufactured goods.

Yet the picture was not uniform across the Roman world, or even across Roman Europe. The range of variation in climate, landscape, and environment from Mediterranean Spain to northern Britain, from the Atlantic coast of Gaul to the Balkans and the Danube, ensured agricultural diversity, and provided distinctly different circumstances of economic potential. Nor was the picture uniform over time. If there is now mounting evidence to argue for both overall and per-capita economic growth, especially during the period 100 BC to AD 200, there are also distinct signs of economic contraction during the third century, and while the fourth century saw a certain recovery, in the fifth century exchange systems in parts of north-west Europe virtually collapsed (Chapter 9).

The study of the ancient economy has been one of the most fiercely debated topics in ancient history, giving rise to divergent views that range from seeing the Roman economy as underdeveloped, with little role for long-distance trade, to seeing it as an early capitalist economy. In the last twenty years the debate has been transformed by the assimilation of vast amounts of archaeological data, shedding light on trade, settlement patterns, production, and consumption. There is no space here to discuss these debates: although there is now greater convergence of scholarly opinion, much remains controversial, and this chapter represents a personal view. Equally, it is impossible to give here a comprehensive history of the economic development of Europe in the Roman period; what is attempted instead is a thematic sketch highlighting some of the main structuring features.

Production

Agrarian production

Northern Europe in the later Iron Age had a mixed economy based primarily on grain, sheep, and cattle. Many communities operated fairly near subsistence, but moderately substantial surpluses of grain and wool were produced in some areas, such as Wessex. A greater diversity of landholding patterns becomes evident in the Roman period than existed either beforehand during the Iron Age or afterwards under the feudal system which emerged after antiquity. At the lower end of the Roman scale the peasant smallholder, eking out a living on a small plot, remains a shadowy figure in the literary sources, and just as much so in the archaeological record. Many inhabitants of villages and small towns will have cultivated small plots in their immediate vicinity. Isolated farmsteads abounded in the Roman landscapes of Italy, Gaul, Spain, and Britain, some owned by their occupants, and others leased as part of larger estates. At the upper end of the scale were the villas, the main engines of agricultural production both in the western Mediterranean and in northern Europe. A villa was an estate centre which tended to combine the amenities of elite urban housing (mosaics, wall-painting, baths) with facilities for crop-processing and storage. Villa estates produced a range of crops and other goods, and may have been self-sufficient in some respects, but always aimed at producing a marketable surplus in one or more crops. They coexisted with tenant farms on the estates, and the villa often provided the central crop-processing facilities for produce of tenant farmers, rendered in kind as rent.

The crops, of course, differed across Roman Europe: the northward limit for olive cultivation runs south of the Alps, and olive-growing was largely confined to southern Spain, southern Gaul, Italy, the Dalmatian coast, and the southern Balkans. Viticulture was, again, most heavily concentrated in the same regions, but it did spread northwards, and here the Romans wrought profound and lasting changes on the diet and palate of north-west Europe that were to outlast the fall of Rome. They introduced the cultivation of the grape, and the making of wine, into Gaul and Germany, and even into Britain: Roman vineyards have been found in Northamptonshire, attested by vine trenches and palynological evidence.

The Roman period saw a spread of cultivars northward through Europe, carried by the army, merchants, and settlers. Their impact is perhaps clearest in Britain, where previously the Channel had acted as a barrier to the natural spread of crops. Here, among the species thought to have been introduced in the Roman period, were vegetables including lettuce, endive, beets, broad beans, parsnips, radishes, turnips, cultivated varieties of cabbage, and an improved variety of carrot. Among the new fruits, in addition to grapes, were new types of cultivated apples, cherries, pears, and plums; and varieties of nut, including the walnut and sweet chestnut. The effect was greatly to increase the range of diet and the variety in cuisine.

Large swathes of the flatter and rolling landscapes of the Northern European Plain are excellent cereal land. It is no accident that all the literary and iconographic evidence for the reaping machine (*vallus*) relates to Gaul. This was a box on wheels harnessed in front of an animal, with protruding blades that cut the stalks of grain so that the ears fell into the box; it would have been suited only to the large flat fields of central and northern Gaul, and not to the hilly uplands and more broken terrain of Mediterranean Europe. Cereal crops provide a steady and relatively low-risk income (compared to olives or vines), although at an unspectacular rate of return. Incomes could, however, be increased by turning part of the cereal production into beer, which commanded higher prices—an increasingly favoured strategy for villas in southern Britain in the second to fourth centuries AD. At villas in Hampshire T-shaped corn-drying ovens often occur in pairs, or with double flues, one for the normal drying of corn before threshing and milling, the other often containing partially sprouted ears of corn, indicating that the malting process had begun, as a preliminary to beer production.

In Italy, the rearing of sheep and goats was the predominant form of stock-rearing, often in transhumant modes in which flocks were moved from lowland winter to upland summer pastures. But with the rise of the villa system, geared towards intensive production to supply urban markets, pork production increased, with pigs reared in sties. At the villa of Settefinestre in Italy a new pigsty was added in the early second century AD. Further north, although the Roman period saw an increase in pork consumption (and therefore, presumably, pig-rearing), cattle predominate, notably in Britain, Gaul, and Germany (King 1999; Chapter 5). This suggests a less agriculturally intensive mode of production in northern Europe, where more land was given over to cattle pasture. The importance of cattle-rearing in the northern provinces is supported by the traces of paddock systems at villas such as Frocester in Gloucestershire. Faunal assemblages also show that cattle on Roman or 'Romanized' (see Chapter 8) sites in Germany were of a consistently larger average size than those on native sites; and that following the end of the Roman occupation such large cattle are no longer found on sites north of the Alps. Either the necessary stock-raising knowledge to breed larger animals was lost in the confusion of the barbarian invasions, or the investment necessary to produce such large animals was no longer worthwhile once the urban and military markets had disappeared (Greene 1986: 77–9).

The intensive modes of production associated with the villa system entailed considerable capital investment, not only in buildings, barns, and processing equipment such as oil- and wine-presses, or corn driers, but also in the landscape. In the Mediterranean regions, the drier climate and thin soils usually meant that irrigation was necessary for orchards and vineyards. The wetter climate and heavier soils of northern Europe had less need of such artificial solutions. Sometimes these schemes were of enormous size: an inscribed bronze tablet from the Ebro valley in Spain refers to the resolution of a dispute between two communities over an irrigation system in the first century BC. A recently discovered inscription, from the same valley, is part of a Hadrianic law regulating the use of a channel irrigation system taking water from the river and supplying users in at least three different districts (*pagi*). The law sets out users' obligations and provides for an annually appointed council to resolve disputes; this clearly anticipates the better-known irrigation systems of medieval Islamic Spain in its physical complexity and need for legislation. Numerous villas in Spain and Italy had their own, localized irrigation systems—often small-scale aqueducts supplying large cisterns that could be used to regulate water delivery to orchards, vineyards, or fields. This is especially clear in the areas of Latium and South Etruria around Rome, where the astonishing level of investment in hydraulic infrastructure in the rural landscape is probably a result of intensive horticulture for the massive urban market of Rome.

In the fourth century BC a programme of draining large areas of the tufa landscape of South Etruria was initiated by diverting streams underground in *cuniculi* (tunnels). The development of artificially altered agricultural landscapes intensified in central Italy in the late Republic with the emergence of the villa system, with programmes of land-clearance, deforestation, and agricultural drainage. Occasional spectacular feats of engineering were attempted under the empire, such as the drainage of the central Italian Fucine lake under Claudius, partly financed by a group of investors who wanted the reclaimed land. In northern Europe the major landscape transformations effected in the Roman period more often took the form of land-reclamation projects, as in the drainage schemes of the Wentlooge Levels in Gloucestershire, and the East Anglian Fenland, partly drained and reclaimed, perhaps as an imperial estate, by means of the Car Dyke drainage scheme.

Despite some claims to the contrary, there was no lack of technological innovation in the Roman period, in agriculture or in other fields. Besides the invention of the Gallic reaping machine (above), the improvement and spread of existing devices all had a cumulative impact on the efficiency of production—innovations in milling devices, oil- and wine-presses, ploughs. The introduction in the Roman period of new agricultural tools, such as the two-handled scythe and new forms of sickles and rakes, all improved labour efficiency. The water-mill, invented in the third century BC, had become widespread across the Roman world by the first century AD (Wilson 2002). For northern Europe, but also for the Mediterranean, the spread of new kinds of water-lifting devices (water-lifting wheels, bucket-chains, and pumps) enabled localized watering of crops from wells with minimal capital outlay. During the first or second century AD the Hellenistic bronze force-pump was re-engineered so that it could be produced cheaply from a single block of wood, and has been found on a number of rural sites and villas in Italy, Gaul, Germany, and Britain.

Mining

The bulk of the Roman world's natural sources of precious metals lay in Europe, rather than Asia Minor or North Africa. The Roman Empire saw massive development of mining activity and metal extraction, especially in Spain and the Balkans. One of the first activities in newly acquired territories appears to have been the almost system-atic exploitation of metal resources, especially of the bullion metals (copper, silver, and gold). In southern Spain, the Carthaginians had worked copper-, silver-, and gold-mines on a large scale in the second century BC, apparently using Archimedes' screws to tackle the problems of drainage below the water table. But the Roman conquest of Spain saw an increase in the scale of extraction, with mines leased to investing companies. The use of hydraulic extraction processes in gold-mining in alluvial deposits, using artificial water channels to erode the overburden and to sort free gold particles from the alluvium by a continuous play of water (ground-sluicing), seems to have been pioneered in northern Italy. In 143/140 BC the Salassi, a tribe of the southern Alps, sparked off a dispute with their neighbours in the plain below by diverting a river for use in gold-mining, as a result of which Rome intervened and brought the area under her control (Livy, *Periochae* 53; Strabo 4. 6. 7, 205–6C). The mines in question are probably those at Bessa, where extensive remains of channels and clearance dumps are associated with set-tlements of the second and first centuries BC. Their operation was leased to *publicani* (companies of wealthy equestrian contractors; see Chapter 2); an indication of their scale is given by legislation lim-iting the size of the workforce there to 5,000, motivated by fears of excessive concentrations of slaves in one place (Pliny, *Natural History* 33. 78).

Under Augustus, the conquest of north-west Spain in 26–19 BC was immediately followed by the massive development of hitherto unexploited alluvial gold deposits using techniques imported from northern Italy, on a truly industrial scale. Virtually every stage of the extraction process was mechanized, harnessing the erosive power of water to play on alluvial deposits and attack the geology of the mining areas. Neither the technology used nor the scale of extraction was equalled again until the nineteenth century. The loc-al population was compelled to work the mines and provide the labour to build the necessary infrastructure, apparently under military supervision. Long-distance aqueducts supplied water to reservoirs from which it could be released suddenly to scour away the overburden by hushing, and separate the gold from the alluvium by ground-sluicing. Vast areas were worked out by such means, and the fan-shaped systems of channels survive where prospection by hydraulic methods was undertaken but found unproductive. At the huge gold-mines of Las Medulas (León), whole hillsides were collapsed by riddling them with tunnels that were then flooded; the collapsed mass was then hydraulically eroded and worked. Pliny's description of long, huge aqueducts feeding mine workings in Spain was probably based on observation of this site (*Natural History* 33. 70–8). In Britain, the one significant gold source, at Dolaucothi in South Wales, was exploited under military control from the Flavian period until the early second century, after which it appears to have been turned over to private, civilian exploitation (Wilson 2002).

By contrast, the other major gold sources in Roman Europe—mostly concentrated in the Balkans (Dalmatia and Upper Moesia) and, after Trajan's conquest of Dacia, north of the Danube—were hard-rock mines which could not be exploited by hydraulic means. These, and the other copper- and silver-mines of southern and central Spain, had to be worked by tunnelling. Their operation tended to be contracted out, and the *lex Vipasca*, setting out legislation for the running of the copper- and silver-mines at Aljustrel in Lusitania, indicates that concessionaires had to yield to the state half of the ore extracted from their shafts.

The activity of these mines formed one of the constraints on the empire's money supply. The conquest of southern and central Spain in the second century BC made unprecedented quantities of copper, silver, and gold available to Rome, and facilitated the spread of coinage and monetization within the empire. This process was accelerated under Augustus with the hydraulic exploitation of the Asturian mines, and Trajan's Dacian wars added important new sources of silver and gold. Traces of atmospheric pollution found in Greenland ice cores show that copper- and lead-smelting (the latter a proxy for silver extraction, as the two metals frequently occur together) peaked during the first century BC and the first and second centuries AD, in concentrations not to be equalled again until the tenth to twelfth centuries in the case of copper (mainly produced by Sung Dynasty China) and the nineteenth century in the case of lead. But for reasons still unknown (the Antonine plague? Moorish invasions? withdrawal of military forces in the civil wars of AD 192?—but *not* exhaustion of the mineral resource), the major Spanish mines ceased working on a massive scale in the 180s and 190s. The empire's resources shrank still further with the loss of Dacia in 265; these events cannot have failed to have had an impact on the money supply, an issue to which we shall return (Wilson 2002).

Artisanal production and crafts

Roman artefacts from archaeological sites tend greatly to outnumber those from the preceding or following periods. In the most basic way, this reflects a much higher level of artisanal production compared with the late Iron Age or the early Middle Ages. Most craftsmen operated on a relatively modest scale; many were free (or freedmen: Chapter 4), but linked by ties of patronage to richer citizens. The elites are rarely to be found directly involved in any production not directly related to landowning (as were agriculture, or brick-making using clay beds on their estates), which alone was considered respectable. Elite ideology frowned on involvement in commerce or trade as ignoble, and legislation passed in the late third century BC limited the size of ships that members of the senatorial order could own. Archaeological evidence indicates, however, that in practice elites may have derived substantial revenue either from the renting out of workshops, or from the profits of production facilities, which they owned, and which were operated through agents.

Production units were typically small, but there were exceptions. At Pompeii and elsewhere workshops frequently occupy rooms in the street frontages of elite houses, along with retail shops. In the Mediterranean cities bakeries, a ubiquitous feature of the urban scene, are often found in such locations. Typically they have between one and four animal-driven mills and a large oven; larger operations, with up to ten animal-driven mills and dough-mixing machines, are known archaeologically from Ostia and Rome. Evidence for bakeries is rarer in northern Gaul and Britain; might this suggest a higher frequency of home baking and less reliance on shop-bought bread in these regions?

Mass-production, however, is clearly apparent in the manufacture of pottery and glassware. Already in the Republic fine black-glossed tablewares had been produced in vast quantities in Campania in Italy, and widely exported and imitated in local productions. Around 40 BC red-gloss fine pottery began to be produced using techniques imported from Asia Minor, initially at Arretium (Arezzo), and then at a series of other Italian sites. This Arretine ware, or Italian Terra Sigillata (ITS), quickly replaced the black gloss wares, and was exported throughout north-west Europe, the Mediterranean, and even reached India. Around 10 BC migrant potters set up facilities making similar wares in Gaul, first at Lyon and then at La Graufesenque (SW Gaul), to supply the markets of Gaul, northern Spain, and Britain; subsequently, further centres were established at Lezoux, in the Rhineland for the supply of the legions on the German frontier, and in Spain.

Stamps on the pots give names of potters or workshop managers, and current thinking supposes that these reflect a system in which landowners would lease production facilities, including workshops, claypits, and perhaps woodland for fuel, to potters (such contracts are known from Egypt). The size of some workshops, with numerous work-places for potters in a row (eleven at Le Rozier near La Graufesenque; twenty-seven at Scoppieto in the upper Tiber valley) suggests that physically these were organized as small manufactories. If, however, the potters leased the facilities, they must have operated as a source of rental revenue for the landowners.

The Roman textile industry seems to have been highly articulated. At Pompeii specialist workshops existed for degreasing and scouring wool, for dyeing it, and for fulling cloth. Spinning and weaving were done partly at home, but also apparently in organized groups. In late antiquity the state operated textile workshops, called *gynecea* (from the Greek for 'women's quarters'; weaving was traditionally a female occupation), to ensure the supply of army clothing.

Workshops for all of these crafts, together with a range of others—metalworking, tanning, fish-salting—are found frequently in urban contexts. There is evidence also for some of these activities at villa sites, probably for market sale over and above the needs of the estate; but the primary location of craft production was in towns and villages.

Labour

Slavery was a structural element of Roman society (Chapter 4). It took many forms, from agricultural labourers on the chain-gangs of *latifundia* (below), through domestic servants, to educated (often Greek) slaves who taught the children of the rich. Slaves might run businesses on their master's behalf, and slaves of the imperial household might be put in charge of substantial sums of money and wield considerable power. We hear of people owning several hundred slaves (Apuleius' wife, Pudentilla, had over 400: Apuleius, *Apology* 93). The image of vast, slave-worked estates or *latifundia* is common in the literature of the late Republic and of the first century AD, and the villa estate at Settefinestre near Cosa in Italy has been claimed as an example. But agriculture was not necessarily dominated by slavery; on most estates it would have been cheaper to maintain a limited core staff of slaves and hire extra labour at harvest time (as was clearly the practice in the world of the New Testament). Slaves were expensive to purchase, as their price represented work that they could do above the cost of their subsistence; they required maintenance, and total costs of ownership may not have been very different from employing waged labour. Slave-staffed estates, tenant farmers, and individual smallholders existed side by side in the countryside. Nevertheless there was considerable demand for slaves, which was met more through trade in captives or slaves imported from beyond the frontiers than from slaves bred at home (Bradley 1994).

Waged labour was regarded as lowly, at least by our elite literary sources, and slave and free artisans might work together. The urban poor at Rome formed a large pool of potential unskilled labour which needed an income, and the large imperial building projects in the capital should be seen not simply as lavish expenditure, but also as a means to circulate wealth among elements of the urban population that might otherwise become restive. In the provinces, the army was sometimes used for civilian construction, such as building the aqueduct at Fréjus, and repairing that at Autun in the late third century. Municipal authorities could also demand a few days' compulsory labour per year.

The size of the labour force grew progressively during the last two centuries BC, as the Roman world increased the territory under its control and acquired new slaves as war captives. Periodically, civil wars and internal strife ate up manpower without providing a further influx of slaves from beyond the frontiers. But the rapid expansion in Rome's empire in the latter decades of the first century BC, and the *pax Augusta* (the Augustan peace), encouraged a general rise in population, which correlated with the intensive economic growth of the first and second centuries AD. This was reversed after the middle of the second century by the Antonine plague, which appears to have had a severe demographic impact. Certainly, the incidence of building activity drops in the 160s; an apparent widespread abandonment of villas in Italy around the end of the second century is also often attributed, although with no real proof, to the plague.

Distribution and trade

Transport

If the Mediterranean has been characterized as a patchwork of topo-graphically fragmented micro-regions, whose very variability and diversity, together often with access to the sea, encourages mutu-al intercommunication—high levels of 'connectivity' (Horden and Purcell 2000)—this is not necessarily true for north-western Europe. Here, the greater uniformity of much of the landscape, with its more gently changing rhythms, on the one hand facilitates overland trans-port between regions, but on the other reduces the incentives for such contact. Much more of the land-mass is further from the sea than is the case in Mediterranean Europe, and the rougher waters of the Atlantic façade do not offer the same advantages to mari-time trade—although that trade was by no means negligible—as the relatively calmer Mediterranean Sea. We should expect connectivity to have been very variable across Roman Europe, with high levels around the Mediterranean and sensibly lower levels in northern Spain, central and northern Gaul, and Britain. A low point might be represented by the Alpine regions (Helvetia and Raetia), with a slight increase over the norm along the Rhine–Danube frontier, owing to the river systems and army communication routes. In the northern Balkans the fragmented topography and distance from the sea limited connectivity, with the exception of the possibilities offered by the Danube. But connectivity also varied over *time*; the creation of road networks and the incorporation of north-west Europe into a single political unit greatly facilitated cultural and economic contact via the movements of people and goods. Similarly, the break-up of the Roman West in the fifth century ushered in a collapse of exchange networks and a reduction in levels of connectivity (Chapter 9).

Available transport technologies and costs naturally affected—indeed, partly determined—the distribution of traded goods. As in other pre-industrial societies, there were great discrepancies between the costs of maritime, riverine, and land transport. It was some twenty-eight times as expensive to move something by land as by sea, and land transport was seven times the cost of river transport. This manifests itself most obviously in distribution maps of archaeological artefacts: in the late Republic, Italian *amphorae* for the transport of wine cluster around the Mediterranean coast, and up the main waterways of central France—the Rhône valley and other major river systems—and the Atlantic coast via the Carcassonne gap. But while road transport was relatively expensive, the costs of overland transport did not *prevent* traded goods ending up on rural and urban sites at considerable distances from the sea or a navigable river. Furthermore, the programmes of road-building that followed the acquisition of new territory by Rome, although initially intended to facilitate troop movement, rapidly encouraged trade. Although the Roman methods of harnessing horses were inferior, in terms of traction, to the medieval horse collar, the combination of poor Roman harnessing with decently paved roads may not have resulted in a worse 'technology package' than the medieval combination of better harnessing and muddy cart tracks (Greene 1986: 17–44).

Similarly, it is often claimed that the Romans operated a sailing season and rarely put to sea in the winter months between November and March. If true, this would have considerable implications for the seasonal availability of traded goods imported from overseas. However, recent research indicates that the true picture is more complex. The sources quoted in support of the traditional view relate (for the Roman period) primarily to warships and to state-owned cargoes, and there is abundant evidence for private merchants taking the greater risks of winter sailing. We should thus envisage something of a winter downturn in maritime trade, but by no means a cessation as far as Mediterranean waters are concerned. The main Mediterranean ports are likely to have seen year-round activity, though winter may more effectively have closed the ports of the Atlantic façade.

Independent trade

The archaeological record provides abundant evidence for long-distance trade in a wide variety of goods; the more genre-bound literary evidence, less so. Not all movement of goods reflects trade; alternative explanations include gift exchange (unlikely for the majority of goods in the Roman period, though true for some; see also Chapters 1 and 10), transfers of agricultural produce between different estates owned by the same individual (especially relevant for the late Roman period); and instances of state intervention and army supply. But the overwhelming bulk of the astonishing quantity and variety of imported goods found on nearly every Roman civilian site, whether farm, villa, village, or town, is hardly explicable by anything other than massive levels of private trade. As illustration, we may take several examples. Italian wine penetrated the markets of Gaul and even reached Britain from the second century BC onwards, long before these regions came under Roman control; redistributive explanations can hardly apply, and we have literary evidence of Italian merchants trading wine for Gaulish slaves (Diodorus 5. 26. 3). Late Republican wine *amphorae* (Dressel form 1A, *c.*150–50 BC) produced at or near Cosa in northern Etruria in Italy, stamped with the mark SES (for Sestius, a senatorial family with estate holdings in the Cosa region), have been found at numerous sites along the coast of northern Italy and southern Gaul, up the Rhone valley, and at a number of sites further inland (Fig. 6.1). A ship of between 290 and 390 tons which sank off the Madrague de Giens in 60–50 BC was carrying a cargo of between 5,800 and 7,800 Dressel 1B wine *amphorae*, many stamped with the mark of a single producer, Publius Veveius Papus, as well as 1,635 fineware vessels. A shipment of this size can hardly be explained as internal redistribution among a single landowner's estates.

Fig. 6.1. Distribution of Dressel 1 wine amphorae with the stamp SES. The amphorae were produced near Cosa, and their distribution reflects the preference for the relatively cheap maritime and riverine routes. But note that some of the examples were found away from these main routes; the higher costs of land transport were not an absolute bar to overland trade.

The so-called Murecine tablets, found in a villa near Pompeii destroyed in the eruption of AD 79, record a series of loans made in the nearby port of Puteoli by a family of bankers in the early and mid-first century AD. In one of them (*TPSulp* 51), dated AD 37, one Gaius Novius Eunus borrows 10,000 HS (= *sestertii*) from the slave of an imperial freedman against security of 7,000 *modii* (46.7 tonnes) of Alexandrian wheat and 4,000 *modii* (27 tonnes) of lentils, chickpeas, and other goods stored in a warehouse at Puteoli; other tablets indicate that he was speculating in commodities imported from Egypt.

The distribution of fine table-pottery is perhaps one of the most striking indicators of the levels and intensity of trade achieved during the Roman period. Italian Terra Sigillata (above) was exported all over the western Mediterranean and up into Gaul and along the Rhine frontier, from 40/30 BC onwards. But from 10 BC onwards imitations made in central and southern Gaul began to capture the northern markets. From the first decade of the first century AD onwards the distributions of ITS and Gaulish Terra Sigillata wares become almost mutually exclusive, reflecting a distinction between the Mediterranean façade of Roman Europe and its north-western European counterpart. When the Italian production dwindled and eventually ceased in the face of competition from imported African Red Slip (ARS) wares from the late first century AD onwards, this market distinction was largely maintained. ARS dominates around the western Mediterranean littoral, but is rare in Gaul, Germany, and Britain. In these latter regions the 'Samian wares' of the central Gaulish workshops were widely traded until the end of the second century, when they ceased production, their place being taken by east Gaulish production which continued to be widely traded until the third century. While such pottery is our most archaeologically visible traded item, it would have travelled together with a wide range of perishable goods (textiles, spices, grain, etc.); its value for the historian is that it provides a proxy tracer for some of these trade flows.

State redistributive mechanisms and state intervention in trade

Not all trade was in the hands of private merchants, with prices left to the market. The state intervened in the trade in major foodstuffs, notably to supply the army, and to assure supply to the city of Rome, whose consumption demand had far outstripped the capacity of its immediate hinterland by the late second century BC if not earlier. A subsidized handout of grain to male citizens of Rome was initiated under the *lex frumentaria* (corn-distribution statute) of C. Sempronius Gracchus in 123 BC, as a popular political measure; the state subsidy was subsequently increased, until in 58 BC P. Clodius Pulcher made the handout completely free. By 5 BC there were 320,000 recipients; three years later Augustus cut the number to 200,000. This was only a part of Rome's total population, but the importance of the measure lay not only in the number of people it directly served, but also in the fact that the assured supply of such a large quantity of grain insulated the market price at Rome, to a considerable extent, from shocks caused by poor harvests in a particular region. By the same token, major expenditure under Claudius and Trajan on harbour infrastructure at Ostia and Portus, the port of Rome at the Tiber mouth, was motivated by the need to ensure safe anchorage for the grain transports, and thus prevent shipwreck of the grain fleets from causing famine and riots at Rome. Much of the grain itself, mainly from Egypt and North Africa (northern Tunisia and north-eastern Algeria), may have been contributed as tax in kind, or as rent on imperial estates, but its shipment to Rome was assured by the state contracting with private merchants for its transport. Claudius offered certain tax privileges to merchants who put a ship of at least 70 tons at the state's disposal in this way for six years (Suetonius, *Claudius* 18. 3–4; Gaius, *Institutes* 1. 32C), and Hadrian granted immunity from liturgies (compulsory municipal services) to shippers supplying the *annona* (grain supply). In the Antonine period one had to own a ship of 350 tons, or five of 70 tons, to qualify for immunity.

Over time, successive emperors added other foodstuffs to the *annona*—olive oil (Septimius Severus), pork and wine (Aurelian). This will have created additional economic opportunities for landowners to supply the state. In the case of olive oil, the state clearly intervened in the supply to Rome long before oil was included in the free handout. The vast mound by the Tiber in Rome known as Monte Testaccio is made entirely of deliberately smashed olive-oil *amphorae*, about 80 per cent of them from south-west Spain (Fig. 6.2). They bear a series of painted inscriptions (*tituli picti*) serving as control marks, recording the weight of the *amphora* empty and full, the name of the estate from which the oil came, the name of the merchant transporting it, and other information. Such precisely controlled information, together with their centralized disposal on Monte Testaccio and deliberate smashing (to prevent fraudulent reuse?), clearly suggests state control. Because the phenomenon begins under Augustus, some two centuries before the inclusion of oil in the *annona*, the implication is that the state was trying to assure a sufficient supply of oil to Rome, perhaps at a guaranteed price, to prevent sharp price-rises in the event of a poor harvest.

The supply of the army was another area in which the state intervened (Chapter 5). In some times and places, though not universally, taxes were paid in grain, or other commodities of which the state had need for military provisioning. But private merchants were also engaged in supplying the lucrative military market, especially where

Fig. 6.2. Monte Testaccio, near the Tiber in Rome. This hill is made entirely of discarded olive-oil amphorae, all of them imported. The majority are Dressel 20 amphorae from Spain, but there are also large numbers of amphorae from North Africa.

there were large concentrations of troops stationed on the frontiers. We have already seen how pottery production centres sprang up to service the Rhine frontier; and the Vindolanda writing tablets record the involvement of private traders in supplying the fort (Bowman 2003). At Domburg and Colijnsplaat (Zeeland) votive altars were erected in the third century to the goddess Nehalennia by traders with Britain, grateful for a safe crossing; these may have supplied military markets.

The incorporation of Europe into the Roman world had a profound impact on the variety and quantity of goods exchanged. Not only were goods widely traded within Europe, but olive oil, fish products, wine, textiles, and pottery were imported into Mediterranean Europe from North Africa, and spices and silks from the lands to the east of the Euphrates. Rome in particular came to rely on imported grain from North Africa and Egypt, and it provided the largest market for luxury goods. But the incorporation of the European provinces within the empire also created new economic opportunities; the empire was a trading space dominated by a single political entity, with a single currency, and based on the Mediterranean. For the Mediterranean provinces, temperate Europe therefore provided vast export markets for agricultural and other produce. The northern European regions were less able to exploit this relationship to the full, but still benefited from increased levels of trade and access to Mediterranean goods.

Consumption and services

The Roman world was characterized by gross social inequality, which became even more accentuated as time progressed. Under Augustus, property qualifications for senators were set at HS 1,000,000, and for *equites* at HS 400,000; decurions (local councillors) in some cities had to possess a minimum of HS 100,000. By comparison, legionary basic pay was HS 900 per annum under Augustus; annual wages for free males were generally between HS 500–1,000 at that period. The elite spent heavily on conspicuous consumption to maintain their social standing. As well as meeting the property qualification, town councillors also had to pay a fee to hold office, and tenure of a magistracy required the financing of gladiatorial displays or other public entertainment. Sometimes, and largely to curry electoral favour, elites financed the construction of theatres, amphitheatres, temples, aqueducts, and so forth in their towns; in gratitude for such acts of *euergetism* or benefaction, the towns erected honorific statues, and inscriptions recording their good deeds. All this created a vast level of demand in the construction and sculpture industries, some of which can be gauged by surviving remains, including building inscriptions which sometimes give the cost of the project. This material provides perhaps the most striking evidence for variations in the level of personal wealth across the Roman world. Building inscriptions show that Europe (except for parts of Italy, notably the cities of the western coast) lagged behind the rest of the Roman world in terms of elite personal wealth. Asia Minor and North Africa produce the largest numbers of building inscriptions, and many of the highest costs known. Spain and southern Gaul come next, with some extraordinarily large benefactions (for example, HS 7,000,000 for an aqueduct at Bordeaux). By contrast, far fewer personal benefactions are known from central and northern Gaul, Germany, or Britain. In Britain the largest class of benefactors is guilds or associations, probably because the cost was frequently beyond the means of individuals there.

The intensive construction activity fuelled by elite euergetism and imperial benefactions, in Italy from the first century BC and in the provinces during the first and second centuries AD, generated enormous demand for building materials, with knock-on effects on employment in the construction sector. Large construction projects increasingly relied on brick-faced concrete, which could be laid by semi-skilled workers, and used bricks produced to standard sizes by a multiplicity of suppliers, thus avoiding the production bottlenecks inherent in ashlar construction dependent on the output of a single quarry. Brick production on such a scale relies on the existence of a large market sustained by substantial building activity. In Europe north of the Alps, fired brick and tile were simply not produced for several centuries after about AD 400, striking testimony to the economic contraction and the cessation of large building projects in the wake of Rome's loss of control of the region (Chapter 9).

Imperial building projects also required the import of coloured and white marbles for columns and veneer; apart from Luna (Carrara), most of the best marble sources were in the eastern Mediterranean. Greece provided the green marble known as *cipollino*, other forms of green and red marble came from the Peloponnese, as well as white marble from Attica and Thasos. Asia Minor was home to a variety of coloured marbles, and North Africa produced the pinkish-yellow Numidian marble. Imperial building projects, at Rome and elsewhere, impressed by their sheer scale and grandeur. They trumpeted a consumption of resources in terms of materials and manpower, and their marble decoration proclaimed Rome's domination of an often non-European world that yielded these beautiful stones.

One of the largest markets affected by competitive social display was in grave monuments; everybody dies, and many wanted to leave a marker of their status. So great was the demand for white marble sarcophagi that standard types were shipped from Proconnesos in the Sea of Marmara to the Dalmatian coast and to Italy in roughed-out form, to be finished by local workshops. Strigillated sarcophagi (so-called from the repeated elongated 'S' design along their sides, which resembles a strigil or scraper) were imported from Asia Minor to Rome, finished in workshops there, and sometimes exported onwards. At a lower social level, graves were marked by stone *stelae* (upright markers). In Italy, southern Gaul, and Spain these show that artisans of modest social standing could nevertheless afford the services of a stone-carver for such decorated monuments. Significantly, carved *stelae* again become rarer in the northern provinces and along the Danube, where they tend to commemorate almost exclusively soldiers (Chapter 5) and merchants.

Many items of conspicuous consumption are largely lost to us—exotic dyed silks and other textiles, furniture, and perfumes generally do not survive in the archaeological record; much gold and silverware was later melted down and reused (but see Chapter 9 for late antique silver hoards). But it is clear from the repeated sumptuary laws setting limits on private expenditure in the late Republic that increasing expenditure on extravagant consumption was felt to threaten the social order. It is equally clear from a letter from the emperor Tiberius to the Senate that in AD 22 such consumption had become so pervasive that the state no longer felt able to check it (Tacitus, *Annals* 3. 52–5). This process finds its archaeological echo in the increasing numbers of imported goods (coloured marble, pottery, *amphorae*) on sites of the Augustan period and later.

The picture of uneven geographical distribution of personal wealth suggested by building inscriptions is broadly supported, at a lower level of social status, by the distribution of more everyday goods. Quantities of pottery on Roman Mediterranean sites are far higher than those in Britain or northern Gaul. By no means all of this variation can be ascribed to the northern European preference for barrels over *amphorae* as transport containers, or to the use of other materials for eating- and cooking-vessels—at some level it reflects a basic distinction between Europe's Mediterranean façade and the north-western provinces.

Yet although fewer artefacts are found on Roman sites of the northern provinces compared with those in the Mediterranean region, they nevertheless greatly outnumber finds of the Iron Age or Medieval periods. Coins, keys, surgical instruments, toilet articles, jewellery, nails, pots, glass, and a range of other goods abound on Roman sites. Even smallish rural sites in Britain are likely to yield imported Gaulish Samian pottery (above). 'Romanization', including the spread of Roman ways of urban living, the adoption of new dietary practices and patterns of consumption, occurred as a result of both top-down imposition and voluntary adoption on the part of the provinces (Chapter 8), but no less important was a kind of early 'globalization' of consumption patterns. Spanish olive oil, Italian wine, and red-gloss pottery were now available, affordable, and desirable as part of the new mode of living. Roman culture was spread as much by merchants as by armies. Measured on a number of crude indices (house construction, public services and amenities, faunal assemblages and other indicators of diet, availability of material goods), standards of living were rising generally from the first century BC, to peak perhaps in the second century AD. Both the archaeological record and calculations based on wages in terms of wheat equivalent suggest that in the first and second centuries AD consumption reached levels not known again until the eighteenth century (Jongman 2007).

Absolute numbers of mammal bones deposited per century show a clear peak in the first century AD for sites in Italy, and for the provinces a sharp rise from the first century BC to a peak in the second century AD, with a decline in the third century and steep drop-off in the fifth. The majority of these bones of cattle, sheep/goats, and pigs are assumed to represent food refuse, and should therefore reflect gross meat-consumption trends. These statistics are not per-capita figures; they will be influenced by wider demographic trends, and thus the third-century decline in meat consumption may be a result of the Antonine plague. Meat consumption rose most quickly and earliest in Italy, largely accounted for by the urban consumption of pork. In the provinces, the rise in consumption broadly correlates with the imposition of Roman rule. Further evidence that Roman control affected diet is provided by King's study of meat consumption across different regions of the empire. Italian sites, especially cities, show a preponderance of pig bones over sheep/goat and cattle. This was a high-status diet, and at Rome was partly subsidized by the *annona* which provided for people's grain needs (although they still needed to have the grain milled and baked until well into the principate), leaving them with more to spend on meat. Roman urban sites in Spain also show an increase in pork consumption by the second century AD. But the further north one goes, the more beef is being consumed—it is the dominant meat in northern Gaul, Germany, and Britain. Greece, by contrast, remained a region where sheep and goat were the most frequently consumed animals (King 1999).

Urban living provided a great stimulus to service industries (including prostitution, entertainment, and the associated animal trade for shows). Besides the ubiquity of bakeries, Roman towns (especially in Italy) are notable for the number of cookshops and eating joints. At Pompeii and Herculaneum rooms could be hired in the baths for dining and entertaining, and at Rome the social need to entertain led already in the early second century BC to the development of a *forum coquinum* ('cooks' *forum*'), where people without their own cooks could engage the services of a cook to provide the catering for a dinner party (Plautus, *Pseudolus* 790; Terence, *Eunuchus* 255–7).

Coinage and monetization

In the Celtic world the first coins were imitations of the gold staters of Philip II of Macedon, copied from coins introduced by returning mercenaries. These had fairly restricted distributions and were used largely for gift exchange, rather than for true monetary transactions. From the late second century BC, cast bronze potin (copper, zinc, tin, and lead) coinage appears in southern Britain, imitating issues of the Greek colony of Massilia (Marseilles), reflecting a move towards the use of money in the incipient urbanism of the *oppida* cultures (Chapter 1). Increasingly in the first century BC, Celtic coinage shows influence from Roman types, but the predominant issues remained gold and silver.

The primary reason for the Roman state to issue coinage was to facilitate taxation and the payment of the army. The first Roman coins were issued about 289 BC, based on the *as*, a large lump of bronze weighing 1 lb, with a variety of subdivisions. During the third century, under the pressure of the Punic Wars, the weight of the *as* was progressively reduced to more manageable levels, and by the late third century gold and silver coins were also being struck; the coinage was now based on the silver *denarius*, worth 10 bronze *asses*; around 100 BC it was re-tariffed at 16 *asses*. Under Augustus the output of gold, silver, and bronze coinage rose considerably, and some coins were struck in *orichalcum* (an alloy of copper and zinc) and copper. The main denominations had the following relationships: 1 gold *aureus* = 25 silver *denarii* = 100 orichalcum *sestertii* = 400 copper *asses*; the *dupondius*, *semis*, and *quadrans* were worth, respectively, two *asses*, half an *as*, and a quarter of an *as*. The *sestertius* was the unit of account, as the largest base-metal coin. Forty *aurei* were struck from a pound of gold, and 84 *denarii* from a pound of silver. Nero reformed and effectively somewhat devalued the coinage, increasing the number of coins struck from a pound to 45 in the case of *aurei* and 96 for *denarii* (Casey 1980).

During the first century AD coins were struck largely from new bullion; in effect, a vast quantity of new coinage was pumped into circulation. This appears not to have had major inflationary effects, probably because much of it was absorbed in the monetization of newly conquered provinces which—at least in north-western Europe—had had little tradition of using money. The economy of Roman Europe became highly monetized, to a degree not seen again until the late Middle Ages, although the use of money remained relatively unsophisticated. Pompeii and Herculaneum provide illustrations of the degree of coin use in Italian cities in AD 79, with a large amount and variety of small change, in the contents of purses, strong-boxes, or the takings of shops; and an abundance of graffiti recording prices of everything from oral sex (2 *asses*) to how much a pair of friends spent on a meal out and some prostitutes ($105\frac{1}{2}$ *sestertii*).

Our sources for the monetization of rural life are better for Egypt and the Levant (where they indicate a thoroughly monetized rural society from the first century AD onwards) than they are for Europe, but Apuleius' *Golden Ass* depicts a monetized economy in rural Greece under Roman rule. The Vindolanda tablets (above) imply that monetization was pervasive in the context of military supply in early second-century northern Britain, a picture amplified by archaeological finds. Coins, especially small change, are common on rural villas, farmsteads, and villages of Italy and the northern and western provinces (monetization: Howgego 1992; Pompeian graffiti: *Corpus Inscriptionum Latinarum* 4. 1469; Herculaneum: ibid. 4. 10675).

This monetization was also possible because of the empire's rich metal resources, exploited by comparatively advanced mining technology (above). But in any economy which does not rely on a fiduciary currency, the physical mineral wealth available sets the limit on how much money can be issued. Nero's reduction of the weight standard for gold and fineness for silver coinage is an early sign of such stress; in 68 he restored fineness somewhat but Vespasian and Trajan further reduced it. Trajan apparently used booty from the Dacian wars, the acquisition of new silver mines in Dacia, and the recall of all Republican *denarii* still circulating (which had a silver content of *c*.96–8 per cent) to finance increased expenditure rather than restoring the purity of the coinage. From then on silver coinage was struck from a mixture of new bullion and recalled coins, and from the mid-second century AD onwards the opportunity was taken progressively to reduce the silver content of the *denarius*. This was probably accompanied by some inflation. Whereas in the first century the bronze *as* was the most commonly used coin for everyday transactions (and thus the coin most commonly lost in antiquity, and most commonly found on archaeological sites), the *sestertius* came into more common use in the second century, and by the time of Antoninus Pius it was being lost in as large quantities as the *as*. By the end of the second century devaluation and inflation meant that the *denarius* had replaced the *sestertius* as the main medium of transaction, and the most commonly lost coin.

Military pay, increased by Septimius Severus and his sons (Chapter 5), had doubled by the end of the reign of Caracalla; this was accompanied by further reductions in the silver content of the *denarius* to 48 per cent. In addition, Caracalla introduced a new coin, the *antoninianus*, thought to have been a double *denarius* but weighing only one-and-a-half times as much. Clearly, the state was feeling the double squeeze of declining output from the Spanish mines and the increasing burden of military pay. These constraints only tightened during the course of the third century, and the silver content of the *denarius* accordingly fell further. Each of the many military coups (Chapter 3) had to be followed by a donative to the troops who had put the new emperor on the throne, and the empire was not acquiring new territory with fresh mining resources to compensate. By AD 249–51, in the reign of Trajan Decius, *antoniniani* were being overstruck on old *denarii*; and following the loss of Dacia in 265, the single largest source of precious metals after Spain, the silver content of the *antoninianus* declined to a mere 2 per cent. The coin-loss patterns on archaeological sites indicate that by this time the *antoninianus* was functioning as small change—a clear indication that the inflationary effects one would expect from such devaluations had occurred.

Aurelian attempted to reform the coinage in AD 273, apparently tariffing the coins above the value of their metal content, but a further reform was necessary under Diocletian. In 286 he increased the number of gold coins struck from a pound from 45 to 60; and in 293 he reintroduced high-quality silver coinage on the old standard of 96 to the pound (like the Neronian *denarius*), with the coin now called the *argenteus*; and in 294/6 he reintroduced large copper coins. He addressed the problem of military costs in part by requiring taxes to be paid in kind. But severe inflation persisted, and in 301 Diocletian issued the 'Prices Edict', which attempted (doubtless unsuccessfully) to establish the maximum prices that could be charged for a wide range of goods and services across the empire. This was accompanied by a further re-tariffing of part of the coinage, without actually affecting its physical composition.

Further devaluations occurred throughout the fourth century, reflecting the fact that mining output was not keeping up with losses from circulation and the state's need for money. Constantine reduced the weight of gold coins in AD 309, striking 72 to the pound; the new coin, the *solidus*, lasted until the eleventh century. Its output may have been facilitated by access to new sources of gold traded across the Sahara from the late third century onwards. But the relationship of gold and silver now fluctuated in reaction to market forces. The fourth-century treatise *De Rebus Bellicis* states that the sequestration and release onto the market of temple treasures by Constantine (it is unclear whether Constantine I or II is meant) caused a fall in the price of gold. But the state seems to have had difficulties meeting its own demand for silver and copper. A new billon coin (i.e. debased silver with a large quantity of copper), the *centenionalis*, progressively declined in weight from 3.0 grams in 318 to 1.7 grams in 348. High-quality silver coinage reappeared in 325, struck on two standards at 96 and 72 to the pound, and the collection of taxes reverted from payment in kind to cash levies. Of course, this was another way of effectively increasing the supply of money, as it increased the velocity of circulation. The base-metal coinage further declined in weight in the late fourth century, to barely more than 1 gram of copper by 402, the date at which the western mints, with the exception of Rome, ceased to strike bronze coinage (Casey 1980).

The state exacted taxes in both coin and kind, the latter mainly as grain or other commodities needed for the supply of the army. Tacitus relates abuses of the tax system in Britain in the later first century AD, when traders hoarded grain to push the price up, causing hardship for the British populace who had to buy this grain to pay their taxes in kind (*Agricola* 19). The anecdote shows that taxation in kind does not equate to a lack of monetization. The extent to which tax was paid in coin or kind seems to have varied regionally, and over time; the third century saw a greater shift towards tax in kind, including some payment of customs dues (*portoria*). Besides a tax on land, and a poll tax, customs dues of $2\frac{1}{2}$ per cent were levied at harbours and on the boundaries between groups of provinces forming larger customs units (e.g. the Gallic or Danubian provinces), and at higher rates on external borders. There were also sales taxes of 1 per cent on auctions and a 5 per cent tax on major bequests outside one's close family, both initially introduced by Augustus to fund the costs of discharging veterans (Chapter 5); the sales tax was reduced to 0.5 per cent by Tiberius and abolished in Italy under Gaius.

Various forms of banking enabled the money supply to work harder by means of credit. Special forms of maritime loans existed, to finance marine trading ventures. Our fullest evidence for banking in daily life relates to Egypt (because of the survival of papyrus documents), but bankers were also to be found in Europe; certainly at Rome (and Ostia and Portus), and in towns where weekly markets were held. We have already mentioned the Murecine tablets concerning loans connected with transactions at Puteoli; the archive of L. Caecilius Iucundus from Pompeii shows the activities of a municipal banker before AD 79. Outside Italy the evidence is thinner, although the Vindolanda tablets show us traders buying large quantities of grain and hides on credit, and operating accounts with their suppliers (Andreau 1999; Howgego 1992; Bowman 2003: 144–6 (*Tab. Vindol.* II. 343)).

City and countryside

In the last two centuries BC nucleated proto-urban communities, *oppida*, with substantial areas enclosed by defensive walls, developed in Gaul, upper Germany, and southern Britain (Chapter 1). Although a visitor from Roman Italy would hardly have considered them proper towns, they do embody some of the functions of towns, and show evidence for differentiated social status, craft manufacture, and limited money-use, although debate persists over whether their function was primarily defensive. In southern Britain, proto-urban centres continued to develop in the first century AD, influenced by cross-Channel contact with Roman Gaul, and before the Roman invasion of Britain in AD 43 the *oppidum* at Silchester had an orthogonal street grid.

The Roman city, with a far greater range of public buildings and amenities, was a locus of consumption, concentrating in a small area high levels of demand that usually outstripped the capacity of the surrounding territory to supply it. But this does not make it, as some have argued, a Weberian 'consumer city', in which the bulk of the funds for consumption was obtained through rents and taxes levied on the rural populace. Such approaches based on ideal types are too constrained by the assumption that city and countryside together formed a self-contained cellular unit. The importance of long-distance trade and the connectivity argued for above demonstrate the need to consider towns within a system of overlapping trade networks, operating at local, regional, and long-distance scales. There is abundant evidence for urban workshops producing a wide variety of goods, not only for the inhabitants of the city and of the surrounding countryside, but also for export further afield. Cities acted as vital markets for their hinterlands, not only to dispose of agricultural produce but also to acquire farm tools, equipment, artefacts, and a wider variety of foodstuffs than those grown locally. Coastal cities played this role on a grander scale, and as import–export points they provided larger local markets than inland cities. Significantly, it is often the coastal cities which yield the most evidence of urban manufacturing activities, again suggesting that their privileged access to an indefinite export market stimulated craft production ('consumer city': Finley 1985: 123–49; Wilson 2002).

The economic stimulus that the city provided to its hinterland is seen in settlement patterns, and most clearly in the villa phenomenon. Because villas were engaged in producing a market surplus, they are found in direct proportion to the degree of urbanization in a particular region. At one extreme stands Rome, with its precociously early development of dense villa landscapes in South Etruria and Latium, engaged in viticulture, flower growing, and intensive horticulture for the urban market. Besides the ordinary requirements of a megalopolis of perhaps a million people, the festivals and lavish banquets held by the elite generated colossal demand for delicacies, and some villas in the *suburbium* specialized in the intensive rearing (*pastio villatica*) of thrushes, blackbirds, fish, and edible dormice and so forth in purpose-built aviaries, fishponds, and *gliraria* (dormouse hutches). At the other end of the scale, on the other side of the Apennines in Samnium, the almost complete lack of villas mirrors a dearth of urban centres; the dominant settlement types are villages. Similarly, there are marked differences between southern and northern Britain; nearly all the villas in Britain are found in the urbanized civilian zone of the south and east, while the militarized northern zone has few villas, and very few towns.

The third century and after

We have already seen that the political turmoil of the third century was accompanied by coinage debasement and inflation. The state's resources were increasingly absorbed by wars, the cost of the army, and additions to the *annona* at Rome to keep the populace loyal (the state went over from handing out grain to distributing bread; Aurelian further increased these distributions and added free pork and subsidized wine). The wider effects on the economy may be judged from several other indicators. The evidence from building inscriptions shows a general cessation in large building projects after Alexander Severus, for both privately funded euergetism and for imperial projects. Apart from defensive walls, which were constructed at many cities—including Rome—across Europe from Carcassonne in Gaul to Tomis on the Black Sea during the middle and later third century, large building projects resume only with the Diocletianic recovery. Municipal elites, crippled by the costs of public building programmes, became increasingly unwilling to shoulder the duties and burdens of public office, and may have engaged less in town life. The rise of the church during the fourth century provided a new institution that helped to fill the gap in local government (Chapter 9). In some regions also the balance of economic power between town and country may have shifted; in Britain, the richest villas are those of the fourth century.

Social inequality intensified after the third century, and while the general standard of urban living falls below its second-century peak, and overall numbers of villa sites in occupation drop, we find more lavishly ornate residences in the very top band. The position of elite landowners was strengthened by Diocletian's reforms to simplify tax-collection, which tied the rural population to places where they were registered, making it impossible for tenants to move. Landowners were successful in getting the government to enforce this against their tenants, although any relationship between this tied 'colonate' and the feudal system of the Middle Ages remains unclear. The late Roman state extended its control over individuals in other ways too, to ensure the supply of goods or services which it could not otherwise guarantee. Certain occupations were made hereditary (suggesting that there was a shortage of labour for such tasks). The state established arms factories and textile workshops (above) to make military equipment and uniforms, items which had hitherto been supplied wholly by the private sector.

The Roman European economy in the perspective of the *longue durée*

Economically, the impact of the Roman Empire on Iron Age northern Europe was profound. For several centuries it transformed it utterly; yet the region reverted with surprising swiftness to economies based on local exchange and raiding after Roman rule collapsed. The establishment of urbanism on the Roman model required an integrated trading network to support it. Ancient transport technologies meant that this was facilitated by maritime and riverine access. The cities of the Mediterranean region, with greater maritime connectivity, were therefore more resilient than their more northerly counterparts when the single political and economic context that had allowed the secure development of long-distance overland trade routes disintegrated. The qualitative and quantitative differences between Europe's Mediterranean façade and the north-western provinces have been a recurrent theme of this chapter, in levels of urbanism, personal wealth, and access to traded goods. Nevertheless, even in the less-developed north, economic activity on these and other measures reached levels not seen in the late Iron Age, nor in the five centuries after the fall of the Roman West.

The Roman world was unique among all pre-industrial western societies in its ability to sustain unparalleled urban development, a standing army, and a larger sector of the population engaged in non-agricultural production than any other society until the eighteenth century. Agriculture was fundamental, but we see both aggregate and per-capita economic growth from the middle Republic onward, accelerating in the late Republic and early empire. This was due to progress both in agricultural technology to sustain a higher number of non-agricultural workers, and in non-agricultural technologies such as mining; and to the political unification of the Mediterranean. Indeed, the economic boom of the first and second centuries AD is arguably partly attributable to the boost to state finances given by the use of advanced mining technologies, on top of a very healthy agrarian base which grew in the provinces under the stimulus of the opening up of new markets as vast swathes of territory came under Roman control.

The economic recession, which was in some regions a crisis, of the third century came about as a complex interplay of internal and external political factors (military coups, attempted usurpations, and civil wars; increasing pressure on the frontiers by barbarian tribes, on which see Chapter 10) and economic causes. These were the lasting demographic impact of the Antonine plague, declining output of mines and eventual loss of some mining territories, inflation, and higher costs of local government as local elites became increasingly unable to shoulder the financial burdens of office. The limited recovery of the late antique period was achieved by heavier taxation, increased state control of the economy, and perhaps to some extent facilitated by access to new gold sources by means of trade across the Sahara, and by the state's acquisition of sacred treasuries on the closure of the pagan temples.

Greece and the Balkan provinces continued under Roman rule into the Middle Ages, with continued maritime exchange. But the loss of Roman control over Britain, Gaul, Germany, and Spain saw a massive contraction or even total disintegration of trading networks. Without these to support them, urban life in the north collapsed, and with them the markets that had stimulated large-scale production. The economic collapse in the fifth century north of the Alps was thorough: it is measured in the disappearance of the large Roman livestock breeds, mass-produced brick and tile to support active construction programmes, and even, in Britain, the production of wheel-thrown pottery. Life persisted in some towns, like Verulamium in Britain, for a couple of generations, but after its abandonment by Rome the former northern fringe of the empire sank to a level of material culture and socio-economic organization lower than that which the Romans had found when they invaded in AD 43. A less intense picture, but following a similar overall trajectory, could be sketched for Gaul and Germany. The political unity of the Roman Empire enabled the creation of trade networks sustaining a highly urbanized world. When that political unity fragmented, with it went all the other defining features of the Roman economy—urbanism, mass-production, high levels of money-use, and intensive trade.

7

Religions

Edward Bispham

BOTH gods of the Graeco-Roman pantheon and deified Roman emperors were venerated across the empire. They were not alone, however, in receiving the devotion of its inhabitants. Local deities survived in urban and rural, public and private, contexts. Moreover, some of these transcended their original confines, moving with administrators, soldiers, merchants, and slaves, to take root in new soils very far from home: thus, the Graeco-Roman cultic melange of Mithraism flourished within the forts of Hadrian's Wall, thousands of miles from its Persian roots. In this situation we cannot hope to define one single entity which is 'Roman religion', or even single coherent phenomena, such as the 'imperial cult'. That is equally true, as we shall see, of the early religion of the Roman Republic; even the eventual imposition of a single orthodoxy across the broad church of early Christianity was by no means a foregone conclusion. We must think of religions in the plural; and unthink 'religion' as we habitually conceive it.

A history divine

> Who, when once he understands that there are gods, does not then understand that by their divine will (*numen*), this great empire of ours has been born, increased, and retained? However much we wish, conscript fathers, to be entitled to feel good about ourselves, nevertheless we have not surpassed the peoples of Spain for population, those of Gaul for strength, the Carthaginians for cunning, nor the Greeks in the arts, nor finally the Italians themselves and the Latins for that very innate and

internal feeling for this race and its land. Yet in dutiful respect (*pietas*) and religious awe (*religio*) and in that particular wisdom (*sapientia*), wherein we understand that everything is controlled and steered by the will of the gods, we have surpassed all races and peoples.

(Cicero, *On the Responses of the Haruspices* 19)

By the late Republic, having survived Hannibal's traumatic invasion of Italy and eliminated all serious opposition to control of the Mediterranean basin (Chapter 2), Roman statesmen were having more frequent recourse to the kind of claim made here by Cicero: Rome's empire was divinely willed. That divine favour was thought to be intimately linked to the exemplary piety of the Roman people towards the gods (the narrative of Roman Republican history in Livy is perhaps the ultimate embodiment of this view).

Roman piety was reciprocal and almost contractual—but contractual in the sense of 'I give if I get', not of 'I give to make you give'; significantly, piety covered proper social relations as well as obligations to the gods (Chapter 4; Cicero, *On the Nature of the Gods* 1. 115 f.; Ando 2003: 11, n. 34, 57–61, 141–6). This analysis of empire as manifesting a successfully executed contractual relationship (legalistic overtones are common in Roman religious contexts) was also tantamount to a claim for the legitimacy of the senatorial governing class. From the aristocracy the priests of the public cults were chosen. They, together with the Senate (of which they were usually members), which had the final decision on responses to religious questions, established an appropriate dialogue with the gods (including interpretation of divine will and displeasure) and mediated Rome's interests so as to promote her success. The favourable assessment of Rome's providential history was effectively a validation of the prevailing socio-political power relations.

In the speech from which I quoted above, Cicero is at pains to equate the threat proposed by P. Clodius to his house on the Palatine hill (which Clodius had consecrated as a shrine to Libertas—Freedom) to a threat to the commonwealth itself. He depicts an attack on Rome's religious institutions, an impiety which is an integral part of wider revolution. The whole community could be damaged by the wicked actions of a single individual, and thus the community often found itself taking expiatory measures to rid itself of guilt by association, and to restore the disturbed reciprocal relationship with the gods. Polybius (6. 56) commented on the punctiliousness with which Romans kept oaths—to breach them was impiety. Cicero amplifies this: a perjurer suffered disgrace, and not all wrongs could be expiated—effaced by purificatory ritual atonement—by the priests (*On the Laws* 2. 22). To understand this emphasis on the community we need to recognize the crucial point that the gods were members of the Roman community too: both dwelt in the city, and both were affected by damage to its legal, social, and moral fabric.

Fifty years and two civil wars later, the Augustan age looked back on the recent fall of the Republic as explicable in terms of the moral failings and impiety of the preceding generations. The civil wars themselves were a fratricidal crime which needed expiation (e.g. Horace, *Odes* 1. 2. 29–30). With the advent of the principate (Chapter 3), proper relations with the gods remained at the core of safety and prosperity, not just for Rome and Italy, but for the empire. In the face of enormous religious diversity, the figure of the *princeps* provided a unifying thread which could be woven into a variety of acts of religious observance (from direct worship to sacrifice offered on his behalf, or to his *genius*—protecting spirit). The centrality within Roman society of the religious figure of the emperor, who included the now-hereditary title of 'chief priest' in his titulature, reflected the enormous changes which had transformed the *res publica* (commonwealth) and its internal power relations.

Together with the divinized figure of the emperor, the official cults of the 'state religion' remained a potent force for expressing the formal and ideological unity of the empire. Refusal to sacrifice to the traditional gods, notoriously a litmus-test for those accused of being Christians, carried overtones of subversive behaviour, suggesting disengagement from Roman society and its norms. From this it was a short step to imagine the creation of an 'underground', a hidden community in the interstices of the existing one, with new values, loyalties, and deities (as in the demonization of the Bacchanalian worshippers suppressed in Italy in 186 BC: Livy 39. 15–16), bringing disrespect to the existing ones, including the emperor. This was a deeply disturbing concept, and the threat, periodically hyped up, was met with brutal repression (Chapter 9). It was, nevertheless, Christianity which survived; perhaps we can detect in the persecutions a sense of panic on the part of the old gods. Christianity, adopted by

Constantine, usurped the position of 'state religion', and itself became central to the ongoing story of the Roman people.

Before we look more closely at various manifestations of religious change at Rome and in the empire, something must be said about approaching ancient religions. They are the most unfamiliar part of the bundle of classical 'legacies' which has come down to shape western civilization, precisely because of the success of Christianity.

The shock of the old

Strictly speaking, there was no 'Roman religion', at least until early Christians needed a catch-all term for non-Christians against whom they were defining themselves, and invented 'pagans'. The religious experiences of Christians and non-Christians were utterly different; the latter lacked the autonomous identity and cohesion which distinguishes the great monotheistic religions. Basic vocabulary illustrates this: many major differences between Roman and modern basic religious concepts are rooted in semantics. While religion means for us an autonomous and totalizing system of beliefs, conduct, and worship, Romans could define *religio* simply as 'the worship of the gods' (Cicero, *On the Nature of the Gods* 2. 8); or, more specifically, it could mean a religious impediment (or a feeling of awe arising from the fear or expectation of such an impediment). In the latter sense, *religio* can be spoken of as something which literally 'sticks to' a person, or to the commonwealth (see Cicero, *On the Nature of the Gods* 2. 11, *On Divination* 1. 30), rather than something which is followed, to which one attempts to attach oneself (Ando 2003: 11, n. 29). Again, the Latin *religiosus* had little in common with the English word *religious* (one of the more frequent words in this chapter). Only in a general and secondary sense could one talk of a person being *religiosus*; the primary meaning (Gaius, *Institutes* 4. 2) concerned places, specifically places associated with the *di manes*, the divine spirits of the dead. The term *religiosus* did not evoke a separate domain which could be clearly demarcated from the secular and everyday. On the contrary, contact with the gods, and thus ritual, permeated all the fields of human existence and activity, from cradle to grave, wrapping itself so tightly around word and action as to make the isolation of 'religious' in our sense very difficult. Ancient religion was a cultural and contingent activity, at least as expressed by the values of city elites. Even the universal veneration of Roman emperors was, in its various different forms, no different, despite becoming a truly imperial phenomenon in all senses.

Even atheist readers will inevitably approach Roman religion having, albeit unconsciously, oriented themselves with reference to Christianity (where Augustine's *City of God* plays a fundamental role in shaping modern attitudes), Judaism, or Islam. These monotheistic religions deal in revelation of a divine truth, the approach to which is mediated by a professional priesthood. In the Roman case, religious and political authority were alike shared within the community: as we have seen, the Senate (and ultimately the people), not the priests, possessed final authority in religious matters: Cicero, *On His House* 136; Livy 9. 46. 6–7). The major monotheistic religions are, famously, 'religions of the book'. Roman religion had texts, most famously the collection of prophecies known as the Sibylline books, but these contained no dogma, only cryptic utterances or warnings which might be applied to specific situations; and they were not Roman, but Greek. When religious books apparently written by Numa, Rome's second king, were dug up in the second century BC, the authorities burnt them (Livy 40. 29; Pliny, *Natural History* 13. 84–6).

Roman religion was polytheistic, that is, it acknowledged many, many gods. Of these, besides the 'Olympian' pantheon there were what German scholars 'christened' *Augensblickgötte*, invoked only for the specific action over which they presided. This atomization of divine–human interaction provided sport for early Christian writers, and is travestied, for example, in Augustine's *City of God* (6. 9: the crowd of deities overseeing the individual moments of the marriage ceremony, from bringing home the bride to wedding-night penetration). There were gods who inhabited natural features (Servius, *Commentary on the* Aeneid 7. 42); although a landowner could not be expected to know whether the deity inhabiting any given grove was male or female, he had to sacrifice to him/her, with catch-all formulae, before doing anything to the grove (Cato, *On Agriculture* 139). Finally, there were yet other gods whose very existence only came to light unexpectedly, but who needed proper reverence (Livy 5. 32. 6–7, 50. 5: Aius Locutius). The main concern of public worship was with managing relations between the community and its gods in the here-and-now, and in the foreseeable future, rather than with revelation of a divine truth, or in salvation after death. This last was, however, a central feature to many cults which later became popular under the empire. These often involved initiation, especially the 'elective' cults, such as those of Isis or Mithras (below). In contrast, Roman citizens related to, and had responsibilities to, the Roman state cults by being born Roman, or becoming one, for example by manumission; one could not 'convert' to them.

Relations between the human and divine elements of the community were managed in several ways (Cicero, *On the Nature of the Gods* 3. 5; further below). Most important among these were: (*a*) ritual actions (including prayers); (*b*) proper observation of the auspices—literally, 'observation of birds'—divided into signs requested from the gods by a magistrate (*auspicia impetratiua*), and spontaneous signs (*auspicia oblatiua*), sent by the gods and reported officially by priests called augurs; (*c*) the taking of proper action in the face of other divine warnings noted by the appropriate priests. Scholars of religion currently concede one major point to those who believe in an inherent decline in Roman Republican religion (see below): what mattered was not what one thought, but what one did, *as long as it was done correctly*; not orthodoxy, but orthopraxy. This emphasis on action rather than internal states is mirrored, for example, by Roman views, already noted, of the *physical* as the medium of contact with the gods. For example, people *and* places could become impure through physical contact, most commonly with death and the dead (a third-century BC sacred regulation for a sacred grove at Luceria in southern Italy forbids the bringing of manure or dead bodies into the grove: *Inscriptiones Latinae Liberae Rei Publicae* 504); purificatory rituals were needed to return to a state of cleanliness.

The observance of traditional religious practices was, for the late Republican elite, not incompatible with radical speculation about the universe, the gods, and their relations to men. In his dialogue *On the Nature of the Gods*, Cicero gives C. Aurelius Cotta the job of putting the torch of Academic scepticism to the theological edifices proposed by Epicurean and Stoic speakers. He also asserts the opinion of 'a Cotta and a *pontifex* (priest)':

What you [Lucilius Balbus] meant by that, is that I defend the views concerning the immortal gods, the rituals, observances, and practices, which have been handed down by our ancestors. Indeed I shall defend them always and always have done so, nor will the arguments of any man, learned or unlearned, at any time, shift me from holding that view about the worship of the almighty gods which I have taken over from our ancestors. (*On the Nature of the Gods* 3. 5)

Note that Cotta places stress on retaining the views about the gods and how to worship them which have come down to him from the *maiores* (ancestors). As important as this traditional aspect is the complete absence of any recognition on Cotta's part that anyone might reach a personally satisfying view about the gods. Part of his piety, part of his identity, is accepting and perpetuating the bundle of ancestral obligations and attitudes which constitutes Roman religion.

Cicero treats divination (techniques to ascertain future events willed by the gods), or some aspects of it, with intellectual scepticism in the second book of *On Divination*, where he is the speaker (the work is, however, more open-ended than some have supposed). He was himself an augur, but in *On the Laws* (2. 31–3) he expresses his belief that the augurs could not really discern the will of the gods by observing birds (although he fudges his position by admitting that they might have once possessed this skill). Some of Cicero's fellow augurs had written books on augury, and at least one insisted that it was not hokum. More importantly, Cicero asserted, drawing on Stoic philosophy, that there was no good reason for denying the validity of divination in general terms. And despite his scepticism in *On Divination* 2, he defends the ancestral uses of divination (which it is part of the 'wise man's' duty to protect, 2. 148, cf. 2. 70), and insisted that divination be retained for its socio-political value. Augural objections buffered against unwelcome political change, by enforcing delay in assemblies or even in extreme situations annulling elections and legislation. Yet the open speculations of Cicero's speakers were atypically daring, and the religious traditionalism of many, even within the elite, was less studied. In an ironic comment on the cessation of exploration in the North Sea and the Baltic, Tacitus characterizes the prevailing lack of enthusiasm: it was deemed more sacred (*sanctius*) and reverent (*reuerentius*) to hold beliefs (*credere*) about the deeds of the gods [here Hercules' northern journeys] than to know (*scire*) about them (*Germania* 34).

Cicero's insistence that augury be retained for the benefit of the commonwealth reminds us that rites carried out on its behalf (*sacra publica*) were inevitably, but not narrowly, political. Polybius, writing of the Romans of his own time, noted the intense interpenetration of the religious with the public and the private: what for fellow Greeks would have been superstition (*deisidaimonia*) was what held the Roman commonwealth together, and was indeed the principal arena in which its strength could be seen (6. 56). He saw piety as a means of social control over the ignorant masses. Equally importantly, members of the elite felt themselves as bound as the masses by the religious constraints which hedged politics around. To be sure, we do find cynical manipulation of religion for political ends, but this is no more than the exploitation of an 'embedded' form of interaction with the gods.

The character of this interaction is well illustrated by the Roman calendar (*fasti*). This was essentially a calendar which organized the year by lunar months; an extra month could be added every other year (a process called intercalation), if necessary, to compensate for the gradual divergence of the lunar calendar from the (longer) solar year. We are able to have a good idea of what the *fasti* were like, since a number of examples, mainly from Italian towns under the early empire, were inscribed on stone—they display minor variations between themselves (local authorities were responsible for deciding what went into their city's calendar). Despite these variations, these versions are based on the public calendar of Rome to a very large degree, and show a significant amount of agreement about its festivals. The major function of the calendar was to map out the dates of the major festivals which constituted the *sacra publica* (many of the older ones were ancient festivals tied to the agricultural calendar, and thus to fixed points in the astronomical year, itself thought of as ordered by the gods, along with the seasons). Festivals of no fixed date, or celebrated by other collectivities within the Roman commonwealth, were not included. A major innovation of the imperial period, correlating to the worship of the emperors, was the insertion of a series of anniversaries within the imperial house as public festivals.

Each day was classified in terms of the kind of civic activities which might or might not take place on that day, or more precisely, some days were apportioned to the gods and others to men, with a few being shared (Macrobius, *Saturnalia* 1. 16. 2–3). About two-thirds of the days in the year were *fasti*, available for public and private business, of which almost 200 were *comitiales*, that is, days on which popular assemblies could meet. Most of the remaining third of the year belonged to the gods (*dies nefasti*, including some sixty days of major public festivals under the early empire). These were days for 'divine business' within and for the community: mortal business ceased.

The importance of public religion for public affairs was not questioned. In this respect Rome was like other ancient communities. At least until the fabric of civic society was tested by military defeat and civil war in the third century AD (Chapter 3), Rome enjoyed a religious outlook which was essentially rational, based on reciprocal obligations suitable for a community, not on fear (those who feared the gods, and always sought to placate them in order to survive at all costs, were deemed to suffer from *superstitio*). Nevertheless, an important caveat applies here, and is indeed more widely applicable to Roman religions. Much of what we know, especially for the Republic, is ultimately derived from official sources (priests, magistrates, senatorial debates). Thus, emphasis of our sources on the *sacra publica*, on priestly colleges rather than individuals, and on the importance of religion for the commonwealth, may be a function of bias towards the elite and the male.

Although Romans talked about 'believing' in the gods, belief did not have the same connotations which it does in monotheistic religions: that is, it did not form half of a clear dichotomy between 'believing' and 'not believing'; it was not intimately connected with *faith*. Romans could talk about believing that the gods existed, or that they had done this or that, rather than of believing *in* a god as we do. Equally, there was no moral code which was specifically religious, or enjoined as an explicit concomitant of religious choice; the closest the Romans came to modern ideas of morality based on religion was the vague idea that the gods (eventually) punished wrongdoing, sometimes only after death. It is important to ask what, then, lay at the heart of Roman religions, if not faith or a moral code. We are otherwise in danger of returning to the nineteenth-century critique, which saw Roman religion as deficient because it was simply an agglomeration of acts.

It has been plausibly suggested that the answer lies in *knowing*, and especially 'knowing how', not believing; remember the tension between belief and knowledge about the gods in Tacitus, and Cicero's emphasis on both *sapientia* (wisdom) about the gods as a distinctive Roman trait, and the 'wise man's' duty to protect ancestral religious practice. To have the proper relationship with the gods, men needed to *know* which rituals were appropriate to which circumstances, how the right rituals must be performed, and why they worked. The priests were crucial here: they were expected to have knowledge, practical and historical, of this body of functioning rules, to advise on problems, identify where breakdown had happened, and suggest how to rectify error. Roman religion was indeed, as has been pointed out, in this sense a collection of *iura*, 'rights' or 'laws', which both parties had to understand and observe. This rational approach entailed a pragmatic flexibility: the possibility that one might have to acquire new knowledge in order to alter or replace that which proved deficient. Roman religion, then, is about knowing where you stand. This makes it empirical and practical, rather than internal, personal, and contemplative; and adds a dynamic strand to traditional conservatism rooted in *mos maiorum* (Ando 2003: 11–15).

sacra publica—the 'state religion'

The antiquarian Festus distinguished between *sacra publica*—those acts of worship of particular deities which were funded by the Roman state and officiated at by members of the Roman priestly colleges—and other types of *sacra*, whether private or tied to specific Roman locales (*On the Meaning of Words*, p. 284L). A number of other writers describe Roman religion in terms of particular acts explicitly placed under the aegis of particular priestly colleges: sacrificial rituals and festivals proscribed in the calendar, to be performed by the priests; advice on the proper conduct of public business from the augurs; consultation of the Sibylline books by the ten—later fifteen—priests in charge of conducting the *sacra* (*quinqueuiri sacris faciundis*); and portents expounded by the (Etruscan) *haruspices* (Cicero, *On the Responses of the Haruspices* 18; Valerius Maximus, *Memorable Deeds and Sayings* 1. 1. 1a–b; Scheid 2003: 129–46, on priests). The key action was sacrifice, 'by which', says Valerius Maximus, 'something is accomplished with solemn ritual, and also the warnings given by prodigies and lightening are expiated' (1. 1. 1a–b).

Fig. 7.1. The Pantheon, Rome (porch and rotunda from north). Probably begun by Trajan, but completed by Hadrian, this was a temple to all the gods of the Roman pantheon, and stood on the Campus Martius, on the site of the earlier Pantheon built by Agrippa, whose dedicatory inscription Hadrian reproduced on the architrave of his temple. This remarkable feat of Roman engineering is the most complete surviving pagan temple (it is today a church, having been consecrated in AD 608 as the church of S. Maria ad Martyres)

The *sacra publica* were not only paid for by the commonwealth, they were for Roman citizens (although only exceptionally, as with major thanksgivings or Augustus' Secular Games of 17 BC, did the authorities desire or achieve anything like total participation). Romans had no need to pay any attention to the deities of other communities (although initiation in prestigious Greek cults, such as the Eleusinian or Samothracian mysteries, attracted Roman aristocrats; we now know that Cicero's uncle was part of a group of Roman officers initiated on Samothrace while returning from campaign in Cilicia in 100 BC). Non-Romans had no business with the celebration of Roman public *sacra*. Like the citizens of Rome, the gods had houses (*aedes*—temples: Fig. 7. 1) and owned property: objects or land dedicated by worshippers. These were denoted by the adjective *sacer*: this was not an attribution of sacredness, but a label which showed the *legal* status of the object or place. There existed a special branch of the law: pontifical law (*ius pontificale*), interpreted by the priests; indeed, originally all legal interpretation and guidance had been provided by priests, not professional jurists. Roman aristocrats had a pathological concern with private property, both its inviolability and the rules governing its disposal, especially by inheritance. These rules held for mortals and gods alike; as private land could be made public and vice versa by the resolution of the community, so sacred objects and places could be taken from the deity (if the proper etiquette was observed) and made 'profane' (*profanus*; Paulus, *On the Meaning of Words*, p. 257 Lindsay; Macrobius, *Saturnalia* 3. 3. 2–4). Equally, sacrifice involved the transmission, just prior to immolation, of the animal from human to divine ownership, a move encoded in the gestures made with the sacrificial knife.

The sacra publica *and their discontents*

That Romans themselves adopted such a straightforward functionalist view of their religious activity inevitably invited attacks rooted in Christianizing assumptions. Nineteenth-century scholarship on the 'state religion', as *sacra publica* are often paraphrased, constructed a paradigm which, despite recent sustained reaction, still underlies many more modern accounts. This is a twofold tale, of purity and corruption, and of decadence and spirituality (debates which worried the nineteenth century after Christ more than the ten before him). Essentially, in this story Roman religion failed to satisfy worshippers' inner needs precisely because it mediated between the commonwealth and the gods, sidestepping the individual. Roman writers speak of a *pax deorum*, perhaps best translated as 'truce with the gods' (Rüpke 2001); sacrifices offered with scrupulous adherence to prescribed words and actions prevented the infringement of the truce, and guaranteed the support of the gods. This was interpreted in the modern era as dreary, cold formalism. It weakened, so the argument went, the pure indigenous core of Roman religion, and opened the door for (Greek) philosophical speculation about the gods, and for 'oriental' or 'mystery' religions—Isis and Serapis, Mithras, Cybele and Attis, Jupiter Dolichenus, and so on—more satisfying to the individual, but undermining 'Roman religion'. Finally, the hollow shell collapsed in the face of Christianity.

This model of decline—analogous to trends identified in Protestant scholarship, where the identification of a pure, original form of Christianity untainted by pagan influences has been used to figure the tension between Protestantism and Catholicism—contains a number of implausibilities. First, the 'weakness' of Roman indigenous religion, and its lack of appeal for worshippers, are largely read into the evidence by modern scholars, seeking in ancient contexts what they assumed to be an essential component of religion on the basis of their own experiences, looking for the culturally specific rather than the cross-cultural. Only the orientation of *sacra publica* for the good of the commonwealth, and the increasing popularity of religions whose origins lay outside Italy, have any basis in the evidence. The inherent conservatism of Roman society affected religion too, but did not impede innovation or the acceptance of new gods (Beard, North, and Price 1998, 1: ch. 2, Ando 2003: 6–8, 193–8). And ritual acts, old or new, were not empty gestures which accompanied worship; they *were* worship, or a large part of it, and moreover communicated important truths about the world. If Roman civic cults were as cold and pallid as modern scholars make out, it is hard to see how they could have lasted three generations, let alone eight centuries, before the Roman people rebelled against the meaningless somnambulism which we must suppose to have passed for their religion (Scheid 2003: 5–8, 11–13: nineteenth-century scholarly orthodoxy). Indeed, the apparent coldness of Roman rites may be recast as a positive expression of Roman propriety, which frowned on unchained displays of emotion. The careful policing of the 'orgiastic' cult of the Magna Mater, imported to Rome in 205 BC from Phrygia (northwest Turkey), is instructive in this respect: Roman citizens could not become Galli, the eunuch priests of this cult (compare Cicero, *On the Laws* 2. 19: the need for official sanction of any new or foreign gods).

Secondly, a 'golden age' of indigenous religious (or indeed any cultural) practices, unsullied by eastern 'temple-trash', is most unlikely given the high mobility of people and ideas in the Mediterranean from prehistory onwards (Horden and Purcell 2000: ch. 9). For example, the coastal site of Pyrgi near Rome has yielded fifth-century BC bilingual (Phoenician/Etruscan) gold tablets, recording the dedication of a sanctuary to Phoenician Astarte, equated with Etruscan Uni (Cornell 1995: 147, 212, 232). The Romans quite happily allowed that some of their religious institutions (for example, the triumph, and extispicy—examining the entrails of sacrificial animals to discover the will of the gods) were borrowings from the Etruscans. Numa, the second king, to whom many religious institutions were attributed, was held to be a Sabine immigrant. There was, and could be, no such thing as a primitive, uncontaminated Roman religion.

sacra priuata

> Privately let them worship those gods whose worship has been duly handed down from their ancestors.
>
> (Cicero, *On the Laws* 2. 19)

When Valerius Maximus listed the proper (that is, traditional) ways of 'paying attention to divine matters', he gives a series of actions or formulae: prayers, vows, thanksgiving, entreaties of signs of divine favour, and sacrifice (1. 1. 1a–b). These actions were by no means confined to *sacra publica*, but formed the essential matrix of all inter-actions with the gods for all individuals across society. Beside and below the religious acts of the commonwealth were forms of worship which served and defined other groups, whether social (household), military (legions and auxiliary cohorts), local (city districts), or pro-fessional (craftsmen). It is perhaps in areas like domestic cult that we come closest to Roman religions which allow for individual anxieties about the supernatural, and which reflect the desire to propitiate it or manipulate it as an individual, not as a citizen or member of a large group. One problem is that this area of religious activity is poorly attested in our sources (above). We have noted Augustine's satirical catalogue of the deities who had to do with a Roman wedding night: he reasons that this throng of helpers ought to cramp the couple's style! But how many real brides or grooms invoked all or any of these deities, at what times and with what rituals? We do not know, but the stresses of life and death must have been mediated for households and individuals by a meaningful interaction with the divine. *Knowledge* was vital for the *paterfamilias* (Chapter 4) in guid-ing his family through these trials of life. Such rituals as the sacrifice to the Lares and Penates (household gods of hearth and larder) are not trivialized for being repeated at every meal. Equally, a range of other information, from amulets and dedications to curse tablets, attests to a wide spectrum of 'personal' relationships with individual deities, which are not explicable in terms of any kind of regimented formalism. These relationships were incessantly and repeatedly instantiated at a range of locations, from altars in the house and garden to those at fountains and crossroads. Nor did they become dormant while men slept: dreams were a common form through which gods instructed men as to their wishes, or answered their queries (although some dreams were recognized as being deceptive); incubation, or sleeping over in the temple of a healing god, especially of Aesculapius, was a common form of healing taken over from the Hellenistic world—the cure was transmitted to the patient via a dream.

North-western Europe

Iron Age antecedents

So far we have concentrated on Rome, noting attitudes and structures, many of which then spread over time through the centres of power and population which articulated the empire, chiefly the major provincial towns. What, though, were the religious experiences of the frontiers, where the Graeco-Roman civilization collided with very different traditions (Chapter 8)? In this section I will examine some aspects of indigenous religious experience in north-western Europe, chiefly in Britain, and attempt to assess what changed, and how, with the coming of Rome.

There is a lot we do not know about Celtic religion: for example, whether or not it, or any regional manifestation of it, involved worship of the sun or the moon. Nor can we say much on how the La Tène populations conceived of the deities they did worship: no unambiguous evidence, for example, for the use of anthropomorphic divine images survives from Britain (one-offs like the Cerne Abbas giant continue to provoke inconclusive debate). If such images formed a focus of cult, they were made of materials like wood, which survive in the archaeological record only in particular circumstances. There are unambiguous images of deities on late Iron Age Celtic coins; but the most common one (found on the coins of all of the British tribes which minted) was Apollo, whose features can be traced back to the fourth-century Macedonian gold *statēr* issue which formed the prototype for the majority of early Celtic coins (Chapter 6).

The Celts clearly drew various distinctions between their deities, even if they never drew or sculpted them; gender is a significant divine variable. Some Celtic tribes enjoyed the protection of female deities. We find Brigantia for the British tribe of the Brigantes, and Andraste figures in Dio's account of the Boudiccan rebellion (62. 6–7). Other female deities are associated with horses, such as Epona (whose cult, however, is too widespread to allow her to be a tribal tutelary deity of the sort just discussed); still others are associated with springs: Coventina at Carrawburgh in Northumbria, Verbeia at the River Wharfe, and Sequana at the source of the Seine in Gaul (also serving as eponymous goddess of the tribe of the Sequani). Unlike their male counterparts, these female deities seem by and large to resist the addition of a Roman name or epithet. The localization of these deities (and here they are like their male counterparts) is one of the striking features of Celtic religion. Few Celtic deities appear to have an international profile (Lug/Lugh is one who did). Inscriptions from Gaul name almost 400 different local deities, but more than three-quarters of these appear only once. Each tribe or locality seems to have had its own deities, mostly overseeing war and trade. It is thus probably inappropriate to speak of a Celtic 'pantheon', which was clearly what Julius Caesar imagined (and would have expected to find) in speaking of Mercury, Apollo, Mars, Jupiter, and Minerva as the principal Gallic deities (*Gallic War* 6. 13–14).

A few dozen British Iron Age cult buildings have now been identified with reasonable certainty from their physical remains. Most were rectilinear in plan, but a variety of other configurations is known. They range in size from quite substantial buildings to tiny shrines (the largest ceremonial spaces of the late Iron Age are those of Eire). Some stood within settlements, others were isolated in the countryside; even those in settlements were separate from other buildings, and some appear to have stood within a sacred precinct (similar to the German enclosures known as *Viereckschanze*: Chapter 1). Various offerings survive, from pottery to personal ornament, from iron bars to animal bones. In no case can we be confident about the identity of the deity/deities worshipped. We also know that Celtic rites were practised at some natural features (as everywhere in prehistoric Europe): Graeco-Roman writers were interested in groves as places of Celtic worship, and we know that springs too were important, although Iron Age antecedents for the popularity of such cult sites in the Roman period are hard to verify, outside a few famous sites such as Bath.

Animal sacrifice was a staple of Celtic religious activity; in some cases various parts of the animals' carcasses were ritually buried, with cattle, horses, and dogs commonly found; by contrast, wild animals occur only exceptionally. More unusual was human sacrifice, which attracted sensational, and thus controversial, coverage in our sources, who record various gruesome methods of execution, from burning in wicker men to impaling. Archaeological evidence suggests a spectrum of ritualized killings, from foundation deposits for hillforts to the ritual killing of the high-status male now known as Lindow Man, recovered from a bog; there is also a grisly variety of methods of killing and deposition of the body, and even evidence of cannibalism. This is all very hard to interpret: were the deceased criminals, war captives, or a 'tithe' selected by the community? What of the severed heads attached to the ramparts of hillforts? They probably had religious significance, and may well be casualties of war, as was probably the case at Entremont near the mouth of the Rhône in Gaul, where a shrine contained skulls fixed to the wall, one with a javelin point in it, as well as sculptures of piles of human heads (third century BC?; Collis 1984: 110–12).

A very important ritual act was the deposition of high-value metalwork in rivers (mainly swords), bogs, and lakes (shields and cauldrons). This constitutes, by a country mile, the most conspicuous element of ritual practice attested from prehistoric Britain from the late Bronze Age through into the late Iron Age (when it seems to enter a decline). The rivers involved are those debouching on the east coast, from the Tyne to the Thames (other areas of Britain saw terrestrial burial of metalwork); lakes and bogs in Scotland, Ireland, and Wales also received such depositions at different periods. Two sites of prime importance are Llyn Fawr in Glamorgan, from which artefacts as diverse as cauldrons and chariot fittings were recovered, dating from about 600 BC; and Flag Fen near Peterborough, used between 1200 and 200 BC, where objects were cast into the fen from a great oaken causeway. A third is Llyn Cerrig Bach on Anglesey, as significant for the late start of depositions (*c.*200 BC) as for the quality of the material (both weapons and jewellery): interestingly, the pattern of dedications seems to dry up only in the first century AD, probably connected with the new Roman presence in Wales.

The religious personnel who officiated in the religions of the Celtic Iron Age attracted rather sensationalist coverage from Graeco-Roman sources, perpetuated in many modern treatments. They were the Druids, discussed by Caesar (who had probably encountered Druids) and other sources, like Strabo (who had not). Druids seem to have been associated with the calendar, and with healing and judication; the famous image of Druids collecting mistletoe for ritual purposes, clad in white, goes back to the Elder Pliny (*Natural History* 16. 95—a rare occurrence, says Pliny, lest we think too quickly of Getafix in the *Asterix* stories). Despite the interest shown in them by the ancient sources, and the fact that they were the focus of Roman attempts to stamp out human sacrifice in Gaul and Britain, the Druids did not operate with complete autonomy in Celtic society: local rulers were probably the key mediators between human and divine.

Romano-British religions

Those Iron Age cult buildings which survived the Roman conquest of Britain were rebuilt as Romano-Celtic temples, more solid structures of which more than 150 are known. They are accompanied by recognizably Roman habits of depicting deities, a culture of religious writing, and the offering of Roman material goods (the deposition of coins, jewellery, figurines, and miniatures—but not weapons—in rivers and pools, known also in Roman Germany, may be related to Iron Age practices). The architecture of these buildings displays enormous variation, from the 'classic' Graeco-Roman (mainly in large towns and forts) to simple structures of various shapes. The Romano-Celtic type, often square or rectangular with a veranda-style portico running round the building, seems to be most common (this is the type familiar from the excavations of the enormous sacred area at Altbach in Trier). Most temple buildings are found in the south-eastern half of the province, but this must in part reflect a bias in archaeological exploration; the military frontier represents another major concentration. There too (but not only there), we find considerable evidence of a range of cult activity focused on the imperial house.

An interesting example of a Romano-British temple is that at Lydney in Gloucestershire, one of a series of almost a dozen temples in this part of Britain which were built from new or enlarged after *c.* AD 200. Another is the temple of Mercury at Uley, where worshippers left curse tablets affixed to the walls of the sanctuary, often aimed at thieves or love rivals, and invoking the help of gods besides Mercury (these tablets constitute a major resource for the study both of these *defixiones* in the northern empire and of 'provincial' Latinity). Yet another type is represented by the sanctuary built within the ramparts of the disused Iron Age hillfort at Maiden Castle (apparently in the 360s AD). All three locations share an apparent remoteness from any settlement, and must have required a considerable journey from worshippers wishing to participate in the rites.

At Lydney, on a ridge above the Severn estuary, stood a third-century temple, a bath-building, a large rectangular structure, and a long range of rooms, some richly equipped with mosaic floors. The last two structures have, on the basis of similar structures in the Greek East and the relative remoteness of Lydney, been tentatively identified as elements of a hostel for 'pilgrims'. The sanctuary was used for the worship of Mars Nodens, named in dedications; but iconographic evidence from the site also shows marine and solar deities and a female figure, as well as the (ubiquitous) Roman woodland god Silvanus, with whom a number of dog figurines may be associated (rather than with Mars Nodens). A miniature human forearm suggests, on the analogy of widespread Graeco-Roman practice, a healing cult as well (perhaps the function of the unidentified buildings was medical). Despite its peripheral location, this was a major sanctuary, patronized and maintained by a wealthy elite, whose multiple concerns involved a range of deities. The sanctuary, unlike some of its neighbours, survived the upheavals of the 360s, when a separatist imperial regime seized power in Britain, and seems to go out of use only in the early fifth century, by which time Rome had formally abandoned her rule in Britain.

The ritual activities practised at these Romano-Celtic temples seem to be culturally hybridized (and in different proportions in different places); but who was doing what to whose deities is not always clear. We find a largely Celtic substrate presented in a Latin vernacular, within a wider Graeco-Roman cultic context. This at least is the impression given by the 'Coligny calendar' from the centre of imperial Gaul. Though it looks like a classic *paragpēgma* (peg) calendar and is written in Latin, it is not *the* Roman calendar. It specifies auspicious and inauspicious days (like its Roman counterparts; see above), but not festivals; the months are Celtic months with indigenous names, and the year starts in summer or autumn, not in January. The mapping of sacred time in the document may be of pan-Gallic application, given that the document bears out some of our other data on the Celtic year. The essential framework of religious activity in the provinces of the north-west was one which presupposed a broad congruity of practice, of sites, and of modes of religious expression (not least the use of Latin), which stood in contrast to the earlier regionalism of the area. One widespread custom was the communal consumption of the sacrificial animal, as opposed to the Celtic disposal by burial in pits (although the latter also continues, or develops, into the Roman period; the burial of sacrificed animals as 'foundation deposits' cannot, however, be seen as particularly Celtic).

Some native practices died out in the Roman period (such as the—already declining?—deposition of weapons in water), but others persisted, including, most strikingly, human sacrifice, despite prohibition by the authorities. Three Roman wells, in London, Hertfordshire, and Bedfordshire, have produced human skulls, two from heads freshly severed when thrown in, the third lodged in a special niche; an adult skeleton was found sealing a cistern at Caerwent. The bodies of two babies were buried in the foundations of a cult site at Springhead in Kent—both had been beheaded. And in a cemetery at Winchester, over a coffin empty but for some coins, were deposited the bodies of two dogs and a young man, decapitated, with his head between his knees, a coin in the mouth (the last a common Graeco-Roman practice). Nor are these the only examples of the ritualized deposition of human remains. The ultimate offering to the gods, the life of a fellow human, continued in some cases to be acceptable in Roman Britain, despite imperial prohibitions.

Rome adopted a laissez-faire policy towards almost all new divinities, and acted to suppress only instances of *superstitio* (above) which threatened the normative practices of society (Christianity, Druidism), and even that not in any systematic way. In most cases encounters between religious systems took the form of mutual rapprochement, as each side tried to accommodate the new gods within its own frame of reference (and by extension, to come to terms with each other). In almost all cases we possess only the Roman side of this process of realignment (a viewpoint termed *interpretatio Romana* by scholars). A common strategy was identification of a Roman deity with a native one, a process referred to as syncretism: thus, Mars and Lenus were seen to be one and the same on the basis of similar attributes and functions: whence Mars Lenus. Whether this is the whole story is another matter: Mars was linked to almost seventy other deities besides Lenus in Gaul, and over twenty in Britain. Yet other deities were not syncretized at all, and for those that were, the process was not inevitable or automatic: in Britain, Cocidius appears four times as often alone as with Mars.

More than regional variation may be at issue here. If Varro was right, that in antiquity the community had logical priority over its gods, then we should expect the formation of new Romano-provincial societies to generate 'new' gods appropriate to their needs. In some cases (as with Romano-British images of horned deities: see Hutton 1993: fig. 6. 12) we simply do not understand the identifications being made, let alone the cultic dynamics behind them.

Traditional Roman deities are found named in inscriptions without a Celtic surname (notably in Britain Jupiter, Mars, and Mercury), as were 'abstract' deities commonly worshipped across the empire (Victory, Fortuna, and so on). The former are mainly attested in the richer, more populous, urbanized south-eastern part of the province, longest exposed to influence from continental Europe. Together with the abstract deities, they also feature in the military zone of the northern frontier. Both elites in cities and Roman soldiers can be reasonably expected to display a more serious engagement with Roman culture in general (and thus cultural systems like religion) than the indigenous peasantry. A similar distribution of texts and objects associated with the worship of emperors comes as no surprise. The colony at Camolodunum (Colchester) was 'ground zero' for this form of worship, with its huge temple to the Deified Claudius. A range of other deities could, as necessary, be assimilated to the emperors' divine powers, whether as alternative manifestations of them, or as co-adjutors. The major cities, the south-east, and the military zone have also produced testimonies of 'mystery religions', from Mithraic 'caves' (most notably the very substantial 'temple of Mithras' found near the Walbrook stream in London in 1956) to a castration device bearing images of Cybele the Great Mother and Attis; but the impression derived from the material remains is not one of a dense penetration of these cults.

Other Roman deities were assimilated to Celtic ones. A set of spoons from a fourth-century AD hoard at Gallows Hill, Thetford, was inscribed not only with the name Faunus, suggesting their use in a ritual associated with his cult, but with a series of epithets in the Celtic language, such as 'Protector' and 'Mead-Maker', as well as personal names, perhaps the worshipper to whom each spoon 'belonged' for the purposes of the ritual (Henig 1984: 59, Webster 1986: 54). This looks very much like an *interpretatio Celtica*, and shows that at the 'micro' level of ritual something far more complex than crude identification of Roman and native on a functional basis was going on. Faunus is here seen as polyvalent, and as having a special and distinct relationship with each worshipper. This assemblage is doubly interesting in that, uniquely, the spoons seem originally to have been Christian, perhaps associated with baptism. Were they later appropriated by pagans? Or is this an instance of absorption of Christian cult into the polytheistic portfolio, a phenomenon attested sporadically across the empire? In this and other cases of syncretism, it may be the *cultural cachet* of the Roman 'equivalent' which leads to its being adopted for worship beside the local deity. Thus, local British deities (some of whom were very local) like Nodens, Thingsus, Condatis, Rigonometis, and Olludius came to occupy a more prestigious position through association with Mars. Religious politics would thus reflect the organization of power and authority within the province.

Then there were deities neither Roman nor indigenous, like the Matres (Mothers, also known by other names) brought into Britain by soldiers transferred from the Rhineland. These three seated goddesses (the Celtic attachment to the number three may have gained prestige by association with Roman triads of deities) are mainly found in Britain in military contexts, or in towns. Confusingly, these military Matres are often spoken of as being associated with particular provinces, or indeed with all of them. Equally, the Genii Cucullati, the Hooded Spirits, may be imported, perhaps again from the Rhineland, although their distribution is wide; in Britain they are found on the frontier and, like the Matres, around Cirencester.

Variety is a defining feature of provincial religious practice, and Roman Britian is no exception: we may take as emblematic the fort at Alauna (Maryport) in Cumbria, which has produced dedications to over a dozen deities, from local gods to manifestations of the imperial power; there are images of others about whom we know nothing. Local and imperial, Roman, eastern, and Celtic are found cheek by jowl, sometimes syncretized, and sometimes aloof from interaction. As ever, most of our evidence was left by the elites and special-interest groups, chiefly the army. What difference was made to the religious life of the majority of the inhabitants of Britannia by the Roman occupation is a question which we are not yet in a position to answer. The burden of proof probably lies with those who think that the answer is 'a lot'.

The empire: the third century AD

The middle of this century was a time of crisis in politics (Chapter 3), but the third century was also one in which new religions like Christianity finally came of age, and in which others, notably the so-called Oriental religions, were in their pomp, beginning with the flood tide of their popularity in the Severan period, which swept them across the empire. It is worth examining the religious 'prosperity' of this period. A new religiosity is often connected with the empire's troubles, as men sought to find a more satisfactory account of their position in the cosmos, and a better earnest of salvation, in an age of gloom.

The rise of the 'new' cults is also 'explained' by the rebarbative austerity of the 'state religion': this account is as unsatisfactory when evoked for AD 200 as it is for 100 BC. Rather, we should realize that the world had moved on, and that Rome had become a global idea and a universal identity after the *constitutio Antoniniana* (Chapter 3). The old cults of the Roman *res publica* had been those of a city-state, and had never been meant to serve the new community, which covered most of the known world (although they could still express a centralizing ideology and identity in this new context—as the Decian persecutions show—and the *princeps* remained *pontifex maximus*). Yet the new situation was propitious for other forms of worship (perhaps prefigured by Hadrian's establishment of the cult of Venus and *Roma* in Rome itself), all of which shared more psychological and existentialist preoccupations. And their rise cannot be understood independently of a religious 'turn' in the leading philosophical schools, especially the contemplative spirituality of the Neoplatonists, who sought mystical identification with the divine, as expressed in the writings of Plotinus and Porphyry.

This branch of philosophy influenced many Christian writers of the next century, including Firmicus Maternus and St Augustine. The Neoplatonist belief that one deity lay behind all the various gods worshipped by men embodied a universalizing tendency (already apparent in some contexts in the Hellenistic period; and note the mid-second-century identification of the Heavenly Maiden (Virgo Caelestis) with the Syrian Goddess, the Great Mother, Peace, Virtus, Ceres, and Panthea ('all-goddess') in a dedication from Hadrian's Wall: *Roman Inscriptions of Britain* 1791) which prefigured Christianity's role under Constantine and his successors, and which in more general terms favoured the new religious climate (and see below on 'solar cults'). An analogous trend has been seen in Philostratus' *Life of Apollonius of Tyana*, written in the later Severan period, recounting the life and travels of the wise man Apollonius from India to Atlantic Iberia. These extensive travels do not simply give pleasure to the reader, they underscore a spiritual journey which surpasses the teachings of all existing religious systems. This experience gives Apollonius a quasi-divine status, making him an advisor to the empire itself, whose boundaries he has surpassed physically and spiritually. The contrast with the localizing tendency of religious writing of the second century, whether inspired by antiquarian interests (like Pausanias' *Guide to Greece*) or contemporary piety, is striking. The earlier outlook stressed local identity in contradistinction to the imperial, which guaranteed the security in which such local interests could be indulged (Elsner and Rubies 1999: 9–15).

In this context the popularity of religions of eastern origin is more comprehensible. A literary and cultural trope in Roman writing treats them with suspicion or contempt, little more than imported occult practice and stargazing; above all, they were incompatible with *mos maiorum*. Some were naturalized by official decree, becoming *peregrina sacra* (foreign cults: Festus, *On the Meaning of Words*, p. 268L), like those of the Magna Mater. Others were simply adopted and practised in Rome without formal sanction: upper-class writers could refer to these cults as 'foreign superstitions'; typical of upper-class attitudes is the hostility of the Elder Pliny to the teachings of the Persian Magi; attitudes to Christianity were similar: Tactius, *Annals* 15. 44; Pliny the Younger, *Letters* 10. 96. 3, who, however, calls it nothing more than 'misguided and immoderate' (96. 8). Yet eastern cults had coexisted with city-state cults in the eastern Mediterranean since the fourth century BC, and had gained ground at the highest levels of Roman society since the late Republic: Marius placed great trust in a Syrian prophetess, Martha, and Sulla had shown his devotion to a syncretism of Roman Bellona and the Cappadocian mother-goddess, Mâ. The Augustan reaction against Egyptian religion in the wake of the war with Cleopatra had subsided by the time of Caligula; Vespasian, whose bid for the throne had begun in Alexandria, spent the night before his triumph in the temple of Isis on the Campus Martius. Formulaic disdain coexisted with considerable enthusiasm for eastern religions: Lucian satirizes eastern gods as illegal immigrants to Olympus (*Assembly of the Gods* 9–10), but he was himself a Syrian Greek, and the satire is really a knowing look at the multiculturalism of the period. Such deities could no longer be harnessed to promote separatism and resistance, as they had during the First Sicilian Slave War in the second century BC, when the slave Eunous of Apamea proclaimed his special relationship with Atargatis. Only in cases like that of Elagabulus did devotion to eastern deities go too far (Chapter 3).

The term 'Oriental' religions is common currency in scholarship, and is not unhelpful—no western cult achieved anything remotely resembling the popularity or spread in the East that eastern cults did in the West. Yet the label invites us to think of eastern cults as monolithic and homogeneous: with initiation as a criterion of participation, personal relationships to the deity, and soteriological characteristics. In fact these cults were very diverse. Their initiations were very different; as were the brands of salvation or rebirth purveyed in ceremonies characterized by noise and costume, colour and emotion, each different from the others.

It is partly to Christian apologetics that, as with the concept of paganism, we owe the idea of unified 'Oriental' religions. Firmicus Maternus' *Error of Profane Religions* is important here—drawing on his Neoplatonist roots, Maternus invented a simple way of classifying the major eastern religions according to the supposed fundamentals of their worship. This scheme made a big impression on the father of the modern study of Oriental religions in the Roman Empire, Franz Cumont. He saw evidence for it in the trend for syncretism between these cults in the later empire, and the fact that known individuals participated in more than one of these cults (but it is clear that they did so aware that each cult was distinct).

One characteristic which these eastern religions do share, at least as we encounter them in the Roman Empire, is their Hellenization (Turcan 1996: 4–7, 23–4): the hymns to Cybele and Isis were in Greek, and all of the cult names of Isis found in her aretologies (lists of her virtues) were Greek, as were the names of the festivals (anticipating early Christianity). The filtering of these cults through a Greek cultural matrix is as old as the eighth-century BC syncretism of Greek Herakles and Phoenician Melqart. The Greek poetess Sappho wrote about Adonis; the Eleusinian mysteries were an important model for the initiatory aspect of all the eastern cults; important too are the Ptolemaic make-over of the worship of Egyptian deities, including the transformation of Isis-worship into an initiatory religion; and the Commagenian remix of Persian Mithraism (the survival of the name 'Persian' for an initiatory grade underscores the cult's deracination). Greek philosophy, astrology, and mythology gave a Hellenic coating to the eastern cults, and an added respectability; equally, these cults lent a more serious aura to astrology. Even the depictions of these deities in art are expressed in the Graeco-Roman artistic tradition; iconography was what distinguished the eastern gods from their Olympian brethren, not style of representation.

Astrology, a largely Hellenic ingredient in this cultural process, is very important (as any student of the cult of Mithras will discover; indeed, some Mithraic scholars have argued recently that it is of cardinal significance). It fused with the indigenous solar theology of the eastern cults (below) to give a deeper cosmic role to themes like death and rebirth, and the cycle of the seasons, and to create a more comprehensible place in the greater scheme for the individual. Interestingly, one of Isis' claims in her aretologies was that *she* controlled the constellations and fate.

In a more direct way, astrology was important for understanding a number of religious systems which had in common the belief—already noted in connection with Neoplatonism, but by no means restricted to the philosophically minded—that it was possible for worshippers to attain temporary unity with god (that is, the divine) through contemplation, and permanent unity after death. For any attempt of this sort, the basic problem was the separation of the human and divine worlds. God was perceived as inhabiting the eternal and unchanging cosmos, the heavens, which contained the stars, the planets, and the moon. By contrast, mortals were confined to the tiny fraction of the cosmos which, in Aristotelian terms, lay *below* the moon (the sublunary sphere)—the earth, where everything was the opposite of the ordered heavens: chaos and chance ruled; everything changed constantly and then perished. Some religions aimed to mitigate the drawbacks of the earthly existence (such mitigation could be sought in several cults) while it lasted.

As the problem was one of physical separation from the divine during life, the solution perforce lay with the soul, not the body. Every soul was, for these worshippers, thought to contain (or to be) a fragment of the god who controlled the cosmos (and who was worshipped, but not in a complacent way, under many different names on earth), and thus to contain something which originated in the heavens (here there is common ground with Stoic philosophy too). The heavenly origin of this divine spark endowed the soul with the virtues or qualities associated with the various planets (reason from Saturn, courage from Mars, passion from Venus, and so on). After death the soul could escape the earthly, physical prison, and returned to the heavens whence it had come.

In the meantime, a number of cults sought to inculcate the hope of rejoining the divinity, and even to encourage the idea that by contemplation the 'divine spark' in the soul might attain brief unity with god. The 'soul' was often considered to be, or to contain, celestial light; and thus, central to managing the proper relation between mortal and divine, and preparing to rejoin god after death, was the worship of a number of solar or stellar deities, whose attributes marked them as belonging to the realm of light. Jupiter Dolichenus (from Commagene originally) and Jupiter Heliopolitanus (from Baalbek in Lebanon) are examples. We have noted the excessive and un-Roman veneration of Elagabulus for Ba'al of Emesa, whose high priest he had been, which undoubtedly played a part in his fall—but the wider importance of this and other solar deities to the whole Severan dynasty, as well as to later emperors, is also important. The epithet 'unconquered' applied to the Sun (Sol Invictus) is also applied commonly to Mithras, and to later emperors. In these important and multifaceted solar and stellar cults, knowledge of the stars and planets, and their influence on the sublunary realm, was obviously very useful, and here we begin to understand the importance of astrology in religion (and in later philosophy), despite traditionalist misgivings. For some it was a sort of road map, a way of understanding, or at least glimpsing, the fate which the supreme solar deity had set out for them; or of at least choosing the least inauspicious times at which to act. The other side of the coin, which also required engagement of astrology, was a series of (often initiatory) cults which promised to free their devotees from the tyranny of fate, and bring salvation.

The popularity of these religions in the third century has been related not just to political crisis in the empire, but also to existential crisis among individual citizens, a sense of rootlessness and impotence which has its origins in the supposed crisis of the *polis* and its civic ideals and cults under the Hellenistic monarchs (fourth to first centuries BC): so, for example, Turcan 1996. In an uncertain world where old truths had fallen by the wayside, these religions, with their (often) full-time priesthoods and initiatory regimes, offered hope of protection not even available any more from the emperor, and more importantly, of salvation.

Yet concepts like the 'crisis of the *polis*' or the 'age of anxiety' may be just that—scholarly concepts, exaggerating processes of historical and cultural change. There are obvious benefits to soteriological religions in an age of upheaval, and we should not deny that those benefits were needed and felt by some; the flourishing of oracles in the third century points in the same direction, perhaps. Yet it would be a mistake to think that only initiates in mystery cults felt that they could get close to their chosen divinities. We noted above, in the context of the Roman *sacra publica*, that *religio* was something that could *attach itself* to mortals, and that the interface with the divine was thought of as operating physically rather than through contemplation. Further, it may be useful to invoke factors like the universalizing trends in philosophy and society discussed above, as well as the benefits of religions which offered solidarity (often expressed through communal dining) to initiates who found themselves crossing a large and diverse Roman empire, often strangers in a strange land. The numerous contexts in which, for example, Isis is proclaimed as active in the aretologies may stand, in a way, for the astonishingly diverse cultural experiences wedged into the lands between the Firth of Forth and the cataracts of the Nile, for the vast bricolage of the Roman Empire. A mobile, supra-local world needed gods of the same ilk, and the eastern gods travelled well: there are over 400 Mithraea known from across the empire, predominantly in Italy and the northern and western provinces, with more awaiting discovery. In doing so, they bound together the scattered and the rootless, the citizens of the *cosmopolis* and those on the margins of society; we may note that the Christian Gnostic sect saw existence as exile. In fact, the appeal of the eastern cults was in these respects similar to that of Christianity, another religion whose emphasis was psychological and existentialist, and to which we now turn.

Christianity

Perhaps the single most significant legacy of Rome for the development of Europe as a whole was the Christianization of the empire; the decisive steps were the universal toleration proclaimed by Constantine in the Edict of Milan in AD 313, and the conversion of Constantine himself (Chapter 9). This set a critical pattern of alignment between temporal and religious authority which, even if honoured in the breach, proved essential for the creation of Christendom. Constantine had only two pagan successors, Julian and Eugenius, neither of whom was able to alter the prevailing dynamics of power—not surprising, according to their Christian detractors, since the true god was not on their side. Constantine's personal attitude remains inscrutable, but he certainly sensed the direction in which the tide of history was running. The ferocity of the Decian and Diocletianic persecutions of the previous century is suggestive of real fear of a religion with powerful support from the floorboards up, across the empire.

In 331 the possessions, and thus the economic viability, of the old gods began to be attacked by Christian emperors; in 337 the first restrictions on pagan sacrifices appeared. Nevertheless, few pagan temples were closed before 357, when a universal order was passed against pagan worship; the reign of Julian ushered in a new period of toleration. The brief reign of Eugenius was followed in 394 by Theodosius' order for the closure of temples and the end of sacrifices.

Thereafter the end came slowly, a gradual decline which lasted until the middle of the sixth century, after which paganism was effectively extinct; it lingered longest among the lower classes, for whom the imprint of the polytheist mentality allowed recourse back to the old gods when the new seemed not to have delivered, a short-termism lamented by church fathers from Augustine in the fourth century to Pope Gelasius at the end of the fifth. The old religions were too diffuse to resist organized Christianity; their adherents could not understand concepts like conversion (preferring syncretism), proselytism, or martyrdom; and their long-standing associations with the civic sphere meant that the weakening of the latter in the late empire undermined the former.

Christianity taught that there was one 'true' god, who was to be worshipped without sacrifice—a major distinction from other religions. Early Christians also reverenced a range of martyrs, holy spirits, saints, and angels, but were careful to distinguish this from pagan practice. These entities did not receive sacrifice; there were no images of them: sacrifice to idols was termed 'idolatry', from the Greek terms *eidōlon* (image) and *latreia* (service, especially to a divinity). The pagans' gods did exist; it was just that they were not gods, but demons leading astray the ignorant.

Early Christians did not have strong views on the existing socio-political order, being more interested in the next world, and having a strong sense in any case of the impending end of the present one. This explains their indifference to existing social hierarchies and cultural customs (for example, marriage—second-best after virginity and chastity; and property). On the other hand, its openness, importantly to men and women in equal measure, contrasted with the increasing rigidity of later imperial society. Women were often the first converts in pagan families (at least at those levels of society with which our sources mainly deal), and female martyrdom was far from infrequent; Christianity did not class women as irrational. This openness offered an advantage over other 'elective' religions like Mithraism, with its small, exclusively male congregations. Its view of the afterlife was attractive and accessible, independent of abstruse initiations or a deterministic theology mired in astrology; its ethical code did not need a philosophical education to be approached. Of course, there were fierce theological debates (themselves alien to the pagan mindset), schisms, excommunications, and bitter infighting (but few executions: Priscillian in Spain in the late fourth century is a rare case). Indeed, Christianity in the age of Constantine was really a collection of Christianities, and still a long way from becoming orthodox. Yet, with its endorsement by Constantine, it became over the fourth century a focus for unity and cohesion, ideological if not political, which even the figure of the emperor no longer provided.

8

The cultural implications of the Roman conquest

Nicola Terrenato

The problem

Few political entities, anywhere, at anytime, have been credited with such a massive and capillary cultural impact as the Roman Empire. Marvelling at 'carbon-copy' inscriptions or bathhouses from Mesopotamia to Hadrian's Wall in Scotland, scholars and general public alike have been awestruck by the apparent homogeneity brought about by the irresistible expansion of Rome. Such a long-lived, relatively peaceful empire, bearer of a pervasive and revolutionary form of civilization, was the perfect precedent to justify medieval and modern expansionist projects of all kinds, from Arthurian Cornwall and Norman Sicily, to the Spanish *conquista* and the British Empire. Never equalled, although always emulated, the thorough acculturation promoted by Rome is still a very powerful icon today. It is, however, only since the early nineteenth century that this perception of Rome has crystallized into an organic, unquestioned form, aligning scholarly frameworks with popular representations. European nationalism seems to have had a specific and acute need for a predecessor like the Roman Empire that would legitimize and reinforce the new, dominant imperialist discourse. It is not a coincidence that it is in the Romantic period that some of the foundations of modern Roman history were laid, by engaged classicists like the Prussian Theodor Mommsen, whose intellectual activity was often vested in the nationalist movements of their time. In a substantial departure from previous historical models, which occasionally left a role for non-Roman agency, these scholars construed the Roman expansion almost exclusively in terms of the triumph of a superior civilization over savage westerners and decadent orientals.

The spread of Roman culture was thus seen as a radically positive development, which forever changed the face of western culture. It supplied a vital ideological prop to several nineteenth-century nationalistic projects of debatable morality, such as the imposition of an official unified culture, replacing a rich regional diversity in emerging states like Germany or Italy. A similar rhetoric worked just as well abroad. European nations participating in the rush for Africa made a heavy use of Roman images, especially in the administration of their dominions (for instance, French colonial commissioners were called *proconsuls*). The early twentieth century only witnessed a further consolidation of the pedestal upon which the Romans had been firmly planted. Francis Haverfield formalized the concept of Romanization to explain the culture of Britain in the Roman period, while Fascist overtones cast belated Italian land-grabs in Africa as the return of the rightful inheritors to the legacy of Rome. In the second half of the century the cultural dominance of Rome was still not radically challenged, decolonization and the decline of nationalism notwithstanding. Rome's law codes or civic ethos may no longer have been exalted in absolute terms, but new materialistic views were still based upon Rome's political, and especially economic, dominance, which in turn was responsible for deep changes in the lands they conquered. In other words, the real motives of Roman expansion can be and have been questioned, but its cultural impact has remained a given in virtually every approach to the issue.

The development of postcolonial studies marked yet another phase in the perception of the ancient phenomenon, one once again modelled after its supposed modern equivalent. Finally, some sort of role in the process was reserved for non-Romans as well. Previously they had occasionally been credited with at best a desperate resistance, but they now become active contributors to forms of cultural osmosis. In the last decade the concept of Romanization has increasingly faced radical critiques, which have tended to reject it as a value-laden term.

For the western provinces, for instance, new models of culture-change envisage the emergence of a brand new make-up resulting from the combination of Roman and non-Roman traits rather than from a one-way transfer. Concepts initially developed to describe modern situations, such as hybridization and creolization, are applied to Roman Britain in particular, in order to explain the cultural implications of the conquest. It is only very recently that some discerning voices have begun to question the modernist presumption, still silently underpinning much of the debate, that Roman expansion was essentially comparable with modern imperialisms. There are, on this view, deep structural differences between post-1750 forms of colonial contact and most earlier ones, including the Roman Empire. For instance, the ethnic polarization that characterizes modern encounters is not at all visible in ancient ones, where there had been contacts, transfers, and exchanges for centuries before political annexation (see Chapter 1). Thus, creolization, which implies the existence of originally 'pure' ethnic groups, can hardly be appropriate to a world like the ancient Mediterranean, where intense cultural interaction has been going on at least since the Neolithic. The kind of colonial encounters that resulted from Rome's expansion largely took place between peoples which had long displayed a number of important cultural similarities or compatibilities.

In a perspective of this kind, what formerly went under the name of Romanization can be cast in a completely different light. Retracing cultural interaction to long before the actual conquest, the relationship between the political event and the changes that happened in connection with it can be analysed in all its long-term complexity. In many current treatments the processes are seen on a flattened temporal scale, typically comparing the situation immediately before the Roman conquest with its aftermath. Besides the modernist assumption discussed above, there is another major bias at work here. Some of the most influential studies of cultural change have focused upon the western provinces, and especially Britain, Germany, continental Gaul, and Spain. This is largely a result of the national points of view of modern scholars, the advancement of archaeological fieldwork, and the overall balance of power in the modern western world. The irony is that, in terms of the Roman Empire, many of these areas were conquered relatively late and can hardly be considered central to the Roman world. There could not have been a truly global Roman empire without Sicily, Syria, or mainland Greece, whereas the addition of the continental western provinces only expanded further the scope of an already unchallenged dominant power.

Thus, our current perceptions of cultural change in the Roman Empire are largely coloured by an over-representation of tardy and peripheral incorporations, which will be conventionally denominated here as the 'outer circle'. Meanwhile, what work was done on cultural change in the Mediterranean inner circle has tended to be informed by different norms and concerns, centring primarily on descriptive treatments of high art and architecture. It is only recently that cross-fertilizations have begun to happen between practitioners dealing with the two geographic spheres, producing very interesting new ideas. The cultural developments in Italy in particular have been recently illuminated by innovative studies that have dealt with the early workings of Roman expansion. A key role in this has been played by archaeological fieldwork, just as had been the case earlier in continental Europe. Crucial data about the rural world, about local power and production, are dramatically rebalancing a picture that relied too much on the public sphere of urban elites. This in turn is prompting a wide-ranging reconsideration of textual evidence, particularly abundant for the Mediterranean region. Better archaeological work has also produced more refined dates, which have often proven problematic for traditional interpretations. In a number of cases, it has been clearly shown how the evidence of cultural change was not chronologically contiguous with the conquest, making the existence of a causal connection much less obvious. Thus, the time seems ripe for a thorough reassessment of the situation, questioning all the strong assumptions made about the diffusion of Roman culture at least since the nineteenth century, if not before.

In the remainder of this chapter it will be argued that the creation of the Roman Empire was indeed connected with substantial cultural changes. Such changes, however, were not the direct, nor the centrally imposed, consequence of the expansion. Nor did they result from the encounter of vastly different cultures, creating new hybrids. In most cases it can be shown that cultural change happens prior to, or independently of, political annexation, to the point where it could be paradoxically argued that it is sometimes the culture-change that drives the conquest, rather than the other way around. Once the

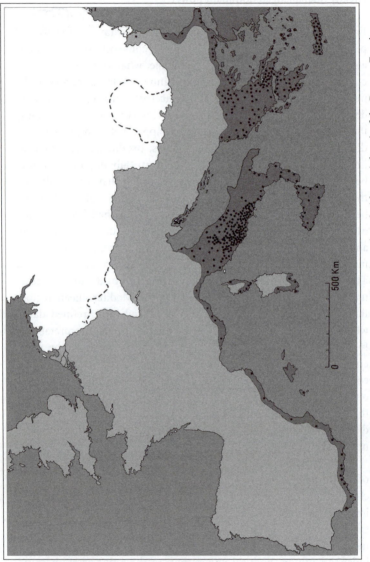

Fig. 8.1. Map showing the 'inner' circle (the core) and the 'outer' circle (the periphery) of the Roman Empire

empire is in place, only limited, interstitial cultural areas will be immediately and deeply affected, while elite cultural fashions will ebb and flow, with only a loose and indirect connection with political events. Global waves occasionally take place, most notably in the Augustan period, but they will sweep across the empire and beyond, impacting core and periphery alike, with a pattern and a tempo that has little to do with the Roman conquest that had taken place centuries before. Only in those areas, such as continental Europe, where the conquest roughly coincides with this cultural trend, will there be an apparent sequentiality, which for centuries has misled scholars based in those areas into assuming a strong causal value, which they have then extrapolated back into the core.

In short, when we look at the culture of the Roman Empire beyond the common data-sets and assumptions, it is hard to describe the process as one of straightforward diffusion of the same universal structure from a centre. The encounter of radically different cultures producing a new hybrid is only a slightly more satisfactory model. What we see instead is a large number of communities engaged in cultural dialogues over a very long time-span, within which the Roman conquest is only one of many relevant episodes. Such cultural negotiation produces different outcomes at different social levels, in different areas and periods, between different age-groups and genders, and even at different stages and in different aspects of the biography of the same individual. It is only by taking such a context-sensitive approach that the richness and significance of the cultural processes associated with the Roman Empire can be appreciated in more realistic and less ideology-laden terms.

With these caveats in mind, it is time to turn to the examination of some of the main cultural areas generally seen as thoroughly shaped by the Roman conquest. The conventional view is that Rome had an active interest in imposing, or at least encouraging, the reorganization and uniformity of the local communities that were one by one being absorbed (review of the literature in Hingley 2005). Political structure, law, language, religion, art, and architecture are all prime areas in which pervasive and long-lasting Roman influence can supposedly be seen. Denying this would seem paradoxical. And yet, taking a fresh look at these areas, and rebalancing these perspectives with what we know of less obvious ones, such as rural culture or social structures, can produce a remarkably different picture, which has deep repercussions for our understanding of the nature of the Roman Empire.

Politics, law, and language

The one Roman imposition that is most easily tangible is, of course, the political one. Without it, it would seem, there is simply no empire. Rome not only pushes militarily and diplomatically for annexation and central control, but even appears to dictate local power structures as well. Even aside from colonies (new foundations organized by the Roman state; see also Chapters 2 and 5), whose entire constitution was shaped by Rome, *municipia* (autonomous settlements incorporated as Roman 'chartered towns' at or after the time of conquest) seem to buy into Roman political culture. Praetors, but also quaestors and aediles (that is, magisterial titles borrowed directly from Rome) pop up in allied cities from the third century BC. Roman influence, combined with new forms of elite self-representation, is very strong and visible in this area. While this is only to be expected, given Rome's central role in the smooth functioning of imperial administration, it is important not to overstate its significance within the local communities.

In Italy, at Umbrian Assisi, for instance, an inscription in Latin was set up in the late first century BC by (among others) local magistrates Nero Babrius and Vibius Volsienus (*Corpus Inscriptionum Latinarum* 1^2.2112). The text, however, is oddly reminiscent of that of an inscription in Umbrian (the local pre-Roman language), set up a half-century earlier by two identically named members of the same families. In other words, the adoption of Roman political formulas can mask the persistence of local power structures and long-standing alliances between established aristocratic clans. These lineages clearly managed to survive and thrive after the Roman conquest, and are now using Latin political terminology to legitimize further their dominant position. Municipal elites showing an ability to adapt and survive are much more common than generally realized, and play a key role in cultural-change processes, which it is important not to oversimplify. While political terminology may appear to be a blatant case of cultural diffusion that may even be intentionally driven by Rome, one should not lose sight of the realities of the actual power-play on the ground, in which local hegemonic families are still struggling for dominance as they had done for centuries, but are now using new Roman concepts to maintain and reinvent their positions. In the inner circle (the core areas of the empire), this change could often build upon existing structures that had characterized city-state politics since the archaic period (late seventh–early fifth centuries BC). Urban magistracies were constantly defined and redefined in response to changing local balances of power and to an evolving global political discourse, within which a measure of constitutional compatibility among the interacting cities had always been necessary. When, in the Augustan period, the equation between two magistracies, the (Etruscan) *zilath* and the (Roman) praetor, is sanctioned, the two terms had in all likelihood been playing off each other for centuries. In these kinds of cultural context, the definitive transition to the Roman system is only the last step in a process of political convergence. Rome's primary concern, in any case, was simply a constitutional standardization that facilitated central administration and political careers that spanned different cities (which, incidentally, existed even before the conquest). The Roman system was chosen more as a convenient federal standard than *qua* Roman. This is clearly indicated by the case of Greek cities like Massalia or Naples, which went on for centuries using their traditional Greek magistracies and political terminology. In this, as in many other areas, Rome was more than willing to accept another recognized standard, and especially the one offered by the *koinē*, the globalized culture common to the Greek-speaking world in the Hellenistic period, as long as it was compatible with the needs of the imperial administration and of inter-city diplomacy and interaction.

The situation was, of course, very different in the outer circle of the empire. Here, non-urban or recently urbanized communities became part of the empire at a later time, when its political structure has firmed up to a much greater extent. Consequently, the transition appears more unidirectional and abrupt. The empire needed quaestors and aediles in each new community, and there was little institutional material in these contexts that could be usefully recycled. Local power networks, however organized, still had a role to play in the new system, by reinterpreting and shaping it to consolidate their social position. The case of the high priest at Lugdunum is very illuminating. This was one of the very few religious and political offices of pan-Gallic significance, and it is promptly re-functionalized by Roman and non-Roman elites as a vital component of inter-provincial government. Grafting the imperial cult (Chapter 7) onto the existing one (but putting it in the care of priests of native descent) represented an acceptable cultural negotiation, that facilitated the acceptance and the management of the new political realities. But, more often, locals and newcomers find themselves holding offices for which there is little precedent, resulting in a rather sharp break in the flow of the dominant political discourse. This was, however, uncharacteristic of the rest of the empire, and a product of the timing and the scale of the territorial acquisitions in continental Europe, which required the rapid establishment of a functional interface with Rome. This level of political discourse is one of the few incontrovertible areas of direct and intentional Roman cultural influence, at least in the provinces of the outer circle.

A related area traditionally seen as central to the Roman cultural heritage is, of course, the law. The main reason for the prominent visibility of Roman legal culture is its deep influence on western modern codes. As always, however, each historical phenomenon must be considered in its own contemporary terms and not with the teleological foresight of its future developments. Roman law emerged in parallel with similar codes within the city-states of the inner circle, between the late archaic and the Hellenistic periods (600–300 BC). There was a great variety of law codes, and indeed they were studied and compared in some detail by ancient authors (from Aristotle to Polybius). It is only with the conquest that Roman law could potentially take on a significance that would go beyond the jurisdiction of the city of Rome. As Rome's Italian alliance formed (Chapter 2), it became essential to determine how much, if any, of the Roman code would apply outside Rome. Within the inner circle of former city-states, Rome on the whole conformed to the expectations created by a long tradition of independence, fully embracing the principle that the European Union today defines as subsidiarity, that is, limiting central regulation to those matters that can only be dealt with at that level, and relying on local decisions for everything else. There is very little trace of any imposition of Roman law (or any other federal law) by Rome. A few exceptional cases may have existed. The famous *senatusconsultum de Bacchanalibus* (senatorial decree on the Bacchanals) of 186 BC (*Corpus Inscriptionum Latinarum* 1^2. 581; Livy 39. 14–18) is traditionally considered to have effectively banned Bacchic festivals in Roman and allied areas alike. While this anomaly is generally explained with reference to the grave political threat posed by the cult, recent scholarship has been arguing for an application of the measure limited to Roman citizens.

Even Latin colonies, which were directly created by Rome, were not subject to Roman law, but were treated instead as allied cities in terms of their legal autonomy. The colonies, of course, tended to adopt codes that were at least compatible with Rome's, but without being subject to any strong pressure to conform. For allied cities in general, the standard procedure allowed each community to import existing Roman laws into their codes, if they so elected. This 'pick and choose' model made for a slow and piecemeal convergence of local laws with Roman, but presumably must have also generated a great variety of hybrids in each city. The full diffusion of Roman law will always remain linked with the progressive spread of Roman citizenship, a process that would only be finally concluded centuries after the conquest (in the first century BC for peninsular Italy, and in the third century AD for the rest of the empire). Thus, far from being a colonial code laid down by the conquerors in their dominions, Roman law remained, for most of the empire's duration, the law of Rome itself, as well as a sort of code akin to the federal one in the United States, in that it primarily regulated interactions happening at a higher level than that of the individual cities. Even among Roman citizens, Roman law always remained a tool primarily used by elites, which never fully replaced arbitrary rulings, customary law, and out-of-court resolutions. The latter, of course, have left very little in terms of written traces, but their extensive presence can be inferred from indirect evidence. The extra- (or even anti-) legal authority of *patres familias* (Chapter 4), clan leaders, priests, and other eminent figures in all likelihood was the primary recourse for the vast majority of legal proceedings anywhere.

Keeping in mind the inherent limits to its scope and application, it is in any case clear that Roman law had a differential impact across the empire. While in the inner circle it intersected and commingled with a rich and long tradition of local codes and jurisprudence, elsewhere the boundaries were much less blurred. In the continental European provinces, communities that had little or no experience of it were rather suddenly exposed to a legal mentality that had been progressively brewing and decanting in the Mediterranean world for centuries. A degree of imposition is occasionally discernible, such as when Roman generals are said to bring the rule of law to wild areas, as with Corbulo's establishment of a senate, magistrates, and laws on the Frisians in AD 47 (Tacitus, *Annals* 11. 18–19). Municipal charters, as is well attested, for instance, in continental Spain, were certainly much more influenced by Rome than had been the case, for instance, in Italy. Here the idea of an impact is more justifiable, although, as in many other areas, the substance of it really came from the Mediterranean world as a whole, and Roman expansion was simply its conduit, through urbanization and citizenship. Here too, however, it was mainly relevant for the affluent and literate classes, who were more detached from traditional ways of life. References to the resilience of customary law are not infrequent, and it would be even less wise to assume universal jurisdiction for the Roman code in the outer circle than in the inner one.

In light of these basic considerations, it should be obvious how the common claim that the Roman legal system changed western culture forever rings rather hollow. In fact, little direct effect outside the empire is really visible. The most cursory look at medieval law outside the Byzantine and Arab worlds reveals how little of Roman practice and thought outlasted the collapse of the western empire. If anything, the situation in continental Europe suggests that there was an active substratum of customary law that was ready to re-emerge again once the overarching imperial structures were dissolved (see Chapters 9 and 10). Whatever afterlife Roman law may have today is clearly the product of Renaissance erudite curiosity and wholesale early modern resurrections, and has nothing to do with the Roman conquest and its attendant cultural processes. The Napoleonic Code is connected with a conscious and instrumental revival of Roman antiquity, down to its female dress fashions, rather than with what Rome had done in the Three Gauls a millennium-and-a-half earlier.

Equally celebrated as a long-lasting and profound influence on modern culture is, of course, the language the Romans spoke itself, Latin, which has remained central to the Catholic church and to scholars everywhere. The sheer size of the Romance-language family and the abundance (rivalled only by ancient Greek) of Latin roots in a wide variety of Eurasian languages can easily be construed in terms of an undying monument to Roman cultural penetration. And yet, just as in the case of law, the issue is made much more complex by our virtual inability to assess the full range of actual practices in antiquity just on the basis of the written record and of distant modern outcomes.

While there is no doubt that Latin became the official language in all the non-Greek-speaking empire, as well as a language that elites everywhere needed to master, it is surprisingly hard to measure its actual penetration much beyond that. In this perspective, much of the debate so far has really only addressed the surface of the problem.

In areas, such as peninsular Italy, that were already widely literate before the conquest, the primary source of evidence has been the progressive replacement of native languages with Latin, especially in funerary inscriptions. Here, the transition can happen soon after the conquest, as in the case of Veneto, or centuries afterward, as in some areas of northern Etruria, but the end-result does not change. At Asciano, for instance, Etruscan epitaphs were still set up in the reign of Tiberius, but subsequently even that community joined in with the rest. While charting chronologically the progress of Latin in this context across the empire has been the dominant approach so far, it is important to remember that all it assesses is the changes in the epigraphic habit of the elites. The language that is chosen on aristocratic epitaphs is clearly a form of self-representation more than a testimony of the actual speech of these people, as is often implicitly assumed. In any case, it does not tell us anything about the practices of the largely illiterate commoners. As is the case in many other cultural areas, the changes that are visible are not a direct result of political incorporation, and even less are they driven by the central imperial government. In many local contexts, the adoption of Latin is probably one of the fashion statements that substantiate elite culture, and as such are largely independent of specific political events. An indication of this is the fact that the variability encountered in elite culture across different communities cannot be explained in the simple terms of greater or lesser acculturation. For instance, the belated use of Etruscan at Asciano takes place in a context that is otherwise in line with neighbouring areas in which Latin was adopted sooner. Rather than being linked with backwardness or conservatism, it should be seen side-by-side with the well-known fascination with Etruscan of the emperor Claudius, or the tragedies composed in Etruscan in the early empire (Suetonius, *Deified Claudius* 42; Varro, *On the Latin Language* 5. 55).

To properly understand the cultural role of language within the context of the inner circle, it must be remembered how elites had long been familiar with the various idioms spoken in the main city-states. Almost all of them—but notoriously, not Etruscan or Punic—belonged to the Indo-European family and shared basic grammatical and linguistic structures. But much more importantly, centuries of contacts, alliances, intermarriages, and resettlements had made most elites multilingual, or in any case very flexible and adaptable. The use of Latin was an option that most aristocrats had had for a long time before it became virtually unavoidable. Rome, itself a multilingual and multicultural city from its very beginnings, only ever pushed Latin as an empire-wide language to be used in dealings with the central government and for official local business. It is likely that Latin was seen as little more than a convenient solution to the new problem of communication and compatibility posed by the Roman Empire. This is also suggested by a seamless use of Greek for the exact same purposes. Wherever—as in most of the eastern Mediterranean, but also in places like Massilia or Naples—Greek was more convenient than Latin as a lingua franca, it was embraced by Rome without hesitation. This particular sphere of linguistic practice was clearly part of the infrastructure that was necessary to run the empire, not unlike the legal and political conventions described above.

Beyond the level of official use and aristocratic display, it is extremely difficult to ascertain the extent of Latin usage and its socio-linguistic realities. There is a distinct feeling that, just outside the narrow cone of light afforded us by the textual sources, a wide variety of conditions obtained. It is enough to remember that, as late as the end of the second century AD, the sister of the Libyan emperor Septimius Severus had so little Latin that she was an embarrassment to her brother when she came to Rome. This shows how there were some elite provincial families that went on regarding Latin merely as a tool primarily used by adult males involved in public affairs. At least in Severan Leptis, neo-Punic clearly remained the first language of elite and commoners alike. If this was the situation in a major port city of the empire, some four centuries after its annexation, one can only imagine what would happen in less central areas. There is very little evidence which incontravertibly shows a massive emergence of native Latin-speakers over the entire life-span of the Roman Empire. It is entirely possible to hypothesize that large swathes of rural-dwellers, and maybe even urban commoners, underwent only a moderate and slow amount of deep linguistic change, and never had Ciceronian Latin as their first language. In fact, in the late Roman period Latin is still far from being a given, but is instead an important cultural element that is actively negotiated and debated, even after it has assumed a key role in Christian religion. As Latin became more and more a liturgical, scholarly, and official language in the early Middle Ages, it is very unlikely to have spread any further than before to peripheral areas and lower classes. The eventual formation of Romance languages, and their gradual diffusion through dialects and variants, should thus not be seen as a direct consequence of cultural changes brought about by the Roman conquest, but rather of the connotation that Latin acquired centuries after the end of the western Roman Empire. Glossing over the mediation of the Middle Ages and the reinvention of the Renaissance, Romantic scholarship created a direct link between Roman culture and the western European one that improperly credits Rome with an impact that it neither had the inclination nor the ability to cause.

A further dimension of linguistic usage is offered by family and individual names. A superficial glance at imperial onomastics may suggest a wholesale conformation to Latin practice. Here too, however, there is much more to the process than the simple diffusion of a hegemonic practice. First, the three-name system (the *tria nomina*) had been developed over several centuries, and before the conquest, within the context of a broad cultural interaction in central Italy. It had not quite crystallized when Rome started expanding, so that the early participants in the alliance had the opportunity of contributing to the system. Upon receiving Roman citizenship (usually in the form of individual grants), many simply took their non-Roman name and made it sound more Latin. Often, linguistic proximity allowed fairly straightforward equations, such as that from Sabine Clausus to Latin Claudius (Chapter 2). Alternatively, long-standing contacts had already established accepted equivalents, such as that between Etruscan Avle and Latin Aulus. Thus a very great number of names that can be declined as Latin nouns or adjectives, while retaining the original root, were created. In this, Latin proved to be a remarkably flexible language, allowing a variety of forms that stay as close as possible to the original word. Such is the case of Etruscan family names ending in -na (like Perperna or Caecina) which adopt the first Latin declension in order to retain the original suffix, even if it is normally reserved in Latin for feminine nouns. Similar is the use of the third declension to preserve the distinctive -ix termination of many Celtic names.

In parallel with that, there is also a diffusion of classic Roman (or central Italian) family names. Freed slaves, of course, account for a large proportion of this phenomenon, since they adopted by default the family name of their former master (Chapter 4). But there are also instances of free and even elite individuals spontaneously changing their name to a more Roman-sounding one. These processes, aside from making it problematic to assume a real Roman descent for all the Julii or the Valerii we encounter, are not actively driven by Rome, but are once again an element of self-representation, linked to fashions, contexts, and social conventions and connections. This is also indicated by the increasing numbers of Celtic names in the middle empire, when being Roman becomes less fashionable than in the Augustan period. Although the evidence is not as rich as it could be, there is also a clear indication of people having more than one name, or using substantially different forms of the same name. This is only detectable from (rare) bilingual inscriptions, or from different inscriptions mentioning the same individual.

The neo-Punic elites of Leptis Magna are again a very illuminating example. A careful analysis of the evidence has revealed husbands that have more Latin-sounding names than their wives, as well as cases of the same individual using a Latin form of his name for a dedication in the *forum*, but a more Punic one for his own epitaph. This suggests that it was common practice to use different names or write them differently depending on the audience. Not surprisingly, names are just another element in a complex discourse about identities and self-representations, so the adoption of Latin-sounding ones does not in the least equate with completely embracing a new culture, but is rather a conscious and context-sensitive strategy of social negotiation. It is also important to remember that these behaviours were not born with, or exclusive to, the Roman Empire; they had been basic tools of long-distance interaction in the inner circle long before it appeared. It is enough to think of Latin Servius Tullius being Etruscan Mastarna or Greek Demaratos being Etruscan Lucumo. A somewhat relaxed approach to personal names became even more common, and spread beyond the elites, in the Hellenistic period, as is shown by a fascinating inscription from Malta set up by the same two brothers in Greek under Greek names and in Punic under Punic names (*Inscriptiones Graecae* 14. 600). In the outer circle there was much less of a tradition of contact, but the pragmatic solutions employed in the Mediterranean were quickly transferred to the new area.

In all this, it is likely that Rome probably saw this issue simply in terms of administrative efficiency. Non-Roman elites needed to have names that were compatible with the Roman onomastic structure for the census and other political purposes, just as they needed to have enough Latin to conduct federal and other official business, or to understand orders in the army. That the chosen convention ended up being close to the Roman original one was in a way less important than its being functional. This is shown by the ease with which non-Roman standards are chosen in other areas. A good example of this is the metric system, where the original Italic foot that was used in Rome was eventually superseded by the (Greek) Attic one to become the imperial standard. In another key area for long-distance interaction, coinage, there is a similar borrowing. The first emissions to circulate widely beyond the city level were coins from Campania that used the Greek weight-system (*didrachmas*). Here again, Rome is more than willing to make use of an exogenous, but well-established tradition as a new norm for the whole alliance.

Two general points emerge so far, and they are worth spelling out. First, Rome is interested in promoting cultural change and homogenization only in some specific areas that are functional to the administration of the empire and to long-distance interactions within it. Secondly, inasmuch as a common culture is taking shape in the inner circle, it is a new creation that is as much Roman as it is a generic form of Hellenism, colonial Greek, Etruscan, or Italic. Some choices, of course, such as that of Latin as the official language, reflect actual power balances and are not coincidental, but they do not involve either the simple diffusion of traditional Roman culture, or a cultural hybrid that is grossly slanted towards Rome, or even one to which only the participants in the colonial encounter are contributing. In fact, the lion's share belongs to the Greeks, who are politically neither dominant nor central in the process. In the outer circle, this cultural assemblage arrives later and in a much more firmed-up form, so that it is easy to construct the phenomenon in simple terms of diffusion, acculturation, or Romanization in the traditional sense. But even there, a full review of cultural variability reveals a much more nuanced picture than is often assumed.

Cities, architecture, and art

Moving on to material culture, pride of place should be reserved for urbanization and architecture, which for many centuries have remained, and are still today, powerful visual reminders of Rome's pervasive impact upon the built environment in most of the Old World. In terms of the very structure of the empire, cities are centrally placed at the intersection between the political and social systems on the one hand, and the cultural and artistic ones on the other. Indeed, urban life comes closest to being a Roman equivalent for the modern concept of civilization, so that it would seem that cities should be fundamental to any definition of Roman culture. This is all the more so, because this is one of the few areas where change is actively and consciously initiated by Rome. There is no corner of the Roman Empire in which the urban system was not reorganized, if not created from scratch, by Rome. Roman colonies, of course, stand out as prime examples of Rome's desire to have more cities on the map, but the imperial action goes much further: existing cities are invariably beautified with monuments and expanded during the time they are part of the empire. In any case, the archetypal value given in modern times to Roman colonies has tended to concentrate on them a lot of the debate on Roman urbanism. The focus has been particularly on the regions that were not urbanized before the conquest (largely in what is here called the outer circle), such as the Po plain in northern Italy, continental Gaul and Spain, Germany, and the Danubian provinces. Here, Rome is often seen as creating outposts of acculturation manned by Roman citizens in the midst of primitive lands, in a move that changes the historical trajectory of those regions forever. The actual rationale behind Roman foundations has been variously interpreted, either in terms of military strategy or of economic exploitation.

All these traditional explanations have mainly been applied to the outer circle and are clearly very influenced by contemporary views held about European colonies. But such an emphasis can be misleading. It is no coincidence that the empire spread to the urbanized areas of the Mediterranean first. Contrary to common perception, the empire did not expand concentrically. Overseas provinces like Sicily, Sardinia, Spain, and even Asia Minor (Turkey) are already firmly part of the empire when Rome is still struggling to find a way of incorporating neighbouring Cisalpine Gaul in the 180s and 170s BC. The expansion process clearly privileges more advanced areas (the opposite of what happened in modern empires), demonstrating that urbanism is a fundamental requirement, allowing a community to become a functional part of the new political entity. Well-defined political offices and public spaces are simply essential for a city-state to be incorporated under the terms of a binding treaty with Rome, and to subsequently negotiating its role within the alliance. Moreover, it is only urbanized elites that will have an interest in the new global political game that is made possible by the expansion, as the case of the Samnites clearly shows. Scarcely urbanized Italian highlanders like the latter (or the Ligurians) will put up a fierce, century-long resistance to the expansion. The well-established tradition of long-distance interaction means that the new, overarching imperial structure can be understood by urban aristocrats as a more complex and more permanent form of the alliances and treaties that had existed ever since the archaic period.

The fact that Rome's first colonies are created in already urbanized areas is an often-overlooked key to understanding the successive spread of urban culture in the rest of the empire. These early colonies are frequently new cities that add to an already dense urban network, as in the case of Cosa in Etruria, or Fregellae in Latium, or they can overlap with existing cities, like Paestum in Lucania, or Satricum in Latium. Typically granted the intermediate Latin right, these centres are populated with a mixture of Romans, locals, and other allies. It is thus clear that, in its original formulation, the Roman concept of colony does not necessarily have the goal of introducing urban culture (although this may occasionally be the case in highland areas), nor that of allowing the resettlement of Roman citizens in large numbers. The aim is rather that of having a city (either new or old) that will be a staunch ally of Rome thanks to the very nature of its constitution. Having a landed philo-Roman (rather than actually Roman) elite in charge of a clearly organized urban community is the ideal building-block of the budding empire. When finally, and almost reluctantly, the empire extends to the first non-urbanized areas, such as the Po plain or the Apennines, it will push for new cities to be created in order to have conditions on the ground that are compatible with those in the rest of the alliance. In this sense, Roman expansion can be seen as a world of coastal cities first coming together and only then slowly colonizing continental areas.

The instrumental rather than dogmatic character of new Roman urbanism is further exemplified by the provinces of the outer circle. Here, in regions that were largely un-urbanized to an extent not known to the Mediterranean (where the presence of cities was the norm), there are two complementary processes visible. One is the frequent emergence of a degree of urbanization just before the conquest. This is discernible in Gaulish *oppida* like Levreux in the Berry, reorganized in the second quarter of the first century BC (see also Chapter 1). This, more than anything else, suggests that expansion often takes place when at least some of the areas to be newly incorporated have developed the necessary infrastructure to be a functional part of the empire. In other words, what has traditionally been seen as 'civilization' is very often as much a cause as it is an effect of the Roman conquest. The flipside of this is the case of large expanses of non-urbanized territory that are, for a variety of reasons, annexed at once, as is the case for large parts of central and northern Gaul and Spain. In these regions, the strategy of urbanization through colonies is probably not viable in the short term, as it would require dozens of cities to be built at the same time. And yet, because the imperial administration needs city-like structures to run these areas, virtual urban entities with little or no material correlate are created. These structures are cities only in name (they are called *civitates*). The physical urban settlement is not there, but the community agrees to behave, vis-à-vis the empire, as if there was one.

Thus Rome's push for urbanization, instead of being driven by military strategy or economic greed, appears to be explicable in simpler and more pragmatic terms. The empire needs polities that conform to what was progressively becoming the standard of the Mediterranean world. This enabled Rome to deal with these communities in time-honoured ways, and at the same time facilitated inter-city elite mobility, a phenomenon that was on the rise, judging by the growing numbers of municipal aristocratic families whose political careers span different cities. Once these entities are in place, it is relatively easy to tip the local political balance in favour of the faction more friendly to the imperial project. This was achieved in colonial contexts thanks to the very nature of the citizenship grants which tied the privileged status of new community to the overall success of the alliance.

Elsewhere, the instruments are those networks of clientele, alliances, intermarriages, and friendship ties of the kind that had long existed between clans since the Iron Age, but which were now rewarded by Rome with citizenship and access to the equestrian and senatorial ranks. In the outer circle such traditions had existed even without cities, and it was not hard to refunctionalize them within the new colonies or *civitates*. Throughout the empire this system was geared in favour of Rome, and provided enough central control even without ethnic Romans being installed in positions of power everywhere, in an extremely significant departure from what happened in many other empires.

When one examines the material counterpart of urban communities across the empire, it is natural to think that what was being pushed by Rome was much more than simply an administrative or political template. Walking down streets that intersect at perfect right-angles and are paved with the same basalt polygons, it is hard not to concur with nineteenth-century scholars who hailed this as a key stage in the formation of western culture. Indeed the grid patterns that repeat themselves from city to city, and even in the intervening countryside, seem perfectly to exemplify the diffusion of Roman rationality. And yet, if we consider the Mediterranean world in a long-term perspective, the situation is rather different. Even aside from the fact that Rome itself never was an orthogonally planned city (to the embarrassment of loyal municipal men like Livy), it is clear that regular layouts were not invented for Roman colonies. There was a long tradition of such planning in the eastern Mediterranean, which was then codified in abstract terms by Hippodamus in the second half of the fifth century BC. Even more importantly, unmistakable orthogonal elements were present in other urbanistic traditions, such as the Etruscan one, culminating in the perfect grid laid out for the fifth-century BC colony at Marzabotto in the Po plain. Other examples come from Greek southern Italy, southern Gaul, the Guadalquivir valley, and so on.

Thus, a wide variety of cultures in the inner circle had been contributing to the definition of a group of standard urban layouts long before the Roman conquest. So when the Romans started creating new cities and reorganizing existing ones, they naturally adopted what by then was a standard design. Far from being modelled after Roman army camps, early Latin colonies like Alba Fucens or Cales in central Italy strictly conform, with their elongated blocks and lack of a primary road intersection, to contemporary Hellenistic norms. That said, the central position of the *forum* and its associated monuments contributes, both in colonies and in other cities, to produce an urban landscape that is self-evident and easily negotiable for a wide range of newcomers. Here again, the Roman empire can be seen, in cultural terms, as the political vehicle that paved the way for a convergence that in the inner circle had been in the works for centuries. At the same time, it also created an infrastructure that allowed aristocratic groups everywhere to prosper, interact, and move over long distances. In the outer circle, on the other hand, there had been some experiments with urbanism, but orthogonal layout had not been a significant component in them. The new cities that were progressively created thus had layouts to the refinement of which the locals had not been contributing, and which must have appeared unfamiliar to all but the better-travelled of them. This is an event whose local significance should not be downplayed, but it is best seen as an old Mediterranean trait (rather than a Roman one) that was progressively transferred to continental Europe.

Individual elements found within the cities are also intimately associated with our general perception of Roman urbanism. Theatres, basilicas, and baths are pervasive sights, which strongly characterize modern experiences of Roman cities, as well as ancient ones. These buildings, however, cannot be considered more intrinsically Roman than the urban layouts that surround them. Quite a considerable proportion of the new architectural types are derived more or less directly from Greek ones, or in any case developed outside Rome. They were adapted and reconfigured in various parts of the inner circle around the time of its incorporation, but they are not Roman, nor solely mediated through Rome. A variety of different Mediterranean cultures is converging on mutually compatible cultural traits and, in the process, apparently paving the way for their unification within a global territorial empire.

Theatres provide a perfect example: having existed for centuries as a distinctive feature of Greek cities, they are rather suddenly adopted across the Mediterranean in the Hellenistic period. Probably through the medium of Greek colonial zones like southern Italy, they appear by the second century BC in cities that are not yet particularly Roman, like Pompeii, and even in distinctively non-Roman contexts, like the Samnite sanctuary at Pietrabbondante. Then the theatre is modified and re-engineered, like so many other building types, as part of the late Republican revolution brought about by the massive spread of concrete (see also Chapter 6), but again showing up outside Rome, for instance at Pompeii, before appearing in Rome itself. The model is finally codified only in the mid-first century BC. The free-standing, barrel-vaulted result, with the shallower orchestra and the fancy stage building, is then diffused to the rest of the empire, including the outer circle, as part of the great Augustan cultural wave. It must not be forgotten, though, that when the new theatres were built in places like Mérida or Orange, the concept of having a permanent stone theatre in the city was barely a few decades old in Rome itself. If this was being Roman, then it was a novel experience for the Romans as well.

Quite often, the Greek original model was transformed more extensively than in the case of the theatre, often merging with Italic architectural traditions. For instance, the *comitium* (the stepped open-air space where elections were held), which had in some form existed in Rome since the archaic period, acquired many elements of Greek Hellenistic *bouleuteria* (council chambers) to become a vital staple of Republican Roman cities. Just like the magistrates that were elected in it, the *comitium*, together with the architecturally unremarkable *curia* (senate house) with which it was always paired, made participation in the alliance possible. This configuration of political topography helped those who sought office in more than one city, by standardizing the material aspects of voting and deliberating. This helps to explain the appearance of standard *forum–comitium* complexes in many Republican cities in Italy and in Latin colonies in particular.

Some building types, on the other hand, were brand-new inventions, such as the quadriporticus (a four-sided portico enclosing an open space) or the basilica (a great roofed hall with clerestory windows). These colonnaded public spaces, destined to enjoy great prominence in imperial cities everywhere, are surprisingly hard to trace anywhere much earlier than the first century BC. The basilica, long assumed to be a Greek import, really has no clear antecedents in any architectural tradition, and it is being pieced together in the inner circle on the basis of a variety of disparate models, ranging from the multi-aisled Hellenistic *stoa* (the colonnaded portico that flanks Greek squares) to the Eastern hypostyle hall (the large covered spaces with many rows of columns or pillars). Its inside-out version, the quadriporticus, is also not seen much before the second century BC, and may derive from the progressive growth of colonnades around squares, combined with the distant heritage of peristyled halls like that at the archaic Etruscan palace at Murlo.

We might continue our survey of architectural types, but it would not change the fact that much of the (over-)celebrated Roman public architecture was not known to Romans as late as the second century BC, when the political unification of the inner circle was virtually complete. Indeed, what is quickly emerging is how the vast majority of what is known as Roman Republican architecture really dates only to the period between the Gracchi and Caesar, and was subsequently codified and spread by capillary diffusion under Augustus. This global development is clearly linked to the existence of a global empire (although not necessarily with the Roman conquest per se), but it cannot in any way be described in terms of colonizers diffusing (or even hybridizing) their own ethnic culture to the lands they conquer, at least as far as the inner circle is concerned. Rather, at a very late stage in the expansion process a new culture emerges, weaving together a variety of old traditions with many brand-new fashions. In any case, it is primarily only relevant to certain highly visible aspects of elite behavior throughout the empire.

Other elements very commonly associated with Roman influence are roads and aqueducts. Their construction starts with the conquest (both the Via and the Aqua Appia date to the late fourth century BC), and they remain a main area of investment from the centre for most of the Roman period. They also represent a sort of public construction that is very little influenced by fashions and trends. In this specific area, the impact of the conquest was clear and visible to all. With the exception of some monumental roads and water channels cut in the rock in archaic and classical Etruria, there was relatively little precedent for this kind of construction, in contrast with urban monuments. An obvious reason for that was that individual city-states could not easily engage in projects whose scope went beyond the territory they could control. Only an imperial power could operate at a regional scale and above the petty interests of each community. And, in fact, roads were always built on Roman public land (*ager publicus*), emphasizing their location outside and across the framework of territorial boundaries. These structures were very appropriate material symbols of the unique advantages that an empire had over the preceding system, and it is not surprising that they were so emphasized by the central government for centuries. They were not only infrastructural and elite-friendly, like municipal charters or *curiae*, but they actually provided a tangible and unprecedented benefit to the entire alliance. At least in the inner circle, however, the primary significance of roads and aqueducts was not that of aweing the natives with a technological marvel. Underpinning this development was a mixture of existing hydraulic engineering, Hellenistic science, and a clever use of concrete for arcades, bridges, and viaducts. What was absolutely new was the presence of a global empire with the staying-power and the political capabilities that were necessary to build up these networks decade after decade. Regulating and reorganizing the interstitial spaces, which had always been beyond the reach of local governments, was the one area where the empire did not need to tread lightly and mediate.

High art provides the perfect illustration of the peculiar role played by fashion, as well as of its independence from the direct influence of contemporary political conjunctures. This was a cultural sphere primarily driven by elite patronage, and in which a unique form of discourse developed with a logic of its own. In spite of that, it has long been at the centre of the debate, and vastly over-emphasized in some modern scholarly traditions, such as the German or Italian ones. The replacement of Celtic abstract art with early imperial classicism has been hailed as a sure sign of acculturation by Romantic and social art historians alike. But if the long-term perspective is taken, it is easy to realize how the process in question was just one of several artistic global trends that characterized the Mediterranean throughout the first millennium BC. The list should include at the very least the Orientalizing (late eighth–seventh century BC) and the Hellenistic periods (late fourth–late first century BC), alongside the early imperial one. Of these, the Orientalizing is particularly instructive, as it takes place long before any imperial expansion, Roman or otherwise, but rather during the formative phase of Mediterranean city-states. In it, the fascination with oriental imports and their local imitations is as strong as any later trend. Cosmopolitan groups, such as the Greeks, Etruscans, Carthaginians, but also Iberians, Illyrians, Lucanians, and even Celts, all show a synchronous development in their elite tastes, which is absolutely remarkable in light of how they are politically completely independent, and only linked by networks of commerce and gift-exchange. Even more surprisingly, the epicentres of this massive wave of goods and styles, located primarily in the cities of the Levant, on Cyprus, and in Egypt, were not involved in any sort of hegemonic project at this time, other than the creation of commercial entrepôts in the West. In other words, there is no obvious political or structural correlate of such a dramatic development in the culture (or perhaps simply the tastes) of aristocracies everywhere.

It is with this sobering example in mind that the following events should be considered. The spread of Greek styles during the Hellenistic period is another global phenomenon. Once again, elites from very different contexts converged upon a well-defined set of aesthetic norms. From the Celtic coins imitating the head of Alexander and Punic tomb-markers in Spain, to Etruscan mirrors and Campanian tomb-paintings, a global trend is very visible, bringing local figurative traditions in different media within the bounds of a shared artistic grammar. The influence of the melancholy pathos and sophisticated poses conjured up by Hellenistic artists was so pervasive everywhere that it almost defies belief. And yet, again, as was the case with the Orientalizing phenomenon, it is extremely difficult to connect this new trend directly with any contemporary political development, especially outside the lands conquered by Alexander. It is not a consequence of the Roman conquest, and it actually has its apogee at a time when politically Greece was virtually irrelevant in the West. As a matter of fact, the Hellenistic cultural wave is not even connected to a peak in the diffusion of prestige items from Greece. Local imitation and influence played a much greater role in this phenomenon, which also reached a broader social group than previous ones, as the mass-production of Black Gloss pottery shows. This form of 'Hellenization' had unprecedented proportions in terms of geographical scope, penetration, and the range of media affected, now including literature, philosophy, and architecture as well as portable items. This great movement, arguably the greatest in antiquity, is not, however, explicable in terms of acculturation with a dominant power, nor can it be said to permanently reshape local cultures in the full, 'anthropological' sense of the word, that is, not limited to elite manifestations. It remained a fashionable trend that drew together different aristocracies (as well as emerging new social actors) in a common discourse, a *koinē* that was not ethnically hegemonic. Its major political significance was probably limited to facilitating contact and interaction across all sorts of boundaries, setting the stage for that elite alliance that was at the core of the Roman Empire (see also Chapter 10).

The subsequent phase in these global ebbs and flows of aristocratic taste took place, notoriously, in the Augustan period. It has been often seen as positive evidence of the diffusion of Roman culture by scholars focusing on those provinces which were incorporated immediately before or during this period, such as continental Gaul and Spain. Looking at the Maison Carrée in Nîmes or at the 'Gypsy' of Mérida, it is perhaps natural to imagine a unidirectional transfer of imagery and forms of artistic expression. But a more extensive review of the evidence does not really support this widespread idea. First of all, Augustan neo-classicism is a novel trend for Rome and for the core of the empire, just as it is for its farthest periphery. In fact, most of the building-blocks that made Augustan culture were of non-Roman derivation, from Athenian fifth-century BC idealizing art to Hellenistic Egyptian imagery. Second, it can easily be observed how this style spread at the same time to lands that had been part of the empire for centuries, like south-east Spain or Sicily, disproving the implicit modern belief that a longer permanence within the empire necessarily resulted in a greater amount of acculturation taking place. In fact, the impact of Augustan fashions is detectable even in regions, such as Britain, that had not yet been conquered (Henig 1995: 27–8). One difference from previous waves is, of course, that this one is consciously initiated and engineered from the centre. But it is essential not to forget that Augustan propaganda is primarily concerned with promoting traditional values and with justifying the new regime, with little discernible interest in replacing local culture with a Roman one. Finally, it would be imprudent to assume that this particular wave had a deeper or longer-lasting impact than the ones that preceded it. In fact, the signs of re-emergence of pre-Augustan elements in the western provinces during the high empire (MacMullen 1990) are an important reminder of the ongoing volatility of aristocratic tastes throughout the Roman period.

When taken together, high art, public architecture, the use of an official language, and formal law create for modern observers an appearance of across-the-board homogenization into an encompassing Roman culture. But a lot of this cohesive package is really confined to political and other exterior manifestations of elite adult males. A lot of it is a derivation, in one form or another, of Greek and other oriental fashions, and it is just as novel for the Roman as it is for any other participant in the empire. Other parts of it have been developed, especially in the inner circle, over centuries of aristocratic long-distance contact across all sorts of cultural and ethnic boundaries. Now, of course, these important symbolic displays have always been connected with prevailing and emerging power structures, as well as with the self-representation of elites everywhere as socially dominant cultural brokers. And yet they cannot be equated with the entire spectrum of beliefs that kept local communities together. The role of customs and folklore (in the sense of non-elite culture and beliefs), while very clear to ancient authors, has been largely ignored in modern scholarship, or included only as a quaint touch of colour. It is true that the extant written record is very heavily tilted in favour of elite culture, but there has also been a reluctance to look beyond the most blatant and visible among the cultural manifestations. Only recently has the picture been progressively rebalanced, especially thanks to new study of settlement and mortuary archaeology throughout the Roman world. New actors are finally beginning to come on to the stage, such as commoners, farmers, women, children, serfs, and slaves. Information of local and domestic cults, magical beliefs, and other ethnological data are diversifying and enriching the traditional perception of culture in the Roman Empire, showing a variety of different world-views and overlapping and shifting cultural identities.

Landscapes and communities

An important role in the new debates has been played by the results of work done on the countrysides of the Roman Empire. Here again, there is a conventional wisdom whereby the Roman conquest brought about a radical reorganization of rural landscapes. Communal lands and small-scale farming are, on this view, entirely replaced by resettled army veterans and, later, slave-run estates owned by absentee landlords engaged in investment agriculture. Centuriation, the geometric grid imposed on some Roman landscapes, is quite naturally seen as the embodiment of the new order wrought by Rome on the conquered lands. The parcels of land formed by these grids extend the geometry of the orthogonal cities to their hinterland, giving a sense of uniformity and order. In recent years, however, a critical look at the available evidence has prompted a considerable nuancing of this picture. Centuriation is only attested in some areas of the empire, and it is most commonly reconstructed on the basis of lines detectable on air photos. This makes any reliable dating of the grid very problematic, even in those cases where the existence of an actual one can be positively demonstrated (such as the Po plain, and southern France). So it is very difficult, even in the case of colonial foundations, to connect with confidence the traces of centuriation with the initial distribution of land to the colonists. Even more importantly, the real nature and function of centuriation has been questioned in recent works (Dyson 2003: 55–60). The presence of two or more overlapping but differently aligned grids makes it unlikely that each corresponded to a radical revolution in land-tenure patterns. And work on the marble cadastral map from Orange has concluded that, at least in that case, the centuriation grid was introduced more as a tool for tax assessment, and a cadastral record of existing holdings, than as a guide to an extensive reassignment.

This resonates with other works suggesting that the foundation of a colony did not always automatically involve the displacement of existing farmers and their replacement with exogenous colonists. In fact, clear archaeological correlates of land distributions have so far proven exceedingly difficult to identify. What has instead been found, in a number of cases, is that small farms created in the early Hellenistic period, often before the conquest, go on being occupied by farmers who stick to traditional customs and vernacular architectures. The spread of these farms, which often display signs of surplus production, is a global phenomenon that does not originate in Rome or in central Italy, but is common to a wide range of Mediterranean contexts, from the Rhône valley to the coasts of North Africa. The cultural relevance of this process is that it suggests, rather than an imposition of Roman models of exploitation onto colonized landscapes, the incorporation of local farming communities without too large a disruption of their way of life. Like the contemporary 'Hellenization' of elite tastes, the settlement of peasants in isolated farms on the countryside seems to be another phenomenon that paves the way for Roman expansion rather than resulting from it.

The outer circle by and large missed out on this particular Hellenistic development (as it had missed out on orthogonal urbanism, for instance), and remained based on hilltop settlements. But it rejoined the rest of the empire for the subsequent wave of rural change, the diffusion of villas. These well-appointed residences, which in many ways acquire a central role in Roman countrysides, are another component of the architectural revolution of the later first century BC and the early first century AD (see also Chapter 6). Contrary to a widely held view, they do not originate in the period of the conquest, nor are they associated with it in any clear way. Early prototypes had existed in the hinterland of Rome since the fifth and fourth centuries BC, but they only reached significant numbers, through a process of exponential multiplication, in the Caesarian and Augustan periods, during which they spread to the whole empire. While this is undoubtedly a cultural element rooted in Roman traditions, the revamped form that is acquired by elites everywhere is again part of the same change in tastes dating to the early empire which we have been examining here. The villas often do not change the nature of land-tenure patterns, nor do they affect the survival of the small farms. The archaeological evidence for *latifundia* (large, sparsely cultivated estates) centring on villas is scarce and controvertible, while it is clear in many cases that local lords directed their traditionally extracted surplus to this new form of conspicuous consumption (as is the case at the palace at Fishbourne in southern Britain, for instance).

The new focus on rural communities is also changing some perceptions of Roman social structure. Many indicators point to the fact that traditional bonds of social obligation remained in place after the Roman conquest, even when the actual lineages that headed them were replaced. Indeed, the long-term survival of small farmers is, at least in some cases, made possible by their symbiotic relationship with the lords to whom they owed their allegiance. The impact of colonial land distributions, for instance, could be softened and deflected by concerned local aristocrats, who could pull strings in Rome to achieve that end (for instance at Volterra: Terrenato 1998). These social processes have a deep cultural significance, because they show entire communities bound together by a hegemonic system of values to which everyone subscribes, even if elites are also at the same time participating in the volatile sphere of fancy fashions. The importance of vernacular cultures should not be underestimated just because the evidence is scarce. The Romans themselves were very aware of them, and very attached to their own. They relied, almost by default, on the structures of power, society, and culture they encountered in each new province to maintain order without the need for their constant direct intervention. Local elites, in this way, found themselves in the role of cultural brokers, regardless of their actual background, between the new global level created by the empire and the traditional ones. So while Rome was keen on promoting a thriving discourse of fashion and novelty among elites, it was equally the staunchest defender of traditional values, at home and everywhere else, as the root of its entire edifice. In this sense, it is the ultimate paradox of the Roman Empire that it resisted change, and fostered such resistance in its subjects, at least as strongly as it embraced new ideas and fashions in other spheres and at other levels.

Conclusion

It should be apparent by now how characterizing the cultural implications of the Roman conquest is a much harder task than previous generations of scholars have tended to believe. Rather than a straightforward one-way cultural transfer, new evidence and new approaches suggest a much richer process that operated differently depending on a number of variables, including time-period, region, social level, gender, age, and so on. A new attention to the early phase of the phenomenon has also contributed to a new image. Although this is sometimes forgotten, for a good half of its expansionist phase Rome dealt with urbanized societies of coastal Mediterranean regions. The core of the empire was thus made of city-states, many of which went back in time as far as Rome itself, or further, and had political and social structures that were essentially similar to each other. Peninsular Italy, southern France, south-eastern Spain, Sicily, Greece, and Dalmatia (to say nothing of Africa or Asia) were brought together, capitalizing on the centuries of interaction between their elites, as well as on a substantive compatibility in their political systems.

Thus it can be argued that, in the case of this 'inner circle' of provinces, the cultural transformations were anything but unilateral. All the elites involved appear to be elaborating a common code, playing around with their existing heritage as well as introducing Hellenistic elements circulating at a global level. While in this way horizontal cultural links were created between aristocracies, the internal structure of the individual communities was much less disrupted, and most ordinary folk remained within the bounds of traditional world-views. What is commonly called Roman imperial culture appears in this light rather as a set of cross-cultural compromises that elites accept in order to interact efficiently within the new political entity. These compromises undoubtedly affected important spheres, such as urban politics and architecture, written law, high art, and official language, but only moderately impacted on others, such as social structures and customary obligations, popular and subaltern culture, as well as vernacular dialects, cults, and imagery.

In the second phase of expansion, from Caesar onwards, a fairly consolidated Mediterranean urban world spread its influence over the rest of western Europe, bringing together lands and peoples that had much less in common. This later process has somehow stolen the attention of most modern historiography (which was, after all, produced in nations roughly corresponding to those ancient peripheral regions), and it is easier to cast in modern colonialist terms. While it is undoubtedly true that ethnic and cultural polarization had a much greater role in this 'outer circle' of the empire, the elements of cross-fertilization and convergence should not be ignored. Urbanization, economic intensification, and political development all took place in the centuries around the conquest, but the precise causal relationships are still debatable. They should also be seen within the context of the Augustan wave which reached everywhere, regardless of when each area had been incorporated. Moreover, only some spheres and some specific sociological groups were deeply affected, again overshadowing often-ignored elements of local continuity.

9

The fourth century

William Bowden

Introduction

IN the context of a study of Roman Europe, the fourth century presents an interesting paradox. The last decades of the third century saw what, with the benefit of hindsight, can be seen as a decisive moment in the history of Europe, when the emperor Diocletian introduced the sweeping reforms that divided the empire in two. Diocletian, as the senior of the two *Augusti* (Chapter 3), took responsibility for the eastern empire, leaving the West to his junior, Maximian. This constituted both a graphic indication and an institutional acknowledgement of where the Roman Empire saw its priorities. The wealth of the empire lay in the East; the West, by contrast, was of secondary importance. The subsequent founding of Constantinople as a second capital further exacerbated the eastward drift of Roman power.

The division of the empire, and its administration's recognition of the fact that the power-base of the Roman world lay in its eastern provinces, is perhaps one of the reasons for the historical antipathy of western scholars towards the later empire. It is, after all, one of the paradoxes of Roman studies that the level of energy devoted to research on the western provinces is inversely proportional to their level of importance in the eyes of the Roman administration. Hence Britain, one of the most exhaustively researched areas of the empire, was generally of marginal significance to the overall well-being of the Roman world, which survived its abandonment of the province relatively unscathed. The gradual fragmentation of other western provinces continued largely unchecked by the Roman administration which, despite periodic campaigns in the West, concentrated its resources elsewhere. Roman studies, however, developed against the background of the nineteenth- and twentieth-century imperial achievements and ambitions of European countries. Eurocentric scholars were perhaps uncomfortable with the fact that the Roman Empire, in which they saw similarities with the colonial ambitions of their own countries (Chapter 8), had placed more emphasis on its activities in the East, a policy which they found difficult to reconcile with the idea of Rome as an essentially European empire. While Rome's earlier eastwards expansion was entirely compatible with the expansionist policies of Britain, France, Italy, and others, Constantine's decision effectively to relocate the administrative heart of the empire to the East sat uncomfortably with the European antipathy towards the Orient more recently highlighted by Edward Said. One historian described the foundation of Constantinople as an 'irretrievable mistake', continuing that, 'while it [Constantinople] became the home and stronghold of what remained of Hellenic culture, [it] was too much exposed to Asiatic influences to escape their dangerous lure' (C. E. Robinson, *A History of Rome from 753 BC to AD 410* (London, 1935), 419).

Of course, the lesser importance of the western provinces in the late Roman period does not negate the importance of research on these more marginal areas of the empire. Indeed, perhaps, this is the raison d'être for study of Roman Europe. Although the events that occurred during this period were perhaps of more significance for the subsequent history of Europe than they were for that of the later Roman Empire, fourth-century Europe offers an intriguing opportunity to examine some of the more peripheral parts of the empire, and by doing so gain a greater understanding of how the Roman world was perceived by those who lived within and without its increasingly permeable borders. Nonetheless, the later Roman Empire was unquestionably a Mediterranean empire, and any narrative history of it is bound to relegate Britain and much of continental Europe into an inevitably supporting role.

This volume, however, is a history of Roman Europe, rather than the Roman Empire itself. As well as placing the Roman era within the wider framework of European history, it allows Europe to act as a prism through which the empire may be viewed (see Introduction). The arbitrary hundred-year period that forms the framework for this chapter allows the adoption of a scheme in which political and religious history, although providing a chronological framework, take second place to a more regionalized approach to the period. Europe and its diverse regions take centre-stage, instead of forming the backdrop to a history in which much of the major action and plot developments are taking place off-stage in the eastern Mediterranean. In particular, archaeological evidence will be utilized to demonstrate how the different regions of Europe changed during the later empire in terms of the attitudes of their populations towards the idea and ideal of Rome; these are changes which can be observed even within the Eternal City itself.

Through the lenses of archaeological and textual sources, the fourth century in Europe appears to have been a period of fragmentation and tremendous change. Like the third century, in traditional historical narrative it is a time of unrest populated by barbarians (Chapters 5 and 10) and characterized by internecine religious and political strife, which, perhaps partly owing to the reasons mentioned above, is often juxtaposed unfavourably with the earlier centuries of imperial rule—the 'Golden Age' that traditionally ends with the death of Marcus Aurelius in 180, which Gibbon famously described as 'the period in the history of the world, during which the condition of the human race was most happy and prosperous' (*The History of the Decline and Fall of the Roman Empire*, vol. 1, chap. 3).

The first decades of the fourth century also saw the official recognition of the Christian faith, and it is the conflict between paganism and Christianity that in many ways forms the frame of reference for the sources for the period, the survival of which is owed in large part to their significance for the history of Christianity rather than for the period as a whole. Gibbon saw Christianity as a key factor in the 'decline and fall' of the Roman Empire, and it has subsequently remained a dominant theme in the historiography of the fourth century, assuming a significance that is unlikely to have been reflected in the lives of most of the population, particularly that of Europe.

Although the western Roman Empire technically survived until 476 (all dates in this chapter are AD), the fourth century is a period in which we can find the roots of medieval Europe. The defeat of the emperor Valens at Adrianople in 378, and the later treaty of 382 by which Theodosius I allowed Gothic federates (Chapter 5) to settle within the empire, are traditionally seen as turning-points in the decline of Rome in the West. It was perhaps, however, the increasingly peripheral nature of the West in relation to Rome's power-base in the East that laid the foundation for the emergence of the barbarian kingdoms of early medieval Europe. The Roman Empire was based in part on a system of shared elite cultural values that crossed geographical divides. In the West this system was progressively eroded by its participants' increasing physical distance from imperial power and their increasing involvement in much more localized power structures, which often included elites of 'barbarian' origin. Indeed, scholarship over recent years has moved away from traditional explanations of 'decline and fall', in which a decadent empire crumbled in response to external pressures, although the reinvention of bloodthirsty barbarians as peaceful migrants has not found universal favour (Ward-Perkins 2005: 5–10). Nonetheless, although weight must be given to the significance of incursions from beyond the frontiers, it may be that the changes in the nature of what it meant to be 'Roman' eventually had a greater impact on the population of Europe.

A brief history of the fourth century

The political history of the fourth century is well known, if slightly confusing owing to both the proliferation of emperors and imperial claimants, and the protagonists' seeming lack of originality in the field of children's names. In order to provide some context for the developments in Europe described in the remainder of this chapter, a brief overview will be provided.

In the year 300 Diocletian had been in power for some sixteen years, the longest period of stable government the empire had seen since the death of Septimius Severus nearly ninety years before. Diocletian's four-way division of power, however, which was introduced in 293, inherently contained the seeds of its own downfall. It was an ideal system only in the unlikely scenario that the participants did not grow too ambitious. When Diocletian and (with less enthusiasm) his co-Augustus, Maximian, abdicated in 305, they were duly replaced by their two Caesars: Galerius, who replaced Diocletian in the East, and Constantius I, who replaced Maximian in the West, with Maximinus Daia and Severus as their respective Caesars. It was then that the problems started, and by 308 there were no fewer than eight individuals claiming the position of one of the two senior emperors.

In 306 Constantius died at York, and his son Constantine, campaigning alongside him in Britain, was proclaimed Augustus by the troops. A compromise was reached, however, with Galerius recognizing Constantine as Caesar to Severus' Augustus. Perhaps inspired by Constantine's success, Maxentius, the son of Diocletian's retired partner Maximian, seized power in Rome, claiming the title of *princeps*, in which he was supported by southern Italy and Africa. Maximian abandoned his retirement to join his son, and successfully drove Severus, who was then marching on Rome, back to Ravenna, where he was captured and later executed.

Maxentius, meanwhile, sought an alliance with Constantine, agreeing to recognize him as co-Augustus and giving him his sister Fausta in marriage. This alliance, however, broke down, when Spain (nominally in the hands of Constantine) declared for Maxentius. Maxentius, meanwhile, had to repel the attempts of his own father to overthrow him following a few months of their joint rule in Rome. The soldiers supported Maxentius, forcing Maximian to seek refuge with Constantine.

Following a failed advance on Rome in 307, Galerius persuaded Diocletian to emerge briefly from his retirement at Spalato on the Dalmatian coast to attend a conference at Carnuntum, also attended by Maximian, who was persuaded that retirement had perhaps been the wiser option. Galerius nominated an old military colleague, Licinius, to succeed the executed Severus as Augustus in the West, in control of Italy, Africa, and Spain (although these were in fact in the hands of Maxentius). Constantine, meanwhile, was demoted to the rank of Caesar and left with Gaul and Britain. Neither Constantine nor Maximinus Daia (Galerius' Caesar in the East) were content with this junior rank, and in 310 Galerius was compelled to recognize both as Augusti, with the result that there were four Augusti reigning simultaneously, while a fifth player, Maxentius, actually controlled most of the West with the exception of Africa, where a certain Domitius Alexander had been proclaimed Augustus.

Maximian, meanwhile, during a visit to his son-in-law Constantine in Gaul, organized an abortive coup while Constantine was away campaigning against the Franks, and was subsequently put to death. The following year, in 311, two further participants fell by the wayside: Domitius Alexander was killed by a force sent by Maxentius, while Galerius died after an illness that he apparently viewed as the revenge of the Christian god for a persecution of his followers. In the wake of Galerius' death, Maximinus Daia reached an agreement with Licinius after taking control of Asia Minor. When Constantine made an alliance with Licinius, however, Maximinus sided with Maxentius.

His alliance with Licinius left Constantine free to face Maxentius in a campaign that culminated with the latter's defeat and death at the Battle of the Milvian Bridge just outside Rome in 312, prior to which Constantine is famously said to have seen a vision of the cross, accompanied by the helpful caption *in hoc vinces* ('herein you shall conquer'). This allegedly inspired him to instruct his troops to paint the Christian *chi rho* monogram (formed from the first two letters of *Christos*, Christ, in the Greek alphabet) on their shields. The *chi rho* symbol was certainly adopted on coinage of Constantine (appearing on the emperor's helmet) by around 319, but whatever the truth of this story, there can be little question of its significance for the subsequent history of the Christian church.

Following his recognition by the Senate as senior Augustus, Constantine met Licinius at Milan in 313 (where Licinius married Constantine's sister Constantia). This meeting also produced the famous Edict of Milan, which proclaimed toleration of the Christian faith. Licinius recognized Constantine as senior Augustus in return for the right to legislate in his own half of the empire. Licinius then went East and defeated Maximinus, subsequently also murdering all the surviving relatives of Galerius and Severus in order to secure his position.

The agreement reached at Milan, although tested by conflict between Licinius and Constantine in the Balkans, endured uneasily until 323, when outright war broke out between the two. This conflict ended in successive defeats of Licinius at Adrianople and Chrysopolis and, although he was initially reprieved after pleas from his wife, he was eventually put to death for apparently plotting against Constantine, who was left as sole ruler of the Roman Empire.

Constantine reigned for thirteen years as sole emperor. After his death in 337, he was succeeded by his sons Constantine II, Constantius II, and Constans. There then followed what Gibbon termed 'a promiscuous massacre' in which nine of the relatives of Constantine's stepmother Theodora were killed, leaving the later emperor Julian and his elder brother Gallus as sole survivors of this side of the family. Constantius is clearly implicated in these events.

Italy went to Constans (along with Africa and Illyricum), while Constantine II was left with Spain, Gaul, and Britain, leaving Constantius with the eastern provinces. This did not last long, with Constantine II soon interfering in his brother's affairs, culminating in his invading northern Italy in 340, whereupon he was killed by Constans' troops near Aquileia. For most of the next decade Constans was based in Trier, from where he campaigned against the Franks (defeating them in 342), followed by an expedition to Britain in 343, of which the purpose is unknown.

Constans was not a popular ruler in Gaul (where he seems to have spent little time after 345), and also lost popularity with the army. Consequently in 350, while Constans was away on a hunting expedition, the commander of two of the leading regiments of the field army, Flavius Magnus Magnentius, was proclaimed emperor at Autun. There was no support for Constans, who was eventually captured and killed, leaving Constantius II as the only surviving son of Constantine. He defeated Magnentius in 353, after elevating Gallus (one of the two survivors of the family massacre of 337) to the rank of Caesar. Gallus, however, only lasted until 354, when he was deposed and executed by Constantius, who had grown suspicious of his junior.

Constantius was now left with an awkward decision as to what to do with Gallus' younger brother Julian, which he eventually resolved by appointing him Caesar in the West, which left Constantius free to campaign in the East. This backfired when the inexperienced Julian proved to be a remarkably successful general in Gaul. When his troops were ordered to the East by Constantius, they instead proclaimed Julian as Augustus, thus placing him in direct conflict with Constantius. Fortunately for Julian, Constantius unexpectedly died while travelling west to face the usurper in 361.

Julian's reign is famous for his attempts to revive the pagan religion, which ultimately had little effect. Following his rather mysterious death while campaigning against the Persians, he was succeeded by Jovian, who lasted less than a year. Jovian had been proclaimed by the army following Julian's death, and this trend continued with the proclamation of the Pannonian Valentinian I, who took charge of the West, leaving his brother Valens in charge of the East. He also elevated his 8-year-old son, Gratian, to the status of co-Augustus to fore-stall doubts surrounding the succession, although when Valentinian died in 375 (apparently in a fit of apoplexy at the rudeness of barbarian ambassadors) the army proclaimed his youngest son as Valentinian II.

Valens was killed in battle against a Gothic force at Adrianople in 378, a moment which is often seen as a decisive turning-point in the history of the Roman Empire, although it is unlikely that it was perceived as such at the time. In the aftermath of Adrianople, Theodosius, a skilled general, was made co-emperor by Gratian in order to counter the Gothic threat.

In 383 the commander of the legions in Britain, Magnus Maximus, was declared Augustus by his troops, and was supported by the troops on the Rhine. Although the Gallic legions were initially loyal to Gratian, they grew disillusioned with his poor generalship against Maximus and defected. The fleeing Gratian was captured and executed at Lyons. Theodosius pragmatically recognized Maximus, who was a formidable leader commanding a major force, until around 387, when Maximus seized Valentinian II's territory. Theodosius launched an offensive to retake the West, capturing and executing Maximus at Aquileia in 388, and restoring Valentinian II.

Owing to Valentinian's youth and inexperience, Theodosius appointed two Frankish advisers, Bauto and Arbogast, to assist the emperor. Arbogast, however, became a de facto ruler, and having probably murdered Valentinian at Vienne in Gaul in 392, he made Flavius Eugenius, a hitherto unknown professor of rhetoric, a puppet emperor. Theodosius, however, made his youngest son, Honorius, Augustus, and defeated Eugenius and Arbogast in battle at the River Frigidus in 394. Following the battle he based himself at Milan, but died in 395, leaving the Roman Empire in the hands of his two sons, Arcadius and Honorius, who ruled the East and West respectively. The 10-year-old Honorius was placed in the care of the Vandal general Stilicho, who at the end of the fourth century was effectively ruler of the West.

This narrative of emperors, usurpers, and battles forms the tra-ditional story of the fourth-century Roman Empire. Diocletian's tetrarchic system did not outlive its creator, and the dynastic principle

(Chapter 3) was re-established by the house of Constantine. This sat uncomfortably alongside a continuation of the system whereby emperors were proclaimed by the army, resulting in a succession of usurpers (like Constantine himself) whose accessions were occasionally legitimized through military victory. The latter part of the fourth century is marked by a series of child emperors, under the protection of 'barbarians' who had risen to become senior figures in the army and administration.

It is perhaps this last factor that gives some indication of the cultural shifts that were occurring in the western empire, particularly in terms of the ways that the elite of the empire were forging new relationships with 'barbarian' leaders in a complex dialogue that affected all participants (Chapter 10). The often confused relative status of the empire's various leaders must have exacerbated the increasingly fragmentary nature of its local and regional power structures. The extent to which the events of this political history really affected many of the inhabitants of fourth-century Europe, however, is debatable; indeed, it is likely that many people were only vaguely aware of them. While the machinations of the various imperial courts should not be overlooked, the diversity of the regions of Roman Europe, whose fortunes appear to be often only loosely tied to those of their nominal leaders, suggests that their effect should not be overstated. The remainder of this chapter will attempt to catalogue some of the divergent responses to the changing political, social, and cultural climates of Roman Europe.

Rome in the fourth century

Perhaps nowhere better illustrates the changing relationship between Europe and the Roman Empire than fourth-century Rome itself, described by one recent commentator as 'a rather drowsy backwater halfway down the Italian peninsula overrun by old families who still thought they counted' (Reece 1999: 166). The capital of the Roman Empire resided with the person of the emperor. Maximian, the first tetrarchic Augustus of the West, was based primarily at Trier and Milan, while Diocletian visited Rome perhaps twice during his reign. Nonetheless, during the fourth century (particularly until the end of the Constantinian period) Rome remained an important location for displays of imperial power and munificence. Indeed, the archaeological remains of fourth-century Rome illustrate a complex dialogue between the early imperial past and the fourth-century present, and the means that its rulers and citizens adopted to adjust to the changing social and political situation of the city within the empire. Rome remained an ideal, an embodiment of Roman life and culture, even if the major political power resided elsewhere, and this is reflected in the attitudes of the emperors towards their erstwhile capital.

The Forum Romanum remained the symbolic political heart of Rome as it had been since the days of the Republic, and as such, it remained the point where the relationship between the imperial power and the city manifested itself; in particular through the medium of monumental building, which, in Rome at least, remained a favoured means of elite self-expression. Despite the emperor's increasingly distant relationship with the city, during the tetrarchic period the Forum (or at least certain areas of it) saw some fundamental work of imperial reconstruction. In 283 and 307 parts of the Forum and its surroundings were damaged by fire. Both events occasioned substantial imperially sponsored programmes of reconstruction, with the usurper Maxentius in particular seeking legitimacy via the traditional path of monumental building in the capital.

The tetrarchic work in the Forum functioned to construct links with the past, reminding the city's population of the absent imperial power and the current rulers' relationship with their predecessors. This traditionalism is reflected in the choice of monuments to be embellished and the building forms used, many of which recalled their predecessors from the early empire. The epigraphic record from the Forum also indicates a self-conscious traditionalism, with inscriptions adopting themes such as the restoration of peace and happiness. An example from the reign of Constantine (*Corpus Inscriptionum Latinarum* 6. 40764a) is dedicated to the emperor: 'To the restorer of happiness | the founder and extender | of peace and author of tranquillity | our emperor Flavius Valerius Constantinus Pious and Fortunate Augustus.'

The tetrarchic use of monumental building to construct a relationship with the past also extended to the building materials used. Although the structure is no longer extant, a monumental arch of the tetrarchic period (almost certainly Diocletian's Arcus Novus), was built using a combination of old and new sculptural elements, in which newer carving was used in conjunction with a series of large figurative panels of the first century on which the heads had been reworked into likenesses of the tetrarchic emperors. A far better-known example of this practice, however, is Rome's most notorious fourth-century monument—the Arch of Constantine, dedicated in AD 315 to mark the emperor's tenth year in office, and to commemorate his victory over Maxentius at the Milvian Bridge in 312 (see fig. 5.1). All the major narrative reliefs on the arch are reused, taken from monuments of Trajan, Hadrian, and Marcus Aurelius.

Since the Renaissance, interpretation of this reuse of earlier material has been inextricably linked with perceptions of the later Roman Empire. The use of salvaged material, or *spolia*, in the Arch of Constantine was seen to reflect ideas of decline and fall, showing the decadence of classical art, with fourth-century artists apparently unable to match the work of their forebears, and consequently forced to borrow sculptural elements from earlier monuments to compensate for their own shortcomings. The Arch, in other words, was representative of the decay of Rome itself.

Other interpretations of the Arch have seen it either as an ideological statement, whereby Constantine deliberately used the earlier reliefs as a device with which to associate himself with great emperors of the past, and in doing so provide his rule with greater legitimacy; or as an act of pragmatism, a means of erecting an impressive structure in a short space of time at minimal expense. There is, of course, no reason for ideology and pragmatism to be mutually exclusive (and most recent commentators on the Arch acknowledge the possibility of both playing a role in its construction). Equally, when viewed in the context of the earlier tetrarchic construction activities in the Forum, the Arch of Constantine appears to be only one aspect of a wider dialogue with the city's past.

The Arch of Constantine was the last of Rome's great imperial monuments, and after the end of Constantine's reign the emperors were infrequent visitors to the Eternal City. The changes wrought by the increasingly distant relationship between Rome and its nominal rulers were exacerbated by the foundation of Constantinople in 326, and indeed, it is following the reign of Constantine that Rome began the process that saw it eventually reinvent itself as the capital of European Christendom. The creation of a rival Senate in Constantinople progressively eroded the standing of Rome's aristocracy, 'the old families who still thought they counted', and who were increasingly sidelined. Throughout the fourth century senatorial status was increasing devalued as it was attached to a growing number of ranks, until by 400 each half of the empire had around 3,000 posts that led more or less directly to senatorial status.

While this devaluation of senatorial standing doubtless rankled with the old aristocratic families of the city, it is also clear that Rome's aristocracy retained immense levels of wealth and privilege. Olympiodorus of Thebes, writing in the early fifth century, tells us that 'each of the big residences in Rome contains everything supposed to be found in a medium-sized city: a hippodrome, piazzas, temples, fountains and different types of bath-buildings. … A house is a town' (cited from R. Blockley, *The Fragmentary Classicising Historians of the Later Roman Empire. Eunapius, Olympiodorus, Priscus and Malchus*. ARCA Classical and Medieval Texts, Papers and Monographs, 10 (Liverpool, 1983), 152). Archaeology in Rome has demonstrated that these descriptions contain less hyperbole than might be imagined. Excavations at the Ospedale Militare, on the Caelian Hill, have revealed a series of residences whose owners are also known from documentary sources. They include the house of Gaudentius, who was named in an inscription found in the *triclinium* (dining-room).

This Gaudentius is also known from documentary sources as a neighbour of Symmachus, whose writings form one of the major sources for the fourth century, and a further grand *domus* (house; Chapter 4) discovered nearby, with a magnificent apsidal reception room, may be that of Symmachus himself. Even the house of Symmachus, however, seems to have been smaller than that of his Caelian Hill neighbours, the Valerii. After the house was burnt during the Gothic sack of 410, no one could afford to buy it from Valerius Pinianus, such was the colossal size of the estate. The creation of palatial private residences, sometimes filling entire city blocks or *insulae*, was very much a characteristic of the towns of the Mediterranean in the late Roman period, although the phenomenon is less marked in western Europe, where grandiose private dwellings were more common in the countryside.

The Roman Senate was also active in the sphere of building restoration, and after the reign of Constantine the Forum was managed and shaped by the Roman aristocracy rather than by the imperial authority. Although a large number of inscriptions dedicated to the emperor have been found, the dedicators were almost all members of the Roman aristocracy. This is particularly notable in areas that had previously been the focus of imperial power, like both the Rostra. While the ruling power was still being celebrated, it was the local grandees who were articulating the means by which this occurred. The Senate was also responsible for the restoration of the Precinct of the Harmonious Gods (*Dei Consentes*) in 367–8, and perhaps also the Temple of Saturn around the same time. As well as taking place at a time when pagan cults had increasingly fallen from favour in imperial circles, it is notable that these monuments both flank the *clivus Capitolinus*, the road that led from the Forum to the Capitol, and which had previously been used by the emperors to ascend the Capitol upon entering Rome, a practice that had by now been abandoned. That the Roman aristocracy continued to ascribe importance to this route further demonstrates that, by the second half of the fourth century, it was they rather than the emperor who were shaping the topography of Rome's political and religious centre. The choice of monuments to be restored, and the large numbers of statues that were moved to the Forum, indicates that the aristocracy was using the Forum and the remains of the city's pagan past to advance a political and religious agenda that was increasingly parochial in focus.

Paganism remained a cornerstone of aristocratic identity in fourth-century Rome, and it was not until 383 that Christianity really became the state religion, when the Altar of Victory was removed from the Senate House in Rome (occasioning protest from Symmachus, then urban prefect and thus responsible for the administration of the city). Rome was also unusual in Europe, however, in the extent to which the Christian religion had been given a monumental form, principally through the great basilicas constructed by Constantine, which are profoundly atypical for the period. As well as the basilica, baptistery, and episcopal palace at the Lateran (originally an imperial palace donated to the church by Constantine around 313), these included a number of churches built over martyrs' tombs in the city's extra-mural cemeteries, the most famous of which is at St Peter's. The churches of San Lorenzo and San Sebastiano on the Via Tiburtina and Via Appia respectively, that of SS Marcellino and Pietro on the Via Labicana (which housed the mausoleum of

Constantine's mother), and of S Agnese (with the associated mausoleum of Constantine's daughter, Constantina), equally bear witness to
the cults that had developed around martyrs' graves from as early as
the second century, and the perceived need on the part of the faithful
to be interred within close proximity to them.

Although fifth- and sixth-century churches and their medieval successors also adopted the basilica plan, these fourth-century churches
should not be viewed exclusively as the start of a specifically Christian architectural form. They are rather examples of Constantine
and his successors (and increasingly the papacy) adopting an already
well-established architectural model for the purposes of constructing
monumental buildings in a Christian context. Indeed, as Constantine
viewed the emperor's position as that of Christ's vicar on earth, so
God was increasingly perceived as emperor in heaven; hence, the
ceremony of Christian liturgy began to resemble that of the imperial
court. Thus it was a natural progression for Christian architecture to
adopt the forms of secular imperial building. As we shall see, however,
this model of building did not extend beyond Rome and the other
imperial 'capitals' (described below), and elsewhere in Europe dated
examples of fourth-century churches are few and far between. It was to
be some time before Christian building was adopted as a widespread
form of elite self-representation in the West outside Italy. Indeed,
even in Rome itself Constantine's churches remained anomalous; it
was not until the later fourth and fifth centuries that further Christian buildings of this scale were erected. Furthermore, Constantine's
churches, much as they dominate the topography of medieval and
modern Rome, were constructed very much on the peripheries of the
city. The 'Christianization' of urban space, which is so characteristic
of the later fifth and sixth centuries in the Mediterranean, was not a
factor in fourth-century Europe.

The wandering imperial 'capital': Trier, Milan, and Aquileia

The decline in Rome's status was in part owing to the fact that, from
the time of the tetrarchy, imperial power and administration was
based wherever the emperor happened to be at the time, as opposed to

resting with the Senate in Rome. The Senate was effectively sidelined by the *comitatus*, the group of 'ministries' that accompanied the emperor in his peripatetic existence. The imperial administration became a vast migratory body, which required a significant infrastructure to cater for its needs. This led to a number of European cities assuming, at least on a temporary basis, the role of imperial 'capital' of the western empire. These included Milan, which was an imperial residence from the reign of Maximian onwards, and which from 373 became, under St Ambrose, the principal Christian centre of the West; and Aquileia, which periodically hosted emperors from Diocletian onwards. North of the Alps, imperial attention was focused on Trier, where emperors such as Maximian, Constantius I, and Constans were based for considerable periods.

In all cases the presence of the imperial court had a marked effect on the built environment of the cities in question. As imperial centres, these towns would have seen architectural embellishment during the fourth century that set them apart from many other provincial cities, including the provision of imperial palaces with large audience chambers. Constantine's basilica at Trier, still standing today, provides some indication of the breathtaking scale of these audience chambers, which provided models of elite architecture that were later adopted by early medieval European potentates such as Charlemagne. The basilica and its associated palace formed only one part of the imperial complex at Trier, which also included a colossal double church (now beneath the present cathedral). The complex was completed by a massive public bath, the so-called Kaiserthermen. This last, however, was never completed, the project apparently abandoned (after Constantine's attention switched to his new capital) until the reign of Valentinian I (364–75), who was based in the city for much of his reign in order to campaign against the Alammani, and converted parts of the unfinished bath complex into a residence. Nevertheless, Trier's role as the capital of Roman Gaul did not long outlast the fourth century, and in 407 the capital was moved to Arles in a direct response to the barbarian invasion of the previous year. Arles itself had also been favoured by the emperors of the fourth century, and was the focus of a church council convened by Constantine in 314. The imperial mint was also transferred from Ostia to Arles in 314, and from 328 the city was given the additional name of Constantina, while Constantius II wintered in the city in 353–4.

Aquileia also functioned as a periodic home for the emperor and the imperial court. In part this was because of its position as one of the principal ports at the head of the Adriatic and the western terminus for many of the major shipping routes from the East. In addition, Aquileia was a key point on roads connecting the East to the West, and also on those that ran north to the Danubian provinces. Consequently, emperors frequently passed through the town en route to one side of the empire or the other, as evidenced by the number of laws which name Aquileia as the place of issue. The city subsequently became a focus of regional administration. As in the case of Trier, this led to a distinctive range of additions to the urban landscape, at least some of which were imperial benefactions: a recently discovered inscription attests to Constantine's rebuilding of the baths. Construction activity was particularly marked in the sphere of Christian architecture: a substantial double basilica was erected in the early fourth century, of which the mosaic pavements can still partly be seen. Aquileia again became a focus of early Christian building in the latter part of the fourth century, particularly during the episcopate of Bishop Chromatius, who was responsible for the early phases of at least three churches.

As at Trier, however, Aquileia's importance barely outlasted the fourth century. In 402, when northern Italy was under threat from Alaric and the Visigoths, the western emperor Honorius established his capital at Ravenna (more easily defended than Milan), and the new Adriatic capital rapidly eclipsed its more northerly rival.

Milan was the most important and well-established of the imperial centres that developed under the tetrarchy and its fourth-century successors. It was strategically placed, allowing the western tetrarchs to monitor both Gaul and the West and the Danube frontier, as well as the activities of their eastern tetrarchic colleagues. It functioned as Maximian's capital, and gained a major new wall circuit, as well as an imperial palace and a circus to make it fit to serve as an imperial capital. Milan's fame lay not only in its role as an administrative and political centre, but also in its growing significance as a Christian city; it became one of the great centres of early Christian architecture. Five huge churches are known from the fourth-century city, including the extraordinary quatrefoil church of San Lorenzo, built sometime before 378, but also the great basilicas of San Tecla, San Giovanni in Conca, and San Simpliciano, and the cross-plan church of the Holy Apostles (now San Nazzaro).

Much of this building occurred under the aegis of the city's most celebrated churchman, Bishop Ambrose. Episcopal office was thrust upon Ambrose in 374 after he quelled a violent crowd during one of the riotous episodes that frequently accompanied changes of ecclesiastical office in the fourth century (the election of Pope Damasus in AD 366, for example, occasioned a massacre in the basilica of Sicininus during which 137 people reportedly died). Ambrose was not yet baptized at the time of his acclamation, but passed swiftly through the ranks of the clergy to ascend the episcopal throne only a week after baptism, in a meteoric career-progression that has seldom been bettered. However unorthodox his election may have been, Ambrose became a towering figure in the Christian West, and is in part responsible for the form and liturgy of the Catholic church as it survives today.

Ambrose also used his position at Milan to exercise a major influence on the emperors who periodically based themselves in the city, and was in part responsible for fostering the growing relationship between church and emperor. In 390 he successfully demanded that the emperor Theodosius do penance after his troops massacred 7,000 people in Thessalonica, and he influenced the emperor's decision to block the reinstatement of the Altar of Victory to the Senate House in Rome (see above), despite Symmachus journeying to Milan to put the senators' case.

Milan, like Aquileia, suffered from the removal of the imperial court to Ravenna in 402, but its importance as a religious centre and its substantial concentration of saints' graves, not least that of Ambrose, ensured that it continued to function as a significant urban centre throughout the Middle Ages. Indeed, it seems that in the cities which served as bases for the imperial court an idea of classical urban life was maintained long after it had become anachronistic in the other towns of the western empire.

'Cadavers of half-ruined cities': towns of fourth-century Roman Europe

It was in fact Ambrose of Milan who provided a description of the other towns of northern Italy, the precise meaning of which has excited

considerable debate among historians and archaeologists. Writing in
the last quarter of the fourth century to his friend Faustinus, who
had recently lost his sister, Ambrose offered the consolation that she
would enjoy eternal life, in stark contrast to the 'many cadavers of half-
ruined cities ... for ever laid low and destroyed' (Ambrose, *Epist.* 39,
Patrologia Latina 16). He describes the desolation of the towns of
Claterna, Bologna, Modena, Reggio, Brescello, and Piacenza, as well
as the desertion of the fields of the Apennines, and the abandoned
fortresses that had previously been teeming with people.

The declining state of the towns of the empire is often linked by the
written sources to the activities of emperors, particularly Constantine,
whom the pagan historian Zosimus blames for the financial ruin of the
cities. It has been suggested by a number of scholars that Constantine
and his successors placed civic revenues (or a proportion of them)
under control of the imperial treasury rather than, as previously,
the town councils, although the extent to which this occurred is a
matter of dispute. The evidence for the confiscation of city revenues is
difficult to interpret, relying to some extent on sources that describe
their later partial restoration under Valentinian and Valens. It is
clear, however, that during the late empire the power and status
accorded to town councils was significantly reduced, and that civic
office became something to be avoided rather than aspired to; election
to the *curia* (the local council) carried relatively little prestige and
could be ruinously expensive, as members of the councils could be
personally liable for any shortfall in taxation.

One result of this, in the West at least, was a lessening of the motivation for building and restoring public monuments as a way of gen-
erating prestige for the benefactor, and thus assisting him in election
to civic office. There is a marked reduction in inscriptions recording
this sort of activity from the early third century onwards (although it
should be noted there is also an overall reduction in the number of
inscriptions of all types). The fabric of the towns seems to have changed
as a result, with many public buildings and public spaces falling into
disrepair. Earlier monumental buildings made useful sources of building material for other projects, and the use of *spolia* (see discussion of
the Arch of Constantine above) is one of the defining characteristics
of late Roman building techniques. This form of architectural salvage
was clearly seen as detrimental to the monumental appearance of
Roman towns, as shown by laws, preserved in the *Theodosian Code*

(a collection of all the imperial legislation issued between the reign of Constantine and 437), proscribing the practice. The repeated legislation against spoliation testifies to the differences of opinion between the imperial administration and its subjects regarding the purpose and nature of towns. To the imperial government, the towns constituted a key part of the means through which taxation was collected and redistributed: consequently they perhaps had a greater allegiance to the concept of the classical town than did many of the towns' inhabitants. Certainly, generosity towards the cities remained an important imperial practice, and gratitude for aid to struggling towns was an important rhetorical device for delivering praise of emperors.

The survival, or decline, of Roman towns in Europe during the late and post-Roman era is one of the questions that has driven archaeological and historical research on the period. Opinion has often been polarized between those for whom descriptions such as that of Ambrose were largely rhetorical, with classical urban life continuing in some towns in a reduced form; and those for whom town life was essentially extinguished in the late Roman period. More recently, however, a consensus has emerged that sees marked regional variation, as towns and their inhabitants responded to changing local circumstances in late antiquity. It is certain that the nature of urban settlement changed significantly in the late Roman period, but the timing and extent of the transformation varied from town to town and from region to region. In some areas of Europe, some fourth-century towns would have looked little different from those of the second century. Other towns, however, had changed dramatically, retaining little of the monumental character which we tend to regard as the leitmotif of classical urbanism (and which was viewed similarly in antiquity).

In Italy, the cities (particularly those of the north) have been the focus of the most intensive research and debate surrounding their survival, and the nature of their occupation between the late Roman and early medieval periods. This research has demonstrated that the towns of Italy followed varied trajectories between the third and fifth centuries. While the towns of Tuscany and southern Piedmont were already showing signs of decline in the third century, it was not until the late fourth century that similar processes affected those of Lombardy and central Piedmont, which were perhaps sustained and stimulated through their proximity to Milan. The picture of decline in southern Piedmont supports Jerome's testimony regarding the town of Vercelli in Liguria, which he describes as being 'sparsely inhabited and half-ruined' (*Epistles* 1. 3).

Archaeological work in towns of Aemilia has also to some extent supported Ambrose's description of their plight. In the cases of nine examples of aristocratic houses, excavated in five different cities, all were destroyed by fire in the third century, and in only two cases were there signs of rebuilding, suggesting that descriptions of ruinous and depopulated cities in the late fourth century may reflect reality as well as rhetoric. Excavation in Brescia, however, has shown that the town's aristocratic houses survived, albeit in an altered form, through the fifth century, as did much of the town's urban infrastructure, including its streets and drains.

The cities of Gaul were also apparently affected by many of the same processes that had affected those of Italy. In the second half of the fourth century Ammianus Marcellinus described Avenches as 'a *civitas* (city) now abandoned, but of no small distinction in former days, as the buildings, though half-ruined, even now testify' (15. 11. 12). While it is clear that many of the towns of Gaul continued to play a key role as administrative and defensive centres, albeit with perhaps reduced populations, it is likely that the urban public life which had been a defining characteristic of the town since the second century progressively diminished in the fourth century. The tradition of imperial munificence towards towns, however, continued into the fourth century, albeit perhaps infrequently; an inscription from Reims commemorating the rebuilding of some baths records that the emperor Constantine paid for the work through his 'customary generosity', while the same emperor was praised by an orator from Autun for his fiscal aid for the town. It may be noted that Avenches, notwithstanding the decrepit state described by Ammianus, was still ranked as a city in official sources in the 380s, indicating that the official perception of what constituted a city may have been more optimistic or more fossilized than was warranted by the actuality.

The towns of Roman Spain (*Hispania*) also saw an apparent decline in locally sponsored municipal benefactions during the third century, although, as in Gaul, occasional imperial assistance was given to cities. In Tarraco provincial officials, rather than the local aristocracy, seem to have maintained the upper *forum* throughout the fourth century, as indicated by a series of inscribed statue bases recording dedications to a number of emperors. In the lower *forum*, however, the basilica was destroyed by fire in the 360s and never rebuilt, while burials appeared within the walls of the lower town as early as the middle of the fourth century, this last phenomenon marking a significant divergence from the classical urban norm, where the dead were buried in extra-mural cemeteries (*necropoleis*). Nonetheless, the town maintained strong trading links with North Africa, attested by the imports of pottery, oil, and fish sauce (*garum*).

Private money in *Hispania*, however, was increasingly reserved for the construction of large country residences, a phenomenon that became widespread in the later empire. Nonetheless, it has been argued that the proximity of these villas to towns such as Taracco and Mérida attests to the continued vitality of the urban centres, notwithstanding a certain loss of monumentality. Furthermore, the presence of imported goods at the villa sites and rural products in cities indicates the continued interdependence of the two.

On the fringes of the empire, in Britain, urban life seems to have reached its apogee around the middle of the third century. After this date the fortunes of the Roman towns of Britain appear mixed, and the evidence has been interpreted in varying ways. In part the argument is a semantic one, with dispute revolving around ancient and modern interpretations of words such as 'town' and *civitas*, and the extent to which the British towns of the fourth century and later would have been recognizable as such to an inhabitant of a Mediterranean region with a longer history of urbanism.

It is certainly clear that some of the towns of Roman Britain underwent substantial changes from *c*.250, and that a number of areas that had previously been occupied fell out of use, for example, the *forum*/basilica at Wroxeter, which was burnt down in the third century and not rebuilt. The picture, however is not uniform; at Caistor-by-Norwich the *forum*/basilica had also been destroyed in the third century but had subsequently been reconstructed. At Silchester, meanwhile, the *forum*/basilica was used for industrial activities from the late third century onwards. There is a similarly wide variation between towns in terms of the use of other public areas such as bath complexes, where a large number appear to have remained in use into the fourth century (for example, at Lincoln), while others were apparently abandoned by the end of the third (as at Wroxeter). The decline of public areas that is characteristic of towns in northern Italy and Gaul, however, does not seem to have occurred with the same frequency in the fourth-century towns of Britain.

Although the public buildings of Britain do not seem to have suffered in quite the same way as those of continental Europe, it is clear that, as elsewhere, the citizens of the province were more interested in spending their money on grandiose country residences than they were in maintaining or augmenting the civic centres of the towns. There is little evidence of new public building occurring in fourth-century Romano-British towns. In contrast, rural villas in the province reached new heights of extravagance in this period (below). As with the Spanish villas, the existence of these sometimes palatial complexes may by default constitute further evidence of the continued relative vitality of urban centres.

It was only in the last quarter of the fourth century (therefore considerably earlier than the traditional date of Rome's abandonment of the province, i.e. 410) that the towns of Britain were partially abandoned. Many towns, such as Verulamium, Chichester, and Canterbury, saw large parts of the public and private cityscape abandoned, while a similar contraction of occupation has also been noted in smaller settlements. As with many other towns in Europe, the late fourth-century Roman towns of Britain would have been barely recognizable as such to a visitor from the second century.

Urban defences

Defence of the cities was a paramount concern for the late Roman administration. City walls were also important, however, for their symbolic and ideological value. Artistic depictions and rhetorical descriptions of cities throughout both the early and late Roman periods place great emphasis on the presence of walls, which were seen as a defining characteristic of towns. Wall circuits tended to be imperial projects, although in many cases it is not clear whether the imperial treasury actually paid for them, as opposed to simply demanding their construction. They were certainly a means by which an emperor could demonstrate concern for cities and their inhabitants, and many of the major cities of Europe had been walled by the end of the third century, including the massive circuit built by the emperor Aurelian at Rome between 270 and 275. A similarly extensive circuit was built to protect Milan in the late third century, while other towns as far away as London also gained major circuits of defences during the third century. The fourth-century walls were, however, particularly in Gaul, also indicative of other changes that were affecting the towns besides the external threat of attack.

The walls are the most striking feature of the late Roman towns of Gaul. In some cases, such as Le Mans, they still stand to their full height and remained formidable throughout the medieval period. They differed markedly from the city walls that had been built until the late third century, in that they often encircled only a small part of the previously occupied urban area. At Tours, for example, the early Roman town covered some 30 ha, of which only 9 ha were eventually enclosed within the late Roman walls (constructed perhaps between 350 and 374); while at Autun the shrinkage was even more pronounced, with a reduction from 200 ha to 10 ha. The contraction of defended areas is also characteristic of the towns of late Roman Spain. The fourth-century circuit at Carthago Nova (Cartagena) enclosed only 5.3 ha, a tiny area by comparison with that occupied by the early Roman city, while a similar reduction may have occurred at Mérida.

This reduction of the defended area is a characteristic of late Roman towns throughout both the eastern and western empire, as walls began to be built for reasons of defence as well as civic identity and status. Although these reduced settlements may often appear to be little more than fortified citadels, even in this later period we should not underestimate the importance of walls as symbols of civic identity in addition to their more functional significance. Thus, although the urban areas (and possibly populations) were apparently shrinking, the perception of these settlements as towns remained, although it may be that this perception was of more relevance to the imperial authorities than it was to the inhabitants (see above).

In Gaul, the reduced urban areas encircled by the new walls, and the types of public buildings that were erected within them (which seem to have been primarily military and administrative in nature), suggest that the function of these towns was changing. Whereas in the first and second centuries they had been places where local elites would compete for status through embellishment of public spaces, their function was now primarily administrative and defensive. A number of small settlements, such as Cambrai and Tournai in the Scarpe valley in northern Gaul, were promoted to *civitas* status (giving them administrative power over the surrounding territory) during the provincial reforms that commenced under the tetrarchy (in which the number of provinces in the empire was increased and administrative areas became smaller). This involved the construction of fortifications and public buildings; indeed, the primary purpose behind this elevation in status seems to have been that of creating additional administrative and military centres. In the case of Cambrai, the new *civitas* perhaps replaced Bavai to the east as a centre of civil administration, as the latter became increasingly militarized, with its *forum* transformed into a fort. There does indeed appear to have been a general militarization of settlement sites, and many of the towns of northern Gaul which survive into the second half of the fourth century are those that appear to have had a military presence. At the *civitas* capital at Arras, for example, the *castrum* was rebuilt in the second half of the fourth century to house what may have been 'Germanic' military units, while the *forum* at Amiens was fortified and partly converted into a vast granary.

Defence in the countryside: the return to *oppida*

As well as the fortification of the earlier towns and the reduction of the occupied areas, in parts of the western empire (and perhaps slightly later in the eastern empire) new settlement sites were established on fortified hilltops and promontories. Although many examples of this, for example, in Italy, Spain and Britain, date to the fifth and sixth centuries, it is clear that the process was also taking root in the fourth century and earlier. It is particularly pronounced in provinces close to the frontiers. The Gallic countryside saw the establishment of a number of new sites in often defensive locations, sometimes reusing the sites of earlier Iron Age *oppida* (Chapter 1). These were the *burgi* later described by the fifth-century writer Sidonius Apollinaris (*Epistles* 5. 14. 1; *Carmina* 22. 101), and seem to have been a response to the increasing insecurity of life beyond the town walls. This insecurity seems in part to derive from the activities of lawless local elements as much as the threat of incursions from beyond the frontier—Sidonius writes of a woman carried off by 'local bandits' (*Epistles* 6. 4. 1). The *oppida*, defended by ditches and stone ramparts, were a feature of the landscapes of Gaul from the period of the so-called 'Gallic Empire' of the second half of the third century onwards. Examples include Echternach in Luxembourg (later famous as the site of the monastery founded by the Northumbrian monk St Willibrord) and the former Iron Age *oppidum* of Vermand in the Somme valley. Possible British examples include the promontory fort at Bitterne in Hampshire and a similar small walled settlement at Horncastle, while a local defensive initiative is also implied at the hilltop villa of Castle Copse in Wiltshire, where earthworks were constructed to link the villa to the Iron Age *oppidum* of Chisbury Castle.

Finds at Vermand indicate that occupation of these *oppida* could be long-lasting. Although little is known of occupation within the interior of the fort, three large late Roman cemeteries have been found on its peripheries. The cemeteries contained 700 inhumations, orientated north–south and accompanied by grave-goods in pagan fashion (Christian burials usually have none). One of the graves was particularly well furnished, including weapons such as an axe, a spear, and javelins, as well as a large and elaborate shield, and it has been suggested that the occupant may have been of barbarian origin but of high rank in the Roman army, possibly even part of an emperor's personal retinue (indicated by traces of purple material lining the shield; for similar cases in continental Europe see Chapter 10).

The extent to which these Gallic *oppida* were military in nature, perhaps garrisoned by *laeti* (barbarians settled within the borders of the empire) or federated barbarian soldiers is a matter of some debate (Chapter 5), as it is becoming clear that the line between 'Roman' and 'barbarian' was considerably more blurred than was once thought: Chapter 10). Hence, grave-goods once considered as 'Roman' or 'Germanic' in nature are no longer considered to be reliable indicators of ethnic identity, and the discovery of 'Germanic' graves at sites such as Vermand (where a small number of burials displayed 'Germanic' characteristics) must be viewed with some caution.

Rather than being formalized military sites, many of these hillforts may have been the result of more local initiatives, although their status and the nature of their occupation remain ambiguous. Other examples of this phenomenon can be seen in the form of small fortified 'villa' complexes, which appear particularly in the area of the Rhine and Danube frontiers. These are often associated with fortified villas recorded in the literary sources, such as that owned by Pontius Leontius described by Sidonius Apollinaris (*Carmina* 22. 101), although the sites that have been identified on the ground are often more like small farms with defensive elements such as ditches or 'tower-granaries' than true villas. These exercises in self-defence again rather emphasize the increasing remoteness of a centralized authority that could not be relied upon to respond with sufficient speed or strength in times of crisis.

The countryside

Despite the apparent growing insecurity of rural life in some parts of Europe, the fourth century saw a transfer of private investment from towns to substantial country residences, although it is to some extent artificial to make a rigid distinction between the towns and the countryside, when both were part of a single overall landscape. The distinction between town and country was never fixed and immutable at any time during the Roman era, but the late Roman period was one when boundaries between town and countryside became particularly blurred. Town walls, which, as we have seen, frequently reduced the size of urban areas, rendered ambiguous the status of those parts of the towns that had been excluded from the wall circuit, while some urban areas saw the introduction of rural activities within the walls. There were, however, clear social distinctions attached to urban and rural living, exemplified in the Roman villa itself. These were traditionally divided into a *pars urbana*, where the owner lived a life of luxurious relaxation, and a *pars rustica*, where agricultural productive activity occurred (the connection of the owner with agricultural production formed a key element of aristocratic identity). Indeed, the villa was the Roman town in microcosm, with its urban centre and rural hinterland.

The traditional view of the late Roman countryside derived from documentary sources (albeit more frequently relating to the eastern provinces) was one that emphasized the oppression of the peasantry by high taxation and rapacious landlords. A. H. M. Jones, whose history *The Later Roman Empire* remains a starting-point for study of the period, painted a pessimistic yet highly influential picture of a 'flight from the land' in which peasants abandoned their farms, unable to cope with crippling levels of taxation. In this he was aided by late Roman descriptions of a deserted and depopulated countryside (although in fact this type of description had been a common device in Roman literature since the late Republic).

Early archaeological field surveys, particularly the South Etruria survey conducted in the countryside to the north of Rome, appeared to bear out this view, pointing to a significant decline in the numbers of rural sites during the late Roman period. However, numerous field-survey projects (including the reassessment of the South Etruria results by the Tiber Valley Project) have effectively remapped the Roman countryside over the course of the last three decades, and the picture that has emerged has become much more nuanced, with a significant degree of local and regional variation in terms of both the quantity and the type of sites that survive during the late Roman period.

In southern and eastern Britain the early fourth-century countryside saw apparently exceptional prosperity, with numerous villas, together with production on an almost industrial scale of glass, metal, tiles, and particularly pottery. The landscape appears to be dominated by these villa estates, of which almost a thousand are known, with concentrations in the south Midlands, Northamptonshire, Hampshire, and Dorset. From around 350, however, we see the rise of the so-called 'palatial' villas, with an apparent corresponding drop in the number of smaller villas, as if some were prospering at the expense of the rest. These 'palatial' villas, of which the best-known example is Woodchester, are perhaps the Romano-British variant of a phenomenon that can be seen throughout the fourth-century Roman Empire, in which a small number of extremely grandiose residences appear in both urban and rural settings, exemplifying the growing power of a small number of individuals. It should be noted, however, that with the exception of Woodchester, the British villas never achieved the size and grandeur of the colossal complexes found elsewhere in Europe.

The villa 'boom' in Britain is mirrored in parts of Spain and Aquitaine in Gaul, where numerous fourth-century villas have been noted, often constructed on a much larger scale than their British equivalents. Away from the coast in particular, the landscape of *Hispania* was suited to the creation of vast estates with accompanying 'palatial' villas concentrated along the river valleys. These villas, such as that found at Montmaurin in Aquitaine, often featured monumental residential quarters decorated with opulent mosaics and collections of statues. The villas of the coastal region tended to be more modest, although, as in Britain, the fourth century saw a number of these sites increase in size and architectural sophistication, while conversely, in others earlier residential areas were turned over to agricultural production and storage.

In northern Gaul the picture is very different. By the fourth century the great villas that had been present in the first and second centuries had gone, to be replaced by much simpler forms of settlement that lacked the grandeur and architectural complexity of the villas. Occupation of smaller sites, however, appears to have continued with much greater consistency, with a certain underlying degree of continuity from pre-Roman settlement structures. At Mondeville and Grentheville in the Calvados region, for example, excavations across an extensive area showed continuous occupation from the late Bronze Age until the fifteenth century. The late third or fourth century, however, did see a change in building styles, in which sunken huts replaced buildings with drystone footings. While the appearance of this type of hut is traditionally associated with Germanic settlers, it has been argued that its appearance here is too early to be associated with 'barbarian' settlers, but instead is representative of typical Gallic construction, which persisted alongside the villas of the Roman period and became predominant in the late and post-Roman periods.

Whereas in northern Gaul it seems to have been the villas that suffered during the third century, in northern Italy the opposite seems to have occurred, and the picture is more reminiscent of that observed in Britain and Spain. Field survey of the area around Verona, for example, appears to have witnessed a progressive desertion of smaller sites, while the great villas appear to have survived into the fourth century. Grandiose northern Italian villas, however, such as those at Sirmione and Desenzano near Lake Garda, barely survived into the fifth century.

In Sicily the fourth century saw the construction of a series of spectacular villas, of which the most famous is that at Piazza Armerina. Like some of the northern Italian villas, and some of those noted in Spain, the Sicilian villas are often associated with *uici*—small settlements that seem to have functioned as minor administrative centres, and which were probably used for the collection of revenues from tenant farmers and wage labourers. This administrative function is also suggested by the discovery of balances and weights at probable *uicus* sites at San Giusto and Metapontum in southern Italy. It is possible that the villas such as Piazza Armerina were owned by wealthy landowners, and played a role in overseeing estates with which the *uici* were associated. In contrast with many of the northern Italian sites, villas such as that at San Giovanni dei Ruoti in Calabria apparently survived as elite residences into the sixth century.

In many parts of fourth-century Europe villas appear to have replaced the towns as the focus of elite display, although in some centres (notably Rome and the imperial 'capitals') grandiose residential structures could still be seen in an urban context (a phenomenon that was more pronounced in the eastern empire). Major residences in both urban and rural contexts were, to some extent, part of the same phenomenon, whereby the focus of display moved away from the public architecture that characterized the early empire, towards a much greater emphasis on private building. The great villas of fourth-century Europe provide a graphic indication of how the display of individual power and status within a private context became of ever greater significance.

Paganism and Christianity beyond the imperial 'capitals'

Luxurious private residences and high-status material culture also form important indicators of the spread of Christianity, as Christian imagery was added to the repertoire of elite display, exemplified by silver plate (such as the hoard found at Water Newton near Peterborough) and architectural decoration (such as the famous image of Christ from the mosaic found in the villa at Hinton St Mary, now in the British Museum). Elsewhere in Europe there is also widespread evidence of Christian belief in the form of Christian epitaphs from cemeteries, although examples of fourth-century churches remain very rare outside the imperial capitals.

The importance of Christianity and the conflict between its adherents and those of the older polytheistic religions during the fourth century has perhaps been overstated (Chapter 7). This is not surprising, since many of the Christian sources for the period have been preserved precisely because they related to this conflict, or could be employed in revisionist treatments of the period and its various protagonists. Equally, however, the early Christian centuries produced a flowering of writing of various genres, which stands in sharp contrast to the poverty of the written sources for the third century. The leaders of the early Christian church were trained in classical rhetoric, which they turned to Christian ends. The result of this is that many of the sources for the period give the rise of Christianity a prominence which is unlikely to reflect the attitude of a majority of the empire's inhabitants.

In fourth-century Europe Christianity was but one religion among many, although one that became increasingly prominent as it was adopted by the imperial power, and became an ever more powerful component in elite systems of patronage and preferment. Outside Rome and the other imperial centres, Christian belief was yet to manifest itself in terms of monumental building. The dating of many excavated churches is extremely imprecise, and the fourth-century dates ascribed to a number of them result more from wishful thinking than convincing evidence.

North of the Alps, towns such as Cologne or Vienne that occasionally hosted the imperial court began to develop Christian cult *foci*, including churches, during the fourth century. Tours apparently had a cathedral by 371–2, in which Martin (the later St Martin immortalized by Gregory of Tours) was ordained as bishop, together with what Gregory terms a 'house church' established by his predecessor Litorius. Fourth-century origins are also claimed for the church at St Bertrand de Comminges, close to the foothills of the Pyrenees, while literary sources record that Flavius Jovinus erected a church at Reims in the second half of the fourth century. It was really only later, however, that a distinct 'Christian topography' began to emerge, with cult sites focused on the cemeteries outside the towns where saints and martyrs were buried, and on the relics of these individuals, which became keenly sought-after in the early Middle Ages. The Gallic towns that survived into the early medieval period were those, like Tours, which developed the additional function of Christian centres, and indeed the administrative map of present-day France (like that of Italy) still reflects to some extent the distribution of late Roman episcopal seats.

The poor evidence for monumental fourth-century Christian cult *foci* from Gaul is mirrored elsewhere in the western empire. In Spain, a cemetery seems to have developed in Tarraco around the tombs of three third-century martyrs, which may have been monumentalized prior to the construction of a church in the fifth century; other fourth-century Christian cemeteries in the region may have had such accompanying *martyria*. In Britain, fourth-century churches have been suggested for a number of sites, including Colchester, where a possible cemetery-church has been identified, and Icklingham in Suffolk, where excavations revealed a probable fourth-century church with what was apparently a baptismal font. A similar building was found at Silchester, although in this latter case a Christian function has not been conclusively demonstrated.

If churches were rare, pagan temples certainly remained widespread throughout much of the fourth century, particularly in Rome, where the Senate formed a bastion of pagan polytheism, and there are examples of restoration or even fresh construction right down to 391, when Theodosius I issued edicts against pagan cults and sacrifice. Indeed, public temples remained inviolable even during the reigns of Constantine and his successors, although public funds were no longer used for their repair after subsidies were withdrawn under Gratian. Paganism remained widespread, and saints' Lives, such as that of Martin of Tours, often describe the subject's attempts to turn the peasantry away from heathen practices. In the region around Trier, for example, archaeological evidence suggests that some village sanctuaries remained active well into the fifth century, despite the series of edicts issued by Theodosius. Indeed, it is these edicts which provide our most vivid characterizations of pagan practice in the late fourth century, criminalizing a man who might 'fear the effigies which he himself has formed, or ... bind a tree with fillets, or ... erect an altar of turf that he has dug up, or ... attempt to honour vain images with the offering of a gift' (*Theodosian Code* 16. 10. 12).

Until the proscriptive edicts of Theodosius, polytheistic religions and Christianity coexisted together, if not in perfect harmony then at least not in a state of perpetual conflict. Burial sites, for example, like the catacombs on the Via Latina in Rome, were in use contemporaneously by both pagans and Christians. The bipolar opposition that we perceive between Christianity and paganism is very much a product of hindsight. In the fourth century the Christian god was one among many, and his followers were generally more concerned with stamping out what they considered heretical practice among their own number than with combating the beliefs and practices of those outside their religion.

Conclusion: being Roman in fourth-century Europe

As was noted at the opening of this chapter, a defining characteristic of the Roman Empire, and one of the principal reasons for its success and longevity, was the rise of a homogeneous elite identity that transcended earlier cultural and geographical boundaries. Its perception of a shared cultural inheritance, its education, and its position within the Roman state apparatus formed the means through which local and provincial aristocracies interacted with one another and articulated their relative status. These shared values were given physical form through architecture, as public buildings within the towns, and private residences in both urban and rural contexts; through epigraphy, in which status could be clearly defined; and through common aspects of material culture, access to which was made possible by the communication system that bound the empire together. In many ways, the changes that occurred in fourth-century Europe that are most visible in both historical and archaeological sources are changes in this elite identity and the ways in which it was expressed.

In Europe, it is hardly surprising that the ways in which elites perceived their own position within the empire changed due to the increasing centralization of power around the figure of the emperor and his peripatetic court, and with the effective removal of the senior imperial position to Constantinople. Both of these factors weakened the relationship between local aristocracies (on whom the administrative structure of the early empire had been based) and the imperial government, and rendered more ambiguous the position of the one in relation to the other. This relationship had never been static, however, and it would be mistaken to ascribe change wholly to these factors. Equally, archaeological and historical sources indicate complex and regionally varied responses to these changes. They ranged from the Roman senators' adoption of the Eternal City's glorious past to shore up their own diminishing status, to the local defensive initiatives adopted in Gaul and elsewhere.

As the relationship with the emperor became more distant and its benefits more ambiguous, the introduction of 'non-Roman' elements into power relations in western Europe clearly had an effect. Power structures became more fluid and localized, and the divisions between 'Roman' and 'barbarian' became blurred (above; Chapter 10). When Julian was proclaimed Augustus by his troops at Paris, they did so by raising him on a shield in the Germanic fashion. Likewise, while the Arch of Constantine balanced the taboo subject of victory in civil war with the reuse of panels emphasizing Constantine's defeat of northern barbarians (a traditional subject of imperial monuments); by the time Pacatus delivered his panegyric on Theodosius' defeat of Magnus Maximus in 389, it was perfectly possible for him to praise the defeat of Maximus' legions by Theodosius' mercenary force of Huns, Goths, and Alans. Roman identity lay in the hands of the victor, and if 'non-Roman' forces were part of that victory they too were subsumed within this changing identity (Chapter 5), becoming a dynamic element of it rather than an 'Other' against which a Roman identity could be constructed or maintained.

It is clear, then, that the ways in which elite identity was constructed, and the ways in which elites viewed themselves within the context of a wider Roman system, were changing. The effect of this on the majority of the population of Europe, however, is more difficult to gauge. For much of the western empire it would be entirely erroneous to evoke Carlo Levi's timeless peasantry, that '[h]istory has swept over ... without effect'. Some regions saw dramatic alterations in settlement patterns during the course of the late Roman period, suggesting that all levels of society were affected by profound systemic changes. Some settlements, however, such as those excavated in northern Gaul at Mondeville and Grentheville, indicate a way of life and mode of occupation that pre-dated the Roman period and persisted beyond it. Responses to Roman hegemony varied throughout the period in Europe, and it is possible that by focusing primarily on the more archaeologically and historically visible aspects of an essentially elite culture we are overstating the impact of Roman rule on all levels of society (Chapter 8). Although there were changes over time, the homogeneous identity projected by elite building and material culture during the Roman period almost certainly conceals a myriad of regional variations that were present throughout the Roman era, and not solely in its later stages.

Nonetheless, changes in the ways that the upper strata of society chose to identify themselves and compete with one another characterize the final period of Roman rule in Europe, as more localized and fluid power structures replaced those of the empire. As Europe became more peripheral to the Roman empire, so the Roman Empire became more peripheral to Europe, with Roman identity becoming merely one increasingly flexible element in the political structures and conflicts that would eventually shape medieval Europe.

10

Peoples beyond the Roman imperial frontiers

Peter S. Wells

Introduction

Most discussions of the peoples of Europe who lived beyond the frontiers of the Roman Empire are based on textual evidence from Roman authors, such as Caesar and Tacitus for the earlier part of the period, and Ammianus Marcellinus and Cassiodorus in the later empire. The available evidence presents the views of Roman and, in some cases, Greek, writers—outsiders' perspectives on the peoples living in the lands on the other side of the frontiers. Roman, and Greek, writers regarded the peoples beyond the frontiers as barbarians, unschooled in the ways of Mediterranean civilization. To learn directly about those peoples, we need to turn to the archaeological evidence. But first I wish to highlight some important changes in modern investigators' understanding of the Roman accounts, to introduce the main discussion.

Roman representations of barbarians

In earlier traditions of research, the surviving texts of Caesar, Tacitus, and other Roman writers were understood as more-or-less accurate representations of reality. Some modern accounts adopt this traditional approach. Thus, Tacitus' *Germania* is still sometimes cited as an ethnography of the peoples east of the Rhine. Later Roman accounts of invasions across the Rhine and Danube, and of long-distance migrations of peoples from northern and eastern Europe, central to the standard narrative of the collapse of the empire, are still commonly accepted as representations of historical reality.

Over the past century some scholars have challenged such readings of the Roman texts, and since the 1980s a new consensus has emerged that the texts need to be examined critically with respect to the perspectives and the political motives of the authors. This is not the place to discuss the development of these new approaches in detail (see Pohl 2002), but a few major points will help to set the stage for consideration of the archaeological evidence.

Barbarian archetypes

Some scholars have argued that for Romans there existed a barbarian archetype, and that all individuals and groups categorized by Romans as barbarians were expressions of this archetype. In this sense, the barbarians were creations of the Roman mind, and to those barbarians were attributed characteristics that were the opposite of the qualities to which Romans aspired. Even more recent accounts use evidence like that of the Greek philosopher and rhetorician Themistius: 'There is in each of us a barbarian tribe, extremely over-bearing and intractable—I mean temper and those insatiable desires, which stand opposed to rationality as Scythians and Germans do to Romans.'

Relations between Rome and the native peoples of Europe were heavily influenced by Roman attitudes rooted in experience of invasions from north of the Alps, memories of which were preserved in Roman oral and, later, written traditions. The Gauls' attack on Rome in 387/6 BC was dramatically described by Livy, writing during Augustus' reign and drawing a lesson from the traditions of the city's earlier history to warn of dangers in his own time. The incursions by the Cimbri and the Teutoni between 113 and 101 BC (Chapters 1 and 2), and their crushing of Roman armies before their own demise in southern Gaul and northern Italy, played a major part in stoking Roman fears about invasion from the north. The catastrophic loss of three legions under P. Quinctilius Varus in the Teutoburg Forest in AD 9 provided another powerful warning about the potency of the little-understood peoples beyond the frontiers of the civilized world (Wells 2003).

Ferriss (2000) identifies four means through which Romans became familiar with the peoples whom they considered barbarians. Elite Romans who were able to read and write and could influence policy, could learn about the peoples beyond Rome's frontiers from texts by writers such as Posidonius, Caesar, and Tacitus. Romans would see representations of barbarians in visual media in Rome, including sculpture and coins. Actual human beings from beyond the frontiers might be seen in Rome as prisoners of war in triumphal processions, in spectacles in the arenas (as gladiators), as slaves, but also occasionally in more respected roles, for instance, serving as imperial bodyguards. Soldiers and administrators had first-hand experience with barbarians along the frontiers, both in fighting and in peaceful interactions. These various mechanisms would allow different Romans to develop very different ideas about barbarians. Unfortunately, only two of these categories are accessible to us: surviving texts and visual imagery; and both require informed critical analysis for their interpretation.

Warlike barbarians

Most of the texts that concern Roman–native interactions focus on military activity, incursions by barbarians across the frontier or Roman invasions of the unconquered territories. With the exception of Tacitus' writings (which themselves need to be treated carefully), we have little information about everyday life, ritual, or other customs among the peoples across the frontier. The limited subject-matter of our written sources results in images of the empire's neighbours as fierce, warlike groups, very unlike the professed ideal of the peaceful, cultivated Roman. Of course, Romans also constructed themselves as military conquerors, and while in this period the idea of an imperial mission and a sense of responsibility arose, the old Republican ideology of military glory was still important; Romans, however, are also *disciplined* (Chapter 5).

Political purposes of the representations

We need to understand the texts as political instruments that strove to portray Roman power and Roman relations with other peoples in the most favourable light. Accounts of long-distance migrations by peoples from the north and east, and of violent incursions into the Roman provinces, were probably often created to explain chaotic circumstances along the frontiers that were in reality mainly the result of conflicts within the Roman political structure (Burns 2003). It has been argued that writers exaggerated the threat of barbarian invasions across the Rhine and Danube during the third and fourth centuries in support of the policies of the military and civil bureaucracies that depended for their existence upon a strong military presence on the frontiers. Some writers may have consciously overemphasized the external threat of invasion in order to deflect concern away from growing problems within the empire.

Pohl (2002) suggests that much of the description of barbarian invasions was literary construct, not representation of reality. There certainly were people moving, and real violence, but, he argues, the invasions and wars were not the essential transformative processes during the late Roman period. Nevertheless, many of the late Roman writers may have believed that the cross-frontier incursions were determining factors in the breakdown of Roman power, because they did not understand the economic and social changes that were happening around them.

In an important archaeological 'test' of historical traditions based on textual sources, a group of scholars has demonstrated that the written accounts of the fall of the *limes* (frontier) in south-west Germany in the mid-third century are not supported by the material evidence. No clear signs of destruction, such as burned layers on settlements or large numbers of graves of war-dead, can be identified that can be associated with this event. Instead, the archaeology indicates a long process of peoples from beyond the frontier moving, apparently unimpeded by any substantial military resistance, across the border into Roman territory, until eventually the cultural character of what had been the imperial lands changed.

Archaeology of the peoples beyond the frontiers

The very substantial and rapidly growing body of archaeological data pertaining to the peoples with whom the Roman world interacted across its European frontiers provides a very different picture of those peoples from that offered by the Roman texts, and from what we see in Roman sculpture, on coins, and in other visual representations, as, for example, on Trajan's Column. Using the archaeological evidence, we can examine the lives and culture of these peoples mediated only by our modes of interpretation. The material evidence comes to us directly from the peoples who made and used the pottery, tools, weapons, and ornaments, and who left them behind as debris on their settlements, or deposited them purposefully in graves or other contexts.

Although the organization of academic disciplines often separates the study of the prehistoric Iron Age from that of the Roman and early medieval periods, the archaeological evidence shows continuity in all respects from prehistoric into historical times. The Roman presence had a great impact on the indigenous peoples on both sides of the frontier, but, as we indicated in Chapter 1, Rome had had powerful effects already during the prehistoric Iron Age. Below I review the most important aspects of the archaeological evidence pertaining to the peoples beyond the Roman frontiers, using specific sites as examples to illustrate the major themes.

Everyday life, economy, and interaction: settlements

In the early Roman period east of the Rhine, settlements were small: individual farmsteads or groupings that we might call hamlets or very small villages. A typical settlement was at Meppen, on the Ems river on the North European Plain. The settlement consisted of three farms, each centred on a large post-built structure about 18 m long by 7 m wide, that included a dwelling for the human occupants and a barn for livestock, above all cattle, but also pigs, sheep, and goats. Ancillary buildings were used for grain storage and as toolsheds. Emmer and other wheats were cultivated, along with barley, millet, oats, and rye; lentils, peas, and beans were also grown. Hundreds of such settlements, which were probably occupied by twenty to forty persons, have been identified east of the Rhine during the early Roman period.

At Flögeln in Lower Saxony archaeologists were able to trace the development of such a settlement over the course of 500 years, from around the time of Christ to the end of the fifth century AD. In the first phase the settlement was comprised of several farmsteads, with dwellings and outbuildings, including workshops. Just beyond the houses, banks constructed of stone and earth defined a system of fields covering 100 ha. Around the end of the first century a village was established, with several distinct settlement areas, each bounded by its own fence and the whole settlement enclosed by a common fence. Archaeologists estimate that fifteen to twenty house–barn buildings stood at any one time, and that the village had a population of some 200–300 people during the second and third centuries. Most buildings were designed to accommodate about sixteen cattle, thus suggesting a village cattle population of between 240 and 320.

In the course of the fourth century the settlement size increased again, and buildings became larger, with a new average of thirty-two cattle stalls per structure. Houses now had two or three separate dwelling areas, each with its own entrance, suggesting that more than one family lived in each building. The excavators note an increase in the number of workshops during the fourth century and a decrease in the number of structures interpreted as granaries. Among the crafts represented by manufacturing debris are iron-smithing, weaving, stone-cutting, and tanning of leather. Analysis of the fields associated with the later settlement indicates intensive fertilizing, suggesting increasingly efficient adaptation to the local soils.

A recently excavated settlement at Kahl on the Main river provides a good example of a farming community from the beginning of the fifth century. Analysis of the associated cemetery suggests an average community size of around 100 people. The settlement was situated on a gentle slope overlooking the Main, an environment that offered lush meadows for livestock. In the excavated portion of the settlement archaeologists uncovered the foundations of thirteen buildings of diverse function and construction, including dwellings, pit-houses (probably workshops), and granaries. Animal bones indicate that cattle, pigs, goats, and sheep were the principal sources of protein, while chickens and wildfowl are also represented. Spindle whorls show that textiles were processed, and iron and bronze workshop debris attests to manufacturing in those metals.

The settlement shows no indication of significant status differences, specialized manufacturing, or importation of exotic materials indicating unusual wealth. In the cemetery, however, small quantities of gold and silver ornaments distinguish some graves, as do imported Roman fine pottery and glass vessels. Weapons, including swords, axes, lances, and spurs, occur in several burials. While the settlement evidence indicates a small agricultural community with modest material culture, a few of the burials reflect material expression of the 'warriors' that loom so large in the Roman texts. The weapon-graves at Kahl are not unusually richly equipped, but they provide an important link between everyday life at a typical settlement and the military aspect that dominated Roman thinking about these peoples. Most importantly, they show that the warriors who loom so large in Roman accounts of the period were members of typical agricultural communities. Their presence at Kahl suggests that these individuals are likely to have worked as farmers and perhaps as craft-workers when they were not engaged in military conflict. Their lives were thus much more complex than the Roman writers imagined (of course, those writers were mainly interested in their military activities, not their peaceful ones).

While Meppen, Flögeln, and Kahl are examples of farming communities, other sites are more informative about the integration of craft-production into economic activities carried out on settlements. A small settlement occupied about a century after the conquest of Gaul at Daseburg (around AD 20–60), north of Kassel in northern Germany, had all of the features of a typical farming village. But the community that lived there not only processed iron and bronze but also lead and silver, showing an unexpected degree of metalworking specialization at this small settlement. The metal-smiths processed bronze and silver to make *fibulae* and other items of jewellery. The working of silver at Daseburg suggests increasing involvement of even small communities in commercial networks along which special products circulated for consumption by elite groups. At the later site of Klein Köris in Brandenburg, one workshop contained abundant remains from processing iron, copper and bronze, silver, gold, amber, and glass. Over 2,040 objects were recovered, including scraps of metal, partly made ornaments, and tools for fine metal-smithing.

Commercial interaction with the Roman world on the other side of the frontier is evident at many sites. Settlements at Erin and Westick, just across the Lower Rhine from Roman military and civil communities, yield evidence for intensive commercial relations across the river. Roman fine pottery, glassware, *fibulae*, bronze vessels, and coins attest to regular interaction from the first to fifth centuries, and to consumption of substantial quantities of Roman goods.

At Feddersen Wierde in northern Germany, near the mouth of the Weser river, excavations reveal evidence for economic and social changes that took place in the context of interactions with the Roman world. When the settlement was established around the middle of the first century BC, it consisted of five large, post-built, house-barn structures along with ancillary buildings, similar to the site at Meppen. But the settlement remained occupied for five centuries, and the community grew in size and in productive capacity. Most notable is an increase in the number of livestock stalls, from ninety-eight in the initial settlement to a peak of 443 in a later phase. At the same time, the number of Roman imports on the settlement increased. A wide range of goods manufactured in the Roman provinces has been recovered at Feddersen Wierde, including coins, *fibulae*, fine pottery, glass vessels, glass beads, and grindstones from the basalt quarries at Mayen in the Rhineland. Imported luxury items include a fan with a carved ivory handle.

The settlement also yields evidence for social change. The number of livestock housed in different buildings diverged, with the largest stall capable of housing thirty cattle, the smallest only twelve. From in the second century AD, one building larger than others was also distinguished by a special workshop associated with it. A nearby horse burial suggests a ritual linked to a special status of the family occupying this house. In the span of time during which Feddersen Wierde was occupied, we can thus identify several interrelated processes—growth in the size and productive capacity of the community, an increase in interaction with the Roman provinces, and an increase in social stratification.

The Roman army stationed along the Rhine and Danube frontiers required vast quantities of meat, as well as leather for tents, belts and straps, sandals, and padding on armour. The evidence for increased stall capacity, growing Roman imports, and emerging status differentiation at Feddersen Wierde can be understood in the context of economic adaptations that such communities made to take advantage of the commercial opportunities offered by Rome's needs for products that could be generated by the native communities. The responses to these opportunities led to changes in local social structures.

At some sites further removed from the frontier, such as Gudme in Denmark and Jakuszowice in Poland, interaction with the Roman world played a role in the emergence of centres of political power. Excavations at Gudme on the island of Fyn, 450 km from the Roman frontier, reveal a complex of settlements, cemeteries, and, at nearby Lundeborg, harbour facilities that show significant interactions with the Roman world, from the first century BC into the fifth century AD (Nielsen, Randsborg, and Thrane 1994). In the Møllegårdsmarken cemetery, over 100 Roman vessels of bronze, glass, and pottery have been recovered. At the main settlement complex at Gudme, Roman silver tableware, a Roman helmet, over 500 Roman silver coins, and remains of a near life-size bronze statue have been found. Recent excavations at the port of Lundeborg show where Roman imports and other goods were unloaded from ships for transport inland, and reveal extensive workshops for the processing of bronze, iron, gold, and silver. As at Feddersen Wierde, at Gudme there is evidence for a close connection between increased productivity, interaction with the Roman world, and local social changes. During the third or fourth century, a 47 m by 10 m timber-frame hall was erected on the site, the largest structure known in northern Europe from the Roman Iron Age. As an increasingly powerful political centre emerged at Gudme, the ruling elites used the material manifestations of their connections with the Roman world as a means for displaying their growing status and authority.

In southern Poland, 300 km from the Rhine frontier, archaeologists have excavated a settlement at Jakuszowice occupied between the first century BC and the fifth century AD. Substantial manufacturing is evident on the site, including ironworking, bronze-casting, the working of lead, tin, silver, and gold, and carving of amber. Extensive Roman imports include fine pottery; *fibulae* and other ornaments, some decorated with silver and gold; glass beads, finger-rings, and game pieces; bronze mirrors; and over seventy-five coins, dating from the late first to the early third centuries. Among the *fibulae* is one of the 'onion-head' type, suggesting relations on a personal level between elites at Jakuszowice and officials of the Roman Empire (within the empire, this type of *fibula* was commonly worn as a sign of office). Richly outfitted burials near the settlement represent members of the local elite who, apparently, oversaw the production of iron (nearby are the Holy Cross Mountains, a source of high-grade iron ore), and perhaps of amber as well, for shipment west or south to the Roman provinces, and who consumed a large portion of the wealth that derived from that commerce.

At Haarhausen in Thuringia, 200 km east of the frontier, archaeologists have investigated a series of pottery kilns dating to the third century AD that are provincial Roman in character, and were used to make Roman-style pottery. This site demonstrates importation not only of objects from the Roman provinces, but also of Roman technical knowledge. It is unclear whether a provincial Roman moved here, or whether a local potter learned the techniques in the Roman provinces. The special significance of Haarhausen is that it demonstrates the exchange of technical information directly between individuals. It indicates that intercultural exchanges very different from those recorded in the texts were taking place between peoples in different parts of temperate Europe. Recent analyses of bronze, silver, and gold objects from burials in regions east of the Rhine show that Roman metallurgical techniques were also being adopted by metal-smiths working beyond the frontier, or, possibly, craftsmen from Roman provinces who had moved across the frontier were making objects in the local styles.

In the late Roman period, from the first half of the fourth century on, a number of centres of political power and economic activity developed close to the frontier, such as at the Runder Berg in southwest Germany and at the Oberleiserberg in Lower Austria. The Runder Berg is one of about fifty known fortified hilltop settlements that were established in the former *Agri Decumates* (the 'Ten Cantons', an area including the Neckar basin, annexed under Domitian to shorten communications between the Rhine and Danube frontiers) in southwest Germany after the withdrawal of the Roman frontier to the upper Rhine. Materials recovered on the site suggest occupation by a group of elite individuals rather than by a farming community. Workshop debris attests to the manufacture of iron weapons and of bronze and gold ornaments. Late Roman pottery and glassware are represented in substantial quantities, indicating that the inhabitants of this site were bringing in Roman luxuries from across the Rhine in Gaul, 150 km to the west.

The principal occupation of the hilltop settlement on the Ober-leiserberg, 20 km north of the Danube river in Lower Austria, began in the second half of the fourth century AD, with the construction of a two-storey stone building modelled on Roman villa architecture. Around the middle of the fifth century, the complex was transformed into a more elaborate form, borrowing from late Roman palace design in the construction of a central building 35 m in length and 17 m wide. The complex included a monumental arch and a columned hall. Most of the excavated material, including pottery, *fibulae* and other personal ornaments, toilet implements, and tools, are of local character. But bricks and tiles, window glass, some pottery, and glass vessels are of Roman origin. This site has been interpreted as the political centre of a potentate who had adopted much of Roman material culture and lifestyle, but whose identity and authority were rooted in local tradition. The Oberleiserberg complex may have been the political base of a 'client king'—ruler of a people allied with Rome, who gained special benefits in exchange for his services in helping to protect this portion of the frontier from attack.

As the few examples cited here show, settlement evidence indicates the existence of many communities with complex economies —diverse subsistence bases along with often specialized manufacturing and commerce. All were integrated into a Europe-wide network through which goods and information flowed. At predominantly agricultural communities such as Meppen and Kahl, materials brought in from outside are relatively few, but other communities were actively involved in the acquisition of goods, from sources including the Roman provinces. At Feddersen Wierde the connection between production of cattle for export and acquisition of Roman products appears relatively clear. Some communities near the frontier, such as Erin and Westick, show intensive consumption of Roman goods. At some more distant locations, rarer Roman materials were displayed and consumed, as at the emergent centres at Gudme and Jakuszowice. The kilns at Haarhausen and the Roman-style palace architecture at the Oberleiserberg show that not only imported objects, but also technologies and architectural styles—and perhaps ideas about the legitimation of power through architectural representation—were often eagerly adopted by peoples beyond the frontier.

Patterns of change in identity and status: burials

Burials provide us with a different kind of information from that provided by settlements. Whereas on settlements, archaeologists study mostly debris left behind from habitation and manufacturing activity—sherds of pottery, fragmentary animal bones, lost *fibulae*, scrap from bronze-casting, and the like—burials are intentionally arranged packages of information. If found undisturbed, a burial can provide insight into the intentions of those members of the deceased individual's community who made the burial structure, prepared the body for cremation or inhumation, selected objects to place in the burial, and arranged them in the grave. Burials are only one part of funerary rituals, but they are the aspect best preserved for us to study. Graves are not passive tableaux in which an individual's prized possessions were buried with him or her. Funerary ceremonies are processes in the creation and expression of social identities and statuses. Participants use these rituals as means to negotiate and reaffirm the statuses and identities of living members of the community, and the rituals are therefore critically important to the future functioning of the community.

Graves in the lands beyond the Roman frontier have been studied much more extensively than settlements. Many thousands have been excavated, published, and discussed in scholarly literature. From the half-millennium of the Roman period we have an immense variety of practice, status, and wealth reflected in the burials. I highlight here some of the principal themes in the burial evidence, especially as they pertain to relations with the Roman world. The vast majority of burials were outfitted modestly, often with no grave-goods or with a few objects of everyday character, such as local pottery and personal ornaments. Information about interactions with the Roman world comes mainly from the most richly outfitted burials, and they form the focus of this review.

In men's graves, weapons were potent symbols of the individual's identity as a warrior. Silver and gold ornament on weapons indicates persons of high status in the military hierarchy, among the native peoples as well as in the Roman army. Roman weapons, or weapons with Roman components, suggest affiliation with the Roman military, perhaps through service in auxiliary units along the frontiers. Inclusion of horse-riding gear, such as spurs and rein dividers, suggests service in cavalry units, Roman or native. Some of the wealthiest graves include personal ornaments of gold and silver, indicating high status in the local society. Sets of feasting vessels of Roman origin, such as bronze, silver, and pottery jugs, bowls, dishes, and plates, point to a close connection between the buried individual and elite Romans, perhaps high-ranking officers in the Roman military. Individual vessels could, of course, have arrived as trade objects, but the presence of complete sets of tableware suggests that familiarity with Roman banqueting practices also passed from elite Romans to the elites represented in the graves. All of these materials can provide information about the social status and the identity of the individual buried. No two burials are alike, and analysis of the patterns of similarity and difference can tell much about the composition of the societies represented by the cemeteries.

Around the middle of the final century BC a new practice of outfitting many men's graves with weapons spread throughout the regions east of the Rhine. The majority of burials were flat graves, with cremated remains and small amounts of metal ornaments, such as bracelets and *fibulae*, placed in ceramic urns. The weapons used in the new practice included iron swords, iron-tipped lances and spears, and wooden shields with metal fittings. In some cases the weapon graves occur in sizeable numbers in large cemeteries, as at Grossromstedt in Thuringia. Since funerary practices communicate a society's values and concerns, this change suggests a new significance for the symbolism of weaponry among the peoples of these regions, and has been linked to the rise of a distinctive martial ideology. As communities east of the Rhine received news of Roman campaigns against the peoples of Gaul, and of Caesar's incursions across the Rhine in 55 and 53 BC, it is easy to understand why weapons should have taken on a new importance as military symbols.

But the new burial practice reflects more than just a response to the threat of invasion. In his account of his campaigns in Gaul, Caesar (*Gallic War* 7. 65) informs us that he hired German mercenary soldiers to serve as cavalry, because of their skill on horseback. Many of the weapon graves east of the Rhine include spurs among the grave-goods, often together with bronze vessels of Roman manufacture. A number of such burials have been identified at Harsefeld, near Hamburg. Some of the buried individuals may have been men who had served in the cavalry with Roman forces in Gaul, their special status represented in their graves by the spurs, and their connection with Rome by the bronze vessels. This sizeable group of men's graves east of the Rhine with weapons, spurs, and Roman bronze vessels may represent individuals who created a special identity for themselves, based on their status as warriors and their affiliation with the Roman world (Wells 2001: 120–1).

Grave 150 in the cemetery at Putensen near Hamburg, dating to the first third of the first century AD, shows the character of high-status burials in this context, and may be that of a chieftain who served as leader of a contingent of warriors in the Roman auxiliary forces. A bronze cauldron contained cremated remains of a man about 30 years old. He was buried with a rich assemblage of weapons, horse-riding gear, bronze vessels, and personal ornaments. Three pairs of spurs were present, together with bronze rein ornaments. Besides the urn there were two Roman bronze casseroles and remains of two local drinking-horns. Personal ornaments included a pin and six *fibulae* of silver, and one bronze and one iron *fibula*. The three pairs of spurs, five vessels, and silver ornaments distinguish this grave from the majority of weapon graves.

Dating to a century later than Putensen 150, and reflecting an increase in wealth displayed on the weapons of elite warriors, is a richly outfitted grave at Hagenow in Mecklenburg-Vorpommern, excavated in 1995. In it was a bronze cauldron with iron rim that held cremated remains of a man about 55 years old. Also in the cauldron was a complete set of weapons of a warrior of this period—sword (bent to fit into the vessel), lance- and spear-heads, parts of a shield, and chain mail, as well as four pairs of spurs made of damascened silver. The sword and shield were decorated with silver, and numerous other silver and gold ornaments were present. Other objects included remains of two drinking-horns and a small bar of gold, as well as unique belt fittings. A bronze belt buckle was coated with finely crafted gilded silver, and a gilded silver plaque was ornamented with figures of humans and horses. The quantity of silver and gold used in the decoration of this man's military equipment strongly distinguished him from the majority of buried males, and represents a considerable increase in displayed wealth over that exemplified by the earlier grave at Putensen.

Further east, at Łęg Piekarski in southern Poland, four graves dating from AD 70–150 are similar to those at Putensen and Hagenow with respect to weapons and precious-metal ornaments, but with a greater emphasis on ornate vessels associated with feasting. For example, with a man's skeleton in Grave 2 were eight bronze vessels, a silver bucket, two silver cups, remains of two drinking-horns, and a set of game counters made of stone.

Two recently excavated burials from the late second and late third centuries, respectively, contained combinations of objects that suggest special relationships with the Roman Empire as well as high status within local societies. These individuals may have been 'client kings' (above). A grave at Mušov in southern Moravia contained a rich assemblage of objects, even though it had been looted in antiquity (Peška and Tejral 2002). The burial, dated to around AD 175, included skeletal remains of two men of similar stature, both about 50 years old. Weapons, horse-riding gear, precious metal ornaments, and feasting equipment predominate among the goods. The weapons include a sword, a shield with gold trim, body armour, seven lance-points, and twelve arrowheads, all of local character. A strap-end of a Roman military belt, along with a variety of other buckles and attachments, links the individuals with the Roman army. Seventeen spurs were recovered in the grave, some crafted in silver and gold. Feasting equipment included fifteen glass vessels, some of exceptionally fine quality, all from Roman workshops. Two silver spoons of Roman origin are the first to be found beyond the frontier in this period. Serving- and drinking-vessels of provincial Roman origin include at least six of silver, eight of bronze, and nine ceramic ones. Silver attachments for two drinking-horns were found. A bronze folding table, a bronze lamp, and gilded bronze attachments for furniture, all of Roman origin, served as accessories to the feasting equipment. Of local origin are a Late Iron Age-style firedog, a tripod, and a hook for handling meat. Sixty items of personal ornamentation including bronze, silver, and gold, were also found. This grave is unusually wealthy in several categories of materials, and it integrates high-status goods of Roman and indigenous origin. Most of the feasting equipment is of Roman origin, but the hearth gear is local. Most of the weapons are local, but the military belt is a sign of service to Rome.

A similarly outfitted burial, about a century later than Mušov, was discovered in 1990 at Gommern in Sachsen-Anhalt. In a stone-covered chamber a man 35–40 years old was buried with a Roman gold coin in his mouth, a gold ring around his neck, two gold *fibulae*, and a gold finger-ring. Near his waist were several silver belt buckles as well as shears and a knife, also of silver. Two gold *fibulae* and one silver *fibula* were near the belt. Near his feet was a pair of silver spurs and silver buckles and strap-ends. Three silver arrowheads and two silver rings were at his left side. At the head end of the grave was a shield with a silver boss decorated with glass and with gold leaf. The boss had been made from a Roman silver vessel, cut and hammered to shape it for this new purpose. At the foot of the grave was a rolled-up leather belt with sheet gold and openwork ornament, and with silver buckles and strap-ends. Among the numerous vessels were a tripod, a cauldron, two wooden pails with bronze attachments and handles, a wooden barrel with bronze attachments and rings, a wooden vessel with silver attachments, two bronze pails, a bronze basin, a silver pail, a silver dipper and strainer set, three glass vessels, and a ceramic vessel. Five Roman silver coins were present, as well as the gold coin. Remains of a game board and gaming pieces were also recovered. The quantities of silver and gold make this burial uniquely rich for its time, around AD 300, and the tripod represents a close association with elite Roman lifestyle.

The patterns—gold and silver ornaments including *fibulae*, weapons and riding gear in men's burials, sets of finely crafted feasting vessels largely from provincial Roman workshops—evident in the well-outfitted graves of the first, second, and third centuries continue during the fourth and fifth centuries, with some notable variations. One change is increased homogeneity of burial assemblages among the well-outfitted graves throughout the lands beyond the Roman frontiers. This greater uniformity indicates that the individuals buried were in increasingly close contact with others across the European continent, and were sharing a common set of signs of status and identity. Another significant change is a decrease in the number of Roman vessels associated with feasting, which had been such import-ant components of rich burials such as those at Mušov and Gommern. Perhaps with the end to the period of relative peace and prosperity enjoyed in the Roman frontier regions during the first and second centuries AD, relationships between leaders beyond the frontier and Roman officials changed. Or perhaps the change was in the ways that elites chose to represent their identities and status, with the emulation of elite Roman lifestyle falling from favour. In any case, these changes in funerary practice and in the ritual that accompanied the arranging of the burials signal a profound shift in the way that elites represented themselves.

At Beroun-Závodí, west of Prague, a grave dating to the final quarter of the fourth century and situated in a large burial chamber may represent a military leader in this region north of the Danube. Buried with this individual were an unusual bronze sword with hilt carved of bone, three spear- or lance-points, a shield, a pair of spurs, several ceramic vessels, and toilet items, including a bone comb. The strong similarity between this assemblage and that of weapon burials further west, closer to the Rhine frontier, has been noted. The sword, with its unique bone handle, suggests special status. Associated with this group of weapon graves in Bohemia are well-outfitted women's burials. For example, the body buried in grave 13 at Pohorelice-Nová Ves, dating around AD 400, was placed in a substantial wooden chamber built around four corner posts, and was outfitted with a considerable quantity of personal ornaments and pottery.

Further changes are apparent in the contents of wealthier burials north of the middle Danube, beginning around the start of the fifth century. Some of the horse-associated ornaments, as well as silver buckles and occasional copper cauldrons, indicate connections with traditions further east. Linking warrior burials of this period all the way from the middle Rhine eastward to Ukraine and beyond are gold neck-rings, with prominent examples in the burial assemblages at Briza in Bohemia and Untersiebenbrunn in Lower Austria. Cloisonné gold-garnet (consisting of small pieces of garnet cut to inlay spaces bounded by gold borders), a technique that originated in gold-working traditions around the Black Sea, appears on buckles and other ornaments at this time, first in south-east Europe and later further west, as at Oros on the Tisza river in Hungary and at Laa an der Thaya in Lower Austria. Sword types in some graves also point to links with lands to the east, such as one in a burial at Szirmabesenyö.

In the second half of the fifth century these trends—growing similarity of grave-goods over great distances across Europe, decrease in objects of 'Roman' origin in burials, and growing popularity of gold-and-garnet ornament and other stylistic features introduced from south-eastern regions of the continent—appear in a series of very richly outfitted graves that represent social, political, and military configurations among the elites at the time of disintegration of the last vestiges of Roman authority. For example, the wealthy graves at

Apahida in Romania, Blučina in Moravia, and Tournai in Belgium share lavishly decorated weapons, goldwork with cloisonné ornament, horse-riding equipment, gold bracelets, gold or silver *fibulae*, and, in two cases, signet rings.

The grave of Childeric at Tournai is of unique significance (see the next volume in this series: R. McKitterick (ed.), *The Early Middle Ages* (Oxford, 2000), 14). Here we can identify the individual buried in the grave, and we know something about who he was and when he died. According to textual sources, Childeric, son of Merowech and father of Clovis, was commander of a contingent of Frankish troops serving to help defend the late Roman Empire in Gaul. He died in 481 or 482. His grave, discovered in 1653, included a rich assemblage of objects that convey his complex role as warrior leader, member of the Frankish confederation, and commander in the service of Rome. His lavish burial with a full set of weapons, abundant gold ornaments, and skeletal remains of a horse, places the funerary ritual solidly in the burial tradition of non-Roman Europe. The gold bracelet links Childeric with warrior leaders beyond the frontier. The gold-and-garnet cloisonné ornament, richly represented on the sword, scabbard, buckles, horse-harness gear, bees attached to a cloak, and other ornaments, connects this burial with the new craft traditions that developed in eastern Europe and spread westward during the fifth century.

The gold onion-head *fibula* in Childeric's grave was a special item probably presented to him to honour his service in the Roman cause, perhaps by the Roman emperor. The signet ring with Latin inscription was of Roman tradition, though the portrait of Childeric shows him with the long hair and spear characteristic of Germanic royal symbolism. The hundred and more Roman gold coins in the grave may be part of payment for his service to Rome. Recent excavations have uncovered three pits within 20 m of Childeric's grave, containing the skeletons of twenty-one horses, almost certainly animals sacrificed as part of the funerary ritual in very un-Roman fashion (Brulet 1995).

Childeric's grave can be understood as a culmination of many of the trends outlined above. During the fourth century, all along the frontier, burials on the two sides of the frontier became increasingly similar, making the distinction between 'Roman' and 'barbarian' ever more obscure (Chapter 9). Tournai is situated in Gaul, yet the grave was primarily non-Roman with respect to burial practice and to the goods placed in it. The set of weapons, gold ornaments, horse-riding paraphernalia, and Roman objects all represent themes traceable from the early weapon graves of the first century BC through to the fifth century AD. No Roman vessels are recorded from the Childeric grave. The mix of local elements, eastern traditions, and Roman ways of symbolizing status in this burial exemplify the complex character of the societies emerging in temperate Europe in the late fifth century.

Deposits of fine metalwork: offerings and treasure hoards

Considerable quantities of material are recovered from deposits commonly referred to as votive offerings, lost plunder, and treasure hoards. Deposits thought to represent offerings to deities belong to a long tradition stretching from the Stone Age to the present day. At a spring at Bad Pyrmont in Lower Saxony, objects have been recovered that were deposited between the first and fifth centuries AD, with particular activity during the fourth and fifth centuries. Among the objects are over 240 *fibulae*, of both Roman and local origin, and an ornate bronze casserole decorated with green and blue enamel, made in Roman Gaul or Britain. Spring offerings such as this one are well documented in the prehistoric Iron Age, as well as in later times.

While Bad Pyrmont was the site of small offerings made over a long period of time, the weapon deposits of northern Europe represent offerings on a much larger scale, comparable to the sites of Gournay and La Tène discussed in Chapter 1. About thirty such sites have been identified in northern Germany, Denmark, and southern Sweden, where large quantities of weapons, along with ornaments, clothing, and other goods, were deposited in ponds and bogs during the Roman period, especially between the late second and the early fifth centuries (see also Chapter 7). These assemblages are generally interpreted as offerings to deities, made by the victors, of defeated armies' weapons as thanks for success in battle, and perhaps to win favour in future encounters. In recent excavations at Illerup in Denmark, archaeologists have recovered, from the 40 per cent of the site excavated, about 100 swords, 1,000 spears and lances, and 300 shields, as well as other materials, most dating to around AD 200. Many of the swords from Illerup and other sites are Roman in manufacture, sometimes with Latin inscriptions on the upper part of the blades.

Other objects of Roman origin recovered in these deposits include coins, jewellery, and other kinds of ornaments.

The means by which Roman swords reached these locations has been much debated. Were they the arms of returning auxiliaries, bringing home with them the equipment they acquired and used in their service on the Roman frontier? Or were they captured in battle against Roman armies, or plundered from military bases during cross-border raids? They may have been trade goods, although trade in weapons was forbidden by the Roman authorities.

Two deposits of metal objects, both dated to around AD 280–300, discovered in what had once been branches of the upper River Rhine, have been interpreted as plunder seized in Gaul by raiders from beyond the Roman frontier and lost as they recrossed the Rhine, travelling eastward toward home. At Hagenbach a cache of 346 objects includes 129 pieces of silver sheet of a kind commonly used as votive offerings, forty-one bronze vessels, twenty-five silver jewellery pieces, eight fragmentary silver vessels, 109 iron tools, sixteen iron weapons, and metal fittings from wagons. A similar deposit at Neupotz contained 1,008 objects, including iron weapons, tools and kitchen implements, bronze vessels, silver votive sheets, and coins. Since the deposition of weapons, tools, metal vessels, and precious metal objects in bodies of water was often done for ritual purposes, it is quite possible that the Hagenbach and Neupotz assemblages were parts of ceremonial activities rather than accidental losses.

Some deposits are comprised entirely or predominantly of precious metals. Caches of gold and silver coins are well represented throughout the lands beyond the frontier from the third to the fifth centuries. A different kind of precious-metal deposit is represented by one found at Pietroassa, west of Buzau in Romania. Twelve gold objects are recorded, weighing in total more than 18 kg., although investigators believe that the original hoard may have been twice that size. Preserved pieces include four ornate *fibulae* in the shape of birds with inlaid stones, a bowl decorated with relief figures, a plate, a jug, two bowls of polygonal shape, and three neck-rings. The style of the objects indicates a date in the early fifth century, a time during which many precious-metal hoards were buried in central and eastern Europe.

The *fibulae* deposited at Bad Pyrmont, the hundreds of weapons dropped into the lake at Illerup, and the hoards of metal objects from the old riverbed at Hagenbach and Neupotz were not hidden for future recovery. But with treasure hoards, whether coins or tableware and jewellery, the interpretive problems are more complex. Such deposits may represent temporary storage of wealth in times of danger, or they may be votive offerings. In support of the first, investigators note unusually large numbers of such hoards from times that textual evidence indicates were plagued by warfare, such as the mid-third and early fifth centuries. But the fact that so many hoards were never recovered might support the second interpretation. We must be mindful that these two possibilities are functional categories that we impose upon such deposits, and perhaps not how people at the time thought about them. We can say with assurance that the deposits of precious metals, such as those in the examples cited here, demonstrate that substantial quantities of wealth were accumulated by individuals or groups during these centuries, and that the communities involved were wealthy enough to be able to dispose of much of that wealth, whether intentionally as offerings to deities or unintentionally by being unable to reclaim the goods.

Dynamics of change from the third to the fifth century

After the Varian disaster in AD 9 and the subsequent campaigns by Germanicus, the textual sources suggest relatively little cross-frontier warfare before the Marcomannic Wars of 166–80, except for the conquest of the the *Agri Decumates* between the upper Rhine and the upper Danube late in the first century, and the Dacian Wars under Trajan at the beginning of the second. These two centuries were times of prosperity in the Rhineland and along the Danube, and commercial relations across the rivers flourished.

Archaeology of migrations

Roman texts mention many migrations of peoples beyond, and into, the Roman frontier regions from the latter half of the second century AD onwards (Wolfram 1997). Modern popular understanding of the late Roman period and the 'Migration Period' is dominated by the idea of massive population movements sweeping across Europe, an image conveyed by historical maps with arrows illustrating these migrations as the ancient authors represented them. But the archaeological evidence for such movements is sparse. We do not find settlement areas that show evidence of sudden abandonment, nor places where large numbers of people established new villages, for example.

As noted above, some scholars argue that much of the portrayal of large armies of barbarians moving through Europe and threatening the Roman frontiers was politically motivated exaggeration, in part for the purpose of maintaining the system of frontier armies and all of the logistical and political support that they required; for example, the texts tend to exaggerate the size of barbarian armies (Wolfram 1997). But as Pohl (2002) reminds us, no matter how critically we approach the texts and no matter how much can be shown to be politically motivated, we are still faced with the fact that some peoples were moving.

Archaeologically speaking, very rarely is there evidence for a landscape suddenly abandoned as if by large-scale emigration. Similarly for immigration, rarely does the evidence suggest rapid arrival of thousands of people from elsewhere. The archaeology of most of the central parts of the European continent is well known. The sudden abandonment or the abrupt settlement of landscapes would be identifiable archaeologically in these regions. Much more often we find evidence, especially in cemeteries, for the appearance of new objects and sometimes new burial traditions that point to another region where these elements are identifiable earlier. Scholars have associated major changes in parts of Poland during the second half of the second and the third centuries with movements of the peoples known as Goths. Material culture associated with the Przeworsk groups (peoples with distinctive types of pottery and metal ornaments who lived in a region centred on what is now southern Poland) appears in eastern Slovakia, on the upper Tisza, and in the Carpathian regions, suggesting incoming peoples.

In the well-documented cemeteries along the upper Danube in Bavaria, however, evidence of new objects and new practices appears gradually over time (below). The archaeology suggests that such gradual movements of peoples settling into new regions were much more common than large migrations. In many cases, there is no recognizable archaeological evidence for a particular migration alluded to in textual sources. In other cases, such as the changes associated with the appearance of the Friedenhain-Přešt'ovice materials (especially the distinctive fine handmade pottery bowls decorated with oval facets or oblique grooves on the shoulder) in Bavaria, archaeological evidence suggests migrations that are not mentioned in any surviving written sources.

While some movements may have been substantial migrations of entire communities, smaller movements occurred more often. Probably parts of communities—a few families—often moved, with others perhaps following at a later time. Some changes can be explained by elites moving from one region to another, introducing certain new styles and types from their homelands, but not entire assemblages. In some cases such elites might adopt the new local material culture; in others, they might stimulate the adoption of their own by locals.

Archaeology of emerging confederations

Historians working with the Roman texts emphasize the disparity between the relatively small 'tribes' of Gauls and Germans named and situated geographically in the writings of Caesar and Tacitus and the much larger groupings represented in texts of the third century and later. Names such as Alamanni, Burgundians, Franks, Goths, Langobards, and Saxons appear at this time, and these have been interpreted to refer to confederations of peoples, or *Grossstämme* or 'mega-tribes', which in turn are understood as the bases for the kingdoms that developed in early medieval Europe. The process of formation of these groups was not described by the Roman writers, because they knew very little about social and political changes that were taking place beyond the frontier. But the archaeological evidence enables us to trace these processes.

Two main developments are apparent. One is the emergence over time of larger cultural areas in which particular forms of settlement, burial practice, and styles of pottery, weapons, and personal ornaments can consistently be identified. For example, in eastern Europe the formation during the third century of a relatively uniform material culture has been observed in relation to settlements and cemeteries over a vast landscape, from central Transylvania in the west to Kiev in the east. This phenomenon has been called the Sîntana de Mureş-Černjachov Culture, after cemeteries in Transylvania and in Ukraine. Much of the material culture, such as the house-barn structures, pottery, *fibulae*, and combs, shows links to the north and west. Burial practices include both inhumation and cremation. Styles that maintained characteristics of the local Late Iron Age groups are apparent, as are forms influenced by Roman craft traditions. In some cemeteries skulls show results of intentional deformation, a practice associated with nomadic peoples of the steppe regions to the east. Certain elements of burial ritual and personal ornaments also indicate such connections. Commerce with the Roman world is apparent in pottery, glassware, and coins. This region of eastern Europe is associated with the Goths in the textual sources, but drawing a direct connection between the archaeological material and a group named by Roman writers is problematic.

Similar patterns of development during the third, fourth, and fifth centuries of large culture areas, with material culture based on elements of diverse origins—some characteristic of the Roman side of the borders, some of the unconquered side—can be identified in other regions of the frontier zone as well. In southern Germany the emergence of common material culture over a wide area is connected with the name Alamanni, and in the lower Rhineland with peoples called Franks.

Patterns of interaction and change: an example on the Upper Danube

To illustrate the character of the evidence that enables us to examine the processes of change throughout the Roman period, I turn to a well-studied context, the formation of the group known as the Bajuwari along the upper Danube. Extensive archaeological research in the region demonstrates the role played by different groups, some local and some from outside, in the formation of a distinctive material culture by the fifth century. Local prehistoric Iron Age peoples are well documented, at major settlement centres at Manching, Kelheim, and Straubing, all on the Danube river, and in numerous smaller communities. Roman armies conquered the region in 15 BC, but not until the latter part of the first century AD is there evidence for the introduction of substantial Roman infrastructure. The troops stationed along the Danube frontier were mainly auxiliaries, many from the region and others from elsewhere. Establishment of Roman military and civil centres brought an influx of Roman pottery, ornaments, tools and weapons, as well as styles of architecture, burial traditions, and ritual practices.

But even at Roman centres such as Regensburg (Castra Regina) and Straubing (Soviodurum), material culture of types characteristic of the local Late Iron Age peoples was common. On settlement sites and in burials, handmade domestic pottery, fine painted wares, and bronze ornaments attest to ongoing manufacture of traditional forms throughout the early Roman period. Burial practices reflect the mixing of Roman and native rituals and grave-goods (Wells 1999: 204–14).

During the second and third centuries special traditions developed on the upper Danube that distinguish the material culture of this frontier region from that of its neighbours. These include distinctive pottery types, known as Raetian Ware, 'grape-urns', and Diota urns, that have no clear antecedents in either the local Iron Age pottery or in interregional Roman ceramics. Also during the second and third centuries, bronze ornaments for military belts, scabbards, and other equipment were made in cast openwork technique, a practice that originated in Late Iron Age ornament, with motifs, such as spirals, that derive from pre-Roman metalworking traditions (Wells 1999: 141–7, 198–204). This phenomenon is not restricted to the upper Danube, but appears widely along the Rhine and Danube frontiers, and even in Britain. It was another element in the interplay of local, Roman, and newly emerging fashions in this frontier region.

During the fourth and fifth centuries, graves in the cemeteries at Regensburg and Straubing show the arrival of new cultural elements. They include finely made, hand-crafted ceramic bowls, broad and flat in form, with distinctive shoulder decoration of oval facets or diagonal grooves. These bowls are associated with the Friedenhain-Přešťovice group, named after cemeteries across the Danube from Straubing and in south-west Bohemia. The Friedenhain cemetery, with its distinctive pottery and burial practice like that at the Bohemian site of Přešťovice, is thought to represent a group that migrated from Bohemia to the north bank of the Danube late in the fourth century. The sudden appearance of this burial complex at Regensburg and Straubing has been interpreted to indicate the presence of soldiers from this population employed as federates, serving in the late Roman defence system on the upper Danube (Chapter 5). Raids during the third and fourth centuries on Regensburg, Straubing, and other places along the Danube are recorded in the textual sources, and they indicate that

Roman authorities hired soldiers from across the river to aid in the defence of the imperial frontier.

Changes in the material assemblages in the cemeteries indicate processes in the transformation of identities within the communities. For example, at the cemetery at Straubing-Azlburg I, beginning late in the third century, some graves were outfitted with traditional provincial Roman material—ceramic or glass urns, small items of jewellery, occasional glass vessels, and oil lamps. Other graves contained materials characteristic of peoples outside of the imperial lands—bronze belt hooks with tongue-shaped attachments, iron tools with suspension rings used with flint for striking fire, and distinctive iron knives. During the fourth century, graves with provincial Roman materials and those with 'Germanic' goods continued side-by-side. In the first half of the fifth century (Chapter 9), Roman-provincial style goods are no longer present, only objects characteristic of the Germanic peoples across the Danube, in particular the distinctive Friedenhain-Přešt'ovice bowls. In the Azlburg II cemetery, 200 m north of Azlburg I, among early fourth-century burials, a western area could be identified in which graves had mostly provincial Roman-type materials, but with some Germanic items, and an eastern area in which men's graves contained provincial Roman goods while women's were characterized by Germanic objects.

In the latest of the major cemeteries at Straubing, Straubing-Bajuwarenstrasse, in which 819 graves have been excavated, the earliest burials have Friedenhain-Přešt'ovice bowls and related goods, such as triangular bone combs, and date to the first half of the fifth century. Graves dated to the second half of the fifth century include materials indicative of a range of connections and identities from this period. They include iron crossbow *fibulae*, miniature silver and bronze *fibulae*, silver earrings, chip-carved strap-ends, and buckles made of rock crystal. This variety demonstrates the diverse origins of ideas and styles, if not of individuals, contributing to the transformation of society here. Several skulls in this cemetery show artificial deformation, indicating individuals who probably came from regions to the east, or, at least, whose parents practised a tradition that originated in central Asia, since such shaping of the skull can only be achieved by treatment in early childhood.

This centuries-long process of immigration, borrowing, and transforming evident in the cemeteries along the upper Danube illustrates the complexity of the processes through which diverse groups from both sides of the Roman frontier came together and created new communities, distinctly different from their predecessors. Near the end of this process, around the middle of the fifth century, we can observe the material manifestations of the character and identity of a man who had probably served as an officer in the late Roman border forces, but who identified more strongly with peoples from the other side of the frontier. At Kemathen in the Altmühl River valley, 25 km north of the Danube, archaeologists excavated the inhumation grave of a man about 30 years of age. He wore a Roman military belt with finely crafted fittings of chip-carved bronze, probably made west of the lower Rhine in north-eastern Gaul. With him was an ornate yellow-green glass beaker, also a product of a provincial Roman workshop. But the rest of his grave-goods mark him as a native of a group that did not consider itself Roman. He had a long iron sword, with silver and bronze rivets, and a shield. Other distinctively non-Roman goods were a pair of tweezers, a piece of flint, probably for striking a spark, and a bone comb. He wore a silver finger-ring. His iron crossbow *fibula* preserved remains of a fur garment. Five handmade ceramic vessels were in the grave, including a bowl of Friedenhain type, probably made north of the Danube near where he was buried.

This burial represents the character of many of the officers of the late Roman defence system along the frontiers. He was a native from beyond the frontier, who identified with his community of origin and maintained much of his traditional material culture. But he also marked his affiliation with the Roman world. Perhaps this man returned home after having completed his term of service and was buried where he died; or perhaps he was brought back to his homeland across the Danube, if he died while serving on the Roman frontier.

New style for a transforming Europe

During the third, fourth, and fifth centuries, at the same time that the larger material-cultural groupings gradually became apparent, a distinctive new style of ornament developed, known as Germanic art. Like the forming cultural-geographical confederations, this style emerged from disparate origins. It was widely adopted by peoples throughout the frontier regions as a sign of new identity, different from both Roman and earlier indigenous patterns. One of the elements from which the new style developed was local metalworking traditions associated with the pre-Roman and early Roman-period peoples, including that known as Jastorf in northern parts of the continent, with its decoration applied to *fibulae*, belt ornaments, ring jewellery, and weapons. Another was ornament of late Roman tradition in the European frontier regions, including the technique of chip-carving, especially on bronze belt attachments, and use of human- and animal-head motifs on metalwork. A third was cloisonné, derived from decorative traditions that first emerged in lands around the Black Sea.

By the fifth century the fully developed and integrated style was taken up by peoples throughout the frontier regions of Europe, from the lower Danube region in the east westward and northward along the Danube and Rhine valleys and across the Channel to Britain. The emergence of this relatively homogeneous style has been connected to the formation of new political systems and to the myths and legends that accompany the creation of new kinds of identity linked to the appearance of new group identities throughout much of Europe.

The archaeology of interaction in the frontier zone

The archaeological evidence provides a very different view of the peoples who lived beyond the Roman frontiers in Europe from that presented in the Roman texts. The large number of objects made in Italy or in the Roman provinces found on archaeological sites beyond the frontier, the great variety of contexts in which they occur, and their diverse character indicate complex interactions of different kinds between the peoples outside the imperial lands and manufacturers and merchants within the empire. The evidence suggests much more widespread and varied interaction between the Roman and the non-Roman worlds than we would infer from the texts. Surely some of these 'Roman imports' were seized in plundering raids, such as those described by the late Roman authors, but many other mechanisms were also involved that resulted in the transmission of Roman products into lands across the frontier.

The archaeological evidence enables us to trace the emergence of larger communities beyond the Rhine and Danube. In many cases, this process was directly linked to interaction with Rome, as is apparent at the settlement of Feddersen Wierde, as well as at the centres of Gudme and Jakuszowice. The emergence of larger political entities is also apparent in the changing character of the richest burials. The graves at Mušov and Gommern show not only much greater wealth than the richest graves before the late second century, but more importantly, they included assemblages of materials that bespeak political power and authority on a much broader scale than do those earlier burials. In these grave contexts too, links to the Roman world are clearly apparent.

But it was not interaction with Rome that *caused* the changes in social and political organization that we see reflected in the archaeology at such sites. The peoples beyond the frontier and those of the Roman world were parts of an extensive network that linked all of Europe. For the farmers and cattle-raisers at Feddersen Wierde, and for the political community of which the man buried at Gommern was leader, interaction with Rome was just one element in complex economic, social, political, and religious transactions. We shall be able to understand and reconstruct these processes in central and eastern Europe more clearly as archaeological research continues to uncover more settlements, cemeteries, and ritual deposits east and north of the Roman frontier.

In the late Roman textual narratives about interactions between the provinces and groups across the frontier, confederations of peoples played major roles. But as a number of authors have demonstrated recently, the names such as Alamanni, Burgundians, Franks, Goths, Langobards, and Saxons, as they were used by the Roman writers, are highly problematical. The peoples so named are rarely defined precisely, and the names are used inconsistently. To a great extent, these named groups need to be regarded as constructions by particular writers in particular circumstances. The archaeological evidence does not support the distinctions suggested, except in a very general way. In the fourth and fifth centuries the archaeology of settlement materials, practices, and grave-goods suggests increasingly common identities, with sharing of material signs and symbols, rather than sharp distinctions between the peoples the Roman writers distinguished with the group names. Some regional stylistic variation is apparent, but it is not as prominent as we would expect from textual evidence.

The increasing similarities in burial practice and in grave-good assemblages during the fourth and fifth centuries, especially in contexts such as the rich burials at Apahida, Blučina, and Tournai, suggest much more the emergence of feelings of common identity among the political elites of that period than of difference. The spread and wide adoption of the style known as Germanic art is an expression of that process. As the Childeric grave illustrates so well, this emergent 'we-feeling' was characteristic by the middle of the fifth century, not only among peoples in the frontier zones east of the Rhine and north of the Danube, but even within the former Roman lands. The challenge for the future will be to develop integrated approaches that enable us to combine what the archaeology can tell us about how the societies beyond the frontiers were forging their own new identities with what the late Roman writers had to say about their northern and eastern neighbours.

Further Reading

Introduction: Edward Bispham

On the European angle, see M. J. Rowlands, 'The Concept of Europe in Prehistory', *Man*, 22 (1987), 558–9; for the Mediterranean see P. Horden and N. Purcell, *The Corrupting Sea: A Study of Mediterranean History* (Oxford: Blackwell, 2000). For interactions between the Greek world, Italy, and the northern European Iron Age, see J. Collis, *The European Iron Age* (London and New York: Routledge, 1984), B. Cunliffe, *Greeks, Romans and Barbarians: Spheres of Interaction* (London: Methuen, 1988); for a contextual approach, K. Arafat and C. Morgan, 'Athens, Etruria and the Heuneburg: Mutual Misconceptions in the Study of Greek-Barbarian Relations', in I. Morris (ed.), *Classical Greece: Ancient Histories and Modern Archaeologies* (Cambridge: Cambridge University Press, 1994), 108–34. For an arresting and well-informed exposition of the traditional view of the impact of Rome on traditional indigenous cultures, see Boris Johnson, *The Dream of Rome* (London: HarperCollins, 2006). For a recent example of a very different view of the imperial experience and its consequences, see D. J. Mattingly, *An Imperial Possession: Britain in the Roman Empire* (London: Allen Lane, 2006). On Egeria and her pilgrimage, see J. Wilkinson, *Egeria's Travels*, 3rd edn. (Warminster: Aris & Phillips, 1999).

1. Peoples of temperate Europe before the Roman conquest: Peter S. Wells

Useful overviews in English of later prehistory include A. F. Harding, *European Societies in the Bronze Age* (Cambridge: Cambridge University Press, 2000), S. Moscati, O.-H. Frey, V. Kruta, B. Raftery, and M. Szabó (eds.), *The Celts* (New York: Rizzoli, 1991), M. J. Green (ed.), *The Celtic World* (London: Routledge, 1995), and K. Kristiansen, *Europe Before History* (Cambridge: Cambridge University Press, 1998). Recent discussions of some major issues in Iron Age archaeology include S. James, *The Atlantic Celts: Ancient People or Modern Invention?* (London: British Museum, 1999), M. Diepeveen-Jansen, *People, Ideas and Goods: New Perspectives on 'Celtic Barbarians' in Western and Central Europe* (Amsterdam: Amsterdam University Press, 2001), and P. S. Wells, *Beyond Celts, Germans and Scythians: Archaeology and Identity in Iron Age Europe* (London: Duckworth, 2001). On the grave at Hochdorf, see the splendid monograph by J. Biel, *Der Keltenfürst von Hochdorf*

(Stuttgart: Theiss, 1985). A good recent summary of the extensive excavations at Manching is S. Sievers, *Manching: Die Keltenstadt* (Stuttgart: Theiss, 2003). A useful overview of the *oppida* is J. Collis, 'The First Towns', in M. J. Green (ed.), *The Celtic World* (London: Routledge, 1995), 159–75. Caesar quoted from *The Gallic War*, trans. H. J. Edwards (Cambridge, MA: Harvard University Press, 1986). On the archaeological evidence for the textually documented Battle of the Teutoburg Forest, see P. S. Wells, *The Battle That Stopped Rome: Emperor Augustus, Arminius, and the Slaughter of the Legions in the Teutoburg Forest* (New York: W.W. Norton, 2003).

2. The Roman Republic: political history: G. J. Bradley

General studies of the Republic can be found in: *Cambridge Ancient History*, 2nd edn., vols 7. 2, 8, and 9 (detailed analysis and narrative), H. H. Scullard, *A History of the Roman World, 753 to 146 B.C.* (London: Methuen, 1980) and *From the Gracchi to Nero: A History of Rome from 133 B.C.–A.D. 68*, 5th edn. (London: Methuen, 1982), T. J. Cornell and J. Matthews, *Atlas of the Roman World* (Oxford: Phaidon, 1982), and M. H. Crawford, *The Roman Republic*. Fontana History of the Ancient World, 2nd edn. (London: Fontana, 1992); note also P. A. Brunt's *Social Conflicts in the Roman Republic* (London: Hogarth Press, 1971) and the useful studies in H. Flower (ed.), *The Cambridge Companion to the Roman Republic* (Cambridge: Cambridge University Press 2004).

For the history of early Rome, see T. J. Cornell, *The Beginnings of Rome: Italy and Rome from the Bronze Age to the Punic Wars (c.1000–264 BC)* (London and New York: Routledge, 1995); note also the more sceptical approach of G. Forsythe, *A Critical History of Early Rome: From Prehistory to the First Punic War* (Berkeley: University of California Press, 2005), and on early Roman society, K. Raaflaub (ed.), *Social Struggles in Archaic Rome*, 2nd edn., (Oxford: Blackwell, 2005); on the archaeological evidence, J. C. Meyer, *Pre-Republican Rome: An Analysis of the Cultural and Chronological Relations, 1000–500 B.C.* (Odense: Odense University Press, 1983), R. Ross Holloway, *The Archaeology of Early Rome and Latium* (London and New York: Routledge, 1994), and C. J. Smith, *Early Rome and Latium: Economy and Society, c.1000 to 500 BC* (Oxford: Oxford University Press, 1996).

On mid-Republican politics and culture, see the studies in F. G. B. Millar, *Rome, the Greek World, and the East*. Vol. 1, *The Roman Republic and the Augustan Revolution* (Chapel Hill, NC: University of North Carolina Press, 2002), C. Bruun, *The Roman Middle Republic: Politics, Religion and Historiography, c.400–133 B.C.*, Acta Instituti Romani Finlandiae 23 (Rome: Finnish Institute in Rome, 2000), and D. Braund and C. Gill (eds.), *Myth,*

History and Culture in Republican Rome: Studies in Honour of T. P. Wiseman (Exeter: Exeter University Press, 2003); on particular issues, see M. I. Finley, *Politics in the Ancient World* (Cambridge: Cambridge University Press, 1983), H. Flower, *Ancestor Masks and Aristocratic Power in Roman Culture* (Oxford: Clarendon Press, 1996), J. W. Rich, 'Fear, Greed, and Glory: The Causes of Roman War Making in the Roman Republic', in J. W. Rich and G. Shipley (eds.), *War and Society in the Roman World* (London: Routledge, 1993), 38–68, N. Rosenstein, *Rome at War: Farms, Families, and Death in the Middle Republic* (Chapel Hill, NC: University of North Carolina Press, 2004).

On the late Republic, see M. Beard and M. H. Crawford, *Rome in the Late Republic* (London: Duckworth, 1985), R. Syme, *The Roman Revolution* (Oxford: Clarendon Press, 1939), E. S. Gruen, *The Last Generation of the Roman Republic* (Berkeley: University of California Press, 1974), and P. A. Brunt, *The Fall of the Roman Republic* (Oxford: Clarendon Press, 1988).

On the nature of late Republican politics, see A. Yakobson, *Elections and Electioneering in Rome*. Historia Einzelschrift 128 (Stuttgart: F. Steiner, 1999), F. G. B. Millar, *The Crowd in Rome in the Late Republic*. Thomas Spencer Jerome Lectures (Ann Arbor, Mich.: Michigan University Press, 1998), H. Mouritsen, *Plebs and Politics in the Late Roman Republic* (Cambridge: Cambridge University Press, 2001), R. Morstein-Marx, *Mass Oratory and Political Power in the Late Roman Republic* (Cambridge: Cambridge University Press, 2004), and J. Patterson, *Political Life in the City of Rome* (Bristol: Bristol University Press, 2000).

Rewarding studies of specific themes in Republican history include M. Beard, J. A. North, and S. R. F. Price (eds.), *Religions of Rome*. Volume 1, *A History*; Volume 2, *A Sourcebook* (Cambridge: Cambridge University Press, 1998), P. A. Brunt, *Italian Manpower 225 B.C.–A.D. 14*, rev. edn. (Oxford: Clarendon Press, 1987), E. Gabba, *Republican Rome: The Army and the Allies* (Oxford: Blackwell, 1976), K. Hopkins, *Conquerors and Slaves* (Cambridge: Cambridge University Press, 1978) and *Death and Renewal* (Cambridge: Cambridge University Press, 1983); for an archaeological case study of changing settlement patterns in southern Italy in this period, see J. A. Lloyd, in G. Barker (ed.), *A Mediterranean Valley: Landscape Archaeology and Annales History in the Biferno Valley* (London and New York: Leicester University Press, 1995); for ecological factors relevant to this chapter, see P. Horden and N. Purcell, *The Corrupting Sea: A Study of Mediterranean History* (Oxford: Blackwell, 2000).

3. The Roman Empire from Augustus to Diocletian: Benet Salway

Volumes X to XII of the second edition of *The Cambridge Ancient History* provide the fullest narrative in English to the period covered by this chapter, with plentiful bibliography and references to sources and relatively recent scholarship: A. K. Bowman *et al.* (eds.), *CAH²*, vol. X. *The Augustan Empire, 43 B.C.–A.D. 69* (Cambridge: Cambridge University Press, 1995); vol. XI. *The High Empire, A.D. 70–192* (Cambridge: Cambridge University Press, 2000); vol. XII. *The Crisis of Empire, A.D. 193–337* (Cambridge: Cambridge University Press, 2005). Less intimidating introductory narratives are provided by two volumes in the Methuen (now Routledge) Ancient History series: M. D. Goodman (with J. E. Sherwood), *The Roman World, 44 B.C.–A.D. 180* (London and New York: Routledge, 1997), and D. S. Potter, *The Roman Empire at Bay: AD 180–395* (London and New York: Routledge, 2004). The most convenient one-volume survey in English is C. M. Wells, *The Roman Empire*, 2nd edn. (London: Fontana 1992), although it ends with the Severans. A wide-ranging thematic introduction to the period from Augustus to Constantine is provided by D. S. Potter (ed.), *A Companion to the Roman Empire* (Oxford: Blackwell, 2006). Numerous collections of translated sources exist; most relevant to the themes of this chapter is B. M. Levick, *The Government of the Roman Empire: A Sourcebook*, 2nd edn. (London and New York: Routledge, 2000). An excellent case-study of the cultural and political development of one area of Europe under Roman rule is provided by G. D. Woolf, *Becoming Roman: The Origins of Provincial Civilization in Gaul* (Cambridge: Cambridge University Press, 1998). On the historical significance of the 'Laws and Rights' coin legend see J. W. Rich and J. H. C. Williams, '*Leges et Iura P. R. Restituit*: A New Aureus of Octavian and the Settlement of 28–27 BC', *Numismatic Chronicle*, 159 (1999), 169–213. The most accessible discussion of the epitaph recently identified as belonging to Tacitus is A. R. Birley, 'The Life and Death of Cornelius Tacitus', *Historia*, 49: 2 (2000), 230–47. A useful discussion of Claudius' speech on the Lyon tablet is to be found in R. Syme, *The Provincial at Rome* (Exeter: Exeter University Press, 1999), 98–113. On the archaeological evidence for Roman city foundations to the east of the lower Rhine, see S. von Schnurbein, 'Augustus in *Germania* and his New "Town" at Waldgirmes East of the Rhine', *Journal of Roman Archaeology*, 16: 1 (2003), 93–107. On the breakaway empire of Postumus, see J. F. Drinkwater, *The Gallic Empire: Separatism and Continuity in the North-Western Provinces of the Roman Empire A.D. 260–274*. Historia Einzelschriften 52 (Wiesbaden: Steiner 1987); the Augsburg victory altar is discussed by the same author and others in *CAH²*, vol. XII, pp. 66, 223, 429, 442.

4. Roman society: Mary Harlow

In 1987 Peter Garnsey and Richard Saller could say in the chapter 'Family and Household' in *The Roman Empire* that, 'The family does not so much as appear in the index of the standard social histories of Rome written in the past decades' (Berkeley: University of California Press, 1987), 126. Since then, however, the situation has changed dramatically and the Roman family has been the subject of a number of general and specialist discussions. The view of the Roman family and society expressed in this chapter is highly influenced by the demographic and social analysis of Saller collected in *Patriarchy, Property and Death in the Roman Family* (Cambridge: Cambridge University Press, 1994). For an introduction to, and comprehensive survey of, the Roman family, see S. Dixon, *The Roman Family* (London and Baltimore: Johns Hopkins, 1992). K. Bradley, *Discovering the Roman Family: Studies in Roman Social History* (Oxford: Oxford University Press, 1992) is a collection of articles that covers, among other relevant topics: the ramifications of remarriage; roles of slaves and non-parent carers; and a case-study of the family of Cicero. On children, the most recent and thorough coverage is by B. Rawson, *Children and Childhood in Roman Italy* (Oxford: Oxford University Press, 2003). This contains reappraisals of much of Rawson's earlier influential work on the history of the family, including lower-class and slave families. Garnsey's article 'Child Rearing in Ancient Italy', in D. I. Kertzer and R. Saller (eds.), *The Family in Italy from Antiquity to the Present* (New Haven and London: Yale University Press, 1991), stresses the need for taking cultural context into consideration when assessing familial relationships in past times. A recent study of the life-course and ageing in Roman society, M. Harlow and R. Laurence, *Growing Up and Growing Old in Ancient Rome* (London and New York: Routledge, 2002), offers a condensed view of many of these themes. The study of Roman women has produced a number of volumes in the last decade, the most lucid of which is S. Dixon, *Reading Roman Women: Sources, Genres and Real Life* (London: Duckworth, 2001). E. Hemelrijk, *Matrona Docta, Educated Women in the Roman Elite from Cornelia to Julia Domna* (London and New York: Routledge, 1999), presents a view of women often hidden in male writings of the period. S. Treggiari, *Roman Marriage: Iusti Conjuges from the Time of Cicero to the Time of Ulpian* (Oxford: Oxford University Press, 1991) is the most comprehensive study on the topic. On patronage, see Saller, *Personal Patronage Under the Early Empire* (Cambridge: Cambridge University Press, 1982), and the collection of articles in A. Wallace-Hadrill (ed.), *Patronage in Ancient Society* (London and New York: Routledge, 1989). On the house and the social use of domestic space, the seminal work has been done by Wallace-Hadrill in a series of articles collected in *Houses and Society in Pompeii and Herculaneum* (Princeton: Princeton University Press, 1994). S. Hales has further looked at the role of public and private in the Roman house in *The Roman House and Social Identity* (Cambridge: Cambridge University

Press, 2003). There is an extensive bibliography of slavery and the lives of freedmen. For an introduction, see K. Bradley, *Slavery and Society at Rome*, Key Themes in Ancient History (Cambridge: Cambridge University Press, 1994); T. Weidemann, *Greek and Roman Slavery* (London: Routledge, 1981). In order to make the source material easily accessible for the general reader, as many extracts as possible in this chapter have been taken from J. Gardner and T. Wiedemann (eds.), *The Roman Household* (London: Routledge, 1991) and J.-A. Shelton (ed.), *As The Romans Did*, 2nd edn. (Oxford: Oxford University Press, 1998).

5. Warfare and the army: Edward Bispham

An excellent introduction is A. K. Goldsworthy, *The Complete Roman Army* (London: Thames & Hudson, 2003); his *The Roman Army at War, 100 BC–AD 200* (Oxford: Oxford University Press, 1996) examines the role of the general in battle. The development of the Roman army up to Augustus is masterfully surveyed by L. Keppie, *The Making of the Roman Army* (London: Batsford, 1984); his 'The Changing Face of the Roman Legions (49 B.C.–A.D. 69)', *Papers of the British School at Rome*, 65 (1997), 89–102, extends his study into the early empire. On Roman arms and armour, the current state of knowledge is set out, beautifully illustrated, in M. C. Bishop and J. C. N. Coulston, *Roman Military Equipment from the Punic Wars to the Fall of Rome*, 2nd edn. (Oxford: Oxbow, 2006).

The cultural dynamics behind Roman imperialism and the militaristic character of Roman society are explored in a classic study by W. V. Harris: *War and Imperialism in Republican Rome, 327–70 B.C.*, repr. with a new preface and additional bibliography (Oxford: Clarendon Press, 1992); T. J. Cornell, *The Beginnings of Rome: Italy and Rome from the Bronze Age to the Punic Wars (c.1000–264 BC)* (London and New York: Routledge, 1995); for the *impact* of conquest on society, see K. Hopkins, *Conquerors and Slaves* (Cambridge: Cambridge University Press, 1978). Important essays on the proletarianization of the Republican legions in E. Gabba, *Republican Rome: The Army and the Allies* (Oxford: Blackwell, 1976); for a different view: J. W. Rich, 'The Supposed Roman Manpower Shortage of the Later 2nd century B.C.', *Historia*, 32 (1983), 287–331. A seminal treatment of recruitment, troop deployments, and much else, is in P. A. Brunt, *Italian Manpower 225 B.C.–A.D. 14*, rev. edn. (Oxford: Clarendon Press, 1987); his analysis of the role of the legions in the collapse of the Republic is also fundamental: 'The Army and the Land in the Roman Revolution', in P. A. Brunt, *The Fall of the Roman Republic* (Oxford: Clarendon Press, 1988), 240–80. A strong challenge to the view which sees the Gracchan agrarian/manpower crisis as provoked by heavy recruitment of peasants for long campaigns is N. Rosenstein, *Rome at War: Farms, Families and Death in the Middle Republic* (Chapel Hill, NC: University of North Carolina Press, 2004), although his own answers are less cogent than his critique of traditional assumptions. The connection between citizen rights and military responsibilities is explored in C. Nicolet, *The World of the Citizen in Republican Rome*, trans. P. Falla (Berkeley: University of California Press, 1992). The best introduction to the imperial army is J. B. Campbell, *The Emperor and the Roman Army 31 B.C.–A.D. 235* (Oxford: Clarendon Press, 1984); on the possible link between army pay, provincial taxation, and economic growth, see K. Hopkins, 'Taxes and Trade in the Roman Empire (200 BC–AD 400)', *Journal of Roman Studies*, 70 (1980), 101–25. For late antiquity see R. MacMullan, *Soldier and Civilian in the Later Roman Empire* (Cambridge, Mass.: Harvard University Press, 1963), and J. H. W. G. Liebeschutz, *Barbarians and Bishops: Army, Church and State in the Age of Arcadius and Chrysostom* (Oxford: Oxford University Press, 1990). An important collection of papers is J. W. Rich and G. Shipley (eds.), *War and Society in the Roman World*. Leicester–Nottingham Studies in Ancient Society (London and New York: Routledge, 1993).

Literacy and Latinity of the Batavians: T. Derks and N. Roymans, 'Sealboxes and the Spread of Latin Literacy in the Rhine Delta', in A.E. Cooley (ed.), *Becoming Roman, Writing Latin? Literacy and Epigraphy in the Roman West*. Journal of Roman Archaeology Supplement 48 (Portsmouth, RI: Journal of Roman Archaeology, 2002); on the diet of the Roman army: A. C. King, 'Animals and the Roman Army: The Evidence of Animal Bones', in A. Goldsworthy and I. Haynes (eds.), *The Roman Army as a Community*, Journal of Roman Archaeology Supplement 34 (Portsmouth, RI: Journal of Roman Archaeology, 1999), 139–50. The recent 'cultural' turn in the study of war is exemplified by L. Hannestad and T. Bekker Nielsen (eds.), *War as a Cultural and Social Force: Essays on Warfare in Antiquity*. Historisk-filosofiske Skrifter 22 (Copenhagen: C. A. Reitzels Forlag, 2001). Veteran colonization: L. Keppie, *Colonisation and Veteran Settlement in Italy, 47–14 B.C.* (London: British School at Rome, 1983). On auxiliaries, see D. B. Saddington, *The Development of the Roman Auxiliary Forces from Caesar to Vespasian (49 B.C.–A.D. 79)* (Harare: University of Zimbabwe, 1982); and for an accessible summary of the evidence revealed by the Vindolanda tablets, see A. K. Bowman, *Life and Letters on the Roman Frontier: Vindolanda and its People* (London: British Museum Press, 2003). On the Roman navy, J. H. Thiel, *Studies on the History of Roman Seapower in Republican Times* (Amsterdam: North-Holland Publishing, 1946) is still useful; for Roman cavalry: K. R. Dixon and P. Southern, *The Roman Cavalry* (London and New York: Routledge, 1992). For the imperial bodyguards:

J. C. N. Coulston, ' "Armed and belted men": The Soldiery in Imperial Rome',
in J. C. N. Coulston and H. Dodge (eds.), *Ancient Rome: The Archaeology of
the Eternal City*, Centre for Mediterranean and Near Eastern Studies, Trinity
College Dublin/Oxford University School of Archaeology Monograph 54
(Oxford: Oxford University School of Archaeology, 2000), 76–118.

6. Economy and trade: Andrew Wilson

The publication of M. I. Finley's *The Ancient Economy*, Sather Classical
Lectures 43 (Berkeley and Los Angeles: University of California Press, 1973;
2nd edn., 1985), sparked a debate which still continues. Important papers in
this debate are: K. Hopkins, 'Taxes and Trade in the Roman Empire (200
BC–AD 400)', *Journal of Roman Studies*, 70 (1980), 101–25; W. V. Harris,
'Between Archaic and Modern: Some Current Problems in the History of
the Roman Economy', in W. V. Harris (ed.), *The Inscribed Economy: Production and Distribution in the Roman Empire in the Light of* Instrumentum
Domesticum, Journal of Roman Archaeology, Supplement 6 (Ann Arbor,
Mich.: Journal of Roman Archaeology, 1993), 11–29; and K. Hopkins, 'Rents,
Taxes, Trade and the City of Rome', in E. Lo Cascio (ed.), *Mercati perman-
enti e mercati periodici nel mondo romano.* Pragmateiai 2 (Bari, Edipuglia,
2000), 253–267. Although twenty years old, K. Greene's *The Archaeology of
the Roman Economy* (London: Batsford, 1986) remains a useful collection of
a large amount of archaeological material that gives very different insights
from the picture provided by ancient literature. P. Horden and N. Purcell,
The Corrupting Sea: A Study of Mediterranean History (Oxford: Blackwell,
2000) is one of the most creative and successful attempts to break out of
the constraints of the Finley-dominated debate over the ancient economy;
it studies communications, trade, and socio-economic contacts across and
around the Mediterranean world; for the evidence from faunal assemblages,
see A. C. King, 'Animals and the Roman Army: The Evidence of Animal
Bones', in A. Goldsworthy and I. Haynes (eds.), *The Roman Army as a
Community*, Journal of Roman Archaeology Supplement, 34 (Portsmouth,
RI: Journal of Roman Archaeology, 1999), 139–50. For the late Roman period, M. McCormick's *Origins of the European Economy: Communications and
Commerce A.D. 300–900* (Cambridge: Cambridge University Press, 2001) contains a valuable and succinct treatment of the late Roman economy, focusing
on Europe. On trade, numerous relevant articles may be found in journals
such as *Journal of Roman Archaeology, Journal of Roman Studies, International Journal of Nautical Archaeology*, and *Münsterische Beiträge zur antiken
Handelsgeschichte*, but comprehensive syntheses are few. The appearance of
The Cambridge Economic History of the Graeco-Roman world, ed. I. Morris,

R. Saller, and W. Scheidel (Cambridge: Cambridge University Press, 2007), now addresses this, and provides much-needed synthesis on other topics (see e.g. the chapter by W. Jongman, 'The Early Roman Empire: Consumption'). On coinage, P. Casey's slim *Roman Coinage in Britain*, Shire Archaeology 12 (Princes Risborough: Shire Publications Ltd., 1980) is a clear introduction to the bewildering vicissitudes of the Roman coinage, with applicability well beyond Britain, while C. Howgego's articles 'The Supply and Use of Money in the Roman World 300 B.C. to A.D. 300', *Journal of Roman Studies*, 82 (1992), 1–31, and 'Coin Circulation and the Integration of the Roman Economy', *Journal of Roman Archaeology*, 7 (1994), 5–21, represent the best available discussions of money-use and coin circulation. J. Andreau's *Banking and Business in the Roman World* (Cambridge: Cambridge University Press, 1999) is an accessible introduction to Roman financial activity.

The case for technological underdevelopment in the ancient world was made by M. I. Finley in his paper 'Technical Innovation and Economic Progress in the Ancient World', *Economic History Review*, 2nd ser., 18 (1965), 29–45. This position, long influential, has since been rebutted in a number of works, notably: Ö. Wikander, *Exploitation of Water-Power or Technological Stagnation? A Reappraisal of the Productive Forces in the Roman Empire*. Studier utgivna av Kungl. Humanistiska Vetenskapssamfundet i Lund, 1983–1984, 3 (Lund: CWK Glerup, 1984); K. Greene, 'Perspectives on Roman Technology', *Oxford Journal of Archaeology*, 9: 1 (July 1990), 209–19; id., 'Technology and Innovation in Context: The Roman Background to Mediaeval and Later Developments', *Journal of Roman Archaeology*, 7 (1994), 22–33; id., 'Technological Innovation and Economic Progress in the Ancient World: M. I. Finley Re-considered', *English Historical Review*, 53 (2000), 29–59; A. I. Wilson, 'Machines, Power and the Ancient Economy', *Journal of Roman Studies*, 92 (2002), 1–32; and, most recently, contributions in *The Oxford Handbook of Engineering and Technology in the Classical World*, J. P. Oleson (ed.), (Oxford: Oxford University Press, 2007). For the contribution of slaves, see K. Bradley, *Slavery and Society at Rome*, Key Themes in Ancient History (Cambridge: Cambridge University Press, 1994).

7. Religions: Edward Bispham

Excellent introductions to religion as practised in Rome, and the Roman cities of the empire: J. A. North, *Roman Religion*, Greece & Rome New Surveys in the Classics 30 (Oxford: Oxford University Press, 2000), and J. Scheid, *An Introduction to Roman Religion* (Edinburgh: Edinburgh University Press, 2003); among Scheid's large body of seminal work, *Religion et piété à Rome*, Sciences des religions, 2nd edn. (Paris: Albin Michel, 2001), is perhaps the most important synthesis. R. Turcan, *The Gods of Ancient Rome: Religion in Everyday Life from Archaic to Imperial Times* (Edinburgh: Edinburgh University Press, 2000), is also useful. More challenging and polemical is J. Rüpke, *Die Religion der Römer. Eine Einführung* (Munich: C. H. Beck, 2001)—now translated as *Religion of the Romans* (Cambridge: Polity Press, 2007). Much more detailed and wide-ranging is the outstanding two-volume work by M. Beard, J. A. North, and S. R. F. Price, *Religions of Rome* (Cambridge: Cambridge University Press, 1998), which deals with all the important aspects of Roman religions from origins to Christianization, lavishly illustrated with textual sources and images. A collection of influential essays on different aspects of the subject is brought together, and provided with stimulating introductory material (to which parts of this chapter are much indebted), by C. Ando (ed.), *Roman Religion*, Edinburgh Readings in the Ancient World (Edinburgh: Edinburgh University Press, 2003); see also D. S. Potter, 'Roman Religion: Ideas and Actions', in D. S. Potter and D. J. Mattingly (eds.), *Life, Death and Entertainment in the Roman Empire* (Ann Arbor, Mich.: Michigan University Press, 1999), 113–67. Early Roman religion: E. H. Bispham and C. J. Smith (eds.), *Religion in Archaic and Republican Rome and Italy: Evidence and Experience* (Edinburgh: Edinburgh University Press, 2000); and for the cultural contexts to early Roman Religion, see T. J. Cornell, *The Beginnings of Rome: Italy and Rome from the Bronze Age to the Punic Wars (c.1000–264 BC)* (London and New York: Routledge, 1995). A provocative interpretation of the worship of the emperors, contextualizing it within the honour system of the family and the community, is provided by I. Gradel, *Emperor Worship and Roman Religion* (Oxford: Clarendon Press, 2002). On 'oriental cults', R. Turcan, *The Cults of the Roman Empire* (Oxford: Blackwell, 1996) provides a lively, although idiosyncratic, introduction. An excellent, well-illustrated introduction to Mithraism is M. Clauss, *The Roman Cult of Mithras: The God and his Mysteries* (Edinburgh: Edinburgh University Press, 2000).

Recent attention paid to Roman religions as cultural systems, rooted in particular situations, has renewed interest in local religions, especially in provincial contexts: on Roman Gaul, see T. Derks, *Gods, Temples and Ritual Practices: The Transformation of Religious Ideas and Values in Roman Gaul* (Amsterdam: Amsterdam University Press, 1999), and G. Woolf, 'The Religious History of the Northwest Provinces', *Journal of Roman Archaeology* 13 (2000), 615–30, and '*Polis*-Religion and its Alternatives in the Roman Provinces', in Ando 2003: 39–54. R. Hutton, *The Pagan Religions of the Ancient British Isles: Their Nature and Legacy*, rev. edn. (Oxford: Blackwell, 1993), is cautious but highly readable on religious practices in the British

Isles in the *longue durée*. For Celtic religion, see M. Green, *The Gods of the Celts*, rev. edn. (Stroud: Sutton Publishing, 1993); G. Webster, *The British Celts and their Gods under Rome* (London: Batsford 1986); and generally for the cultural context, J. Collis, *The European Iron Age* (London and New York: Routledge, 2000) ch. 9; for Roman Britain, M. Henig, *Religion in Roman Britain* (London: Batsford, 1984). Valuable essays, many dealing with the European empire, are found in M. Henig and A. King (eds.), *Pagan Gods and Shrines of the Roman Empire*, Oxford University Committee for Archaeology, Monograph 8 (Oxford: Oxford University Committee for Archaeology, 1986). The interaction of Christianity and traditional polytheistic religions is the subject of exhilarating treatment by R. Lane Fox, *Pagans and Christians* (London: HarperCollins, 1988), and the world of early Christianity is brought to life by K. Hopkins, *A World Full of Gods: Pagans, Jews and Christians in the Roman Empire* (London: Weidenfeld & Nicolson, 1999). For the implications of mobility and regional diversity for the study of ancient religions, see P. Horden and N. Purcell, *The Corrupting Sea: A Study of Mediterranean History* (Oxford: Blackwell, 2000).

8. The cultural implications of the Roman conquest: Nicola Terranato

An excellent recent review of the scholarship on Romanization is in R. Hingley, *Globalizing Roman Culture: Unity, Diversity and Empire* (London and New York: Routledge, 2005). The papers in J. Webster and N. J. Cooper, *Roman Imperialism: Post Colonial Perspectives*, Leicester Archaeology Monograph 3 (Leicester: School of Archaeology Studies, University of Leicester 1996) and D. J. Mattingly (ed.), *Dialogues in Roman Imperialism: Power, Discourse and Discrepant Experience in the Roman Empire*, Journal of Roman Archaeology Supplementary Series 23 (Portsmouth, RI: Journal of Roman Archaeology, 1997) offer a representative cross-section of different opinions; for an earlier approach see R. MacMullen, *Changes in the Roman Empire: Essays in the Ordinary* (Princeton: Princeton University Press, 1990). For the different traditions in Italy and in the western provinces, see S. J. Keay and N. Terrenato (eds.), *Italy and the West: Comparative Issues in Romanization* (Oxford: Oxbow, 2001). For individual provinces: G. Woolf, *Becoming Roman: The Origins of Provincial Civilization in Gaul* (Cambridge: Cambridge University Press, 1998); M. Millett, *The Romanization of Britain: An Essay in Archaeological Interpretation* (Cambridge: Cambridge University Press, 1990); M. Henig, *The Art of Roman Britain* (Ann Arbor, Mich.: University of Michigan Press, 1995); S. J. Keay, *Roman Spain* (London: British Museum Press 1988). For the political implications, see M. Torelli, *Studies in the Romanization of*

Italy, ed. and trans. H. Fracchia and M. Gualtieri (Edmonton: University of Alberta Press, 1995). Cities and architecture are discussed in P. Gros and M. Torelli, *Storia dell'urbanistica. Il mondo romano* (Rome and Bari: Laterza, 1988), and P. Gros, *L'Architecture romaine*. 1. *Les Monuments publics* (Paris: Picard, 1996). For the non-urban world, see N. Terrenato, 'Tam firmum municipium: The Romanization of Volaterrae and its Cultural Implications', *Journal of Roman Studies*, 88 (1998), 94–114; S. L. Dyson, *The Roman Countryside*, Duckworth Debates in Archaeology (London: Duckworth, 2003). For longer-term cultural influences, R. Jenkyns (ed.), *The Legacy of Rome: A New Appraisal* (Oxford: Oxford University Press, 1992).

9. The fourth century: William Bowden

The principal work on the history and administration of the late Empire remains A. H. M. Jones's *The Later Roman Empire 284–602: A Social, Economic and Administrative Survey* (Oxford: Blackwell, 1964). Detailed thematic treatment of the period can be found in A. Cameron and P. Garnsey (eds.), Volume XIII of the *Cambridge Ancient History*, 2nd edn., *The Late Empire, A.D. 337–425*, 2nd edn. (Cambridge: Cambridge University Press, 1998). A useful shorter introduction can be found in A. Cameron, *The Later Roman Empire*, The Fontana History of the Ancient World (London: Fontana, 1993). For a 'revisionist' approach to the end of the western empire, see now B. Ward-Perkins, *The Fall of Rome and the End of Civilization* (Oxford: Oxford University Press, 2005) and P. Heather, *The Fall of the Roman Empire: A New History of Rome and the Barbarians* (Oxford: Oxford University Press, 2005).

For recent scholarship on late Roman Europe, see now the volumes in the series *Late Antique Archaeology*, in particular W. Bowden, L. Lavan and C. Machado (eds.), *Recent Research in the Late Antique Countryside* (Leiden: Brill, 2004), and W. Bowden, A. Gutteridge and C. Machado (eds.), *Social and Political Life in Late Antiquity* (Leiden: Brill, 2006), from which many of the examples cited here are drawn; these volumes also include extensive bibliographic essays. See also the publications of the European Science Foundation's 'Transformation of the Roman World' project, in particular W. Pohl (ed.), *Kingdoms of the Empire: The Integration of Barbarians in Late Antiquity* (Leiden, Boston, and Cologne: Brill, 1997) and G. P. Brogiolo and B. Ward-Perkins (eds.), *The Idea and Ideal of the Town Between Late Antiquity and the Early Middle Ages* (Leiden, Boston, and Cologne: Brill, 1999). There is also a wealth of accessible literature on the archaeology of late Roman Britain and Europe. Recent examples include A. S. Esmonde Cleary, *The Ending of Roman Britain* (London and New York: Routledge,

1989; repr. 2000); J. K. Knight, *The End of Antiquity: Archaeology, Society and Religion AD 235–700* (Stroud: Tempus, 1999); and R. Reece, *The Later Roman Empire* (Stroud: Tempus, 1999). On early Christian architecture, the principal work remains R. Krautheimer, *Early Christian and Byzantine Architecture*, The Yale University Press Pelican History of Art (New Haven and London: Yale University Press, 1986). On changing urban and rural life in Europe (among a vast body of literature), see N. Christie and S. T. Loseby (eds.), *Towns in Transition: Urban Evolution Between Late Antiquity and the Early Middle Ages* (Aldershot: Scolar Press, 1996), and N. Christie (ed.), *Landscapes of Change: Rural Evolutions in Late Antiquity and the Early Middle Ages* (Aldershot: Ashgate, 2004).

10. Peoples beyond the Roman imperial frontiers: Peter S. Wells

For overviews of interactions between Romans in the European provinces and the peoples whom they considered barbarians beyond their frontiers, see H. Wolfram, *The Roman Empire and its Germanic Peoples*, trans T. Dunlap (Berkeley: University of California Press, 1997), and T. S. Burns, *Rome and the Barbarians, 100 B.C.–A.D. 400* (Baltimore: Johns Hopkins University Press, 2003); on Rome and Arminius, see P. S. Wells, *The Battle that Stopped Rome: Emperor Augustus, Arminius, and the Slaughter of the Legions in the Teutoburg Forest* (New York: W. W. Norton, 2003). On Roman perceptions and representations of these peoples, I. M. Ferris, *Enemies of Rome: Barbarians Through Roman Eyes* (Thrupp: Sutton, 2000). Themistius quotation from P. Heather, 'The Barbarian in Late Antiquity: Image, Reality and Transformation', in R. Mills (ed.), *Constructing Identities in Late Antiquity* (London: Routledge, 1999), 236. For an anthropological approach to Roman–native interactions, see P. S. Wells, *The Barbarians Speak: How the Conquered Peoples Shaped Roman Europe* (Princeton: Princeton University Press, 1999). On general issues of archaeology and identity, P. S. Wells, *Beyond Celts, Germans and Scythians: Archaeology and Identity in Iron Age Europe* (London: Duckworth 2001). For peoples and archaeological sites in northern Europe, see P. O. Nielsen, K. Randsborg, and H. Thrane (eds.), *The Archaeology of Gudme and Lundeborg* (Copenhagen: Akademisk Forlag, 1994). For a clear statement of changing perspectives on these centuries, see W. Pohl, 'The Politics of Change: Reflections on the Transformation of the Roman World', in W. Pohl and M. Diesenberger (eds.), *Integration und Herrschaft: ethnische Identitäten und soziale Organisation im Frühmittelalter* (Vienna: Verlag der Österreichischen Akademie der Wissenschaften, 2002), 275–88. An excellent analysis of migration myths is by A. S. Christensen, *Cassiodorus,*

Jordanes and the History of the Goths: Studies in a Migration Myth (Copenhagen: Museum Tusculanum Press, 2002). On the connection between the new styles of ornament and myths associated with the formation of new societies, see L. Hedeager, 'Migration Period Europe: The Formation of a Political Mentality', in F. Theuws and J. L. Nelson (eds.), *Rituals of Power: From Late Antiquity to the Early Middle Ages* (Leiden: Brill, 2000), 15–58. For a model of a publication of a grave of what appears to have been a 'barbarian king', see the three-volume work by J. Peška and J. Tejral, *Das germanische Königsgrab von Mušov in Mähren* (Mainz: Römisch-Germanisches Zentralmuseum, 2002); and on the grave of Childeric, see R. Brulet, 'La Sépulture du roi Childéric à Tournai et le site funéraire', in F. Vallet and M. Kazanki (eds.), *La Noblesse romaine et les chefs barbares du IIIe au VIIe siècle* (Paris: Musée des Antiquités Nationales, 1995), 309–26.

Chronology

*c.*1,200 BC	Beginning of Late Bronze Age in Europe.
*c.*1000 BC	End of the Late Bronze Age in western central Italy; earliest settlement on the site of Rome.
*c.*800 BC	End of Late Bronze Age in temperate Europe.
*c.*900–450 BC	Period of 'Halstatt' culture in central Europe.
*c.*800–500 BC	Development of central-place settlements in upland temperate Europe.
*c.*720–580 BC	'Orientalizing' period in Italy.
*c.*800–50 BC	Iron Age in temperate Europe.
753 BC	Traditional date of foundation of Rome by Romulus.
*c.*650–625 BC	First phase of Roman *forum* laid out.
*c.*600–500 BC	Archaic period in central Italy.
*c.*550 BC	Rich elite burial at Hochdorf, representative of late Hallstatt burials.
*c.*530 BC	Vix *krater* made in southern Italy.
509 BC	Traditionally, expulsion of the last Roman king, establishment of the Republic; first treaty between Rome and Carthage.
504 BC	Arrival of Attus Clausus and the Claudii in Rome.
496 BC	Roman defeat of other Latins at Lake Regillus.
494 BC	First 'secession' of the *plebs*; institution of the plebeian tribunate.
493 BC	Cassian treaty regulates relations between Rome and other Latin cities.
486 BC	Attempted tyranny of Sp. Cassius.
477 BC	Disastrous expedition of the Fabii to the Cremera river.
474 BC	Etruscan hegemony in Italy weakened by Syracusan naval victory off Cumae.
451 BC	*Decemuiri* appointed to draw up a law code (XII Tables).

*c.*450 BC	Start of 'La Tène' cultural horizon.
450 BC	Secession of the *plebs; decemuiri* deposed.
439 BC	Attempted tyranny of Sp. Maelius.
(?) 437 BC	Cornelius Cossus dedicates the *spolia opima.*
*c.*400 BC	Pay introduced for military service; possible introduction of new voting procedures in *comitia centuriata.*
396 BC	Capture of Veii after long siege.
390 BC	Crushing Gallic victory at the Allia leaves Rome exposed to attack. Rome sacked by a Gallic war-band.
389 BC	Roman treaty with Massilia.
385 BC	Manlius Capitolinus suspected of aspiring to tyranny, tried and executed.
378 BC	'Servian' walls built around Rome.
367 BC	Licinio-Sextian laws (among other achievements) open consulship to plebeians, ending patrician monopoly.
348 BC	Romano-Carthaginian treaty renewed.
343–341 BC	First 'Samnite War'.
342 BC	One consulship now reserved every year for a plebeian.
341 BC	Outbreak of Latin War.
340 BC	Manlius Torquatus reputedly executes his son for disobedience on the battlefield.
338 BC	End of Latin War, dissolution of Latin League, extensive reorganization by Rome of territory now under its control, using various institutional mechanisms.
334 BC	Cales, first of a new type of Latin colony, founded.
327–304 BC	Second 'Samnite War', including shameful Roman surrender at the Caudine Forks in 321.
326 BC	First Roman coinage, minted in Neapolis, issued; *nexum* outlawed in Rome.
323 BC	Death of Alexander the Great in Babylon; conventionally the start of 'Hellenistic' era.
313 BC	Latin colony sent to island of Pontia.
312 BC	Censorship of Appius Claudius Caecus; construction of Via Appia and Aqua Appia begun.
311 BC	Naval officials known as *duumuiri nauales* first appointed.

304 BC	Cn. Flavius as aedile publishes procedures of civil law, and the religious calendar; equestrian parade (*transuectio*) introduced.
300 BC	Major priesthoods now all open to plebeians.
298–290 BC	Third 'Samnite War'.
296 BC	Temple built to Bellona in Rome.
295 BC	Rome defeats Etruscan, Umbrian, Samnite, and Gallic coalition at Sentinum.
294 BC	Temple of Victory built in Rome.
291 BC	Cult of Aesculapius introduced into Rome from Greece.
290 BC	Territory conquered from Sabines by M'. Curius Dentatus distributed to Roman settlers.
c.287 BC	Secession of the *plebs*; 'Struggle of the Orders' ended by the Hortensian law.
281–275 BC	South Italian city of Taras calls in Epirote king Pyrrhus against Rome; the Pyrrhic War continues until Pyrrhus' defeat at Beneventum; he withdraws to Greece.
273 BC	Latin colonies founded at Cosa and Paestum.
270 BC	Regular issues of Roman coinage begin.
268 BC	Roman advance in Italy reaches Adriatic with conquest of Picenum.
264 BC	Roman conquest of Italy effectively complete; outbreak of First Punic War following Roman support of Mamertine mercenaries in Sicily.
256 BC	Short-lived success of Regulus' invasion of Africa.
241 BC	End of First Punic War after Battle of the Aegates Islands, Rome gains control of substantial areas of Sicily; last Roman rural voting tribes created.
c.240 BC	Livius Andronicus active at Rome, beginnings of Roman literature.
237 BC	Rome seizes Sardinia and Corsica while Carthage is distracted by internal conflicts.
232 BC	Tribune C. Flaminius settles Roman poor on land captured from Gauls in north-east Italy.
c.230 BC	Carthage begins to bring the Iberian peninsula under its control.
229–228 BC	First Illyrian War.

227 BC	Roman territory in Sicily made into a province; number of praetors increased from two to four.
226 BC	Ebro treaty delimits Roman and Carthaginian spheres of influence in Iberian peninsula.
225 BC	Major Gallic invasion of Italy defeated at Telamon in Etruria.
222 BC	M. Claudius Marcellus dedicates the *spolia opima* after killing the Insubrian king in single combat.
218 BC	Hannibal invades Italy from Spain, via the Alps; start of Second Punic War, Hannibal wins Battle of the Trebia; Roman offensive against Carthaginians in Spain; Claudian law, regulating senatorial involvement in commercial shipping.
217 BC	Hannibal defeats Roman army at the Battle of Lake Trasimene.
216 BC	Hannibal inflicts crushing defeat on Romans at Cannae, defection of Capua to Hannibal.
212/11–205 BC	First Macedonian War, ended by the peace of Phoenice.
211 BC	Romans recover Capua; Roman alliance with Aetolian League against Philip V of Macedon.
*c.*206 BC	Regular appointment of two praetors for the Spanish campaigns begins.
204 BC	Hannibal recalled to defend Africa.
202 BC	Scipio Africanus defeats Hannibal at Zama, ending Second Punic War.
*c.*200 BC	First history of Rome by a Roman (Fabius Pictor) written, in Greek; last ritual depositions of metal objects at Flag Fen in Britain.
200–197 BC	Second Macedonian War ends in Roman victory at Cynoscephale.
197 BC	Demarcation of two fixed provinces in Iberian peninsula (Nearer and Further Spain).
196 BC	Roman proconsul Flamininus proclaims 'freedom of Greeks' at Isthmian games; human sacrifice banned at Rome.
195 BC	Consulship of Cato the Elder.
194 BC	Roman army withdrawn from Greece.

191 BC	Roman forces return to Greece to oppose the Seleucid king, Antiochus III.
*c.*190 BC	Rome begins to recover control of Po valley, intensification of Roman colonization of Italy.
189 BC	Romans defeat Antiochus III at Magnesia.
188 BC	Humiliating terms imposed on Antiochus by Peace of Apamea.
187, 184 BC	Trials of the Scipiones for peculation.
186 BC	Roman Senate suppresses the popular worship of Bacchus across Italy.
182 BC	Orchian sumptuary law.
181 BC	Last Latin colony founded, at Aquileia.
180 BC	Villian law defines clearer career structure for Roman magistracies.
177 BC	Roman colony founded at Luna.
171–168 BC	Third Macedonian War between Rome and Perseus, ends with Roman victory at Pydna.
170 BC	Triumph of C. Claudius marred by silence of allied contingent after distribution of booty to the advantage of Roman soldiers.
167 BC	Dissolution of Macedonian kingdom into four republics; direct taxation permanently abolished in Rome.
163 BC	Fannian sumptuary law.
157 BC	Roman colony founded at Auximum in Italy.
149 BC	Rome declares Third Punic War against Carthage.
148 BC	Anti-Roman rebellion in Greece and Macedonia.
147 BC	Scipio Aemilianus elected consul in contravention of the Villian law, for the attack on Carthage.
146 BC	Romans (under L. Mummius) sack Corinth to end revolt, and Carthage to end Third Punic War (under Scipio Aemilianus).
143 BC	Didian and Licinian sumptuary laws.
139 BC	Rome defeats Lusitani under Viriathus; secret ballot introduced for elections.
137 BC	Secret ballot introduced for judicial proceedings in the assembly.

133 BC	Celtiberian centre of Numantia falls to Scipio Aemilianus after a major siege; Attalus III leaves his kingdom to the Roman people; tribunate of Ti. Gracchus, ends in his violent death.
129 BC	Secret ballot introduced for legislative assemblies; senators excluded from equestrian order.
129–126 BC	Former Attalid kingdom annexed as province of Asia Minor.
125 BC	Revolt and destruction of Latin colony of Fregellae.
125–123 BC	Rome intervenes against Saluvii on behalf of Massilia.
123–122 BC	Tribunates of C. Gracchus: among other legislation, corn law provides subsidized grain for urban poor at Rome, extortion law creates standing court (*quaestio*) with an entirely non-senatorial jury.
121 BC	Killing of C. Gracchus after the passing of the 'Final Decree' of the Senate.
120 BC	Province of Narbonnese Gaul created from conquered lands.
113 BC	Migrations of Cimbri and Teutoni begin.
112–106 BC	War with Jugurtha, king of Numidia; after disgrace of Bestia (111) and Albinus (110), the more capable Metellus is appointed commander (109).
107 BC	Marius consul for the first time, given command against Jugurtha by popular vote; secret ballot introduced for treason trials.
105 BC	Roman army destroyed by Cimbri and Teutoni at Arausio in southern Gaul.
104–100 BC	Marius holds consecutive consulships to deal with the Germanic threat.
103 BC	First tribunate of Saturninus, radical legislation in favour of Marius' veterans passed.
102 BC	Marius defeats Teutoni at Aquae Sextiae in Gaul.
101 BC	Cimbri defeated at Vercellae in northern Italy; province of Cilicia established.
100 BC	Saturninus tribune for second time; Marius forced to suppress him after a violent campaign for re-election.
96 BC	Cyrene (Libya) incorporated as a province.

95 BC	Licinio-Mucian law establishes standing court to identify Italians who have illegally usurped Roman citizenship, provoking considerable hostility.
91 BC	Outbreak of the Social War.
90 BC	Italians still loyal to Rome granted citizenship by the Julian law.
88 BC	Sulla marches on Rome to safeguard his tenure of the Mithridatic command, from which a popular vote has recently removed him; Marius and others flee and are declared public enemies; Mithridates of Pontus invades province of Asia, massacring Romans and starting First Mithridatic War.
87 BC	End of Social War; Marius returns to Italy and seizes Rome in bloody coup.
86 BC	Marius elected to a seventh consulship, dies soon after; faction led by Cinna and Carbo remain in power until 82.
85 BC	Cinnan army sent out east to engage both Sulla and Mithridates; Sulla makes peace of Dardanus to end First Mithridatic War; his army winters in Asia in notorious luxury.
83 BC	Sulla lands in Italy; first Civil War ends with Battle of the Colline Gate in 82.
83–82 BC	Second Mithridatic War.
82–81 BC	Dictatorship and reforms of Sulla; institutes proscriptions.
74–66 BC	Third Mithridatic War.
73–71 BC	Servile insurrection led by Spartacus, ended by Crassus and Pompey.
70 BC	Pompey and Crassus consuls for the first time, major elements of Sullan settlement abolished or reformed, notably restoration of powers of tribunate and ending of senatorial monopoly on juries.
67 BC	Tribune Gabinius proposes Pompey for major command to combat piracy; granted in the teeth of senatorial opposition, the command is a spectacular success.
66 BC	Command in Third Mithridatic War transferred to Pompey by popular vote on proposal of the tribune Manilius.
63 BC	Disturbances in Italy and conspiracy in Rome, associated with Sergius Catilina, suppressed under the leadership of the consul Cicero.

62 BC	Pompey returns from his eastern campaigns, but becomes bogged down in Roman politics.
60 BC	Informal agreement for mutual cooperation between Pompey, Crassus and Julius Caesar.
59 BC	Julius Caesar elected consul, introduces a package of reforms, many favourable to himself or his allies; Pompey marries Caesar's daughter Julia.
58 BC	P. Clodius elected tribune of the *plebs*; among his reforms he establishes free grain dole (*annona*) for citizens of Rome; Cicero exiled; Cyprus annexed and added to province of Cilicia.
58–51 BC	Julius Caesar's proconsular command in Gaul and Illyricum, conquest of Gaul.
57 BC	Recall of Cicero; Pompey obtains task of supervising corn supply; Caesar's campaigns against the Belgae and Nervii.
56 BC	Agreement of Pompey, Crassus, and Caesar renewed in meetings at Ravenna and Luca; Caesar's campaign reaches the Atlantic coast of Gaul; Cicero defends Caelius in court on charge of public violence.
55 BC	Second consulship of Pompey and Crassus reasserts ambitions of the three dynasts; major provincial commands for Pompey and Crassus, and extension of Caesar's command.
55–53 BC	Caesar undertakes expeditions to Britain, and beyond the Rhine.
53 BC	Crassus killed and his army destroyed at Carrhae during an invasion of Parthia.
52 BC	Virtual anarchy in Rome leads to appointment of Pompey as sole consul; revolt of Vercingetorix in Gaul; Pompeian law on provinces introduces mandatory gap between magistracy and pro-magistracy; in consequence, Cicero is forced to become governor of Cilicia in 51.
49 BC	Caesar crosses the Rubicon, starting the Civil War with Pompey and the conservative clique in the Senate; civil conflict dominates the next nineteen years.
48 BC	Murder of Pompey in Egypt following his defeat by Caesar at Pharsalus.
46 BC	Caesarian victory over Pompeian troops at Thapsus in Africa, suicide of Cato the Younger; Caesar's temporary dictatorship extended to last ten years.

45 BC	Caesar defeats last Pompeian army at Munda in Spain, ending the Civil War.
44 BC	Julius Caesar made dictator for life; assassinated (Ides of March).
43–33 BC	Mark Antony, Lepidus, and Octavian elected triumvirs for the restoration of the Republic, and serve for two five-year terms.
42 BC	Battle of Philippi ends hopes of republican revival; death of Brutus, Cassius, and other tyrannicides.
41–40 BC	Disputes over confiscations of land for settlement of veterans after Philippi escalates to Perusine War between Lucius Antonius and Octavian.
c.40 BC	Production of Arretine/Italian Terra Sigillata pottery begins.
36 BC	Octavian defeats Sextus Pompey in Sicily, and removes Lepidus from power; this success allows him to tighten his grip on power in Rome.
31 BC	Octavian defeats Antony and Cleopatra at Actium.
30 BC	Suicides of Antony and Cleopatra; Octavian enters Alexandria, end of Civil Wars.
29 BC	Return and triple triumph of Octavian.
28–27 BC	Octavian regularizes his constitutional position in the 'First Settlement', receives the name Augustus.
26–19 BC	Conquest of Asturia; Rome begins hydraulic gold-mining in north-west Spain.
23 BC	Second constitutional 'settlement': Augustus resigns consulship and receives substitute powers, including tribunician power.
19 BC	Cornelius Balbus last man from outside the ruling family to hold a triumph.
18 BC	Julian laws on adultery, marriage, and child-rearing.
16–15 BC	Conquest of Alpine tribes, including area around Manching on the Danube.
16–13 BC	Consolidation of Roman occupation of west bank of the Rhine.
13 BC	Augustus' first reform of the army.
12 BC	On the death of Lepidus, Augustus becomes chief priest.

12–7 BC	Conquest of Pannonia.
c.10 BC	Gaulish pottery workshops established at Lyon.
9 BC	Altar of Augustan Peace (vowed in 13 BC) dedicated.
2 BC	Augustus named 'father of his fatherland'; cuts *annona* recipients to 200,000.
AD 1–10	Gaulish Samian production starts at La Graufesenque.
c. AD 1–33	Burial of local chief and probable auxiliary commander at Putensen.
AD 6	Further army reform, creation of military treasury fed from dedicated tax revenues.
AD 6–9	Major Pannonian revolt suppressed by Tiberius.
AD 9	Ambush and destruction of Varus' legions at Kalkreise in the Teutoburger Forest; Papian and Poppaean law mitigates some of the harsher provisions of the Julian laws of 18 BC.
AD 11–34	Tenure of Poppaeus Sabinus as governor of Moesia.
AD 14	Death of Augustus, accession of Tiberius, revolts among the Rhine and Danube legions; revolt followed by Germanicus' campaigns against the Germans until AD 16.
AD 19	Germanicus, Tiberius' adopted son, dies in the East in suspicious circumstances.
AD 20	Trial of Cn. Piso for treason after the death of Germanicus.
AD 20–60	Occupation and metalworking at Daseburg.
AD 22	Senatorial debate on luxury; Tiberius advises against setting limits on conspicuous consumption.
AD 31	Sejanus first equestrian to reach the consulship, falls in a palace plot soon after.
AD 37	Tiberius dies, succeeded by Gaius 'Caligula'.
AD 41	Gaius assassinated, Claudius proclaimed emperor by the praetorian guard.
AD 42	Claudius begins construction of a new harbour at Portus; abortive revolt in Dalmatia.
AD 47	Corbulo's political settlement of the Frisii.
AD 48	Claudius' speech to the Senate advocating the admission of Aeduan Gauls.

AD 55–64	War between Rome (under Corbulo) and Parthia for control of Armenia.
AD 60–61	Boudiccan revolt in Britain.
AD 61	Notorious senatorial debate, and punishment, of a senator's slaves after his murder.
AD 66–74	Jewish revolt, includes capture of Jerusalem and Massada.
AD 68	Provincial revolts against Nero, who commits suicide, ending Julio-Claudian dynasty; Civil Wars break out.
AD 69	Victory of forces loyal to Vespasian over Vitellius ends the Civil Wars, and leads to the accession of Vespasian and start of Flavian dynasty.
AD 79–81	Vespasian dies, succeeded by Titus.
AD 81	Titus dies unexpectedly, bringing his brother Domitian to the throne; Tacitus enters the Senate.
AD 85–96	Domitian at war with Dacian king Decebalus.
AD 96	Assassination of Domitian, Nerva chosen as *princeps*.
AD 97	Tacitus consul.
AD 98	Death of Nerva, accession of Trajan, start of Antonine 'dynasty', lasting until 192.
AD 101–2	Trajan's First Dacian War.
AD 105–6	Second Dacian War, ending in conquest and access to Dacia's rich silver and gold deposits.
AD 112–17	Construction of Trajan's harbour at Portus.
c.AD 112–13	Tacitus proconsul of Asia.
AD 113	Trajan invades Parthia, conquering Mesopotamia briefly.
AD 117	Death of Trajan, accession of Hadrian, who gives up Trajan's eastern conquests; Roman Empire at its greatest extent.
AD 122	Hadrian's Wall begun.
AD 131–5	Bar Kochba revolt in Judaea.
AD 138	Death of Hadrian, accession of Antoninus Pius.
AD 161	Marcus Aurelius and Lucius Verus succeed Antoninus Pius.
AD 162	Lucius Verus' successful Parthian war.

AD 165–9	Antonine plague, with recurrences in the 170s and 180s.
AD 160–88	Notable increase in military activity within the empire, especially Marcomannic Wars.
AD 171	Moorish invasions of Spain.
AD 175	Revolt of Avidius Cassius in Syria.
c. AD 175	Wealthy burial at Mušov of elite individuals with probable service record in Roman army.
AD 180	Death of Marcus Aurelius, accession of Commodus.
AD 192	Death of Commodus leads to brief period of political confusion.
AD 193–7	Civil War sees proclamation of Septimius Severus as emperor, and his final victory.
Late 2nd cent.	Output of Spanish gold-, silver-, and copper-mines dwindles; many gold-mines abandoned.
c. AD 200	Dense deposits of Roman arms, armour, and other metalwork at Illerup.
AD 211	Septimius dies, succeeded by his sons Caracalla and Geta (murdered late December).
AD 212	Caracalla's Constitutio Antoniniana grants Roman citizenship to those free inhabitants of the empire who do not then possess it.
AD 215	Introduction of the *antoninianus* silver coin.
AD 217	Assassination of Caracalla; elevation of equestrian Macrinus to the purple, followed by period of civil conflict.
AD 222	Severus Alexander comes to the throne, bringing a period of stability.
AD 229	Second consulship of Cassius Dio, with Severus Alexander.
AD 230s	Start of increased pressure on Roman frontiers.
AD 235	Assassination of Severus Alexander, Maximinus Thrax chosen emperor.
AD 238	Opposition to Maximinus precipitates the 'year of six emperors', including Gordian I and II.
AD 238–44	Reign of Gordian III, ended by his murder.

AD 240s–280s	Height of 'third-century crisis', chronic political and military instability.
AD 244–9	Reign of Philip the Arab.
AD 248	Philip celebrates Rome's millennium.
AD 249–51	Reign of Decius after his victory over Philip; he is the first emperor from a northern European province; his death in battle against the Goths leads to further military instability.
AD 253–60	Valerian and Gallienus emperors.
AD 260	Valerian captured by Persian king Sapor I during Roman reverses in the East.
AD 260–8	Reign of Gallienus.
AD 265	Loss of Dacia, with its gold- and silver-mines; radical debasement of *denarius* to silver content of *c*.2 %.
AD 268	Deposition and murder of Gallienus opens the way for domination of the throne by equestrian military officers, starting with Claudius Gothicus (268–70).
AD 270	Aurelian obtains the throne, ruling until 275, and restores political and military stability, including the suppression of the breakaway Palmyrene empire under Zenobia; builds Aurelianic walls of Rome; reforms of the coinage (273).
AD 275	Murder of Aurelian by his officers brings Tacitus to the throne, followed (276–82) by Probus.
AD 284	Accession of Diocletian.
AD 293	Diocletian standardizes silver and gold coinage.
AD 294/6	Diocletian reforms the billon coinage.
c. AD 300	Outstandingly rich burial at Gommern.
AD 301	Diocletian's Edict on Maximum Prices, and retariffing of existing coinage.
AD 305	Diocletian and Maximian abdicate; replaced as Augusti by Galerius (East) and Contantius I (West), with Maximinus Daia and Severus as Caesars.
AD 306	Constantius I dies at York; his son Constantine proclaimed Augustus by troops; recognized as Caesar by Galerius; Severus becomes Augustus; Maxentius (son of Maximian) seizes power in Rome, joined

by Maximian. Severus executed; Maximian fails to overthrow Maxentius.

AD 307 Conference at Carnuntum; Maximian retires again; Licinius replaces executed Severus as Augustus in the West. Constantine demoted to rank of Caesar.

AD 310 Constantine and Maximinus Daia recognized as Augusti.

AD 311 Death of Galerius.

AD 312 Constantine defeats Maxentius at the Milvian Bridge outside Rome.

AD 313 Edict of Milan. Constantine and Licinius proclaim religious toleration for the Christian faith; Licinius recognizes Constantine as senior Augustus. Licinius defeats Maximinus in the East.

AD 314 Council of Arles. Constantine attempts to resolve 'Donatist' controversy.

AD 317 Constantine's sons, Crispus and Constantine, made Caesars, as is Licinius' son (also called Licinius).

AD 323 War breaks out between Constantine and Licinius; Licinius defeated at Adrianople and Chrysopolis.

AD 324 Licinius (although previously pardoned) is executed on a charge of treason.

AD 325 Constantine convenes Council of Nicea to debate relationship between God and Christ. Nicene Creed formulated, stating that Christ 'is of one substance' with the Father; Arian doctrine outlawed.

AD 337 Death of Constantine; succeeded by Constantine II (in Spain, Gaul, and Britain), Constans (in Italy, Africa, and Illyricum), and Constantius II (in the remainder of the East).

AD 340 Constantine II invades Italy; defeated and killed by Constans.

AD 350 Constans deposed by Magnentius and killed.

AD 351 Gallus (nephew of Constantine I) made Caesar by Constantius II.

AD 353 Magnentius defeated by Contantius II.

AD 354 Gallus deposed and executed by Constantius II.

AD 355 Gallus' brother Julian made Caesar in the West.

AD 360 Julian declared emperor by legions in Gaul.

AD 361	Constantius II dies. Julian left as sole emperor.
AD 363	Julian killed while campaigning against Persians; succeeded by Jovian, who reigns only seven months.
AD 364	Valentinian I becomes emperor in the West, with his brother Valens as emperor in the East.
AD 367	Valentinian names his 9-year-old son Gratian as co-Augustus.
AD 375	Death of Valentinian I. Succeeded by Gratian and Valentinian II.
AD 376	Arrival of the Huns in central Europe.
AD 378	Valens defeated and killed by Goths at Adrianople.
AD 379	Theodosius made co-emperor by Gratian.
c. AD 380	Egeria's pilgrimage from Spain to Palestine.
AD 383	Magnus Maximus declared Augustus by British legions. Gratian killed by Gallic legions.
AD 387	Magnus Maximus invades Italy (deposing Valentinian II).
AD 388	Theodosius defeats and executes Maximus at Aquileia, and restores Valentian II.
AD 392	Death of Valentian II, probably at hands of Frankish adviser, Arbogast, who effectively ruled the West, with Flavius Eugenius as puppet emperor.
AD 394	Arbogast and Eugenius defeated by Theodosius at the Battle of Frigidus.
AD 395	Theodosius dies leaving the empire to his sons, Arcadius (who takes the East) and Honorius (who takes the West); Vandal general Stilicho rules the West on behalf of 10-year-old Honorius.
c. AD 400	Oustandingly wealthy female burial at Pohorelice-Nová Ves.
AD 402	Western mints, except Rome, stop striking bronze coinage.
AD 410	Goths under Alaric sack Rome; Honorius advises Britain to see to its own defence.
AD 469–78	Spain overrun by Visigoths.

AD 476   Last western emperor, Romulus Augustulus, deposed; Odoacer creates Ostrogothic kingdom of Italy.

AD 481/2   Death of Childeric.

AD 533–54   Eastern emperor Justinian launches reconquest of Italy and North Africa.

AD 537   Justinian redefines criteria for membership of Senate.

Maps

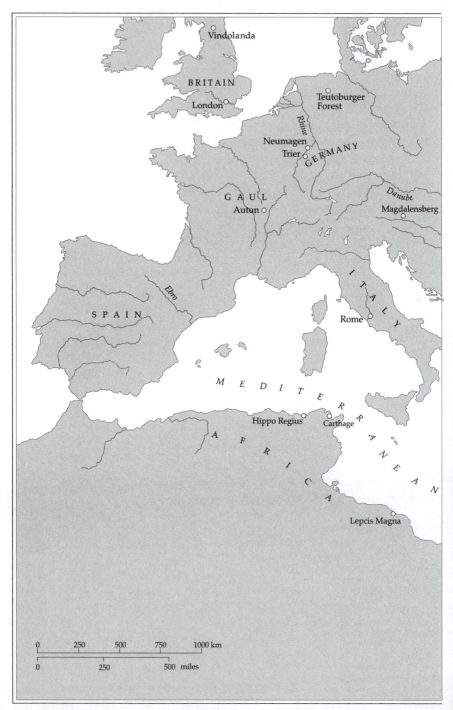

Map 1. Roman Europe—general map

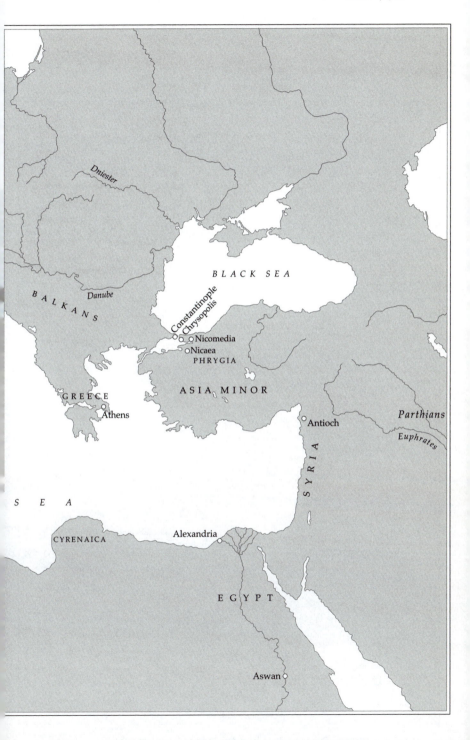

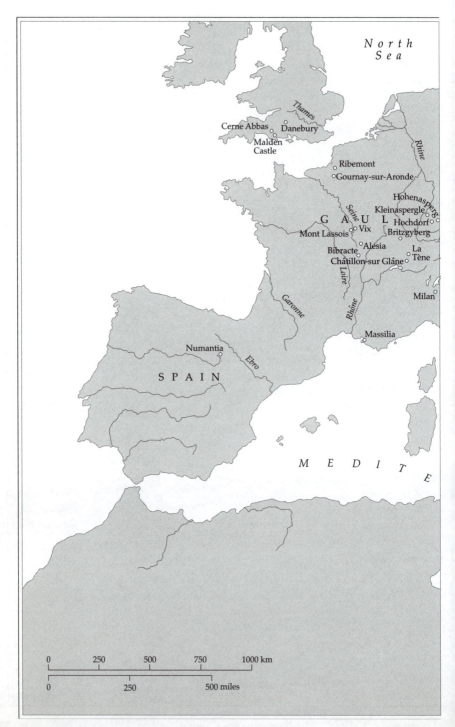

Map 2. Roman Europe—Late Iron Age Europe (chapters 1–2)

Klein Köris
Biskupin
Vistula
Dnieper
Elbe
Libence
Glauberg
Závist
Alanding
Kelheim
Passau
Hart an der Alz
Heuneburg
Danube
Smolenice-Molpír
Magdalensberg
Stična
Danube
I T A L Y
ETRURIA
Perusia
Assisi
Cosa
Veii
Gravisca
Tiber
Rome
Pyrgi
Arpinum
Lavinium
Cales
Luceria
Ardea
Naples
Fregellae
Minturnae
Cumae
Pompeii
Herculaneum
Paestum
Samothrace
Ilion/Troy
A S I A
GREECE
Athens
Eleusis
SICILY
M E D I T E R R A N E A N   S E A
Carthage

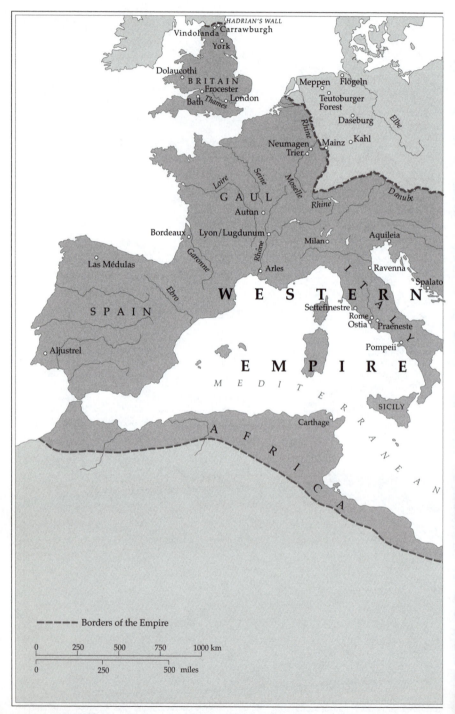

Map 3. Roman Europe—the Roman Empire (chapters 3–10)

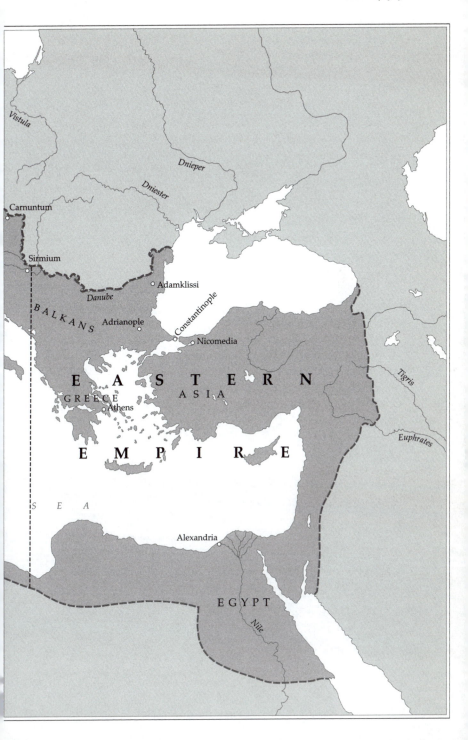

Index